STANDING NAKED
IN THE WINGS

Anecdotes from Canadian Actors

Compiled
and Edited by

Lynda Mason Green and Tedde Moore

Toronto   Oxford   New York

Oxford University Press

1997

Oxford University Press
70 Wynford Drive, Don Mills, Ontario M3C 1J9

Oxford New York
Athens Auckland Bangkok Mumbai
Calcutta Cape Town Dar es Salaam Delhi
Florence Hong Kong Istanbul Karachi
Kuala Lumpur Chennai Madrid Melbourne
Mexico City Nairobi Paris Singapore
Taipei Tokyo Toronto Warsaw

and associated companies in
Berlin Ibadan

Oxford is a trade mark of Oxford University Press

Canadian Cataloguing in Publication Data

Main entry under title:

Standing naked in the wings : anecdotes from Canadian actors

Includes index.
ISBN 0-19-541195-1

1. Actors – Canada – Anecdotes.   2. Theater – Canada – Anecdotes.
I. Green, Lynda Mason.   II. Moore, Tedde.

PN2307.S72 1997   792'.028'092271   C97-931367-8

Design: Brett Miller
Jacket Illustration: Alain Massicotte
Formating: Indelible Ink

Copyright © Oxford University Press Canada 1997

1 2 3 4 – 00 99 98 97

This book is printed on permanent (acid-free) paper ∞ .
Printed in Canada

CONTENTS

ACKNOWLEDGEMENTS

Without the support and encouragement of the following people, the realisation of this book would not have been possible: Paul Lima (Paul Lima Communcations) for website design and technical support, Robert and Marion Green and Kyah Green, Don Harron, Christopher Plummer, Vanessa Harwood, the Ben Lennick Archives Committee (Dan McDonald), Margaret McGann (2M Communications), Marcia Bennett, Esme Markle, Ruth Lima and Bruce Buckley, Monica Parker and Gilles Savard, Sean McCann, Alfie Scopp, Alan Pearce, David Smith, Len Starmer, Chris Braden, Zoë Carter, and Trisha Langley.

We would also like to thank: Actra, Canadian Actors Equity Association, Academy of Canadian Cinema, The Screen Actors' Guild of America (Los Angeles), Canadian Consulate (Los Angeles), The Stratford Festival (Jason Miller), The Shaw Festival (Christopher Newton), the CBC Talent Bank, and CBC photographer Fred Phipps.

French translation services were donated by Marc Beaugrand-Champagne, Anne Douville, and Karen Gusto, B.A., M.A., (Jean-Louis Roux material).

Last but most definitely not least we wish to thank all the actors who dug into their hearts and memories and took the time to send us their stories.

We are grateful for permission to include excerpts from the following (page numbers indicate where they appear in this text). Pp. 42–3, 143: from BERNARD BRADEN. *The Kindness of Strangers* (1990). Toronto: Hodder & Stoughton. Used by permission of Curtis Brown Group and Barbara Kelly. Pp. 318–19: ROBERTSON DAVIES. Tribute to Robert Christie is used with the permission of Pendragon Ink. Pp. 98–9, 128–9, 200: from AMELIA HALL. *Life Before Stratford: The Memories of Amelia Hall* (1989), edited by Diane Mew. Toronto: Dundurn Press. Used by permission of Diane Mew. Pp. 3, 189, 205: from MARTHA HARRON. *Don Harron: A Parent Contradiction* (1988). Used by permission of Martha Harron. Pp. 135–6, 199, 242: from BRUCE LAFFEY. *Beatrice Lillie: The Funniest Woman in the World*. Copyright © 1989. Published by Wynwood Press, a division of Baker Book House, Inc. Used by permission. Pp. 127–8 (Martin Short) and pp. 58, 289 (Dave Thomas): from DONNA MCCROHAN. *The Second City*. New York: Perigee Books, The Putnam Publishing Company. Pp. 326–7: NICHOLAS PENNELL. Letter to the Stratford Company is reprinted by Permission of The Stratford Shakespearean Festival Foundation. Used by permission. Pp. 20–1 (Kate Reid and William Shatner): from GRACE LYDIATT SHAW. *Stratford Under Cover: Memories on Tape*. Toronto: N.C. Press Ltd, 1977. Pp. 67–8, 122, 168–9, 207–8, 325–6: from TONY VAN BRIDGE. *Also in the Cast* (1995) edited by Denis Johnston. Co-published by Mosaic Press, Oakville, Ontario; and the Academy of the Shaw Festival, Niagara-on-the-Lake, Ontario. Used by permission of Tony Van Bridge and the publisher.

Every effort has been made to determine and contact copyright owners. In the case of any omissions, we will be pleased to make suitable acknowledgement in future editions.

INTRODUCTION

It is in the nature of actors to tell stories, whether it is in a theatre speaking the words of a playwright to an audience of a thousand or having coffee with friends. Among us, there is a venerated tradition of trading tales of our misadventures at work or exchanging any of a litany of big and small absurdities that come with 'being an actor'. Invariably someone will say, 'Why the heck doesn't someone collect these? Wouldn't they make a wonderful book!' As it has happened, the 'someone' has turned out to be us. After more than two years of gathering, sorting, filing, transcribing, organising and editing, we sat down to select from bulging files containing over a thousand stories.

Along the way, our sense of connection and reconnection with other actors had a very powerful impact on both of us. As we worked through the submissions, we began to sense that the cumulative impact of these stories, every one filled with warmth, generosity, wit, and tenacity, was a great deal more than the sum of its parts. Not only did it reflect a sensibility unique to our acting community but it began to take on a deeper meaning and a remarkable poignancy. Some of the voices that would speak from these pages would never be heard again. Nicholas Pennell died during the course of our work, followed by Bruno Gerussi, Barbara Hamilton, and many others. What had begun as a fun project that we thought people might enjoy, had become very personal and very important to us.

Our actors are well known and respected world-wide for the depth and breadth of their experience. Some of the actors who have so generously contributed their memories to this book may be unfamiliar to you by name, but if you attend the theatre, listen to radio, watch TV, or go to movies you have likely seen or heard most of them. Some were born here and made careers elsewhere, some were born elsewhere and have chosen to settle here.

Contrary to the Hollywood myth, few actors, no matter where they work in the world, ever make much more than a modest living. So why do we do it? Perhaps some answers lie in these pages. Perhaps ultimately it doesn't matter. We are actors. We are a family. We share the knowledge of that startling rush each time we step onto a stage and the swell of gratitude as we step off, buoyed and embraced by applause.

We two, who have been entrusted with our community's remembrances, are privileged to present them here. This book is an affectionate tribute to our mentors, teachers, colleagues and, of course, our audiences, all of us forever bonded by our love and respect for the work.

Lynda Mason Green and Tedde Moore
http://web.idirect.com/~canuck/canact.html

I

Auditions or 'Just have fun with it'

ELVA MAI HOOVER
Where shall I begin?

There I stood on the raised platform of Hart House, squinting into the darkness, wondering what to do next. It was 1959, I was fifteen years old, and I was auditioning for the National Theatre School of Canada.

I had never acted in my life outside of lying to my mother. Although I liked books and movies, I had never actually seen a play. What got me there? An ad in the *Toronto Star* that offered the possibility of free tuition if you were accepted. I'd dropped out of high school and was working at the Bell Telephone and knew only one thing...I didn't want to work at the Bell for the rest of my life.

They sent me a list of possible audition pieces and I read the plays. I chose 'Juliet', of course, and 'Joan of Arc' from Jean Anouilh's *The Lark*. The opening speech started with 'Where shall I begin? I'll begin at the beginning.' There followed a month of learning the speeches. I was not a flamboyant girl so it never occurred to me to say them out loud as I was working on them. I sat in my room at night, or on the john at work, with my eyes closed and my lips working, trying to remember the author's words though I was not always totally sure how to pronounce them.

The day arrived and Jean Roberts, that den-mother of the Canadian theatre with her wonderful Scots burr and quiet ability to take charge, ushered this cowed, skinny kid onto the stage. I peered into the darkness and could vaguely see three figures seated behind a table with a single lamp. Nobody said anything. I waited. Still nothing happened. Finally I understood that no instructions were forthcoming. I began my audition piece, if not out loud, at least in a whisper:

'Where shall I begin?...'

A male voice with an unfamiliar melody, one I'd never heard before, spoke. It was Powys Thomas.

'Anywhere you like, love.'

'Oh...... then I'll begin at the beginning.'

And that is how my life as an actor began.

LARRY DANE to LINDA GORANSON when she was
bemoaning 'losing' a part:
'You didn't lose anything. It was never yours to begin with.
A part is only yours after you get it.'

RICHARD MONETTE
On rejection letters

When I was a young actor I auditioned several times for Stratford and, in fact, was
rejected three times at the beginning before I was accepted. I kept the letter that the
producer at the time wrote me saying that there was no place for me in the
company. I had it framed and I keep it over the toilet beside the letter that invited
me to become Artistic Director of the Stratford Festival. So you see, it pays to stick
around.

Now when I have to write rejection letters myself, I try to tell actors not to feel
too badly and that I have three myself from this place.

It's so hard for actors, but there are just so many places that you have to fill, and
there is no guarantee that you are ever making the right choice. As a colleague once
said to me, 'The theatre takes what it needs, not always what you have to offer.'

ALFIE SCOPP
That time of my life

In the late forties Fletcher Markle was directing a play for the New Play Society in
Toronto. It was *The Time Of Your Life* and it had a fabulous cast, all people that I had
only heard of and never dreamed of working with. There was a part up for grabs
and the male students at the Academy of Radio Arts, who were physically right for
the part, were invited down to read for it. I had only been learning how to act for a
couple of months and I had never in my life been on a stage.

About sixteen of us auditioned. They ran through the list until it was my turn.
I had no idea of the set-up, never having done such a thing before. I just went out
on the stage and read my part. Fletcher was in the theatre watching.

'Uh, yes. Thank you. I wonder if you'd mind doing it again? But this time
would you mind facing the audience?'

I turned around, my nose still buried in the book, did it again and left. The
next day, posted on the board at the Academy was the notice that I had gotten the
part. Such is blind faith.

MARCIA DIAMOND
My first movie audition

When I first moved to Toronto in 1948, I took a job as a baby-sitter. I lived in and was paid $50 a month. After a couple of months of running to auditions between obligations, I received a call from the National Film Board.

'Your name was given to me as a likely prospect for a film I'm directing.' Later in my life I would have asked more about the project, but at that point I just thought *movies*! I was thrilled. David Bairstow wanted me to see him at 2:00 p.m. that day.

In a mad dash I washed and set my hair. Put on the make-up and my skinniest blue wool dress. I wore very high heels and a navy coat with a white fox collar and a little navy hat with a feather in it. You didn't go anywhere without a hat back then. I felt gorgeous. I even got a taxi because I didn't want to arrive with a hair out of place. I've been a character woman from the time I was eight years old. I have never been a leading lady in my whole life, but this day I worked hard on trying because I wanted to be in the movies.

At the National Film Board offices David Bairstow came out to meet me. He took one look at me.

'Oh, I've made a mistake, Miss Diamond. Somebody has told me about you all wrong. I'm sorry, but you're not what I'm looking for.'

'Oh? What are you looking for?'

'I'm looking for a tough factory nurse.'

Well, I stepped out of the shoes, whipped off the hat, and tore off my earrings. I took the lipstick off my face with my arm and I walked up to him and whacked him across the back.

'There. Am I tough enough for you?' I got the part. Thirty-five dollars a day!

DONALD HARRON
Early Hollywood days

I spent my time doing screen tests with young hopefuls, including a handsome young Texan named Ty Hungerford, changed to Hardin by the studio. We did a scene together from *The Philadelphia Story*, with me in Jimmy Stewart's role and Ty in Cary Grant's. Afterwards, Ty slapped me on the back and said, 'Ah thought yew played it more comical, while ah jist played it more swave!'

GERALDINE FARRELL
Auditions in California

I got what I thought at the time was a big audition for the part of the best friend on a (post-*Cheers*) Shelley Long sitcom. I was very excited. I could not sleep all night. Like a cartoon character, dollar signs were in my eyes—ch-ching!, ch-ching! I was sure my life was about to change forever. The series would run for ten years...Shelley Long!...Oh! my God! In my head I bought a house, a car, clothes, I had parties. I was nuts.

I got to the audition sleep-deprived, which did not leave me exactly looking my best. And on top of that, for some weird reason, I was shocked to realise that I was *not the only one auditioning*. Somehow I had got it into my head that they were going to give me this job, boom! that day. They'd take one look at me and say, 'Fabulous! You're our girl!' In fact, they were reading half the female acting population of L.A. On top of that, this audition was just a preliminary reading. We would not even meet the producers.

To make a long story short, the part went to Teri Garr. Who knew I would be up against *Teri Garr*! I mean, please. Why in heaven would they choose her over me? Let's see. Teri Garr...famous, blonde, adorable, quirky, *famous* comedic actress from film and TV who is *famous*...or me...funny, quirky, adorable, completely *unknown*, brunette, musical comedy performer who's just arrived from Canada...it could happen.

The series lasted for six episodes and was cancelled. I got over it.

GORDON CLAPP
On getting *NYPD Blue*

I had been in [producer Steven] Bochco's files. I had done a *Civil Wars* and *Cop Rock*. I had also read for the role of a Mafia task force guy very early on when they were doing the pilot for *NYPD*, so I had some history with them.

When I went in to read for the show, the character 'Medevoy' was not a continuing role and was never meant to be. But as they were about to start shooting episode three, they began to realise that only the two leads were detectives. The rest were uniforms and the lieutenant. They were going to have to fill the detective squad room. I think they planned these to be recurring characters on day contracts, not regulars.

They sent my agent the sides* for a guest role, a good scene and, as an afterthought, they also gave me a scene where this guy Medevoy sets up for a joke with the series lead, 'Sipowitz' (Denis Franz). It was a nothing, a couple of little tiny lines, a couple of pages.

Normally I like to spend a lot of time with a script and really prepare well, but the sides had come in late and I had also been working on something for another audition, so I really didn't have time to prepare as I would normally. I looked at the sides, looked at the guest role and thought it was nice. I looked at the Medevoy gag and thought, 'What are they sending me this for? It's nothing.' Then I noticed that the script said that Medevoy was 'at his desk'. That's in the squad room...where these guys live. I thought that if I did something good with this, it could turn into something.

The scene would be with Denis Franz' character, one of the leads. He's a pretty scary guy; maybe Medevoy could be a little nervous about dealing with him. The scene was about Medevoy asking Andy Sipowitz to take care of his dog. It occurred to me that, in his nervousness, he might stammer a bit. So I frivolously decided to have him repeat almost everything he said twice. A very simple request turned into, 'Andy. Andy. Ya gotta hel...ya...ya gotta help me out. Ah, ah...my wife's in Cleveland. My wife's in Cleveland and ah...I got the dog. I got the dog. He's in the car.'

As I was leaving, David Milch, the producer/head writer, said, 'Great choice, saying everything twice. Yeah. Yeah. That's good.' But I didn't hear anything for about a month. Then they called and offered me Medevoy. They said it might become a recurring role but that I was on for one episode for now. That was all I knew.

When I got to the set, all these people, producers I had met before doing other things for Bochco, came up and said that they loved the stuttering thing and that they were going to do something with the character based on that. From then on, I did a scene here and there, or a few scenes every other episode and the role slowly built.

* Pages of script to be read at an audition.

JOY FIELDING
Hollywood auditions

During my auditioning days in Hollywood, I rarely had the chance even to open my mouth to read for a part before being dismissed as too tall, too short, too pretty, or not pretty enough. At least in Canada, they were reasonably polite about rejecting me. In Hollywood, it was a different story altogether.

I remember one particular incident. I had been sent to audition for a part in a motorcycle movie which was to star a pre-*Sundance Kid* Robert Redford. I no sooner walked into the producer's office, my long hair curled seductively around my face, my dress short and low-cut, my legs bare, when the producer shouted at me from across his desk.

'What's the matter with those casting people? I told them I wanted sex! You know sex?—Big tits, big ass!'

Stunned speechless, as only a good Canadian girl could be, I backed my 'little tits, little ass' out of his office without a word. My father later said that I should have told the producer that *he* was a big enough ass for the two of us. Why can't you ever think of those lines when you need them?

Eventually I used that line after all—in a book. So, things really do have a way of working out...just like my mother always said.

LISA LANGLOIS
Parting ways in Hollywood

Early in my career, I was 'discovered' by a network during a nation-wide search and placed under a development contract. There was great publicity attached to this highly touted program. Early on, an executive from the network made some suggestions about my audition technique.

'You know what I think your problem is, Lisa? I think that you don't let guys think that they have a chance with you. So I think...that you should wear a dress and...don't wear underwear. Sit with your legs open. Let the guys think that they have a chance with you.'

I was stunned. I told him that I didn't need to do that, that I had more talent than that. Tears darted to my eyes as I somehow found an escape to my manager who waited outside the office. For years afterwards, I was a nervous wreck when I had to do any publicity or auditions for this network.

Apparently the 'flasher' audition technique is indeed practised in Hollywood. An acting coach later related a story about an actress who is now highly regarded and very successful. After this actress left the audition, the director, a very well known English gentleman, turned to the casting director.

'Did you know that she wasn't wearing any underwear and that she kept opening her legs?'

'Oh, she does that all the time. Everyone knows that.'

'Well,' he said, 'she can't think very much of her face.'

ROBIN GAMMELL
On how to get a job from Steve Bochco

I was invited to read for a part on *Murder One* some time ago. I had worked for Steven on *Hill Street Blues* so we knew each other. In the Bochco building, a very nice building at Fox, I was sitting in an atrium going over my lines when in walked Steven Bochco. I looked up and did a double take.

'Steven, I thought only mortals came through the front door.'

He stopped for a moment, took in what I had said with all innocent, pleasant intentions, said, 'Fuck you!' and walked on.

I thought I'd pretty much blown the job at that point.

I heard later that Steven had walked into the room where they were auditioning and said, 'Robin Gammell's out there. Hire him. Don't audition him, just hire him.' They did audition me, nevertheless, but they also hired me.

MONICA PARKER
On nepotism

I auditioned for Alan Parker, who is not in fact a relation, for the strangest script I had ever read. It was called *The Road to Wellville*. I auditioned once, I auditioned twice, three, four times. It was always exactly the same, always on tape. I wore the same outfit, hair the same way, everything.

I started to wonder if this was some kind of perverse fetish for him because he had never asked me to do anything different. Finally I said, 'Alan, your last name is Parker. Somewhere we're related. I've waited my whole life for nepotism. Just give me the job.'

And he did.

GERALDINE FARRELL
Lassie stays home

I once auditioned for producer Mark Tinker. It was to be a 'guest' role on one of the big series. As I walked in to read I glanced toward one of the corners and noticed two beautiful animals, a Collie and a little Lhasa Apso, lying there curled up sleeping. A fraction of a second later I realised that they were not breathing. These animals were stuffed!

Of course, I couldn't think of anything *else* for the entire audition. I was completely thrown. I became fixated on the weirdness of having your pets stuffed! I can only assume that they couldn't bear to be separated from them when they died, but I'm a pet lover and I wouldn't, I couldn't do that. It was just too strange.

In any case, I completely blew the audition.

ROBERT ITO
On being cast in *Quincy*

Originally, I was not on the list of people invited to audition for the role of the assistant, 'Sam Fujiyama', on *Quincy*. Another Asian actor and I were already well known to the people at Universal Studios and we had hoped to have an opportunity to try out. We finally insisted that we be allowed to meet the producers.

My friend went in and read with Jack [Klugman] and they liked him very much. They were just about to leave when they decided to let me read anyway. Which I did. I assumed by their behaviour that my friend had got the job so I was just happy to have had an interview.

Five days later, I collected my unemployment cheque and took my wife out for a dinner. When we got back, the phone was ringing off the hook. My agent told me that they wanted me down at Universal for a costume fitting right way. I asked him, 'What's the part?' He said it was a lab technician. So I said they could find me a size 40 regular lab coat and I would wear my own clothes. I was to be at the studio at 7 a.m. the next morning ready to work. They handed me a script as I went through the gate to the studio. I didn't know what I was doing, a TV show, a test, a movie. I had no idea.

When I was called in to do some blocking, Jack Klugman was there, and I realised that this was a test. As I walked in, he asked who I was. I said my name and that I was reading Sam Fujiyama. He said, 'Oh.' That was it.

We did the scene, an autopsy scene. We moved around the table discussing the cadaver very intimately. We were very reverent, respectful of the body. We treated it as if it was the source of secrets yet to be revealed. In any case, the scene went well. There were no hitches or problems. At the end of it, he said, 'You'll do.' And walked away. I didn't understand what he was talking about. I found out only later that Jack had had casting approval.

The next day on set, he came rushing over to me. He had just seen the rushes. He grabbed my face in his hands. He was very excited.

'We can do this! This is going to work. We know exactly what to do.'

Apparently there had been some concern about doing a show about a coroner's office which involved dealing a lot with death and corpses. They thought it might be a hard sell for the after-dinner slots, but because we had been so respectful of the corpse, they felt confident that it would work.

It was my first TV series and I worked on that show with Jack for seven years. He was a tough guy sometimes. He gave 100% and expected everyone else to do the same. Sometimes he would get a little tense. Occasionally I would give him a 'zotz' of Shiatsu massage and that would relax him. We got along pretty well. And I will never forget what he did when he found out about my contract for the show.

I was taken on effectively as a day player and as my part was expanded the contract was never upgraded. I pestered my agent, but three years into the show, the stand-in for Jack was still making more money than I was. When Jack heard about it, he was so mad.

'Fire your agent. I'll get my agent to represent you and we'll fix this.'

So that was how I ended up with Abby Greshner, one of the top agents in Los Angeles. And he made sure the contract was improved.

ALBERTA WATSON
Film auditions

Auditions are not usually fun and very rarely easy but at some point in your career, you stop trying to second-guess the people who will be on the other side of the table. You pretty much decide what you want to do, you prepare well and you do it.

The character in the film I was auditioning for was a New Yorker. I had lived in New York for many years. I was appropriately dressed, clear about my choices, everything was ready. And...of course, I was nervous. (I don't care who you are, you're nervous.) Usually there are anywhere from two to six people behind the table but on this day, there must have been 12 people on the other side of the tables. The director, maybe five producers, casting director and miscellaneous assistants...*everybody* was there. We did the 'Hellos' all around, all very polite. Then they asked me to stand in the hot spot 10 or 15 feet away. The lights and the camera lens were directed at me which meant that they could see me but I couldn't see them. It feels much like an interrogation scene in an old war film. It's unnerving but you more or less get used to it. Just as I was about to start, the director put up his hand to stop me.

'I know you probably don't like this....'

'Yes.'

'But I want to give you a direction. I want you to be as New York as you can be.'

Now...I was married to an Italian/American New Yorker and was pretty familiar with the rhythm, attitude, and speech patterns. I knew what to do with her. I don't mind getting direction *after* they have seen what I have brought to the audition, but to give direction before I have begun effectively negates my work and undermines my preparation. It assumes that I don't know what I'm doing. To me, it was insulting. I resented it. I was silent for a minute...and then I said, 'Fuck you'...which of course, was what any good New Yorker worth her salt would have said in that situation.

There was more silence for what must have been 10 seconds but felt like an hour. Then the director just smiled. He loved it. A few days later, he offered me the job. But it happened that I was in the lovely position where I could turn him down because I had, in the interim, been offered a better job.

DON FRANCKS
Too what?

In the early sixties, CBC Television was doing a production of *Death Of A Salesman*, by Arthur Miller. The director called me into his office. He said he was very interested in me.

'A lot of people are talking about you. I think that you would probably be the one to play "Biff" in my production of *Death Of A Salesman*.'

'Gosh, thank you very much. Sounds wonderful. I'm very enthused about this.'

'Good. Of course you know *Death Of A Salesman*.'

'Well, I know there's a movie about it and I know that it's a very, very important play. I know that it is being performed and will continue to be performed in theatres throughout the world.'

'But, you have *read* it.'

'No, I haven't read it.'

'And you call yourself an *actor*?'

'Well, no, I mean, I don't know. I act...sometimes.'

'How can you be an actor if you haven't read *Death Of A Salesman*? It's a classic!'

'If I read every book that was called a classic I would spend the rest of my life reading and I'd never act.'

'You're much too modern for me. Good day!'

SAUL RUBINEK
Auditioning at the CBC

In 1968, I was a 19-year-old actor just out of theatre school. In those days, CBC was pretty much the only game in town for television work. If you couldn't get seen there, you were screwed. It took me until 1976 to finally get an audition.

A casting director there had a little lap dog that went everywhere with her. She kept it in her office in a bottom drawer and I remember getting the distinct impression that if you were not nice to her dog, you didn't get in. Once during the interview, the thing yapped at me.

I didn't get another audition at the CBC for six years.

MICHAEL MILLAR
Here's the line

In the early '80s I was doing a lot of theatre but precious little film or TV. I was working steadily but wanted to expand my horizons. The auditions started to trickle in but it seemed impossible for me to get a CBC audition.

I was near the end of a tour of *Billy Bishop Goes To War* and feeling very confident and probably a bit cocky when I actually got a call to audition for a role in a CBC movie starring John Vernon. I figured the good press I'd received had led to this audition and approached it eagerly. I went to the fifth floor at 750 Bay and found the room crammed with contemporaries, all looking a bit annoyed. When I asked to see the sides I was told 'You won't need them, here's the line.'

'The *line?* What do you mean *the line?*' Then I saw all of the actors who were also waiting, many, like myself, with 10 years experience or more, to read for the role of a waiter who only says: 'More wine, Mickey?' I was more than a bit pissed off. I was at that time in the midst of a run, performing in one of our great one-man shows, one that required versatility and discipline, not to mention memory, and I could not understand why I was being asked to read for the measly role of a waiter. And why would they even audition any of us for such a small part, I wondered. Just look at their résumés and ask them, or throw a stick out here and whoever catches it gets the part. Lord knows any one of us could have done it. Why drag us down here for one line? *One line! And then on top of that to have to read for it. 'Read for it.' I thought, 'Why? Why read? Do they think I'm going to screw up one line, three words! "More wine, Mickey?"'* C'mon!

So, in I went. They were very nice and tried to make me comfortable by asking me what I'd been up to. I told them and they seem suitably impressed. Then came the big moment. They asked me to read the line. 'I'll show them,' I thought. So I looked directly into the camera and said with all of the authority of an experienced, confident maitre d': 'More nine Wickey?'

Oh, so that's why they audition for even the smallest parts.

After the laughter died down...I was told I had the role.

LISA LANGLOIS
Quincy Jones?

When I was very new to Hollywood, I had an audition for *The Slugger's Wife*. After I had read for the part, the casting director asked me if I could sing. I replied that I didn't know, that I had sung in the shower as well as in church. Evidently, it was the right answer because while I was home in Hamilton for the Christmas holidays, I received word that I was to prepare an 'R&B' song for the film's director Hal Ashby.

I didn't even know what R&B *was*, as I shuffled through the albums that I had left behind in storage. Nor did I know where I would find an arranger in steel town over the holidays. I settled on a Joe Cocker tune and found an accompanist from the local Holiday Inn piano lounge.

Once back in Hollywood, I found myself waiting on a sound stage with a very experienced but slightly moody musician who, like so many others, had not yet had his break. The assistant director appeared and said, 'You don't have to sing for Hal Ashby now. You're just going to go directly to Quincy Jones' house in Bel Air and sing for him there.' The name sounded familiar to me, but I turned to the musician and asked, 'Quincy Jones. He's big, isn't he?' The musician graciously replied, 'Yeah. He's big.' He continued, 'And you're gonna catch him in a good mood this morning. He's just been nominated for six Grammy Awards for Michael Jackson's *Thriller* album.'

MICHAEL MILLAR
The coin toss

I had been doing *Bus Stop* at The Gryphon in Barrie with Catherine McKinnon and so met and played tennis with her husband, Don Harron. Near the end of the run, Don asked me if I was interested in TV. I assured him that I was. 'Good' he said, 'because I've just written something that I think you'd be perfect for. I'll call you.'

Well, a few weeks later, I got a call to read for the lead in Don's new teleplay. I was very excited; this was pretty early in my career and though I wasn't always as sure of myself in auditions as I would've liked to be, this was, I felt, possibly a career-making role. I read it and loved it. This *was* my role! Down I went and I read. It went well. I got a call-back. I read again. It went even better, I thought. Then Don told me it was down to two people and I was one of them! 'Just be confident,' he said.

Don was very pragmatic and had a great deal to share if you were smart enough to listen. The big day came and in I went. I felt confident, I felt that Don was behind me but I also felt that the director wasn't that keen on me, but who can tell? There was a strange atmosphere in the room. My rival had just left and there was obviously something going on, but I dismissed that and focused on the job at hand.

It seemed to go well but I felt that the director was searching for something, some reason to deny me the job. After the read, he stared hard at me for a moment then said 'How old are you?' Well, I'd lost a few jobs because of that question and since I was three years older than the character I declined to answer. I didn't think it was an appropriate question but the director became quite hostile and asked again.

'How *old* are you?'

'The same age as the character.'

He threw himself back in his chair and said to his assistant, 'Tell him to leave.'

I was quite taken back by this behaviour, more so because this director was also an actor and seemed quite unconcerned with the effect his questions and actions had upon me, a fellow actor. I left feeling more than just a little disappointed.

I didn't get the role and I wondered if it all came down to that question or if there was something else I'd missed. I didn't know. I came to the conclusion that I had failed somehow, the age thing didn't really matter. The role was mine for the taking and I had somehow screwed up, but how? Doubt in my abilities took over and from then on, whenever I went to an audition I'd always second-guess myself. I was always looking for whatever it was that I'd missed so I could exorcise it. I was so full of self doubt and questions at every audition that soon I was screwing everything up and getting little or no work at all.

About a year later I was in the upstairs lobby at the Bayview Playhouse and who should I see but Don Harron. If anyone could tell me what I had done wrong it would be this man. He was there, after all, he'd seen the dreadful call-back and he was an astute observer with a wealth of knowledge to share. So I went over to him. We had a chat and then I blurted it out:

'Don, this has been bugging me for over a year now. Tell me, where did I screw up?'

'You didn't screw up,' he said, 'I wanted you, the director wanted the other guy, so we tossed a coin. You lost.'

I've never let losing a job affect me since. I learned more about 'the business' that day than any other day in my career.

GUY SANVIDO
The right place

Once when I was sent to an audition by my agency, when I arrived a young lady with a clipboard asked me what I was doing there. I was not on her audition list. I looked around and everybody else was in their mid twenties. It appeared there had been some mistake. She went back into the room anyway, presumably to discuss the matter with her clients, came out again, and led me back in to see the director and three other people around a table.

As I stood there with eight eyes looking at me, the director came out with 'Hey, maybe we could make "Walter" an older guy. What do you think?' They told me to leave my picture and résumé, which I did.

As I came out of the room, a receptionist said I was to call my agency right away. They'd sent me to the wrong audition and I was to hightail it to another address. So off I went to the right address and auditioned there as well.

Ironically, I got the part of Walter, for the commercial I was never intended to read for, and which turned out to be not just one commercial but nine, and I didn't get the one that I was originally intended for!

KENNETH WELSH
If you say so

When I arrived in New York it took me a year and a half to get a job in the city. When I did, I started on Off Broadway doing very interesting plays, among them the play by Canadian writer David French, *One Crack Out*.

Soon after, I worked with a wonderful actor, whom I still treasure, the late John

Aquino. He told me he'd got a part in a new play going on at the Public Theatre and that there was a part in it just right for me.

'But the director's weird, so you gotta come in and look weird. Wear a suit and...some galoshes.'

I followed his advice and got the part. The play was the North American pre-mière of Sam Sheppard's *The Curse Of The Starving Class.*

PAUL SOLES
I *am* Rappaport!

On a visit to New York I went to see Herb Gardner's play, *I'm Not Rappaport,* on Broadway, starring Judd Hirsch. Thirty seconds into the play, I was out of my chair, killing myself laughing and thinking, 'I've gotta do this play. I've gotta do this play.' I came back to Toronto, called my agent and told him I'd like to see if anyone had the rights to do this play.

'Oh, yeah. The Mirvishes are doing it at the Royal Alex. Didn't you know?'

'No, I didn't, but I gotta get an audition.'

'But, Paul, that part's for an 82-year-old!' I was 56 at the time.

'How old do you think Judd Hirsch is, who's doing it in New York?' My guess was that he was at least ten years younger than I was and he'd just won a Tony for his work in the role.

I did my audition for the director, Guy Sprung. I felt pretty good about it. The feedback from Sprung was that he thought I was great, just too young. I knew many other people wanted the part, too, so I just went home and watched the papers every day to see who had been cast.

I had to go away. I went. Months went by with no word. I came back to Toronto and decided to make a last attempt. I called Beverley Cooper-Seely, who did the incredible make-overs for Second City, and asked her if she could help me. I needed a wig and make-up to make me 82. I went to a thrift store, got a costume and called up my agent to ask him to get me five minutes with Sprung.

All made over and looking wonderfully old, I walked into Toronto Free Theatre to see Sprung. He was standing at the top of the stairs. He saw me and burst out laughing. We talked for five minutes and three weeks later I got the call. I had the part. Apparently I'd been third or fourth down the list.

In my life that was the only part I have really wanted. The only time I knew in my bones, this was the part for me. Indeed, it turned out to be the great experience of my professional life.

MICHAEL HOGAN
Still auditioning

At the beginning of our careers Richard Donat and I had these 'life' conversations. They would be about things like where we were going to be in twenty years. We would talk about how we were living life just the way we wanted. We felt great. We had no insurance policies, no furniture, and no debts. We swore we would never be bogged down with belongings.

Some number of years later Dick and I got to thinking about things. We realised that he and Maggie had a farm in Nova Scotia and an apartment. Susan and I had the place in Toronto and the farm. We figured out that by then, between us, we had seventeen beds, five TVs, eight couches, all these *belongings*. Things didn't seem to be turning out quite as we'd imagined.

Around that same time, there used to be a casting place on Yonge Street in Toronto where the usual gang would meet to do auditions, Dick, Booth Savage, David Fox, myself, the whole crowd of us. We'd sit around, read our sides, smoke cigarettes and try to distract each other.

One day I had to go there to pick something up. When I walked into the room who did I see? There was Tony van Bridge, Paul Craig, Larry Reynolds, all these guys 20 years our senior. There they were still doing exactly the same stuff that Neil Munro and Dick and I were doing when *we* got called in to audition! I was stunned. I raced right over to Dick's.

'You'll never guess what I just saw. I just saw us 20 years from now! Sitting in that room looking over our sides and smoking cigarettes. The same thing!'

Well, some of us stop smoking from time to time but, by God, we're still auditioning.

Nope. Not what we imagined.

MICHAEL HEALEY
Tom?

I once thought about changing my name, making it more actor-y. When I was in my second year in theatre school I had some résumés printed up calling myself M. Thomas Healey.

That year we students were all given auditions for Toronto Free Theatre's *Dream in High Park,* with R.H. Thomson directing. I arrived with plenty of time to spare, and sat down to wait with the others. The door opened, and R.H. Thomson stuck his head out.

'Tom?' he said. 'Is Tom here?'

Silence.

'Poor little sap,' I thought to myself, looking around like everyone else. 'He's late. He's blown this one.'

REX HAGON
Nude auditions at *Brompton Place*

The audition was for a television series that was to be Canada's entry into the soft porn TV market, produced by Global TV and some production company from

Chicago. All the actors auditioned on the understanding that there would be some nudity in the program.

After the first clothed audition, if they were interested, there was to be a second audition that would involve taking our clothes off and showing ourselves to the production people. Presumably they were looking for physical defects or unsightly tattoos. Perhaps they just wanted to be sure we would really be able to take our clothes off in public.

For the second audition the 'lucky' ones found themselves gathered together in the lobby of Global TV. We got fairly giddy. We were trying to crack jokes. We had all pumped ourselves up by telling ourselves it didn't matter or that we didn't care. Among the chosen were several people who were very active on the council of the Toronto Branch of ACTRA, as well as other recognisable, seasoned professionals. Everyone there knew that they would have to walk down into that studio and take off their clothes! We weren't exactly sure what to expect because *none of us had ever done this*. Some of us were mature people for whom standing around naked in a studio was not high on our list of things to do.

My turn came and I took the long walk into the dark studio. Sitting in a semi-circle were the executives from the production companies, the director, the hairdresser, the make-up artist, and a female representative from ACTRA there to see that all was handled properly, pardon the pun. Last but not least was the female casting director who had cast the whole thing.

'Could you just go behind that screen and come out when you're ready?'

'Oh, yes. Sure. No problem.'

I walked behind the screen and there was the group dressing gown hanging forlornly on a hook. I stood there taking off my shirt thinking, 'Good God, I've worked in the business for all these years to do this? Well, just be cool. You can do it.'

So I did it. I stood there, completely naked, and let all these people look at me, and everyone else did the same. All I could think of was that the casting director and someone who worked in the ACTRA office was going to see our genitalia. Well, we all got our roles so I guess the genitalia passed muster. The series, mercifully, didn't last.

LINDA GORANSON
Behind Door #2

A few years ago, I heard about auditions for a play that had in it a part I thought I might be very well suited for. I really wanted to get the part, so I fought for an audition.

As it happened, the night before, I had been flown to Ottawa to do Bruno Gerussi's cooking show as the guest celebrity. They sent a stretch limo to the airport and I was given the star treatment all the way. I was feeling pretty full of myself by the time I got home. I just knew that I could go out and *get* this job. Back in Toronto, I arrived at my audition the next morning at 10 a.m. I was pretty tired but I had worked very hard to prepare. I had chosen my wardrobe carefully and done heavy dark eye make-up which I felt the character would have worn. I walked into the audition feeling pretty good and did my piece. When I had finished, the director (who shall remain nameless) spoke to me.

'Linda, I brought you into this audition because I thought you could bring something new and wonderful to the part. Obviously you can't. So thank you very much.'

I was so shocked, that I stumbled to the door, opened it, closed it and burst into tears before I realised that I had gone into the *broom closet*. There had been two doors side by side and I had stumbled blindly through the wrong one.

By then I had totally disintegrated, sobbing, in the closet and I *couldn't go out*. I decided to wait him out. I was just going to wait until he went away. Meanwhile tears were pouring down my face through the black eye make-up which by that time was smeared everywhere. I still couldn't stop sobbing. At the same time, I was trying to put my ear to the door hoping that he would leave. I knew that he knew that I was in there. But there was nothing that could make me leave that closet until he was gone.

Finally I realised that he was not going to leave and that I would *have* to come out of the closet. There were other people auditioning and I couldn't stay in there all day...as much as I wanted to. So I thought I'd open the door and try to pretend I was invisible and find my way out. I cracked open the door.

He was still there...sitting behind the desk. He hadn't moved. He had sat there staring at the door, apparently waiting to see how long it would take me to come out. He stared at my face which, I discovered later, was just about black from streaked eye make-up. By then, I had slightly more control over my gasping but I could still barely speak.

'I got the wrong room.'

'I know.'

'So where's the door?'

He pointed...and I left.

PATRICK McKENNA
Dead man dancing

As a veteran of The Second City Theatre Company, I used to carry the burden of not being recognised in the acting community as a 'legitimate' actor. Second City is successful, it's popular, but it's not 'real'. So when Don Shipley, then the Artistic Director of the prestigious Grand Theatre in London, Ontario, invited me to audition for his new show, *Barnum*, I was a god amongst my peers. I was to have a prepared song and dance clothes. I had neither. But I did have two days!

The day came. Little did I know I was about to be taught the difference between a singer, a true singer, and a guy who, in his cups, thinks he sounds a lot like Elvis. I strutted into the audition, which was being held in the hallowed Stratford rehearsal space. Other actors filled the room...with just their voices.

I was dead.

People began singing renditions of *Memories*, *Miss Otis Regrets*, *Ole Man River*, and even a jazzed-up version of *Oh Canada*.

I was dead.

I was far too embarrassed to sing my pseudo-witty, almost clever little Second City ditty, so...I sang the scales. The musical director complimented me on my arrangement of the *Do, Re, Mi* standard and how cleverly I had made each individual note sound the same. Even I knew that wasn't a compliment, but all my quivering lips would allow to pass was 'Thank you'.

I was so dead.

I thought that if I walked back to my seat coughing and gingerly touching my throat, people might think, 'Oh, he can really sing. It's just that he has recently come out of a throat operation and his vocal cords haven't had time to properly heal yet. What a brave guy!' Instead, most of them had that look on their faces that people get when a lunatic gets on a bus with them, that Please-God-don't-let-him-sit-next-to-me look. I went straight to the back of the room, sat down and prayed that if spontaneous combustion were a true phenomenon it should please burn me up now. Instead, we moved on to the dance portion of the day.

I was dead.

It was on this day that I also learned that the title 'singer/dancer' is not as uncommon as I had once thought. The room was practically full of them. I say 'practically' because I knew that I could not sing or dance, so technically it couldn't have been full. Again I made my way to the back of the room, as might a beginner that had mistakenly walked into an advanced jazzercise class. No matter how hard I tried to hide, it seemed that amongst the neon green and purple spandex ultra lightweight Danskins that revealed far more than I ever wanted to know about these people, my torn Boston Bruin hockey sweater and sweat-stained, over-sized, grey fleece track pants made me stand out.

I was dead.

The choreographer bounced up to the front of the room with a 'don't start with me' look that I haven't seen since I was nine years old and my father woke up with a hangover on New Year's morning. Our dance captain introduced himself and then proceeded to speak in a half lyrical, half voodoo language that all the other people in the room seemed to understand. He finished with, '...On my count...One, two, three and...'

The music started and practically everyone started to move. I was frozen. My brain went numb and the veins in my forehead began to swell to the point that people might have thought that I had four ears!

Dead man...*dancing!*

Then the weirdest thing happened. I began to dance, dance as I had never danced before. It was that bad! I leaped when they leaped, turned when they turned and 'step-ball-changed' with the best of them! Well, most of them...some of them...okay, there *was* one guy there that danced like me but he was a delivery boy dropping off fruit and sandwiches for the director.

Finally the music stopped and the unthinkable happened. The terrible man at the front of the room yelled.

'I want everyone to turn around and watch the man in the hockey shirt at the back. He is the only one doing it with any life!'

Every Arthur Murray-trained eye in the room turned and glared at me. It was at this exact moment that I realised that Depends undergarments are not just for seniors.

'One, two, three and...'

The music started and so did my feet. I jumped, hopped, turned, tripped, hopped some more, crawled a bit and smiled a lot, all the while internally screaming, 'Kill me, kill me now!'

The music stopped, the dancers all nodded their acknowledgement of my steps and away they went, 'One, two, three and...' Now everyone was dancing...*just like me!* I *loved* it! Over sixty of Canada's finest musical performers suddenly looked like they were auditioning for the lead in 'The Jerry Lewis Story'! I wasn't dead! Man, that was *living!*

I didn't get a part in the show, but I did sneak into a rehearsal. Bruin hockey sweaters were all the rage.

SAUL RUBINEK
Sorry, not interested

In 1968 in Toronto the only theatre where you could get paid real money at that time was something called Theatre Toronto run by Clifford Williams. I arranged to try out for an apprentice position, which meant I would probably carry a spear.

My standard audition pieces were a medieval piece, 'Bosola' from *The Duchess of Malfi* and a Renaissance piece, 'Malvolio's' letter scene from *Twelfth Night*, both of which are lengthy.

In the middle of the audition, I began to realise that it was not going well. I was boring. It was awful. Clifford Williams and a couple of others were barely looking up. I knew I was dying in this audition but somehow I *had* to save face. I had somehow to come out of this with some dignity intact. So I stopped abruptly in mid sentence.

'What did you say your season was?'

Boy, did heads look up. Suddenly everyone was looking at me. Finally I've got them. I repeated the question. They were completely thrown.

'Well, we're doing *The Deputy* and...' they continue to list their season. I listened, nodding.

'Nah, I'm not really interested.'

And I left.

2

Beginnings, Mentors, and Influences

FRANK SHUSTER
Brass tact

I was born in Toronto and when I was about six, sometime in the '20s, my movie projectionist dad ran a movie theatre. There were no baby sitters at that time so I was brought up in the theatre. My mother sold tickets, my older sister took the tickets, and I was just the little kid who sat around. I learned to read from the subtitles on the films. At the end of the night, after I had lifted the seats and looked for pennies, my father often had to carry me home because I had fallen asleep.

As a kid I watched Chaplin, Buster Keaton, Harold Lloyd, all the greats. I loved comedy and the whole family liked show business. My mother loved music and we went all the time to concerts and shows. When I got to Harbord Collegiate there was show business there and I met Johnny Wayne. In the middle thirties Harbord used to do Gilbert and Sullivan operettas. Then at the University of Toronto we naturally ended up in the *UC Follies*.

After graduating we started in radio. Then, in 1942, when Johnny and I joined the army, the *Canadian Army Show* came along. All the army knew was that they wanted a radio show first and then a stage show. There was no specific unit at the beginning so they gathered together some enlisted performers and musicians and posted us all in Montreal.

The commanding officers knew Shuster and Wayne from our years on radio. By then we'd had a couple of different programs, so Johnny and I ended up writing most of the music, book, and lyrics for the show. Although the army offered me a commission, they didn't offer Johnny one. I told them we were partners and had to be the same rank, so we both started off as sergeants. We never got any further because we were trouble makers. You see, nobody in the army knew much about show business. Even the men who were our commanding officers. So we would sit around the discussion table with all these majors and captains, and boss the brass around.

In order to make this a unit the brass had to make a good show and they could tell we had the instincts for the business so they were kind of afraid of us. Every now and then the brass would ask 'How about a Spanish number?' They really seemed to like Spanish numbers. We would say 'What for?' The colonel would say 'How about this?' And we would say 'No. That won't work.' They had to believe us. This was a show so we were going to be honest. We didn't want to be in a lousy show. They had to trust us but they didn't have to promote us.

MARTIN LAGER
If not me, then...

All through my younger years, my mother had always been supportive of my amateur theatrical endeavours. I had studied with various teachers and been very active in amateur theatre. I then took it upon myself, as all hopeful actors had to do in the mid-1950s, to do a CBC drama audition before Casting Department Chief, Eva Langbord. I passed! I made *the* decision. I would become a professional actor.

My mother was appalled. Her fondest hope for me was that I might become a pharmacist and perhaps eventually earn as much as one hundred dollars a week, surpassing even my tailor father's average weekly stipend. Years later, I learned from my sister the lengths to which my mother had gone.

Fearing for my sanity, my mother made an appointment to meet with the psychologists at the Jewish Child and Family Services Agency. She gave these learned specialists chapter and verse of the situation, detailing the family history and the aberration of an offspring who wanted to be an actor and was about to enter the unseemly profession of the theatre. Perhaps, she suggested, the problem stemmed from the marriage of grandparents who were first cousins. After many hours of consultation, the psychologists returned their verdict. They advised my mother that despite her understandable concern, they felt that there was little they could do in respect of her son, the budding actor. But...they were very anxious to see *her* again!

In the end, my mother was my staunchest fan, travelling miles to see my performances wherever they would be, and she was continually amazed that I could actually make money while acting. I don't suppose she was ever sure why the psychologists thought it was she who needed the help. Everyone knew that one had to be deranged to practise this perilous career. Who knows? Perhaps she was right.

KATE REID
I thought I couldn't do it

Mr Guthrie said that you must be able to speak ten lines in one breath. When you hear something like that, you think, oh my God, I could never do that. I never had the privilege of working with Dr Guthrie, but he remains in my memory as a great man.

I was allowed to sit in on a couple of his rehearsals of *Julius Caesar* before I was with the Company. Sitting in that tent and just watching him rehearse people like Don Harron, Lorne Greene, Lloyd Bochner, and Frances Hyland was extraordinary. I thought: 'Oh no. I can't. I know I can't do that.'

In a strange way, it's like watching soap shows of which I am an addict. I have been asked a few times to do soap shows, but I think: 'Oh no, I can't do that. No.' And you know, I really didn't think I could do Shakespeare. And I still am not sure if I can. Quite honestly, and I am not really undermining myself.

This very young girl was given to me to take me over and over my lines. Her name was Roberta Maxwell, who I think will be, if not is, one of the major voices of the North American theatre. She was a tyrant, as far as my learning every comma, if, and but.

George McCowan and Jean Gascon directed *Othello* together and I got so confused by it. I said: 'Oh please fire me. I don't know what I am doing. Just let me go.' They just said: 'Oh shut up, just do what you are doing.' [Douglas] Campbell kept saying exactly the same thing: 'Just do it and be quiet.' So I did, and you know, I guess I was better then than I have ever been. I just wanted to get away from it but they believed I could do it.

Drama professor GORDON PEACOCK to KEN WELSH
and his fellow students:
'Some of you in this program want to be actors. That's not enough.
Unless you *have* to be an actor, switch your program.'

WILLIAM SHATNER
Oh, I had dreams

My first recollection of acting was in a summer camp that my aunt ran in the Laurentians up near Ste Agathe. I can recall a parents' visiting day, a Sunday, when we put on a skit. It must have been during the War because it had something to do with the War. The subject matter must have touched the people watching because I can remember people crying, the parents crying. It was my first sense of the kind of thing that can be effective on the stage.

When I graduated with a Bachelor of Commerce in June of 1952, Bruce Raymond, whom I knew through McGill, offered me a job as an assistant manager with the Mountain Playhouse on Mount Royal. Norma Springford ran the theatre and there was no opening in the acting Company at the time. Jack Creley and Barry Morse were the leading members of the Company. I spent half the season up-front watching these two experts work, especially in light comedy. To a great extent, I learned a good part of what I know about timing and comedy by osmosis, watching these two guys work. During that time I was losing tickets, dropping money, and making a complete mess of the books, to the point where they fired me as the assistant manager, and hired me as the juvenile.

SAM PAYNE, Artistic Director of the Candian Repertory Company
to a very young actor:
'A theatre is no place for a young lad; you should be
out in the open air!'

CHARMION KING
Birth of The Straw Hat Players

My final year at the University of Toronto, in 1947, was the first year that Robert Gill ran the Hart House Theatre. He started with only two productions that included Henry Kaplan, Don and Murray Davis, myself, and many others. For the following summer Gill invited eight or so of us down to the Woodstock Playhouse in New York as apprentices for a season of summer stock. There was no pay so we had to support ourselves. At first, we weren't even allowed to act. We just did everything else! Later American Equity relented and we were allowed to play some smaller roles.

At the start of the season we were part of a group of 20 apprentices but after the second week there were only eight Canadian apprentices. The Americans all left in droves because it was hard work, expensive, unrewarding, and on and on. The composition of the acting company was two juvenile actors, two leading actors, two character actors, and imported stars for the leads. Frances Bavier who played the aunt in *The Andy Griffith Show* on television was the regular character woman. We did eight shows in eight weeks.

One night, towards the end of the season, Donald Davis and I were sitting on the curb of the main drag of this tiny town, talking about what we were going to do. He had to go back to university but I had graduated. Although I had an offer from an agent in New York, what I really wanted to do was go back and do just what we'd been doing all summer. 'We could run a theatre.' If Mickey and Judy could do it, so could we. And there was no summer stock company in Ontario at that time. As we talked about it I decided to go back to take an MA instead of going to New York.

There on the curb we mapped out just how we could make our theatre work. We started with ten people including a business manager and a property person and an investment of $400 from Murray and Don. I had read that Port Carling was the centre of the golden ring of cottage owners and the Davis family had a lot of connections up in Muskoka because they had a summer home there. Our digs were a big barracks at the Muskoka Airport where the Norwegians had been housed during the war. We were able to stay there for $2 each a week because another Davis cousin ran the airport! And the Davis family also owned a truck so we could move the shows from town to town.

The following summer of 1948 we opened The Straw Hat Players in Jackson's Point, then moved on to Beaverton, then up to Gravenhurst, and on to cross-country tours and into Canadian theatrical history.

SANDY WEBSTER
If I can do this, I can do anything

In the late fifties I was experiencing a pretty thin stretch. A friend described a job that might interest me. At that time movie houses were involving their audiences in various promotional schemes. This particular gimmick involved about twelve of Toronto's larger cinema theatres. They were to give away a very elaborate set of dishes to the audience member holding a ticket with the winning number.

The campaign ran about ten weeks, and on one night of each week there was a draw at a central theatre. All twelve theatres were to be in touch by phone at a certain time. About an hour into the film the lights would come up. Someone would step out from behind the screen or the wings, and explain the deal. The audience had to be kept amused and entertained while a stage hand carried out the phone. It would ring, the person would give 'tonight's lucky number', and the holder of that ticket number would win the dishes.

This was the job my friend described. I was to get paid five bucks for each night—good money in those days—and I jumped at the chance.

It was just as awful as you can imagine. The audience was really hostile. They would let out a groan when the projection stopped. I had prepared material, all the jokes I could think of or steal from Bob Hope, and I would talk and smile as if my life depended on it. The phone would *never* ring when it was supposed to. Sometimes I had to fill for an extra ten minutes! When I did pick up the phone, I heard eleven other guys screaming 'Where the Hell have you been?' At least there were eleven other souls suffering elsewhere.

It was such a cacophony of static and voices and operators I never once heard the number. So I would just hang up the phone and reel off a seven-digit number from my head. Praying, even as I was doing it, that nobody had such a number or I would have been in deep trouble.

Finally, I told my friend I couldn't do it again. He begged me to do it just once more, until the present cycle was finished. I had a foreboding that on that very night my phoney numbers would be discovered. Nine times out of ten was pretty lucky. But I was still broke, so I said OK.

Then along came my chum Alex McKee. He had been a first-stringer on the vaudeville circuit in the early part of the century, a very capable and wonderful actor. I spilled the whole story.

'Why do you come on to the stage from behind the screen?' he asked. 'Lurking back there until the time comes is akin to facing a firing squad, isn't it?'

'Yes, yes, it is!' Understanding at last!

'Don't do that. Stand at the back of the theatre. When the film is stopped and they all start to moan or boo, start running down the aisle, shouting and screaming.

The general gist of this is to reflect something of their feeling but at the same time to be full of life and fun and some kind of salvation. When you get to the front of the theatre, vault over the footlights. Then, you need to catch your foot on the foot-lights. You can do a pratfall, I take it?'

'Oh, yes. Sure.'

'Well, that's it. After attracting attention to yourself, you take that fall. It's got to be really loud, as if you've broken every bone in your body. Lie there for a bit. Pull your-self together and slowly get up. I think you'll find the atmosphere's very different.'

I did exactly as he said. It worked like a charm. Even before I hit the floor, there was a huge gasp from the audience. Mind you, when I hit the bloody floor, I thought I *had* broken every bone in my body. I didn't have any trouble lying there. I played it to the nines and staggered to my feet. As I turned to face the audience, they broke into thunderous applause! The material was no better than it had been on any other night, but it didn't matter *what* I said. They laughed at everything.

I had the script in my hand, as usual. And, as usual, the phone didn't ring on time. So I just threw the bloody script away and that brought the house down. It was pretty much the same drill after that. I didn't hear the number, so I made up another one. Thank God, there was no winner that night either. I went to the box office and picked up my five bucks. Walking down the street that night I had never felt so good.

RICHARD MONETTE
On Eleanor Stuart, a great teacher

Eleanor Stuart was a very famous teacher. She taught Plummer, Colicos, Martha Henry. She was at the National Theatre School and appeared at Stratford doing 'Volumnia' opposite Paul Scofield.

I went to her when I was about sixteen. 'Mr Monette,' she said—she always used to call me Mister, '*why* do you want these classes?' I wanted these classes of course to learn voice production because I didn't go to theatre school. Also I wanted to get rid of my accent which was then a conglomerate of Italian, French, and English. It was most bizarre and it suited me for absolutely no work at all. I wanted to clean that up and I wanted to improve my voice production.

'Why have you come to me?'

'Because I want to be as great an actor as Laurence Olivier or John Gielgud.'

'Oh, Mr Monette, we have a *great* deal of work to do.'

Months later, I remember cracking open the spine of a script so it would lie flat and she said, 'Mr Monette...would you like it if I did that to *your* back?' She taught me respect for books, respect for words, respect for the theatre, respect for the work and ultimately, respect for life.

Eleanor had a huge influence on my life as an actor. We would spend an entire hour on one line of verse. I remember spending one full hour specifically on the line in Romeo's text, 'The yoke of inauspicious stars' when he's in the tomb. We looked up every word. We discussed the idea of stars and fate. It was an hour of *work*. She was Spartan in her discipline. I learned the most important lessons of my life in the theatre from her, but especially this:

'You do not become An Actor until you have twenty years experience.'

And she was right. It is very true. You can be a star. Shirley Temple was very talented and a great success at six, but you don't become An Actor simply from success.

AUGUST SCHELLENBERG
All this and caring too

My background was boxing, dock work, waiting, clubs, not theatre. Even so, I knew I was a story teller. I'd learned to listen from the many hours I had spent in clubs in Montreal. If theatre was about telling stories and listening, life as an actor would certainly be better than the lives I had already lived.

I began my new life as an acting student at the National Theatre School. During our first student summer session in Stratford, two fellow students (Ann Anglin and Bill Mockeridge) and I were rehearsing a short play. It was a student workshop, something we did on our own and directed ourselves. One day, as we worked, a stocky man with a mane of white hair came into the rehearsal space and asked if he could watch. We didn't know who he was but he seemed quite at home so we said, OK, sure.

He watched with deep concentration. When we finished the rehearsal, he asked us if we were expecting an audience and we said, well, yeah. The next day he had found some chairs and there he was setting them all out in rows. Then he asked us about lights, did we want lights? Well, yeah, that would be great. And soon enough he was hanging lights and devising lighting schemes to create cell bars or whatever else he felt would augment our little performance—which went off much better than we could have managed without his help.

That night we students received our first invitation to a performance on the Stratford main stage. There onstage, playing one of the solid supporting roles that comprised much of his enormous body of work, was our mysterious helper. It was none other than Mervyn Blake, the dedicated actor we soon came to know and love as 'Butch'.

JAYNE EASTWOOD
Thanks, Mr Christie

My first professional theatre job was *Marat/Sade*. I was an ensemble player and understudy to Vivien Reis, a role which, I am ashamed to say, I didn't take too seriously. Well, sure enough, she got sick and, God help me, I was *on*!

Much to my surprise, it actually went rather well, with the help of some improvising on the part of myself and my fellow thespians.

After my first night Robert Christie, a marvellous and much respected veteran actor, invited me to his dressing room, and complimented my performance. He said, 'You were very good. I didn't think you could do it. Remember one thing, though.

Always bring your voice up at the end of a phrase or sentence.' I thanked him, but I thought, 'Oh, man! How technical, how old school. Give me a break. I work from within, man. Don't give me that Stratford bullshit!'

I soon discovered that he was quite right. Ah! the arrogance of youth.

KENNETH WELSH
Who? Me?

In 1965 I graduated from the National Theatre School and auditioned for Stratford, Ontario. My audition was for John Hirsch, who'd been a teacher of mine at the theatre school. I dried. I had to start over three times. I thought, 'Well, that's it. I'll never work at Stratford.'

Incredibly I was offered an 'as cast' contract and was called for 10:00 a.m. on an April Monday, in Stratford. Early that morning, I said good-bye to my wife and drove from Toronto to Stratford in my old Volkswagen bus. Not early enough or fast enough, because I didn't get there until 10:10. I came in the backstage door and was greeted by the stage manager, Thomas Bohdanetzky.

'You're late! Here's your script. They're doing your scene and these are your lines. They're all onstage waiting for you.'

Waiting? For me? Lines? I thought I'd be a walk-on or something. It turns out I was to play someone called 'Captain to Talbot' and I had this big, energetic speech in the first scene of *Henry the VI*! Thomas showed me where I was supposed to make my entrance. I walked through the door, holding the book right up to my nose, desperately trying to see what I was supposed to say. I was on the Stratford stage. John was impatiently waiting for me.

'So, what are you waiting for? Come down the steps, come through these people and end up over there!'

I thought, 'OK, that's what I'll do.' I quickly glanced up and saw that they were all there: Bill Hutt, Tony van Bridge, Bill Needles, Powys Thomas (my teacher and mentor), Leo Ciceri, Max Helpmann. The entire general staff of the Stratford acting company was onstage looking at me!

I threw myself into the task. I came charging down the stairs reading out my lines. I tripped over the coffin of Henry the Fifth, broke the handles off and landed face down, spread-eagled on the stage. There was a long silence. Nobody moved. Then Bill Hutt came over and enquired gently, 'Are you all right?'

That was my entrance onto the Stratford stage

DENISE FERGUSSON
MTC, John, and the Fort Garry Hotel

John Hirsch 'discovered' me at The Village Playhouse in Toronto in 1961. I had just graduated from Carnegie Tech—there was no National Theatre School in those days. John came backstage when the show was over and asked me to play 'Raina' in *Arms And The Man* by Bernard Shaw at the MTC! I said sure. Was I ever surprised when the contract came in the mail and I found out MTC stood for Manitoba Theatre Centre and that it was in Winnipeg!

When the door to the plane opened, I had my first blast of 40-degree-below-zero air. We stayed at a hotel across from the train station called The Fort Garry Court and it was awful. I used to have to look out my door before I went down the hall to the bathroom because there was a man who used to chase me. It didn't occur to me to tell the management. I just thought that was the kind of thing that happened when you were 'on tour'. By the time we got to the end of the run a terrible smell in the hallway kept getting worse and worse. It turned out that somebody had died in one of the rooms.

The MTC was then using the old Dominion Theatre. There were big pillars all through the audience, and when you played there you had to get used to seeing people peering around these pillars to watch you. And you couldn't put the lights on around your dressing table mirror during the performance or you would blow the circuits.

The rehearsal period would be punctuated by John's snapping his fingers if you didn't go fast enough, a habit he kept all his life. You knew the rehearsal was going *really* badly when he disappeared into his seat and all you could see were his feet on top of the row of seats in front of him!

The costumes in those days weren't quite as elaborate or well made as they are now. I had a very diaphanous nightgown under which I was to wear a petticoat. Having just come from theatre school and having done some method work in New York, I thought it would add to my sense of realism if I didn't wear any panties. After all, Raina is in bed when the 'Chocolate Soldier' comes in through the window of her room.

Opening night my petticoat started to slip off. By the time I got out of the bed I couldn't clutch it any longer so I wiggled out of it and gave it a kick under the bed. While all this was going on, and it couldn't have lasted longer than a couple of seconds, I swear to God, from the back of the theatre I heard: Snap. Snap. Snap.

It didn't bother me. It somehow helped me to pull myself together. I grabbed a sheet off the bed and got on with the show. Afterwards I complained to the wardrobe department about the costume but I was too embarrassed to admit that I had left my panties off!

MICHAEL HOGAN
Drafted

My father was a prospector so we wandered in and out of Temagami when I was growing up. Then we settled a while in North Bay where I went to high school. I was out of school for a bit, then went back to get my junior matric exams so I was a little older than the other students.

One day, as I was walking down the hall, one of the English teachers caught up to me.

'Hogan, we had a meeting of the drama department last night and we have decided that you are going to be in our play this year.'

'Well, ma'am, I don't think I will. I've never seen a play in my life. I've no desire to see a play, let alone be in one.'

'That's OK. We've decided that you are going to do it.'

And, of course, the teachers were after me in every class I went to.

'I hear you're going to be in the play, Hogan.'

'Well, actually, no sir, I'm not.'

'Well then, maybe another couple of laps around the gym, Hogan.'

The Head of the English Department talked to me a lot and eventually I agreed to do it. I played 'Sir Thomas More' in *A Man For All Seasons*. And I loved it. I got right into it.

TANYA MOISEIWITSCH to RON HASTINGS:
'Just remember, dear, it's "play".
We're doing plays.'

KATE TROTTER
The question

I was a serious university student with plans to do a Masters at York and then a Doctorate at Birmingham on Film Criticism. The sweet and very dear John Brooks (father of Pamela Brooks) had told me that he thought that I ought to try out for the National Theatre School in Montreal. I had never heard of it but, being a well brought up farm girl who seldom disagreed with her elders, certainly never out loud, I signed on to audition.

I vividly remember auditioning for Douglas Rain and the look in his eyes as he asked me when I had decided that I wanted to be an actress. I searched inside my soul for the right answer, because when you are asked such a question by such a man you know you must answer with respect, not just for the man, but for the theatre's traditions and history. However, I had a dilemma...this was my very first audition. And I didn't think I *did* want to 'be an actress', whatever that was.

Those eyes continued to look at me so intently over those glasses...that '2001' voice* was still ringing in my brain. Then something hit me. I told Douglas something I had never told anyone else in my entire life.

'I was doing a student production of *The Seagull* in my first year of university and I was so overwhelmed by the role of "Nina" that I would find the same spot every night before the opening curtain and promise Mr Chekhov that if he would only please help me get through this performance that some day I would play his "Nina" properly. That was when I promised myself that I would be an actress.'

I had never spoken those words loud enough to even hear them myself until then.

I have never had the chance to make good my promise to Chekhov. But I have remained grateful to this day that the artist in Douglas Rain had the generosity to listen so keenly to one young girl's soul.

* Douglas Rain was the voice of HAL, the computer in the movie, *2001, A Space Odyssey*.

CLARK JOHNSON
How I got the bug

I was nine or ten when my mother took me to my first audition. Oddly enough, I got the part. It was a revival of the Broadway musical *South Pacific* with Mary Martin. The tour began in Toronto at that barn of a theatre, The O'Keefe Centre. Finally, after what seemed to me like decades of rehearsals, opening night arrived.

My character 'Jerome' opened, or should I say a beach ball opened the show. At curtain rise, an assistant stage manager tossed the ball from the wings. I was scripted to follow it downstage, catch it, and throw it to my sister (understudied by my real sister, Molly). Maybe the stage manager had a boost of opening night adrenalin, or maybe I was slow off the jump, but the ball sailed off the stage, bounced off the forehead of a cellist in the pit and into row three or four of the house. I froze in horror at the footlights. Fourth wall* hell!

After what seemed like hours to me, a quick-thinking patron tossed the ball back up to me. And that's when I threw out my very first of many, many career ad-libs.

'Big wave,' I cracked.

I got a nice house chuckle, I sang my number, and that's when it hit me.

The O'Keefe is a monster of a place. It seats three thousand fannies and that night we played to capacity. The wave of applause washed over me like the warm South Pacific sea. My mother said my face lit up like the lights on Broadway. I stood there letting the applause caress me. It was so wonderful that I almost forgot to exit.

* On a stage set, the invisible 'wall' between actor and audience.

WENDY DONALDSON
Opening night

My first professional job, fresh out of acting school, was at White Rock Summer Theatre (1983). On opening night of *Arms And The Man*, I hit the deck for my first scene, uttered my first line, and then suddenly heard an horrendous pounding noise. It was so loud that I couldn't hear another thing. It was so loud that I had to watch Corrine Koslo's lips to understand what she was saying. When they stopped moving I knew it was my time to respond.

I was furious. What techie would hammer something backstage during a show?! I would have a few choice words for someone later, as soon as I had a chance to find out who was responsible for the racket. Somehow the scene proceeded . . . then it hit me. *It was me!*

I was so nervous that my heart was pounding like a tympanum. The blood was pumping straight to my ears, deafening me!

MICHAEL IRONSIDE
Skid marks

In Canada in the '70s, when I wasn't acting, I did all kinds of jobs to stay alive. I did grip work on sets, craft service, anything that was available. Sometimes I would get to do a couple of days as an actor and then a few days on the same picture on the crew hauling cables. Once when I was making deliveries with Bob Wertheimer, who is now a producer, to the set of *Stone Cold Dead,* I wore a ski mask to keep the director from finding out that one of his actors was also crewing. He called me 'the Phantom'. What was really great was that the crew would never tell him who I was because they were protecting me as one of their own.

I was dead broke. The roofing business (where I also picked up work) was slow, none of the things I had auditioned for were happening. I was getting tight to the belt, so I phoned a friend of mine and asked if there was anything on a crew somewhere. She said that there was but that it was only a fourth wardrobe assistant. I asked what I had to do. She said that it was basically doing laundry on *Nothing Personal*.

This picture starred Donald Sutherland, Suzanne Somers, Roscoe Lee Browne, Dabney Coleman, Saul Rubinek. It was a typically '70s picture, a bad imitation of an American picture with a bloated budget, a bad script, and an armload of American stars dropping in to do cameos.

It was my job to do Donald Sutherland's personal laundry every night...by hand. What made it more difficult was that for some reason I couldn't use phosphate soap. I had to use goose grease soap every night to try to get the skid marks out of Donald Sutherland's underwear.

I was not having a good time.

I did that for two weeks. Then I found myself hired as an actor for a bit on the same film. I was to play a brusque motorcycle cop with a lot of 'attitude' who was to pull Donald's character over for speeding and tell him to get out of the car. It was a nothing scene but I had the 'attitude' down without too much trouble.

When we finished the scene, Donald came up to me and said, 'You are fabulous to work with. What were you using as a base for all of this? Your animosity was very real.' I smiled, remembering those skid marks, and said, 'Nothing.'

NICHOLAS CAMPBELL
Landing on *A Bridge Too Far*

When I was a young actor in England, I was so broke that I was calling bingo numbers in Tottenham for food money. One morning my agent, Hazel Malone in London, called to say that Sir Richard Attenborough wanted to see me at his home, Beaver Lodge in Richmond.

From where I lived in London, it took about two hours to get there by subways. I was up around 4 a.m. to make it in time. When they showed me into the house, they took me to the kitchen and actually gave me breakfast. As I was sitting there, in came Sir Richard with two scripts, one of which he left on the table. We chatted for a minute about hockey or something, then he got up and said, 'Well. Very sorry. I have to go. Lovely talking to you. Sorry it can't be more.' And he started to leave.

'Sorry it can't be more? Does that mean I got the part?'

'Yes.'

I looked at it and there were actually a couple of scenes for me in this huge movie!

I was so excited I went home and called my mother. She asked if I had a contract yet.

'It's *Sir Richard Attenborough*, Ma!' She still wanted to know about the contract. I told her I couldn't talk to her and put down the phone.

It was Friday morning of a long weekend when my agent called again. As far as I knew, I was supposed to be in Holland to start shooting on Wednesday of the following week, so I was surprised when she told me that the casting director wanted to see me right away. I got down there within the hour and read the scene for her. At that point, I didn't know whether I had the job or not. So I asked her. 'We just want to make very sure. Dicky liked you but...' and she muttered something. I figured they were bringing in someone from the States and were trying to let me down easy.

I went home and was in tears when the phone rang. It was my mother asking if I had signed the contract yet. I didn't *know*. The next two days were hell. I had no money at all. I don't remember if I ate. By Monday, it was OK. I had the job.

I arrived at the airport in Holland. It was the beginning of the movie. All I knew was that a lot of big stars were in it. There must have been twenty-five huge guys from the U.S., Britain and Europe in this movie: James Caan, Sean Connery, Robert Redford, Laurence Olivier, Michael Caine, Maximilian Schell, Anthony Hopkins, and so on. It was a who's who. The press was waiting at the airport expecting some of these big stars. They didn't know who the hell I was but they started flashing anyway, I guess, just in case. Next thing I knew, I was doing all these interviews. All I wanted to do was get out of there because I was kinda hungry. When I finally got to the set where I thought I could grab something from craft services, I was sent to a wardrobe fitting instead.

I walked into the room for the fitting and up on the shelves were rows of wardrobe baskets and prop boxes with names on them. There in alphabetical order were 'James Caan', 'Michael Caine', 'Nicholas Campbell', 'Sean Connery'. And my brain seized. Wait a minute, wait a minute. Wind this back. What happened there? I started at the beginning again. In the midst of all these big names, there I was!

It was the biggest moment of my life. It hit me like a brick. I just stared at my name on that box. For once I completely forgot about food.

FRANCES ROBINSON-DUFF, acting teacher,
to AMELIA HALL:
'Always the "too little", never the "too much".'

DENISE FERGUSSON
Leo Ciceri

Leo Ciceri was my mentor. He took me in hand by saying, 'I'm going to be hard on you.' But I felt that it was because he thought I was worth it. I was playing 'Clara' in *Pygmalion* by George Bernard Shaw. Leo was 'Professor Higgins' and Pat Galloway was 'Eliza Doolittle'. I learned so much from observing both of them. Leo was a wonderful actor. He was also a teacher. He saw that I was interested in teaching as well. He said, 'You must do this too. You have a responsibility to do it. If you are articulate and can pass the lessons on, you *must* do it.'

I remember particularly one performance of his at the Long Wharf Theatre in the States. I had been invited down to play in Anouilh's *The Rehearsal* directed by Ivan Brown. They couldn't find an actor with the elegance and humour and sensuality and vitality that Ivan felt was necessary for a particular role. I suggested Leo because Leo was all those things. Ivan had seen his work at Stratford and became very excited. Leo came down and he gave a definitive performance, absolutely brilliant. He had an amazing intelligence coupled with animal magnetism that is quite unusual.

Leo passed much, much too soon. His car went out of control on a particularly hazardous section of the highway between Kitchener and Stratford. He had been to pick up a friend at the airport and they were driving back to Stratford. His friend survived but Leo and his dog Chich were killed. I was working at the Shaw Festival at the time. The one o'clock news came on and the first item was news of his death. He would have loved that. He would have loved being the first item on the National news.

I talk about Leo to my students. I show them pictures and try to pass on some of the great legacy he left those who were fortunate enough to have known and worked with him. He taught us that integrity is everything in the theatre, that technique is a springboard and not an end in itself. He was a complete person. He investigated. He was meticulous. He was a robust extrovert. He would reach out and grab the audience and the other actors and haul us into the experience. He had a lust for life. By example he showed us that it was OK to be single in this life, to love and enjoy our work. That it was essential to care, to show your passion.

He hasn't really left. Every time I pass the spot where he was killed I experience a little wave of feeling. When I am working he taps me on the shoulder and reminds me of things. Robust energy like his can never leave us.

KATE TROTTER
On Roland Hewgill

I remember doing *Twelfth Night* as a very young actress. I played 'Olivia' and Roland Hewgill shone as 'Malvolio'. I still smile when I recall our first preview.

I was sure I owed it to Roly to inch my way down stage of him so he could be favoured upstage during our scenes together. I was, after all, very young and *very* inexperienced and he was...well, *Roly Hewgill!* Well, I inched down...and he inched down. I inched further. Perhaps he didn't see that I was giving him the focus, I thought. He simply inched down opposite me, continuing to share the focus. This went on for the entire scene until we were almost out of our light.

When we went off stage, that teacher of many lessons took my hand and, chuckling, said, 'That scene is about the two of us and we will play it equally. If you like, we can go and sit in the audience's lap, but if you are going to play "Olivia", my dear, you must take your place on the stage, for her sake!'

Like all the really great actors, I have never ever seen Roly steal a scene. He demands that you share the stage...that you always play a scene together.

DOMINI BLYTHE

I had the great good fortune to spend four years at Stratford working with the amazing Dame Maggie Smith. In all, I did eight plays with her. The first season I was so in awe that I could hardly speak to her. I had grown up in England watching all her remarkable performances at the National Theatre and in the West End, not to mention her film work.

By our second season working together, 1976, I had become a bit more relaxed around her. Our first production that year was Noel Coward's *Hay Fever* and then we opened in *As You Like It* by Shakespeare. In *As You Like It* I played 'Celia' to her 'Rosalind'. It was an absolutely stunning production directed by Robin Phillips. It looked like a Gainsborough painting.

Throughout the play the character of Celia supports the character Rosalind. It is Celia's job to feed the lines so that Rosalind will get the laughs. After a few weeks of playing in this glorious production, Maggie started doing things onstage that, at first, I completely misunderstood. She would cut me off before I had finished the last word of my line. Sometimes I would hear her sighing heavily behind me. I respected her so much that I didn't want to go to her and say, what's the problem.

The message I got was that there was a problem and that I was the problem.

I thought that it must have something to do with the way I was playing the scene, so I started to experiment. Then one night, after the scene had gone much, much better, she came into my dressing room and said, 'That was wonderful. Do you know *why* it was wonderful?' I was beginning to get the point. I was either throwing the ball, figuratively, too high or too slow or so low that she couldn't catch it, accidentally making it impossible for her to do *her* job in the scene.

She kept giving me these signals until, very gradually, I began to learn how to play it. How to throw the line so the volley would work. Nothing was said. Except that every time it felt right because the scene had a proper buoyancy, she would come into my dressing room and say, 'That was wonderful. Do you know why? That's what's important. Do you know why?'

Eventually I began to know 'why' on a gut level because she was teaching me on a gut level. I loved her so much for that. I loved her for two reasons. One, because I have rarely met a person who worked as hard as she did, who loved the work to such an extent that she would not let anything go by. Two, because I realized that she respected me enough to not just give up on me. She wanted me to be better than I was and she did it in such a way that I was able to *do* it. It was a huge learning experience. This is not something you can sit down and talk to an actor about. You have to feel the rhythm of the scene. Having experienced this I took a huge leap forward in everything I did thereafter.

ALBERT SCHULTZ
What's in a name?

[An excerpt from a speech made by Albert at Bruno Gerussi's memorial service, in Toronto, 1995.]

When I was 16 years old and I was in love with the plays of Shakespeare, I used to dream that, one day, I would play 'Romeo' at the Stratford Festival. I had never been there but my mother had and she told me about it. In fact, she had a couple of books about it by Robertson Davies.

I pored through these books. There were a lot of pictures of Shakespearean actors with really impressive names. Most of them seemed to have 'Thing Names': William Hutt, Eric House, Douglas Rain, Donald Harron, William Needles, Roland Bull and that incredible, lofty beauty, Frances High-land. And, then Bam! I saw him. It was Bruno! Bruno Gerussi, from *The Beachcombers*.

Some of you may remember the picture...Bruno as 'Grumio' in *The Taming of the Shrew*. He's slumped down low and sexy in a chair, pelvis thrust forward, hands jammed in his pockets. Jauntily sitting a-top that mass of black curls is, yes, a boating cap. It's as if Bruno had drawn that cap in later to say 'Yeah, that's me. Nick the Greek, in my younger days.' And, of course, his shirt is open just enough to say, 'Although I'm doing a Shakespearean play, I still have one serious chest of hair.'

The picture is all confidence, all ease. All terribly reassuring to a boy in the foothills of the Rockies who, like Bruno, didn't have a 'Thing Name' but who did also want so much to be a Shakespearean actor. Even though Bruno was, in my mind, Canada's biggest star, the nature of his appeal was such that he was one of us. If Bruno did it, then maybe I could too.

GORDON CLAPP
On listening

I was in Kurt Reis's workshop many years ago. He was about to direct *Death Of A Salesman* in Winnipeg at MTC and I wanted very much to play 'Howard', the boss's son, who is supposed to fire 'Willy Loman'. It was one scene. He put me through hell for this part even though I was his star pupil in the class; he made me beg him. Finally he gave in and I got the part.

In the first couple of rehearsals, I was really having problems. I was acting up a storm, but for some reason it wasn't really working. The guy who was playing Willy was an old regional theatre dog named Thomas Hill, who since he was 20 had made a career of playing 'King Lear' and Willy Loman in every regional theatre in the country. A wonderful actor, he was a Willy Loman like I had never seen. He was real middle America, not the little Jewish guy from Brooklyn or the blustery Lee J. Cobb version from the movie. This guy was so real, he just *was* Willy Loman. There was so much pathos in the look of him, in how he moved and spoke, and in the optimism that Willy kept trying to resurrect.

I was having a very hard time in the scene. It was basically my scene. I had to control it and drive it but I would look at the guy and I couldn't fire him. I couldn't act with him because he was just too real. I just wanted to say, 'Here, you take *my* job. I'll quit.'

Kurt found this all very funny but he was very frustrated with me. He came to me after rehearsal.

'I don't have any time for this. If we have to get some extra rehearsals...I don't know. We might have to bring in someone else because I'm not getting the feeling that you're in control of this situation. You're retreating through the whole scene. This guy has got you by the balls. You never recover and I don't understand it.'

He terrified me, but he couldn't help me. At the same time, I had to find a way of dealing with this, so I went to Tom Hill.

'You know, a lot of actors, when they are having trouble, it's because they aren't listening. They're not listening to what's going on in the scene. They're thinking too hard about what they're gonna do and how they look. They act listening real good but that kind of thing doesn't really do anything for you.'

I, of course, thought he was talking about someone else, but I thought maybe I'd try to apply that to my own performance. It proved to be a big turning point for me. I don't think I ever quite got the scene to what it should have been but it sure made a huge difference. And...I wasn't fired.

MICHAEL IRONSIDE
On doing Dad

I had an opportunity on the television series *ER* to play a continuing character called 'Wild Willy Swift'. They had originally conceived the character as arrogant and kind of hard-assed. I wanted to play it a little differently, more of a 'tough love' character, which was fine with them. I did not tell anyone that I was basing Willy on my father.

Other than learning the lines, the only preparation that I ever did for that part each day was to just sit quietly and get a sense of my Dad and just trust that.

When the second show aired, my sister called me.

'You're doing Dad.'

'Yeah. What do you think?'

'It's very good. It's him. It's a real person. It's really *him*.'

I was dying to know my father's reaction.

'So...has he seen it? What's he think?' She laughed.

'Ah...no. He's watching the hockey game.'

3

Support Staff

FRANK SHUSTER
Who *are* these guys?

Ed Sullivan knew what the hell he wanted. He had a great instinct for talent and for knowing what the audience would like. He just had a knack. He was what we call a 'civilian', nothing to do with show business. He had a regular column in a New York paper, so he knew what was happening. You can be sure if someone had done something special that week, they'd turn up in the audience for his show that Sunday night. Sullivan had an hour to fill so he would pepper it with something for everyone, covering all the bases, and he kept very tight control over all the acts.

Wayne and Shuster were the only people who ever had a contract that said that Mr Sullivan was not allowed to edit us. The only reason we signed with him was because we were allowed that privilege. When you're brought up in show business in Canada and everybody is starting out knowing nothing together, you have to rely on your instincts. Johnny and I loved The Marx Brothers and we loved movies. When we wrote a sketch, it was never a three minute skit. Our material was 20 minutes, or 18 minutes long. That was our style. All our sketches were really one-act plays. And we had to do what *we* did to make it work.

Our New York agency, MCA, would say to us, 'Give us five minutes and you can work anywhere.' We told them we'd call them if we thought of anything. There were a lot of variety shows on the air at the time. The agents just couldn't figure us out. 'Who are these guys who refuse everything?' We had a great attitude. We lived in Toronto. We already had a gig, and it was working for us. We didn't need to travel. We thought maybe someday someone will come to us and say do it your way. And that's what Ed Sullivan did.

It was 1958 and I got a telephone call at home in Toronto at 7 a.m. one morning from MCA agent Burl Adams in New York. 'This is Burl. I'm in New York. I want you to get dressed, call your partner, hop a plane and get down here in twenty minutes. Ed Sullivan wants to talk to you. Delmonico Hotel. Be there.' We thought, what the heck. So we did it.

In Sullivan's elegant hotel suite I remember there was a beautiful Renoir on the wall behind him. I was thinking, 'There's no red sticker on it. Is it his?'

I felt remarkably cool. I'm pretty good under stress. Johnny was vibrating. Sullivan started the meeting. 'I like what you guys do. It's fresh and it's different. I would like you for alternate appearances for a year.' That was 26 appearances on the biggest television show in North America! We were dumbfounded. We thought maybe three, but he had been carried away by what we did.

I was bold because I was thinking ahead to the things that might come up if we started with him.

'Mr Sullivan, we do long sketches, 14 minutes, 18 minutes.'

'I know and I don't like that.' Well, he didn't like it because he was well known as a butcher: cut, cut, cut. That's the way he ran his show. Then he told us a story.

'When I was working as a kid in Port Chester, New York, in the 1920s, I was called in to the city to work for the New York *Globe* as a sports reporter there. After two weeks I was called in by the editor. "Sullivan, what the hell are you doin'? What's this crap you're writing? This is not the way you wrote in the Porchester paper!" I said, "Well, I'm in New York now, with Damon Runyon," and I listed off all the names of the wonderful sports writers of my time. "I'm just trying to write like them." The editor replied, "Look, I hired a kid named Sullivan because I liked the way he wrote. I don't want you to try to write like somebody else. Do it your way!"'

Sitting around the table with us at this meeting was the head of MCA, East Coast, and all the top agents at MCA, guys like David Begelman and Freddie Fields. They were thinking, 'What's going on? Sullivan wants *these* guys for *this* crazy contract?' It was unbelievable. This important man was telling us how wonderful we were and how we shouldn't listen to anybody.

Johnny was the guy who usually talked all the time at meetings but, this time, it was me who wanted to make sure.

'Mr Sullivan, supposing you come to us and say you don't like something, what do we say?'

'If you don't like something I said, you tell me to forget it.'

I wish that meeting had been filmed because all these big, big guys were all sitting there with 'Whaaaat *is* this?' plastered all over their faces. We accepted Sullivan's offer. After that meeting, Johnny had a gold coin struck that said 'Do it your way! Sullivan.' He used to throw it on the table whenever there was any trouble.

The first sketch we did on the Sullivan Show was great, *Julius Caesar*, ran 14 minutes, big hit. The second show, *The Scarlet Pumpernickel,* ran 17 minutes. Seventeen minutes in a show that was bing, bing, bing! So, Sullivan came over to me and said, 'You know that scene in the Bastille, do you think that's important?' I told him I thought it was and he said, not unkindly, 'All right, you son of a bitch.' Deep down he must have been saying 'Oh, God. Did I get into trouble here!'

Eartha Kitt was on our second show, too. We were standing in the wings a few minutes before showtime and she said, 'What have you guys got on Sullivan?' I said, 'What do you mean?' She said, 'Look, I had two songs, I've got one song. Tony

Bennett had a medley of four and a half minutes, he's cut to three minutes. You've got eighteen minutes! *Who are you?* What are you doing here?' All I could think of to say was, 'He likes us.'

DON FRANCKS
Best can only be one thing

When I first went to Hollywood, my manager, Mace Neufeld, a wonderful man, took me to see the head of Universal Pictures. 'Mr Universal' sat behind his big desk.

'So, you're from Canada. You know, we really like Canadians. You people have done so many different things up there and you're not just pretty faces. So, what do you like to do best?'

'Well, I like to act and I like to sing and I like to dance and I like to do mime and I like to paint and I like to write music and I like to sing jazz,' and he's starting to look funny at me but I continued, 'and I like to do stand-up comedy and I like to tell stories.' I just kept going, talking about how one thing enhances the other.

He leaned forward and said, 'Hey! Hey! I asked you what you liked to do best!'

'I like to do it all. It's like flowers in a garden. They're all different sizes and colours and smells.'

He turned to Mace, 'Look, I asked this guy what he likes to do.'

'I like to do it all.'

'Well you *can't* do it all.'

'Well, thank God my name isn't Chaplin!'

Mr Universal turns to Mace again and says 'Who the fuck *is* this guy?'

'Excuse us, please. Don, let's just step outside for a moment.'

Mace took me outside the office to the hall.

'Don, where are you?'

'I'm at Universal Studios.'

'What do they do at Universal Studios?'

'They make motion pictures.'

'And what is it that you like to do?'

'Well,...I guess,...I like to make motion pictures.'

'That's right.'

We went back into the office. Mr Universal said, 'What is it you like to do?'

'I like to make motion pictures.'

'Let's talk.'

MICHAEL IRONSIDE
The first day on *Extreme Prejudice*

The first big American film I had a lead part in was *Extreme Prejudice*, directed by Walter Hill and starring Nick Nolte, Powers Booth, Rip Torn, and myself. It was a huge film, with a huge cast. We were shooting in El Paso, where I remember vividly that the parking signs in front of the city hall were so damaged by bullets that they were unreadable. I thought, 'Man...This ain't Toronto.'

We had had, by the first day of shooting, two wonderful weeks of rehearsals during which we, the cast, and the director had had a very congenial time. Everyone was friendly and I was very comfortable. The very first day, the very first slate of the film was a bank heist scene. We were set up on the street in El Paso. I was supposed to pass from off camera right and walk towards the bank around a Brinks truck and into the bank. Walter was sitting just to the right of camera and I was standing beside him, between him and the camera. They slated it and they called the roll. I was in a state of bliss until that very moment. Suddenly it hit me! Just over there was Nick Nolte, and on the other side there was Powers Booth talking to someone in make-up and then there was Rip Torn. You have to understand that I was and am a huge fan of Rip Torn.

This all happened in the split second that Walter was saying 'Action!' He tapped me on the leg for my cue...and I froze! It was the very first slate on the film and I completely seized. Everyone was waiting. The earth started to shift under me and I had a sensation of vertigo. I truly thought I was going to faint, so I grabbed the arm of Walter's chair. Walter said, 'Cut!' Then, quietly to me, he said, 'What's wrong?' I was in such a state that I just blurted out the truth. 'I'm really frightened. I feel like I've forgotten everything. This is the real deal here. I'm playing hard ball with the big boys here.' Which was pretty embarrassing because my mike was live and the sound guys were recording me.

Walter, looking like Winnie the Pooh in dark glasses and a hat, reached up and took me by the arm and he said, 'Me too. Every time I start a project I always feel like they're gonna catch me. Because I don't remember anything. It takes me about two or three days of faking it before I get the strokes back.' I said, 'Yeah. I feel like I have completely forgotten how to act.' He said, 'But I don't need you to act. Right now all I need you to do is walk from here, around that truck and into the bank. Do you think you can do that?' I said, 'Oh yeah, sure.' So the second slate went up and I did what I was supposed to do. But for some reason when Walter called 'Cut!', I just started to laugh and couldn't stop for about five or ten minutes.

BENEDICT CAMPBELL
Getting the chop

Sitting in the stalls of the theatre one day with my father [Douglas Campbell] and Neil Munro, I witnessed the near murder of an artistic director.

We were doing a production of *Mother Courage* that was not going particularly well, or at least, that was the opinion of most members of the company. The director was beginning to get as frustrated with us as we were with him.

The scene that was being rehearsed was not particularly complicated, but tensions were running a little high. Derek Ralston, who was playing 'the Chaplain', had either just finished or was about to begin singing the Chaplain's Song, a very complicated piece of music. Derek was very nervous about the song. To make matters worse, he was required to chop a pile of wood at the same time. He felt that the logs were too big for him to chop easily and he let this be known in no uncertain terms. He wanted shingles to chop. He felt that they would be easier and allow him to concentrate on the words and music, instead of worrying about whether he was going to chop off his hand or foot. No one seemed to be paying much attention to his complaints, so he became a little more vociferous.

From behind our vantage point, we just heard the director yell out, 'Oh, for Christ's sake, Derek! Just get on with it.'

'I beg your pardon?'

'It really isn't that difficult. Let me show you.'

At which point, the director proceeded to mount the steps to the stage. A fairly *sotto voce* conversation took place, punctuated with gestures from Derek and the director.

'Well, I'm not the fucking actor! *You* figure out how to chop them!'

'That is what I've been trying to explain, if you just got me something I *could* chop everything would be fine!'

'Just cut the fucking logs, Derek!'

Now Derek had taken about all the verbal abuse and mistreatment from this person that he could take. Before another word could be exchanged, a move of such forcefulness occurred that it threatened to become either serious drama or high comedy. Derek swung his hatchet over his head and started to advance on the disbelieving director.

Neil, Dad, and I got to our feet in one synchronised gasp, too stunned to make any other move. It was an electrifying moment, made absolutely hilarious by the image of the director high-tailing it for the back of the auditorium as fast as his feet would take him, hurling obscenities over his shoulder.

ALBERTA WATSON
On Michael Apted

My agent asked me to audition for a series pilot. I said, No. But I happened to be in New York shortly after that and the director of the pilot, Michael Apted, was also there, so I agreed to meet him. I had heard wonderful things about him and I was interested in meeting him even if I did not get the job. We got on like a house on fire. We did a test deal, I went back to L.A....and to make a long story short, I did not get the job.

A while after that, I got a lovely letter from Michael. He made me feel like an equal, a peer. He expressed respect and appreciation for what I had done and regret that it had not worked out. It was a very gracious thing to do. A few months after that, he was in Toronto shooting a film. When he heard that I was in Toronto, he phoned me and invited me to the set where he introduced me to Hugh Grant and Gene Hackman (who, not incidentally, made my knees weak when I saw him).

Michael was so giving and straightforward that I felt as if I had known him for years. He made me feel that he respected the effort that I had put into the work.

There are very few directors, even if they feel that way, who will take the time to let you know. And it is the directors who do take the time to do that, who make me willing to go farther in the work, risk more, work harder, give more than I ever thought possible. The respect and generosity that he gave me made me feel trusted and that I could trust him. And that kind of relationship can do more for a performer and their performance than anything else can.

I have heard other actors say that they would do anything for Michael Apted and I understand why. He's a decent human being and—an added bonus—a talented director.

SUSAN WRIGHT to SHIRLEY DOUGLAS when asked her opinion
of a certain director with whom Shirley might be working:
'Do you need the money?'
'Yes.'
'Borrow it.'

BERNARD BRADEN
One pillow is much like another

[This conversation took place during rehearsals for the 1949 West End production of Tennessee Williams' play A Streetcar Named Desire, *directed by Laurence Olivier.]*

The only person who argued [with Olivier] from time to time was Vivien Leigh.

'Puss,' she'd say, 'are you absolutely sure you want to cut that line?'

'Puss,' he'd reply, 'absolutely.'

And on we'd go. I wondered if Tennessee Williams had agreed to let Sir Laurence make these changes. He hadn't. There's a point in the play where Blanche [Vivien] asks Stella [Renée Asherson] how she can bear to live with an oaf like Stanley. Stella replies, 'There are things that happen between a man and woman in the dark that sort of make everything else seem unimportant.'

One day Renée read the line, and Sir Laurence said, 'I'm afraid that line will have to go.'

'Larry,' said Vivien, 'you must be joking!'

'But I'm not, Puss, I'm not.'

'Not only is it the most important line in the play, it's the *point* of the play!'

'A London audience will laugh, and we can't afford a laugh here.'

For the next five minutes, they went at it hammer and tongs with neither giving way. Then Sir Laurence, realising that the cast was being treated to what had become a family row between the theatre's best known husband and wife, called a halt.

'We must get on with the rehearsal, Puss. We'll hold this in abeyance and discuss it later.'

For the rest of the play Vivien gave a very sulky reading. Next morning we were all on tenterhooks, awaiting the crucial moment. It came, and Renée read the line. As the reading continued, Lyn [Evans] leaned into my ear and whispered, 'There *are* things that happen between a man and woman in the dark that sort of make everything else seem unimportant.'

Perhaps [Olivier] understood the play better than I thought.

WAYNE BEST
The actor's unerring tact

Many years ago I was hired to do an episode of *Night Heat* that was directed by the inimitable George Mendeluk. In one particular scene, I was supposed to be dead, having been savaged by Dobermans, and I was required to 'play dead' on a coroner's slab. Since the scene was between the actors who were discussing my demise, they needed my face to be exposed and my eyes open in a fixed stare with the rest of my body lying naked under a sheet. This meant that for the entire interminable scene I had to hold my eyes open while I held my breath and remain perfectly still.

We were taking a break between set-ups when George walked over to make a comment to the actors and to give me a word of encouragement as well. As George spoke to me he reached over and gave me a few pats. Because he was looking at my head he did not realise that he had been gently patting my penis. My eyes crossed and I sat up. Suddenly I saw his expression change and he said, 'I'm patting your dick, aren't I.' I said, 'Yeah, you are.' The sound guy, who was probably the only person who had actually heard this conversation, fell apart. He literally had to leave the room before he could recover his equilibrium.

I had the opportunity to audition for George some time later. Thinking I was being witty, I said to George, 'I remember you, you patted my dick.' George did not laugh. Needless to say, I did not get that job.

GORDON CLAPP
On getting it right

Because of the way I came onto *NYPD Blue,* 'Medevoy' was never written up as part of the series bible. Before Medevoy was established as a continuing character, before any of the episodes that I had done had been broadcast, Medevoy was evolving from a miscellaneous 'cop' character. And that was the case in this particular episode, which ended up being a week's work for me.

The director, Brad Silverling, was doing his first episode of the show. Every time we did a take, he'd come up to me and say, 'I want to do it again. OK? Let's do it once more. It's fine. I just want to get it right.' So he did this several times. I wasn't sure what he was talking about, but we did it over and over until he seemed satisfied.

Months later I found out the reason that he'd made me do it over and over again. Apparently when he had gone into the editing room, he had said to one of the editors, 'I had a lot of trouble with this guy. He had a really weird stutter. So can we cut around that?'

The editor had to explain to him that that was part of the character, that the character stammered and I, as a person, did not stammer at all. He had thought that I was just struggling with a natural affliction and was screwing up the takes because of it.

RON HASTINGS
The gift

Being in a poor production poses a lot of problems for actors but it is really crushing when the director, who has guided you through the performance, is unsupportive as well. One always makes the best attempt one can to be as good as possible when opening night arrives, no matter what one 'thinks'.

After the opening night of this particular less than successful show, the director arrived backstage with words so negative and destructive they cut to the bone. We had just struggled through an evening of desperation and were terribly vulnerable to any comment. That such thoughtlessness came from our director was too much.

I had bought her an opening-night gift. It was a plant. I didn't give it to her. I took it back to my home and put it in the spare room. And, although I know this is cruel, I didn't water it. I just watched it wither up and die.

WILLIAM NEEDLES
The measure of man

When the Stratford Festival was started in 1953 there had not been that much Shakespeare performed in Canada. The audiences were not so familiar with it that they had preconceived ideas of how it should be done. Tyrone Guthrie took advantage of this when he decided to direct *The Taming of the Shrew* in a very original way. His inspiration was the Wild West and he wanted to have some fun. The actors who formed that early company were, to a great extent, the same actors who formed the company of radio actors at the CBC.

Mavor Moore was to play 'Petruchio' but he had some misunderstanding with Mr Guthrie. So, as the understudy, I was suddenly dropped in as Petruchio. I was hopelessly unprepared and inexperienced. The terrific production and direction held me up. Ironically, because I was barely up to the job, there is a picture of me in that production that appears in dozens of Shakespeare books and now I am famous for that role. In the picture I am on a 'horse' with two well-known fellas fore and aft, Roland Hewgill and Jack Northmore.

Tony Guthrie was a towering figure. When I was rehearsing *The Taming of the Shrew* there were some days when my acting was OK and some days when it was really awful. When Tony would yell at you it was like lightning striking: Wrong! Go back! Get on the text! You can't invent Shakespeare! Can't hear you! Louder! I'd practically be in tears by the end of it. Then, when the rehearsal was over, and we'd come out of the tent to head home, suddenly you could have this big figure loping alongside of you. He'd throw his arm around you and say with a chortle, 'Didn't go very well this afternoon, did it? Never mind. Go home and rehearse in the shower. One's voice sounds much better there. Come back and astonish me in the morning.'

ERIC HOUSE
Dwellings

When Bill Hutt and I appeared on stage together in *The Taming of the Shrew*, Guthrie, in a playful mood, couldn't resist dubbing us 'those two desirable residences', a reference to the absurd up-scale property ads in the London Sunday papers. (Many years earlier, on the first day of a class at North Toronto Collegiate, Bill made a better joke at roll-call; it went, 'House?' 'Sir.' 'Hutt?' 'Sir. No relation.') But to continue this game, Guthrie might have noted that there was also a Mews (Peter) and a Holmes (Ed) in the company and that we shared a dressing room with Bill Needles and Doug Rain. Six substantives in one dressing room. It's a record that stands, I believe, to this day.

ROBIN GAMMELL
The patience of Guthrie

Although the Stratford Festival is host to an audience from all over the world every year, the town of Stratford is still a very small town in every sense.

I will never forget one occasion in my first season in the fifties, when Tyrone Guthrie was directing *The Merchant Of Venice* with Freddy Valk. We were in technical rehearsals, doing a scene where Franny Hyland as 'Portia' is greeted as she returns to Belmont after her triumph in court. Lou Applebaum had written stunning music for the show and Guthrie had hired some ladies from the local choir to be a singing chorus. The effect was magical.

The rehearsal went late into the wee hours of the morning partly because Guthrie was having trouble getting the ladies from the choir to move gracefully across the stage. Of course, they had not had any experience that required them to *move* at all while they sang, which is what the director required. One particularly plain woman struggled with the movement until an exasperated Guthrie finally blurted out, '*YOU...fucking goosey girl!*' Then realising that he had reached the very end of his civility, he stopped the rehearsal, announced that they would pick it up the next day, and abruptly left. They must have finished at about 2:00 or 3:00 a.m.

The next day I woke at my digs at about 7:30 a.m. and went down for breakfast. And as the landlady was bringing in the food she said, 'Did you hear what Mr Guthrie called Mrs "So and So". I have *never*...in all my life...!'

In the space of time from the end of rehearsal, when most people were presumably asleep, to an hour before I had had my breakfast, the story had circulated through town and arrived at the house where I had been boarding.

JACK NORTHMORE
Doing his 'thing' at Stratford

In 1954 an article appeared in the Toronto newspapers: 'Anyone over six feet tall wishing to play a soldier at Stratford this summer may see Mr Cecil Clarke'...etc. etc.

I was the first one there, all six feet three inches of 'starving actor'. When Mr Clarke found out that I had had stage experience and knew about 'stage left' and 'stage right', he hired me on the spot. I was to be Captain of the Guards (no words) in *Measure For Measure* and 'as cast' in *The Taming of the Shrew* and *Oedipus Rex*. I looked forward to a wonderful summer working for Tyrone Guthrie and meeting Mr James Mason, who was at the time at the peak of his fame as a film actor.

On the first day of rehearsals for *Measure For Measure*, all of the soldiers were issued eight-foot poles which would later become spears, pikes, halberds, etc. Mine was to become the rather large 'standard', a huge black lion, for 'The Duke's' (played by Lloyd Bochner) army.

Mr Clarke, Tyrone Guthrie's production manager, had been promised that one day he could direct a show. This was to be it. Mr Clarke was a very serious and methodical person. No doubt he felt the pressure of his debut as a director keenly. He was, as well, at a loss as to how to help Mr Mason adjust to the vocal projection required for the stage. Things had not been going very well. As a result, he would tolerate no fooling around or joking.

Mr Clarke could not tell the soldiers apart and identified us by the weapons we were to carry. As standard-bearer, I was without a weapon to identify me. In a very British accent, Mr Clarke would say to me, 'Oh, yes, yes, yes. You're the one with the big "thing", aren't you?'

No one dared to make a sound. But there was much shaking of shoulders and stifled laughter.

This way of referring to me and the part I was playing continued all through rehearsals, much to my embarrassment. However, I confess I loved the publicity. If you have no lines, you must be noticed somehow!

At the dress rehearsal, my pole was replaced by a standard which was about ten feet high with a huge emblem on top. We came finally to rehearse the curtain calls. The principals were to be sent off upstage and to the wings. Next the townspeople divided in half and were to exit into the two tunnels. Then the soldiers were to exit, half into one tunnel and half into the other. I was left alone on stage.

Mr Clarke 'hmmmmmm'ed for a minute or two, then said very seriously, 'We'll never get that big "thing" of yours through the tunnel with all those people, will we?' He paused, then, 'Well, come downstage centre and lift that big "thing" over your head—you can, can't you?—and we'll shine the spot on it.'

Great screams of laughter swelled from backstage and the tunnels. Mr Clarke was not at all amused and made his feelings quite clear. I, the lowly standard-bearer, had to stand there alone at centre stage holding my enormous prop and maintain a straight face.

TONY GUTHRIE to LLOYD BOCHNER. In rehearsals for *Richard the Third* for the first season of The Stratford Shakespearean Festival, Lloyd kept mispronouncing the name 'Buckingham'. Guthrie wanted him to say 'Bucking-um' but Bochner kept saying 'Bucking-ham'. After a couple of admonitions Guthrie dashed up on the stage and said: 'Look here, there will be no more Fucking-ham Bucking-ham!'

ROBIN GAMMELL
On Greek tragedies

I played 'Cassandra' and 'Electra' in Tony Guthrie's production of *House of Atrius* at The Guthrie in Minneapolis in the '50s. Douglas Campbell, as a chubby 'Clytemnestra' and 'Athena', and Len Cariou were also in the cast. It was one of the most extraordinary productions ever mounted at that theatre and still lives vividly in many memories. In mine, however, it lives for less glorious reasons.

Tanya Moiseiwitsch had designed stunning costumes, long flowing robes with full masks. Many of the cast were on stilt-like platform shoes as well. The effect of all this was stunning for an audience. The difficulty for the actors was that the masks were large and heavy and prevented any ability to see at all beyond a very narrow range straight ahead of you. This combined with the flowing robes, a raked stage complete with ramps, and unusual footwear meant accidents were pretty much inevitable.

Opening night, we are at the scene where I, as the beauteous Cassandra, was accompanying 'Agamemnon', as his prize. We arrived up from the vom (vomitorium)* in a sort of chariot. It had a front that dropped like a military landing craft when the 'soldiers' unroped it, allowing us to 'disembark'. Agamemnon has his welcoming home speech and a scene with Clytemnestra during which she is to entice him to what will be his murder. As soon as he disappears, 'Cassandra' is to fling herself into a paroxysm of prediction of impending disaster and doom.

Unfortunately, the guys who had unroped the chariot had dropped one of the ropes in front of me where I could not see it. As I charged forward, I tripped and sailed across the stage, ploughing a furrow across the polished stage floor with the front of my mask, almost falling into the gutter on the other side. I leapt up and continued with the scene nevertheless.

We finished the first act, and I raced backstage to change into 'Electra' for the *Oresteia* in which Len played 'Orestes'. Guthrie, six foot six inches of seersucker suit, running shoes and no socks, came back to my dressing room and said, 'Never mind, dear boy. Never mind. Looked exactly as if you had planned it. Very nice recovery. Now, here are some notes for Electra.' He must have thought that would distract me, but of course, if you are about to go on opening night, notes are the last thing you can hear. Meanwhile in the next dressing room, another actor who was sharing with Len Cariou came back and succinctly explained to Len what had happened. 'Gammell!' He slapped one hand off the other in an imitation of my skid across the stage. 'Opening night! Flat!' and repeated the gesture for emphasis. Of course, Len was concerned and wanted to know how I was. He poked his head out his door and as Guthrie was leaving my dressing room, quietly inquired, 'What, ah...what's going?...is he...ah...ahyah...what happened?' I heard Guthrie's voice as he turned back to Len and replied in a slightly pained, exasperated tone, 'Yes, yes. All right. Cassandra tripped on the front of her frock and fell flat, silly cunt.'

* Ramped entrance to stage from beneath the audience seating.

SCOTT WENTWORTH
Oh, pith on it

In Richard Monette's first production at Stratford, *The Taming of the Shrew*, William Needles was playing the 'Pedant'. He and Richard had decided that the Pedant should stutter: 'I've been to PPPPPadua and I've been to PPPPPisa...' Bill was up-roariously funny in the role. Richard had him enter down one of the aisles carrying a parasol and wearing a pith helmet. When he got to the stage he'd start the scene.

The actors were gathered for the note session at the end of the last rehearsal, spread out in the empty theatre. On stage, Richard was giving us notes and illustrating the things he said.

'Bill, when you come in down the aisle for your first entrance, don't wear the pith helmet because the lighting designer says we can't see your eyes. More importantly, when you start the scene you've got to be a lot "spacier" because the stutter is only really funny if you're spacey.'

Then Richard began to act out what he meant. He started getting laughs from the company, so he kept on going with the scene. Richard is a talented comedic actor and his imitation of Bill playing the Pedant was hilarious. Finally he said, 'So, Bill, it should be more like that. OK?'

There was a pause, then Bill said, 'So, you don't want me to wear the hat at all?'

SHARON NOBLE
Breakdown at MTC

For the production of *Cyrano de Bergerac* that starred Len Cariou in the title role at the Manitoba Theatre Centre in 1975, the director was the legendary Jean Gascon. Supporting cast included the cream of Canadian thespians: Roland Hewgill, Jack Medley, Dixie Seatle, Alexe Duncan, Doreen Brownstone. Len's wife, Susan, was playing 'Roxanne'. The fight director was the late Patrick Crean, a gentleman of the old school, instructor to Errol Flynn and Basil Rathbone. I was playing 'The Foodseller' in the opening and 'A Nun' in the final scene.

In rehearsal one day, we came to the scene where Robert Benson, as the baker, 'Ragueneau', had come to deliver the message that 'Cyrano' had been injured and was dying. Ragueneau stood upstage right to explain, in a distraught, trembling voice, the injury which had felled his dearest friend.

Director Gascon listened approvingly, then interjected in his distinctly French accent, 'Good, good. Now, break down.' Bob obligingly hunched his shoulders and increased the agony in his voice, continuing to tell his story. Gascon nodded again and again directed, 'Excellent. Now, break down.' Bob allowed his shoulders to shake and great sobs to issue from his throat. He was almost incapacitated with sorrow. He fell to one knee in Ragueneau's pain. We wondered how much more he could endure and still be able to repeat the lines. Yet the director seemed unsatisfied.

At last, Gascon arched his body toward Bob and gestured grandly with both hands as he repeated the instruction once more, 'Yes, *yes!* Now. Break *downstage.*'

The light went on in everyone's head, including Bob's, and without a pause or a break in thought, he moved downstage to finish his great monologue to a round of applause from the cast and crew.

ROSEMARY DUNSMORE
On John Hirsch at Stratford with *Streetcar*

In 1982, with John directing, we moved into rehearsal for *Streetcar Named Desire* in which I was to play 'Stella'. They had brought in Billy Peterson from Chicago to play 'Stanley'. He became the 'new boy'. John is notorious for being *very* good with the new person and, of course, that new person falls in love with him as I did in my first year. As this was my second season working with John, now it was Billy who could do no wrong. John in one way or another made it clear daily and often that I was single-handedly *ruining* it.

We were in rehearsals and about to take a lunch. As John was the artistic director of the theatre, people would descend on him. Everyone, administrative people and so on, wanted something or other from him. As a consequence, the entire cast and all of these other people were milling around waiting, when John decided to devise an improv exercise between Stanley and Stella (Billy and myself) to help us get at the heart of the scene that we had been exploring. He wanted me to hit Billy, hard, to really hit him as hard as I could. It was a badly conceived exercise and I was already so pissed off that I just hated doing it. I had never been so angry in my life. I was not seeing 'red', I was seeing '*white*'!

At lunch I walked past John. I was so angry that I was not even aware that anyone else was in the room. I remember walking by and screaming at him, 'You do it! *YOU DO IT! YOU* hit him! And see if *YOU* can discover anything! Why don't *YOU* go and do something...!' All these people were around. He said something or other, I can't remember, but we were yelling at each other.

This is so uncharacteristic, so abnormal for me that I was just shaking from the shock. But I remember stomping out, wheeling around in front of all these people. I pointed my finger at him and said, 'John! *John! Sometimes you can be a real fucker!*' and stormed out the door.

As soon as I got out the door, the silence hit me. I guess I was giddy from adrenalin, but I started to laugh...until I realised that I had forgotten my purse...and there was *no way* that I could go back in there. I was just going to not eat. I had no money, no keys. I was enough of an actress to know I could not ruin *that* exit. So I just had to hang around the parking lot until someone came out to feed me lunch.

Then we came back from lunch. Billy didn't understand it at all. He thought I was some kind of a weird prima donna. I came back 20 minutes late. John was there playing at the piano. I walked in the door. He stood up, he came over, he apologised to me very loudly in front of the entire company, and I never had a problem with him again. Instead, he focused his hostility on another actor. I guess he just needed someone to vent on.

BILL GLASSCO to RICHARD MONETTE: After a particularly
good rehearsal at Stratford involving Richard and the luminous
Brenda Donohue, Monette asked Glassco, 'Why can't I act like Brenda?'
Glassco replied:
'Because when you act you make it complicated.
When Brenda acts, she goes right to the jugular.'

DAVID FERRY
That old Canadian rag

Just the other day I was in a production of *A Winter's Tale* with Moira Wylie directing, and my old pals Douglas Campbell, Tom Hauff, and Nicki Guadagni. We were talking about Stratford. Moira passed on a story about my friend Michael Mawson working with director Richard Rose, in the Young Company at Stratford.

Richard Rose told the company that he wanted the Shakespearean language used to be 'Canadian Shakespeare'. He didn't want any of the British pronunciations. 'For instance; If you have to say the word Duke, say "Dook". I don't want to hear any of this "Dyouk" stuff.'

'I'm sorry, I can't do that, Richard,' said Mawson.

'What do you mean, you can't do that?'

'Well, if I said "Dook", it'd make me "pook".'

GEORGE SPERDAKOS
What a man

I first encountered Sir Robert Atkins when I went to London, England in 1956. One of those antique actor/manager/directors still left from the old days, he was a distinguished, portly gentleman of 70 with an extraordinary, plummy voice. Sir Donald Wolfit was another such a one. These characters actually felt that they owned Shakespeare. They spoke of him in the present tense as if he was a great friend and they'd just had breakfast together.

I had heard about Sir Robert and his Regents Park Open Air Theatre, in the centre of London, from another Canadian actor named Neil McCallum. I pursued Atkins and got an audition with him. He was doing *Twelfth Night* and *As You Like It*, then, later on, *Hamlet*. I saw him at least five or six times before he made his decision. Each time he auditioned me he would speak to me in ever so round tones.

'Don't quite know how to handle this, ole son. I should use one of me own for this, you know, a Brit, but I am looking for a fine, fiery young actor to play Laertes.'

By the time I had finished my series of auditions for him, I had done half of Shakespeare!

'Very good, very good, ole son. Let me think about it.' He'd look me in the eye, give me an equivocating wink, and then he'd murmur to me, *sotto voce*.

'I've got a lot on me mind. Just hold on.'

I did, but only just. Finally, I was chosen to be in the company. I was asked to play 'Charles, a Wrestler' and 'William' in *As You Like It*, the 'Sea Captain' in *Twelfth Night* and, of course, the tantalising possibility of 'Laertes'. I was thrilled.

The 'Rosalind' was played by a beautifully nubile young British actress of some fame called Belinda Lee. She was England's answer to Marilyn Monroe. It wasn't long before I realised that this guy, Atkins, was an old lecher and had gone quite gaga for Belinda. He was an Elizabethan in every way. While we were rehearsing, every time we got to the Charles the Wrestler scene, I'd be 'acting my socks off', as Atkins used to say, but Atkins was trying to impress Belinda Lee! I would open my mouth to say my line and he would interrupt me.

'Wait. Stop. Stop, ole son. Let a *man* show you how to do this.'

Of course I wasn't cast as Laertes in *Hamlet,* but was given several smaller parts instead. The old bugger had conned me. I will never forget him or that season in the park so long ago.

TRISH O'REILLY
A 'fraction' too long

The year I was at the Banff Centre for the Arts our final show was Kurt Weill's *Street Scene*. Michael Mawson was directing and the conductor was Peter Stanger, from Britain. Peter was a gentle and rather proper man, a very fine musician, but an absolute stickler for detail. His favourite phrase was 'a fraction'. Could that be 'a fraction' faster? Could you hold that just 'a fraction' longer?

Difficulties developed in the show over the melodramas (dialogue with musical underscoring) since Peter regarded his role as conductor to be that of 'guardian of the sacred score'; nothing was to be altered in any way. 'Kurt Weill wrote it that way for a reason and we must treat every note with the utmost respect.'

Michael, however, had spent months working with a group of performers who were primarily singers, attempting to instill in us an awareness of authentic impulse and staying in the moment, to improve our acting skills. He struggled to gently undo our conditioning to time things to the music and take our impulse from the score. Instead he taught us to actually react to each other.

Street Scene is a wee tad corny and stilted at the best of times, and Michael was determined not to let us fake it and do silent-film 'face acting'. However, that was just what the melodrama sections seemed to call out of most of us. Michael decided that for 1990s purposes, many of these sections would have to go. He had not reckoned on the 'guardian of the sacred score'.

There were clashes in rehearsal over this and rumours of even more passionate altercations behind closed doors. One day in rehearsal, we were doing the little scene where 'Sam' and 'Rose' are talking on the stoop in the evening. As they are saying goodbye Sam asks Rose for a kiss good-night. At this point in the score, there are at least eight bars of rhapsodic melody building to one glorious orgasmic chord. I assumed, probably correctly, that the kiss should happen on the chord and I, therefore, had *a lot* of time to fill.

So there we were. Sam screwed up his courage and asked, 'Rose, would you kiss me?' 'Why sure, Sam,' I simpered sweetly, turning back from the door. I paused significantly (*eight bars*, remember...), then I stepped off the stoop and hesitated again, and finally began to walk shyly, slowly toward him. I still had about two more measures to fill when Michael exploded.

'What the hell are you doing? Just walk over and kiss him!'

'But Michael,' I pleaded, 'there's a lot more music and there's a big climax, and I thought I should kiss him right at the high point.'

Michael wheeled around to Peter.

'Is that true? How much music is there? Play it for me.' Peter played the exquisite, lush and interminable passage in question. Michael just about burst a gasket.

'For God's sake, Peter! She's got time to give him a blow job!'

I nearly hurt myself trying not to laugh. Peter was genuinely offended and if the atmosphere in the rehearsal hall had been just 'a fraction' more tense, I have no doubt that there could have been a murder.

ORSON WELLES to ALEXIS KANNER, while rehearsing a
scene for Welles' film of Shakespeare's *Henry the Fourth,*
called *Chimes at Midnight.* Alexis was playing 'Hotspur' to Welles' 'Falstaff':
'That was a very interesting entrance you made, Mr Kanner.
Much more interesting than the entrance you will make when
we shoot this scene. Please always remember, it is I who own
the grocery store and it is I who will sell the groceries."

NICHOLAS CAMPBELL
Keep the duck

When we were shooting *Diamonds* we used to take it upon ourselves, in the first
season especially, to 'depart' from the script. Tony Rosato and I would just wander
off into improv and drive everybody crazy.

Sonny Grosso, the producer of the show, had also been the producer of *Night
Heat.* He had been a cop in New York City for many years and was the real-life
partner of Popeye Doyle on the bust that the movie called *The French Connection* was
based upon. Roy Scheider played him in that movie opposite Gene Hackman as
'Popeye Doyle'.

Once Sonny got so pissed off at me for changing the lines that he came down
to the set just to show me his cop licence.

'Why can't ya stick to the lines? Do I hafta show yas my badge? When CBS's got
a problem with *Diamonds*, is it Nicky Campbell that they are callin'? Nah.'

'But Sonny, the stuff's not funny.'

'I personally looked at it this morning. It's funny. I made some cuts. It's funny.'

'But Sonny, you cut half the joke. You got the first part of the joke here, which
isn't funny, and you cut the second part of the joke which is the funny part.' He'd
get so mad.

I fought with the writers so much in the first year that Sonny finally hired a
new head writer. We flew down to Los Angeles to meet him and when we walked
in, I realised that the guy had cerebral palsy. Now Sonny was always playing practical jokes on me. I never knew when the guy was serious, so I thought for a minute
that he was using this poor guy to play some kind of cruel joke, or that he'd hired
an actor to set me up.

This guy, his name was Nick Arnold, had a lot of trouble talking. Nevertheless
he proceeded to tell me this story:

'You have a hunter and you have a farmer. The hunter is out duck hunting. He
shoots a duck but it falls and lands in the farmer's field. The hunter goes to pick up
the duck but the farmer says, "Hold it. You shot the duck, yes. But it landed on my

property. Around here that means that duck is mine." Hunter says, "No. Where I come from, he who shoots the duck, keeps the duck." The farmer asks how he wants to settle this. Hunter says he doesn't know and asks the farmer what he suggests. The farmer says, "OK. I'll kick you in the balls as hard as I can and then you kick me in the balls as hard as you can and who ever stands up to it better, keeps the duck." They agree. Boom! He nails the hunter in the balls. The hunter goes down for twenty minutes. He finally recovers enough to have his go at the farmer. The farmer looks at him and says, "Keep the duck.'"

It took him forever to tell the story. And at the end of it, I was laughing and I looked at Sonny like, 'What is this?' Sonny explained that this writer had created *Welcome Back, Kotter,* and that he'd written for Johnny Carson when he was sixteen years old. He had a solid list of credits. Sonny thought the guy was a genius and it turned out that he really was the new head writer.

For the rest of the year, every time I got a bee in my bonnet about a script not working or not being funny or whatever, he'd say, 'Keep the duck.' It became a catch phrase for the whole production that year.

Nick Arnold was the greatest gift Sonny could have given me or the show. He was the funniest guy I ever met and he turned out to be a brilliant head writer.

SARAH TORGOV
On *American Gothic*

The teen horror movie, *American Gothic*, was about a group of kids downed in a plane crash and trying to survive on an island where they are being stalked by a serial killer. Everybody in the film gets killed except my character, the only one to survive the ordeal. In a lot of ways it was probably the most fun I have had on a shoot, but a lot of weird, strange, and not so pleasant things happened as well.

We were shooting on a small island north of Vancouver, and once we arrived on set in the morning by boat, we were pretty much stuck there until wrap. Early in the shoot, one of the cast members got drunk on the set while we were shooting and destroyed a day's work. They fired him. Because they'd already shot some film of him, they had to alter the script and kill his character off earlier. They still had to shoot his death scene so on his last day they decided to punish him.

When it came time for his death scene, the shot required that he lie in the bottom of a boat that had a lot of water in it and be slowly pushed from shore. The director made this guy lie soaking wet and freezing his buns off in the bottom of that boat for hours. They did everything to prolong the time he had to remain soaking in that boat. They told him he couldn't move because they had to maintain continuity. Then they'd reset the lights, change the roll, call tape run out from the sound cart. I don't even know if they were using film for some of it.

Another actor, from Los Angeles, was annoyed that he did not have a private Winnebago. It seemed to mean a lot to him. Personally, I enjoyed having some company. But apparently he decided to make things pretty unpleasant for the other actor, a very nice guy, who was to share the Winnebago with him. So he went to the bathroom, wiped himself and left the used toilet paper strewn through the trailer.

The producers punished him by killing his character next with a skewer through the ear. They poured a horrible mixture of dye and glycerine all over his face and hair and made him lie on a filthy, basement floor for hours while the crew took breaks and delayed.

It's a good idea to behave professionally on a shoot. If a crew wants to make your life miserable they can do it, but that kind of thing doesn't happen very often.

GARY FILES
Stage hands

In the early days of the Manitoba Theatre Centre at the old theatre, the members of the fire brigade were also stagehands. They would eventually become too old to be fighting fires and as they retired, they were shifted to backstage work. The youngest of these men were close to 60 and the oldest was in his 70s at least.

We were doing *The Snow Queen*. Elva Mai Hoover was the beautiful 'Snow Queen'. I was playing a wild, evil madman who leapt about on different levels of the set. At one point, I was to leap onto a large rock and be very scary. The children in the audience loved it. One day I leapt on this rock, which was not supposed to move, and it suddenly went sailing off under me...right off stage into the wings! My terrifying 'AH HA!Grrrrrrraaarrrrll, arrrrrgh!' gained in pitch and became a terrified, 'RRaaaarrrr-iiiieeeeeeeiioooo-yyyeeeee-aaaaahhhhh!' What the hell was this!

Another stagehand explained it to me, an outraged and blustering actor, like this: 'Oh, that's Ernie. He has to take the rock on, eh. Ernie's about 84 and he can't do it. It's too heavy. So we put little wheels on the bottom of 'er.'

Unfortunately, this was before there were lockable wheels. And, not being trained in theatrecraft, it had not occurred to him that this might pose a problem for me.

MAVOR MOORE
Sticking it to the crew

As a young actress, around 1910, my mother, Dora Mavor, was playing in a production of Shakespeare's *Richard the Third*. The American actor/manager Robert Mantell (pre-John Barrymore) was one of the great stars of the day, especially in melodrama. He was manager as well as actor on this particular tour and he was having a terrible time with the incipient unions. This was before Equity, the actors' union, and before the stagehands' union had been organized. So every manager had a really strife-ridden relationship with the stage hands and even, sometimes, the actors. The actors, interestingly, were the last to organize themselves in 1913. The stagehands and the musicians formed their unions first.

On this tour the stagehands had been having a severe fight with Mantell about wages, among other things, and they had been doing odd things to mess up the show. On the night concerned, at the intermission, Mantell, in full costume, came out through the curtain split. He announced to the audience that they were having certain problems backstage and he begged their indulgence. As he was standing there making his speech, he saw a bump travelling along the curtain behind him. The stagehands were trying to find Mantell in order to push him into the pit.

As he watched the bump coming along, Mantell simply drew his dagger (which in those days was a real one) from the scabbard of his costume. When he figured the bump was behind him he turned and jabbed the dagger through the curtain. There was an awful yelp but the show proceeded without further incident.

MONICA PARKER
Advice from an L.A. agent

In my early days in L.A., I had a meeting with a very big agent. This woman spoke in a Bronx accent that could cut through stone. As I sat down with her in her office, the first words out of her mouth were these:

'I'm only taking this meeting because I was asked to do someone a favah, because I wouldn't nohmahly see a person like you because I usually deal with people who are, ya know, like twenty and undah, twenty-three and undah, twenty-four and undah. But I saw yah tape. You're cleahly talented. So this is what I'm going to do. I'm going to give you this advice as a freebie, because I wouldn't nohmahly meet with you. This is what I'm thinking. I'm thinking the hai-ah....the hai-ah's awl wrowng. It's not the one colah. Out in California, we do the one colah blondes. Lightah, lightah, brightah. And your clothes...very east coast. You need to go lightah, lightah, brightah. So really and truly, what I think you should do is go home, lose 60, 70, 80 pounds, and then when you come back, we'll tawk.'

I decided that what I would do was send in a friend of mine, Linda Renhoffer, who was a stunning blue-eyed pale blonde with a fabulous body. I would tell her to say she was me and that I was back, 'lightah, lightah, brightah'.

MONICA PARKER
Early days: agents in L.A.

Bernie Brillstein, a very big manager in L.A., called me into his office, and the conversation went like this:

'So I saw your tape, kid, and it's good. It's really good.'

I thought, 'Great!'

'So what is it that you want to do?'

'I want to be "that actress" that you see in every single movie. No one knows her name, but everyone says, "There's that girl again. She was in that other movie. Who is she? There she is again!" I want to be the actress who works all the time but no one knows who I am.' I thought that was the greatest thing in the world. I could have a life and still be a working actress. He looked at me, obviously baffled by my idea of an acting career.

'That's what you *want?*'

'Yeah,' I said with all the dignity I could muster, 'That's what I want.'

'You're in the wrong office.'

I went away feeling so hurt and indignant.

Eight years later, I woke up and it hit me. Oh my God! I was supposed to say, 'I want to be a fucking star!' It had never occurred to me. That's the difference. I was so Canadian, it took me that long to get it, to understand entitlement, to understand that I had the right to expect to have the whole thing. It was a major revelation.

BRIAN GEORGE
Commercial actor

I used to do commercials. I loved it. I had a chance to do some interesting characters, funny stuff. I managed to avoid the truly hokey, silly stuff and never had anything but a wonderful time. I was very lucky and I made a good living at that for a while. But I became known as a 'commercial' actor and had a great deal of difficulty getting any TV, film, or theatrical work. Part of that was my ethnicity and my apparently incongruous English accent. Whatever the reason, I was delighted to be invited by my agent at that time to a reading of a play that she was producing.

The reading was a lot of fun and I enjoyed myself very much. After the reading, my agent looked at me with astonishment and said, 'Brian! I didn't know you could *act*. I thought you were just a commercial actor.'

I left that agency the next day.

DONALD HARRON
And so it goes in showbiz

[Don was offered a role on Broadway in the première of The Tenth Man *by Paddy Chayefsky which he eagerly accepted. The next day his agent said...]*

'Forget about the whole thing. A much bigger offer has just come in. Lerner and Loewe have written a new musical based on T.H. White's *The Once And Future King,* and are looking for a Lancelot.'

'It's one of my favourite books, but what does this have to do with me?'

'You don't understand, it's all together. It's called *Camelot* and they've already got Richard Burton and Julie Andrews as Arthur and Guinevere. They auditioned Laurence Harvey and Chris Plummer for Lancelot, but now they're interested in *you.*'

'Marty, are you crazy? I've just landed a part I love in a play I love, with a director I love!'

'Yes, but Donald, musicals pay a lot better than plays, and you get to do this great number called *If Ever I Would Leave You.*'

'I can't even sing!'

'What do you mean you can't sing?! Everybody's raving about that blues number you did in *Look Back in Anger*!'

'Marty! Forget it! I can't sing to save my life, be happy with what you've got. And if they're looking for a Lancelot, tell them to phone CBC in Toronto and ask for a guy named Robert Goulet.'

Marty Baum was an agent, not a referral service, so he tracked Goulet down in Bermuda and brought him to New York. When Bob got the part, Marty split the commission with Goulet's agent, who hadn't bothered to propose his unknown client for a starring role.

DAVE THOMAS
How about this, then

The single most successful example of building a cheap set, leaving it there, and letting two oafs talk in front of it was the McKenzie Brothers. This deft stroke answered not only financial considerations, but also the problematical issue of Canadian content. Doug and Bob McKenzie (Dave Thomas and Rick Moranis) were born when Andrew Alexander came back from yet another of those long-winded discussions he'd had with the CBC about what is Canadian content, what is Canadian comedy. One of those long-drawn-out philosophical chats that they like to have. And if you've got a Mountie in a sketch, that somehow resolved the problem.

Andrew came into our offices on Richmond Street one day. Joe Flaherty and I were the head writers at the time. And Andrew said the CBC wanted Canadian content in the show. I said, 'What do you mean, Canadian content? We're going to Alberta to shoot it. It's going to be a complete Canadian production. There are only a couple of Americans in the cast. How much more Canadian can it get? Do you want us to put a map of Canada and sit in front of it drinking beer, wearing tuques and parkas?' He said that would be great. And we compromised and put a Mountie beer mug on the set. Originally, we just did it as filler for the Canadian version of *SCTV*, which was two minutes longer than the American version. Then it caught on.

It caught on as a perfect spoof of community-access television and therefore, another type of programming *SCTV* could satirize. The McKenzie Brothers delved deep into issues of the day. 'Like, how come there's only eight parking spaces at takeout doughnut places?' 'Today, we're going to show you how to stuff a mouse in a beer bottle because, like, we heard of this guy who got a free case of beer for finding a mouse in a bottle.'

Bob and Doug spoke Canadian by ending sentences with *eh*? 'What do you think of that? Beauty, eh?' They invented a word, *hoser*, because they had to be able to insult each other with something permissible on TV. We found ourselves in a situation, being guided by standards and practices, and needing some sort of expletives to deal with each other the way these brothers would in real life but couldn't on the air. This was sort of our alternate language. I had heard the verb *to hose* which had various connotations as all those obscure words do. *Hoser* we came up with specifically for the show.

CHUCK SHAMATA
'Chowk' and De Trial Of De Swarta-Fitch: The true story

In Canada, in 1970, movie production barely existed. There wasn't much work for young actors, especially those of ethnic extraction. Including me. Especially me. Still, I hung on tenaciously to my dream of a successful acting career in international movies. That's when Armando showed up with his plan to produce the first Italian-Canadian-Feature-Motion-Picture-Co-production, to be written, directed, and produced by Armando Arugala. His script was called *The Trial of the Swordfish*, or, as Armando pronounced it, *De Trial of de Swarta-Fitch*. The title was allegorical.

[Unfortunately, limited space prevents us from publishing this story in its incredible entirety. Chuck had a number of indications that the film might be something of a small-time operation. Everyone seemed to be working for free, but he badly wanted this starring role in an international feature film. And he got it.

Eventually Chuck, a young leading lady from Italy who could not speak English, a continuity person named Blanche, a cameraman named Peter, and Armando, the 'producer', found themselves after many adventures in a small town in Calabria, Italy, awaiting the commencement of 'principal photography'. They waited, and waited. For days. Usually in the local bar.]

One morning, just after the bar opened, Armando entered, walked over to us and announced solemnly, 'Tonight we shoot!' I actually spluttered my Bloody Mary.

'Today is de feast of Santa Caterina. Big celebration! Dere will be fireworks explodin' over de sea. Think of it! The fireworks reflected in de beautiful blue Mediterranean! We are so lucky to get dis!' He was gushing.

'We will shoot a scene on de pier, where Chowk will plead wid Marina in de foregroun', while, in de backgroun', de fireworks are explodin' over de Mediterranean...'

'But there's no scene like that in the script.'

'Now dere is.'

'Well, why am I pleading with her?'

'Chowk, jus' be tranquil. Don' worry. You will plead.'

'But Armando, how can I plead if I don't know what I'm pleading about?' His face was getting red again. I was getting on his nerves.

'Madonna! Why you gotta problem? Chowk, jus' *plead*!'

'The problem is, Armando, I won't know what to say!'

He stepped up to me and yelled in my face, 'Nobody's gonna know what you're sayin' anyway. We don' have no sound!'

We arrived at a photographically strategic but remote pier late that afternoon. Despite the circumstances surrounding our location shoot we arrived in good spirits at the prospect of actually doing work of any kind. The equipment truck had not yet arrived, so Armando decided to rehearse Marina and me.

'Marina, you sit on dat little post. Chowk, you will be on your knees, in fronna her, pleadin'.'

'On my knees?'

'Chowk. Jus' be tranquil! Plead. On your knees.'

'Okay. Just please tell me what the pleading is in connection with?' For an instant I thought he would hit me, but with obvious effort he contained himself, turned, and walked away. Then Marina glared at me and I thought *she* would hit me. That was the end of the 'rehearsal'.

An hour passed and still no equipment truck. Armando re-appeared, tense and angry. 'Da camera truck gotta lost,' he said, then walked away again. Marina, confused, looked at me and shrugged her shoulders. I slowly and clearly said to her 'No camera. No camera.' A sad expression appeared on Marina's face. She shook her head, looked into my eyes and touched my hand. Blanche, who had overheard me, came over and whispered that I'd just told Marina I didn't have a hotel room.

Another hour passed. The sun went down. Still no camera truck. The fireworks began. Then ended. Still no camera truck. Armando walked around with a pasted-on smile, as if he'd planned things to happen just this way.

Finally the truck arrived. Armando, already having said that we would insert the fireworks later, 'optically', told Peter where to put his camera. Marina was perched on the post. I went to my knees, ready to plead. Armando waited for us to begin until Peter reminded him to say 'action'.

'Action!' Armando announced. Then, Marina turned to me. She was Theda Bara. The back of her hand went to her pained forehead. Tears appeared imminent. Her lips quivered, tried a weak smile, then quivered again. She was clearly able to deliver a plethora of emotions at whatever the hell it was that I was pleading about. In fact I wasn't pleading at all. I guess I was in something like shock.

Then, I couldn't help it, I began laughing. I knew it was a rude thing to do and I felt badly, but couldn't stop. When I turned away from Marina to hide my laughter, I noticed that the camera was running without an operator. Peter was a few feet away, doubled over, shaking, trying to bottle his laughter. Then I caught sight of Armando. Steam was rising from his large head and shooting from his ears. He didn't think it was funny at all.

That beginning was the beginning of the end—figuratively and literally. No other footage of that great Italian-Canadian epic film *De Trial of de Swarta-Fitch* was shot.

FRANK SHUSTER
There's more to life than what?

Johnny Wayne and I didn't like to travel. *Wayne and Shuster* enjoyed working at home. In 1948, we even managed to talk the head of NBC, East Coast, into taping a radio series in Toronto.

'Toronto? What is that? Some kind of dance?' He acted as if he'd never even heard the word.

In 1968, when *The Ed Sullivan Show* came along, it was perfect for us. We'd fly to New York, do a show, and the following day we were back in Toronto. People couldn't believe their eyes.

'What are you doing here? You were in New York last night!'

'That's last night. Today, we're back home.'

MCA, a huge talent agency of the day, were our agents and also the packagers of *The Ed Sullivan Show*. They wanted us to do more work for them directly.

'Let's make a buck off you guys,' was the refrain.

MCA took 10% off the top of the Sullivan show so, at the time, they weren't actually making money off *Wayne and Shuster*. They kept offering us this show, that show, but we would turn almost everything down. We didn't need it if it meant leaving home.

Johnny and I had agreed to meet with MCA any time on the condition that 'money', 'cars', 'villas in the South of France', or whatever, were not used as part of any argument put forward about what *Wayne and Shuster* should do. We told them we could only be won over by some reason more important than 'money'. One morning I had a meeting in New York with the MCA agent Marty Kummer, who was one of the best agents there.

'Frank, give me the bottom line. I know you guys are very content with your life in Canada but, you know, if you come to the States, you will...you will...become...truly...international stars! Your careers will...will flourish!' he continued in desperation. Then he looked intently at me and said, 'You know, there's more to life than happiness!'

We just looked at each other in silence. I didn't know what to say. That moment is just frozen in time. As he said the words, I could see this very bright man grappling with the inanity of what was coming out of his mouth. It was very funny to me because, in the States, 'money' seems to be the only reason for doing things. If you take that away, they don't know what to talk about.

4

Kids and Animals

DAVID GARDNER
My favourite review

It was early in the '50s. The Straw Hat Players, located in Gravenhurst and Port Carling, had undertaken to do Shakespeare's *A Midsummer Night's Dream*. This was a fairly ambitious project for a summer theatre with limited resources and a short rehearsal period. Our post-war *Dream* was a low-budget, modern-dress production directed by a free-spirited Englishman named John Blatchley. Murray Davis played 'Oberon' in a golden bathing suit and I was 'Bottom' in shorts and a tartan shirt. When bully Bottom gets turned into an ass, the head gear was a WW II gas mask that had miraculously sprouted ears.

Budget restrictions also meant there would be a small cast. There were no subsidiary fairies or 'corps de ballet', no troupe of neighbourhood kids to play 'Titania's' minions. Instead, I mimed the little creatures crawling over my body and tickling me from within my shirt. To learn their names, I held each one up to my ear one at a time at the tip of my fingers, listening hard as they told me who they were. A triangle sounded in the wings and I translated 'Cobweb', 'Pease-blossom', 'Mustard-seed' and 'Moth'. It was a delicious moment to play.

After one of the matinees, we were taking off our make-up in the large assembly room underneath the Gravenhurst Opera House, when we had a young visitor. A little girl of four or five stood with her mother by the curtain that separated the men from the women. We said, 'Hello' and asked her if she had enjoyed the play. She nodded, yes. Then shyly, with a look to Mom, she ventured over to my chair and mumbled a wonderful request. She wondered if she could meet the fairies.

I exchanged a quick glance with my fellow actors and replied softly, 'I'm terribly sorry but they are sleeping right now, in their box, and they can't be disturbed. They use up so much energy doing the show that they have to nap before the evening performance.'

I hoped that she would understand. She did. Then, quite simply, she said that whenever I was talking to them on stage, she had seen them. My mouth fell open. It was a moment of incandescent purity and it remains the one review that I will treasure forever.

MAJA ARDAL
Inga and the Barbies

I was performing the one-woman show, *Female Parts* by Dario Fo and Franca Rame at Toronto Workshop Productions. It was in the very early '80s. My daughter, Inga, was five or six years old. These four tough-talking feminist plays are pretty hard for an audience to take, especially with 'Medea' at the end, hurling rage at her husband, and threatening to kill the children after he has taken up with the 'other woman'.

Inga wanted to see the show one day, and nothing would dissuade her. I tried to explain about Medea and she reassured me that she knew it was 'only a play'. The audience was sparse, to put it mildly, and Inga, in her nice pink dress, sat to the side and seemed to soak up every moment. She was unusually silent on the way home, and I figured it had all been a bit too much for her.

The following weekend, Inga insisted on coming back to the play with me. I was surprised, given her non-committal response last time. She put on another of her nice 'going out' dresses, made me do her hair, and then went upstairs to her room. A few minutes later, I heard an awful bumping coming down the stairs. Inga had a huge garbage bag. She said she was bringing her Barbies and stuff. Of course, I thought, she just wants to be with Mum and play backstage, not watch the play again. I patiently helped her down to the car, with what seemed the entire contents of her bedroom.

When we arrived at the theatre, I was told that attendance was going to be pathetic *again*. I went backstage, leaving Inga to hang around in the empty theatre. When I came out minutes later to warm up, Inga had unloaded the contents of the garbage bag and placed stuffed animals, baby dolls and Barbies in prime seating in the audience area. She turned proudly to me after placing her two best Barbies in the centre front row.

'Look, Mum. I brought you a audience.'

Nobody suggested they be moved, and the straggling audience politely avoided the 'best' seats. That afternoon, I played to 10 people, and twenty-four 'special guests'. Inga sat proudly in the front row, flanked by two rather well-dressed Barbies. It was not easy doing Medea that day, especially speaking lines like, 'Give me the weapon! And desperate Medea, drive, drive the knife into the tender flesh of these children...the blood...the blood...'

But as Inga said...'It was only a play.'

RICHARD CURNOCK
Been at it since I was five

The Italia Conti Academy, the famous acting academy for children in London, was attended by Noel Coward and Gertrude Lawrence among others. Miss Conti always wore red and was very frightening, and she wasn't a very good actress. I was taught by her sister Bianca Murray who was a brilliant actress. She used to demonstrate acting and could have been a wonderful professional.

The two of them would go around this very poor part of central London, Holborn, and find kids playing in the gutter. And Miss Conti would say, 'Where's your mum? Where do you live? I want to talk to your mum.' If they were bright and she could see something in them, she'd train these children, then take a 20% cut of the money they earned. She was a bit naughty like that. Jessie Matthews was there. Conti had found her in the street, dancing to a barrel organ. Jack Hawkins was there. Some wonderful actors were there; a lot of them were later lost in the war.

I got there because my sister and I had rheumatic fever when she was seven and I was five. She was told by the doctor to take ballet and my parents were journalists and couldn't afford a ballet school. They could just afford to send her to the Conti Academy. Miss Conti said, 'I'll take her if I can have him,' because she had a hard time finding boys.

It was a pretty dreadful place. Some of the kids were rough and awful but they taught us all the basics of acting there. How to pull a punch, how to stab someone and not hurt them. How to step forward on the right foot if you're kissing a woman, there's a certain way to favour her. All that kind of thing that's considered old-fashioned and corny these days. I think it would prevent some of these silly accidents we have if these things were still drummed into students.

SHIRLEY DOUGLAS
Kiefer's first job

When he was nine years old my son Kiefer was asked to play a substantial role with a professional company on the Los Angeles stage. Like any parent, I put every possible obstacle in his path. No missing school. No hockey for the duration of the run. All homework to be completed on time...etc. This did nothing to dissuade him.

He worked hard, learning endless amounts about the Holocaust, which was the topic of the play. He just threw himself into it. And on opening night he was wonderful, just wonderful. And I thought, well, there it is.

I asked him about the experience and he said, 'Mother, it was great...and I never want to do it again.'

TANJA JACOBS
Goings-on at the castle

In 1987 I was performing in a play by Howard Barker called *The Castle* for The Necessary Angel Theatre Company. It was an extraordinary play, one that asked a lot of performers and audience alike. Among the cast of terrific actors was Tedde Moore. After a matinee, one afternoon, she kindly offered to drive me home. In her excellent station wagon was her young son who had come along to meet her.

Noah had not been brought to see the show. It was a wordy piece. He had, however, heard a great deal about the show. He was four years old.

Noah was sitting in the back in his little safety seat and I was sitting in the front passenger seat. As we were driving along, out of the blue he asked me, 'Um, uh, Tanya. Is it true that you show your bare bum in the play?'

I couldn't tell a lie. In fact it was true that there was a scene in the play where I flashed my bum in an insulting gesture at a character I disliked intensely. It was a very dramatic moment. After a moment, I said, 'Yes, Noah, it's true.'

Noah took a moment to think about it and then asked me, very seriously, 'With poop coming out?'

Tedde and I nearly slid off our seats. I almost died laughing. Barker would appreciate the image, that's for sure.

DIANA ROWLAND
Merde

My son was about five years old and just starting to pick up swear words (certainly not in our home), finding in them the source of secret giggles and humour. One day, as I was preparing for an audition, he wished me good luck. I explained to him that it was bad luck to say, 'Good luck!' to an actor. He asked how you wished someone good luck, then, so I told him that there were a few ways of doing it—'Break a leg', etc. Then, remembering his new-found delight with the illicit swear words, I conspiratorially told him that there was another word that actors used sometimes but it wasn't very polite. Of course, he was intrigued and listened with rapt attention as I explained that the word was 'merde' which was a naughty French word. After much pleading on his part, I whispered its meaning—'shit'. He giggled and wished me 'merde' with much enthusiasm.

A couple of weeks later, I was on my way to another audition. I was halfway out the door, having already said goodbye, when my son urgently called me. As I turned, he looked me directly in the eye and said 'Fuck you!' It took me a moment to realise how proud he was that he had remembered the 'naughty word' that would wish me luck....

JOYCE GORDON
She may look like a princess

It was 1969, the early days of the Young People's Theatre in Toronto, and I was in *Rumpelstiltskin,* produced by Susan Rubes, the founder of YPT, and directed by Robert Sherrin. We were playing in the charming little theatre in the Colonnade on Bloor Street. This was an intimate space with a steeply raked auditorium, very conducive to encouraging our young audiences to feel 'part of the action'.

Kenny Wickes was 'Rumpelstiltskin', Alan Royal was the 'Prince', and I was the wicked and imperious 'Queen'. It was a fun role with a wonderfully villainous song that I boomed out, trying to frighten the children.

At one matinee, in the third row centre, was a most angelic looking little girl. She was dressed in a white frilly dress, with lace and ribbon trimmings. Her long black ringlets framed an adorable face. She looked like a picture-perfect five-year-old princess at her own birthday party. No sooner had I made my entrance and launched into the first few bars of my terrifying aria, when this little angel's voice rang out loud and clear, 'Aaah, fuck off!'

Need I say how difficult it was for the company to carry on?

GARRICK HAGON
Flashing

I was a kid of 12, very green and naïve, playing the Prince of Wales in the première Stratford Festival production of *Richard III*. Just before the grand opening night, I watched Tyrone Guthrie directing a photo call for the press. The best set-up seemed to be the scene in which Alec Guinness advanced towards the throne for the first time, an orb in one hand, a sceptre in the other. Kicking myself for forgetting my camera, I went home, got my precious box Brownie, and raced back to the theatre for the final tense dress rehearsal that afternoon. I finished my own scenes early in the play (the Prince having been dispatched to the Tower with his brother), then I snuck into one of the front rows of the theatre and waited, my camera in hand.

I knew the scene I was waiting for—the coronation scene, the glorious shot I had seen them take at the photo call. Guinness was advancing slowly, carefully, downstage, his eyes glued hungrily on the throne that would soon be his, his mouth curling in a slight, triumphant smile. I eased my camera out from under the seat and clicked. The flash reverberated round the auditorium.

There was an awful silence. Guinness stopped dead. I froze in my seat, suddenly realizing what I had done. Guinness turned towards where the flash had come from, and in an icy voice said, 'Don't ever do that again.'

I crouched down behind the seat, mortified, wishing I could fall into the pit and never come out. When the intermission came, I crept towards the exit door. Just as I was going out, a hand descended on my arm. It was Guthrie, leaning over to whisper in my ear, 'Never mind, Garrick. You learned something today, didn't you?' I looked up. Guthrie didn't even seem angry that I had brought his rehearsal to a halt. I burst into tears and headed out the side door.

AILEEN TAYLOR-SMITH
On saving Mommy

In a production of *Bus Stop* in Gravenhurst, Donald Sutherland was playing the young cowboy to my 'Cherie'. On this particular evening, we were both happily unaware that my young son was in the audience. When we got to the part where the cowboy was to throw 'Cherie' over his shoulder and exit, a small, familiar, and very clear little voice asked, 'What's that man going to do with my Mommy?'

The house fell apart laughing.

SUSAN DOUGLAS RUBES
On *The Diary of Anne Frank* at YPT

We brought our good friends Eli Wallach, Anne Jackson and their daughter, Roberta up to Toronto to do *The Diary of Anne Frank* at the Young People's Theatre some years ago. Kate Reid, Robert Joy, Paul Soles and Henry Beckman were also in the cast.

The first matinee curtain of the first week after we had opened was about to go up. I was sitting in the office working when Annie came in, very upset and said, 'We can't do the show. We can't do the show.' I asked her what the problem was. I thought someone was sick. She said, 'We're all right but there is a kindergarten out there!' I couldn't understand what she meant. She said, 'But there are all of these, these, these *kids!*'

I told her that it was the mandate of the theatre to do productions for children and that during matinees we often had school tours booked in. She was very upset. She was worried that the show would give them nightmares, that they would not understand it, that they would squirm and talk and that the show would be terrible as a result. I explained that the parents knew the content of the show and that they would not have allowed their children to attend if they were worried. I asked her to please continue with the show and that if she found that the children were misbe-having or causing a problem, she could send the stage manager for me in the office and I would come down and speak to them during the intermission.

The curtain went up and I waited. I went down to the back of the audience to see if there was any indication of a problem. The kids were quiet and attentive, absolutely spellbound. So I went back up to the office at the intermission and waited to see if the stage manager would come up. No one came, no one called.

At the end of the show, Annie and Eli came out after the bow and talked to the children to allow them to ask questions. They talked to the audience for about half an hour. And when they came back into my office they were very excited. They immediately wanted to go out and discuss this marvellous experience with the kids. They had never been so surprised and delighted by an audience in their lives.

Later they did the play in New York. For that production, they stipulated in their contracts that school children must be invited to attend the matinees, because the school children they had played for in Toronto had been some of the best audi-ences they had ever had.

TONY VAN BRIDGE
Ah, youth

[After making a huge success as 'Falstaff' at the Stratford Festival, Tony was invited to the River Street Theatre in Boston to play the lead in Brecht's Galileo.]

During an early rehearsal when I was trying to get 'off book'—a difficult time, as all actors know—I had a long speech to the young prince, played by a boy of twelve. He sat on the throne, his court about him. The speech was getting along famously, but I dried. The prompt came immediately and like a pistol shot, not from the prompter, but from this twelve-year-old who had no script anywhere near him. I thanked him coolly. (And I thought of W.C. Fields who, when asked how he liked children, answered, 'Fried.') The boy never got another chance. I buried that scene in my head for keeps. At the next rehearsal, having fixed the young prince with a steely eye that dared him to so much as draw breath, I delivered the speech word-perfect and at lightning speed.

DIANA ROWLAND
Only in the theatre? Pity!

When my daughter was two years old I had the opportunity to work at Theatre New Brunswick and the Neptune Theatre in a co-production of the Graham Greene play *The Return of A.J. Raffles*. The cast featured Sir John Neville and Roland Hewgill and was directed by Malcolm Black, all of whose talents I admired and respected. Though the role required nudity, I had no qualms about accepting it. During rehearsals, my daughter was around the theatre a lot, as she loved being there and was never any trouble. I hadn't realised how much she had absorbed until one afternoon during the run, when I had taken her to a local park.

Because she was hot, I suggested she take off her dress and run through the sprinkler that was watering the grass. She did so, then begged me to join her. I explained that I couldn't take my clothes off because adults weren't permitted to run around without their clothes on. She seemed to have trouble understanding this concept, then suddenly brightened and said, 'Only in the theatre, Mum?'

NOAH SHEBIB
Just wondering

I started television and film acting a few years ago when I was ten. It is so much fun. The only problem I've had so far, besides sometimes getting *really* cold, has been with worms. That's the one thing about auditions. I really hate it when you go in to an audition and the director asks you some casual little question like, 'Noah, are you scared of bugs or perhaps worms?' Naturally, I ask, 'Why?' and of course he responds 'Just wondering.' Well, obviously I don't want to kill my opportunity of getting the job, and in fact I am not afraid of bugs or worms, so I say, 'No, I'm not.' *That* was my mistake.

The phone call arrives to say I got the job on *Goosebumps*. They send me the script. I read it and sure enough it is all about a kid who is really into worms. It looks like fun. I don't mind playing with some worms. Shortly after my six o'clock call time, I make my way to the set, unaware that fate awaits me....

The director and the crew are all waiting for me.

'Noah, I'm going to have to ask you to...ah...put your face in...in some worms.'

'OK. But are you sure the rubber won't ruin my make-up?'

'Noah, I'm going to have to...ah...ask you to...ah...put your face in, ah...in some...real worms. *Please*! For the sake of the shot?'

I turn my back to him, to think, and see the whole crew looking at me with these puppy dog faces. In my mind I can hear everyone shouting. 'Please, Noah, don't let us down.'

'Let's just get this over with! OK?'

There were hundreds and hundreds of worms all over a pillow that I was to be sleeping on. I had to put my face in this pile of worms! I swear to God they were about to go up my damn nose! Hell! That was the only word for it, maybe even more revolting.

I swear if it wasn't for my love of the business (and concerns about my professional reputation) I never would have done it.

GREG KRAMER
Please, Sir...?

I was sitting front of house at the final dress rehearsal of Vancouver Musical Theatre's 1983 production of *Oliver* (in which I was playing 'Fagin'). My entrance wasn't for a few scenes yet.

For the first time, the props department provided real 'gruel' to be served up to the orphans. There were a few wary faces when they saw there was actually something to eat (instead of miming as they had earlier during rehearsals). They were required to eat the entire bowlful within a few bars of music during the song 'Food, Glorious Food'. The kids sat down at their tables and proceeded to wolf down their meal as rehearsed.

The 'gruel', cold porridge, was an unpleasant surprise.

One kid must have started the barfing, which, like a chain reaction, took hold of the entire cast of kids. In short order, all of the kids were vomiting everywhere. The topper, of course, was when 'Oliver', green-faced and trembling, approached 'Mr Bumble' with the immortal line: 'Please, sir, may I have some more?'

For the remainder of the run the gruel was, mercifully, changed to a more palatable pudding.

REX HAGON
Lively child on live TV

My brother Garrick, who is eight years older, was a child actor and he kind of blazed the trail for me. I accompanied my mother down to his auditions and it was inevitable that I would get into it too. I was five and a half when I did my first TV show, *Follow the Rocket King*, a science fiction show for the director Henry Kaplan. I had 50 lines! That's a lot of lines for a little kid.

There's a story my mother enjoyed telling about me in live television. I had the great pleasure of doing an Arthur Haley show called *Time Lock*, about a young boy who gets locked in a vault that can't be opened until morning. His parents are incredibly distraught.

On the night of the live-to-air show, I was in my vault sitting on my stool waiting for my next scene. Quite forlorn, a single bulb overhead. Outside the vault the adult actors were getting so pumped up that, as a kid, I was just drawn to watch it. I quietly left my little stool and walked around the set to the back to see what was happening. Would they get that little kid out of the vault? Completely forgetting that that little kid was me!

It was my mum, sitting at home, watching the show, who noticed the back of my head on camera. As my cue approached, I went back into the vault for my scene, like the little pro I was. Years later Aileen Seaton, the actress who played my mother, told me her part of the story.

The doors had finally been opened. She rushed into the vault choked with emotion. I was sitting on my stool under the light. With tears welling up in her eyes, she embraced me, her dear little son.

From my position I could see that she had missed her light. My mouth right beside her ear, I whispered to her, as she was emoting like mad, 'You're not in your light. You've got to get in your light.' She said she could have killed me! I'm not surprised.

SHARON NOBLE
On the Fuller Brush Wolf

In the late '60s, I was touring through Florida in a play called *A Thurber Carnival*. Since their father was directing and I was acting in the same production, my three small children were taken along on the tour. They had attended many rehearsals and, being little sponges, had soaked up all of the dialogue and music and they were permitted to watch the performances in each locale if they had not fallen asleep.

One evening we were performing to a particularly responsive audience which was laughing and applauding through the show. During a segment of the play entitled *The Wolf And Red Riding Hood*, Thurber's 'Wolf' comes to the door pretending to be a Fuller Brush Man. I, as narrator, spoke both 'Red Riding Hood's' line when she sees the Wolf's tail through the window, 'Who is it?' and then the Wolf's reply, 'It's the Fuller Brush Man, and this is my brush!'

Unfortunately I was on auto pilot that night and the words that popped out of my mouth were, 'It's the Fuller Brush Man and this is my *tail*.' I realised my mistake the moment that I said it, but it was by then too late. I hoped no one else had noticed.

However...my precocious five-year-old daughter, Regan, stood up in the third row, turned to the house and stated, 'That's my Mommy...and she made a mistake.'

The house went right up. She was a bigger hit than the play. Fortunately for us, there were a couple of nuns in attendance who discreetly removed all three children from the theatre and entertained them until the show came down. When we went to fetch the children, I asked Regan how the rest of the evening had gone for them. She replied with a smile, 'Just fine. The penguins gave us ice cream!'

REX HAGON
Little Rex's late night song

The CBC used to have a variety show that came on after the hockey games on Saturday nights starring the singer Juliette. One day we were called up and I was asked if I would sing, with Juliette, a popular song of the day about Davy Crockett.

Because the show was live and done late in the evening, and as I was only seven, my mom was a little concerned. She wanted me to have a nap in the afternoon. I just couldn't settle down to sleep so she found a sleeping pill and gave me a half, or maybe even a quarter. I still couldn't sleep and then it was time to go to the studio.

We got to the rehearsal at six. I felt a little drowsy but otherwise cheerful. Nonetheless, my mother thought it wise to give me a chocolate bar, hoping the caffeine would help counteract the effects of the pill. She also kept me walking up and down the halls to keep me going till the hockey game ended and the show could start.

We got on the set and the word came down that it was time to begin. I was seated on a stool behind the piano so the camera could see me. I heard 'And now, here is Rex Hagon to do the Davy Crockett song! Hi, Rex!' 'Hi,' I chirped perkily. Billy O'Connor was at the piano and started the opening chords and away we went. Juliette and I started singing and there I was on my stool, bright as anything, my old performance self.

I don't think I got much further than 'King of the wild frontier...' when it occurred to me that it would be very nice to just slowly put my head down on the piano. I promptly fell asleep and slid completely from view right onto the floor!

There we were, live TV. The cameraman didn't know whether to go down or up. Juliette looked over and just laughed and carried on. There's the picture; this big close-up of a beaming seven-year-old, smiling away, brush cut and all, just disappearing from the shot. Gone.

My poor mother felt suitably guilty and told the story on herself for years.

MICHAEL MILLAR
Tricky Dicky

At university in the '70s, our program was quite versatile and many areas of theatre were explored. One area I had reservations about was children's theatre. I wasn't comfortable with it, but Blaine Parker had written a play called *Tricky Dicky Deuce*, and looked forward to helping us with the audience interaction.

Interaction was the key to this show. 'Tricky Dicky' (played by me) was a detective who had a mystery to solve and the children in the audience were going to help him do that.

When a scene was over, the actors who left the scene were not to retire into the wings but to sit in the audience with the kids, ask them questions, let them participate and generally be 'one of them'. I didn't feel comfortable with this but

Blaine felt it would bring the children closer to the characters. Blaine explained it would be good for us as actors to 'wallow in their innocence' and perhaps get back in touch with a more pure part of ourselves. Reticent as I was, I thought I'd give it a try. The only way to learn is to experience. So, we all practised and on opening day were greeted by a theatre full of cherub-faced youngsters who seemed as eager as us to get the play going.

When my first scene ended, I, as Tricky Dick, picked up my squirt gun (Dick's weapon of choice) and headed out to the audience. I sat beside a freckle-faced eight-year-old who stared at me with eyes of wonder. He smiled. I smiled back. I asked him if he had any 'information' but he just stared at me. Then a big grin crossed his face. Blaine was right, I thought, this is a wonderful way to connect with these kids and I began to ease into a more comfortable state. The boy then looked at me and grinned wider. Never been this close to an actor, I thought. I guess he's pretty excited. Then he gleefully shouted out 'Tricky Dick!' 'Yep, that's me.' I answered. 'Tricky Dicky Deuce!' He shouted even louder. Isn't that cute, I thought. His teacher tried to shush the boy but I continued. After all, we were trying to encourage this kind of participation. The child then looked at me and shouted at the top of his lungs, 'Tricky Dicky Douche-Bag!'

Well, we lost it completely. Even the actors laughed.

Critic of the future.

I then had to go back up on stage amid all that mirth, but before I left I couldn't resist using the weapon I'd been given and I squirted the little hellion in the face. The next words that came out of this tyke's mouth were anything but childlike. The play resumed after the teacher had removed the little brat.

'Isn't theatre exciting?' Blaine said to me after the show.

CHRIS WIGGINS
Lon Chaney Jr and children on set

Lon was a big, strong, and very active man while he was shooting the television series *The Last Of The Mohicans,* but he was not a young man. The physical action of shooting an adventure series in winter, riding horses, leaping out of trees and so on was very tough on a man his age. It was also fairly common knowledge that he had had a problem with alcohol, but the sweet, generous, protective side of him shone through around children. He had grandchildren whom he adored.

There had been in one episode a sequence involving an Indian attack on a wagon train, where the attackers were dragging away a young mother who was reaching back screaming, 'My baby, my baby!' The baby, who was being played by this actress's real two-year-old child, was sitting among some charred ruins and was expected to cry piteously, 'Mama! Mama!' as Mom was being dragged off screaming. However, the child did not react as expected. She seemed to think it was all a lovely game and simply sat contentedly and giggled.

The director was not getting an appropriate reaction. So the AD (assistant director) decided that he could get a reaction from the child if he did something to her real doll off camera while they shot. The AD began tearing the doll apart with a pair of pliers while the cameras rolled on the child. The ears and the nose and the arms and hair were being viciously ripped off this little girl's favourite doll. Well, they got their screams all right. The child was hysterical.

As this was in progress, Lon came around the corner of a building and saw it all. Walking behind Lon, I didn't see what was happening. I only saw him take off, tackle that AD with a shoulder, and knock him down. There were yells and screams from everyone. Lon just lost control. He had to be held back by four or five men, myself included, because we could see that he was literally, seriously trying to kill the guy. I have been in the army and there is a difference between someone who is mad and wants a fight and one who is ready to kill. Lon would have killed him. And believe me, Lon was a fantastically strong man. It was not easy to pull him off.

The AD said, 'Hey whattsa matter! Whatareya, crazy? We're just trying to get a picture. Just trying to get a picture!' The director realised what had happened. He folded up the first AD and called immediately for a car. He said, 'Get him outta here. Get him to the airport! Get him out of the country! Out!' And that was exactly what they did. He never came back.

Lon didn't start to settle down until the guy was off the set. He went straight over to the child who was purple in the face from screaming and terror. He picked her up gently and walked off with her, trying to calm her down. The mother came over to take her daughter and started to speak, 'Who would have thought...' when Lon cut her off and looked as if he might backhand her. She backed right away. He was furious at her for letting this happen. Instead, he turned and walked off with the child and did not return for almost an hour until she had calmed down completely. Even then, he would not hand her over to the mother. He gave her to someone else. He wasn't even going to speak to her.

The director came to Lon and said, 'Hey, Lon, we'll buy her five dolls.' To which Lon said, 'You think that's what it's about? You think that is what the child wants?' He was completely disgusted and deep down angry about all the crap that he'd seen happen over many years. Nothing else mattered; animals, bystanders, children, extras, actors had been injured, maimed, or had even died in the name of 'getting the shot'. The dehumanising cruelty that existed, and still occasionally exists in the business, had built up in him and this incident had triggered the release of a deadly rage.

MARTIN JULIEN
Candy and the Boy Scout

I acted in my first professional show in 1971 when I was ten years old. I played 'Buddy', the wolf cub, in a family musical called *Be Prepared* by Victor Sutton, about Girl Guides and Boy Scouts out on a camping trip. It was presented over Christmas at the Factory Theatre Lab above the garage on Dupont Street. John Candy, who couldn't have been more than twenty years old at the time, was 'The Scoutmaster'.

I made my first entrance swinging a big silver whistle on a cord, singing the opening number with the entire ensemble. I remember the first applause as thrilling. I decided I was a great actor.

Unfortunately, because there was no backstage washroom access, during one performance I peed my pants behind a flat. I was terrified. John Candy, as choreographed, had to carry my soaking torso piggy-back through the final number. He was very kind and forgiving afterward, but I think this experience may have driven him to the relative security of big-budget Hollywood movies, where child stars carry their toilets with them.

VLASTA VRANA
Something a-p'ffft

In 1972 when I was the second assistant director on *Alien Thunder*, a film being shot in Saskatchewan, we had built an entire Indian village. The long, lingering, opening shot was of Jack Creley, playing an Indian agent, driving a gig into town. A gig is a little carriage with two wheels, like a sulky, so the horse's ass is right in front of your face. Jack and his rig were to start way in the distance and trot along, clop, clop, clop, into the village.

We set up the whole shot running three or four cameras. Everyone was strategically hidden in the bushes when the director called 'action'. Jack was to be stern-faced and, if you know Jack, you'll understand just how stern that was, *really* stern. As the gig got a little closer, every step the horse took, we could hear a fart! Along came this horse farting in the rhythm of a trot, phht-*phht*, phht-*phht*, phht-*phht*, and there was Jack's incredibly stern face, two feet from the horse's ass! Jack held it. He never broke his concentration.

It was a great take for Jack. But I think *we* lost the take on all four cameras. One guy had a hand-held camera and his shot was totally gone. We just became hysterical behind the bushes. Everybody was dying. All you could hear were people sobbing and trying to hang on 'til the shot was supposed to finish.

ELIZABETH SHEPHERD

When I played 'Cordelia' at Stratford, Ontario, in an early William Hutt *King Lear,* I died right downstage front and centre. I chose, for optimum effect, to die with my eyes and mouth open. Stratford is a summer festival and there are often troubles with flies in the theatre, a fact I had not reckoned with in my creative exuberance.

One matinee, after I had died, a fly started crawling up my neck, over my chin, around my lips and into my mouth! It was disgusting. I tried to flick it out with my tongue with no success. That evening, in an effort to avoid such an event again, I sprayed myself liberally with insect repellent—only to discover to my dismay that the repellent got right up my nose and created an almost overwhelming desire in my inert body to cough and sneeze!

SHELLEY PETERSON
Animal wrangling

The highlight of my days at Western University's Talbot Theatre might just be my adventures in animal husbandry.

I was asked to be in a crowd scene with a spider monkey on my shoulder to add 'colour'. That monkey was the most horrible, malevolent, disgusting, vicious creature God created. My friends and family will confirm that I love animals, but that monkey was lucky to survive the run. He would scream raucously, 'Chi! chi! chi! chi! chi!' as he scratched my face and neck and pulled bunches of my hair out by the roots in his efforts to escape. Once he peed on my shoulder to distract me long enough to get away. But his most embarrassing activity was what he did while he sat on my shoulder, where he was supposed to be. For there, beside my right ear, he gleefully masturbated.

After the monkey, I thought walking an elderly drugged horse across the stage would be a piece of cake. Wrong.

My mother delivered Sir Nigel to the stage door at the appointed time in the dark of night. I, dressed in my gaily brilliant peasant costume, rushed outside to help her unload him from the trailer. He allowed himself to be led toward the hastily constructed stage door ramp. He was suspicious, but my mother pushed on his rump, I pulled on his halter, and together we convinced him to move. He took a step onto the ramp and suddenly his weight splintered the plywood and his foot crashed through. Terrified, he leapt into the air and through the stage door, dragging me behind.

At the best of times a horse once frightened takes a while to calm down, but now he was faced with even greater horrors. The bright stage lights after the pitch black of outside would've been enough. Add the roar of the surprised and delighted audience, well, it was too much. Sir Nigel, ancient and normally ever accommodating, rolled his eyes, frothed at the mouth, and dropped a load of manure on centre stage. That done, he hastily made his exit, stage right, never to return to show biz.

DAVID McLELLAND
Bat in a hat

I was playing Colonel Pickering in a production of *My Fair Lady*, directed by Allen MacInnis at Neptune Theatre in Halifax and Centaur Theatre in Montreal. Our Halifax run went well, then we had a short break before the opening in Montreal, where we had a week of rehearsals to bring us up to speed in the new space. On the first day, cast members were amazed to see a bat flying around the theatre. 'Don't worry,' stage management assured us, 'they don't come out during shows.'

If only someone had informed the bat!

Our first public preview was to a pretty full house and we were off to a great start—until the bat made its first appearance with a couple of low flybys. Robert Seale, playing 'Henry Higgins', managed to ad-lib a little and keep the show moving.

Then came the famous Ascot scene. Imagine, if you will, women in elegant gowns and large, fancy hats, men in top hat and tails, and a bat flying back and forth across the stage, gradually swooping lower and lower. Our musical director/piano player, Lisa St Clair, ran off the stage because she thought that her hat, which had little tufts of fur on top, would attract the bat. The audience was howling. Cast members scattered this way and that. Any pretence to maintaining character in the scene was completely gone, as one by one we lost it and began to crack up ourselves.

Finally the bat slid to an exhausted halt centre stage. He and I looked at each other, perhaps *both* of us wondering what to do next. Well...the show must go on...so I whipped off my top hat and dropped it over the bat...to even more laughter and applause. Paul McQuillan, who played 'Freddie', then slid the hat off stage to the waiting hands of stage management. More applause. Eventually, we were able to regain our composure and the show continued.

The bat, for those who might be concerned, was taken to Montreal's Biodome to their resident bat colony where he remains, as far as I know, well and happily beyond the glare of theatre spotlights.

THEA MacNEIL
Mr Pesty

In the summer of 1980, I was playing 'Louisa' in *The Fantasticks* at the Gryphon Theatre.

There we were, my love interest and I, hand in hand, eye to eye, singing our love duet when in one ear, I could hear the loud buzzing of a fly. I held my focus thinking this little pest will just buzz on by but instead, while I was nicely shaping the vowel 'O' for my 'You are love. . .', in pops Mr Pesty. Without missing a beat I spat him out between breaths. Unfortunately I found myself having difficulty controlling an impulse to laugh, though I realized that I still had another chorus to sing. My shoulders must have been heaving up and down and my eyes watering because after the curtain my partner turned to me and remarked on my apparent emotional intensity.

'Boy, you were really into it today.'

He'd no idea what had really happened.

GREG KRAMER
One from the carp

Horizontal Eighty, the short-lived but legendary Toronto company, was staging Witold Gombrowitz's *Ivona, Princess* of *Burgundia,* at the Queen Street Mental Health

Centre. It's the story of a repulsive girl whom the Prince of Burgundia decides to marry, against the wishes of his family. Merely by being herself, placid and unresponsive, Ivona wreaks havoc in the kingdom. The King plots with the Lord Chancellor to kill her. They decide she will choke to death on fish bones at a state dinner.

As a key part of the set, director Vladimir Mirzoev wanted a huge fish suspended ten feet above the stage in a tank. Engineers were called in to make certain the beams in the ceiling would support the weight. The tank was hoisted aloft suspended by aircraft cables, and filled with water. An enormous live carp was found and installed in the tank. We named him Ivan.

Ivan was a big hit. He was well cared for by cast member Brian Macdonald. But he became the worst kind of scene stealer, swimming back and forth ferociously at just the right (or wrong) moment. Although we all loved Ivan, we hated standing beneath his tank.

On closing night, Ivan was especially active. I was about to make my entrance as the King when I heard gasps from the audience, followed by a deep silence. Then, exclamations of 'Oh my,' and hoots of laughter. There was the 'Prince' (Jeffrey Max Nichols) and his 'Advisor' (Robert Eaton) and, suddenly on the stage between them ...Ivan, flopping about in a fishy frenzy. The carp had made his leap for freedom.

Boldly, the Prince wrestled Ivan up off the floor and into his arms, almost losing him. Then, with fish firmly in his embrace, he took one giant step onto the nearby piano bench, then to the top of the piano and hoisted Ivan back into the tank with a tremendous splash. Wild applause, whistles, and bravos.

When the din settled, the dripping Prince delivered his next line:

'I could never do that before!'

The house came down.

LYNDA MASON GREEN
Star treatment

In the 1980s it seems that every actor in Toronto had done at least one episode of *The Littlest Hobo*. We all knew that it was a production done on a shoestring and that the only continuing cast member was of the canine persuasion. I was a guest lead playing a rodeo veterinarian.

In one particular scene, my last of the shoot, my character was to enter the stall of an extremely bad-mannered stallion and be threatened by flying hooves. I would then be knocked down and subsequently saved by the valiant intervention of 'Hobo', the heroic German Shepherd of the title.

Naturally, since we were shooting in a real stable, the remains of what would normally have been deposited in any stall were still to some degree present. There was no straw, nothing but bare stable floor and the lingering pungency of equine 'water'. Mario Azzopardi, the director, explained that he wanted me to roll around on the floor screaming in terror. I suggested (hopefully) that there would normally be straw on the floor of an occupied stall. Privately, I couldn't help feeling some dismay at having vounteered to wear my own clothes, including a very expensive pair of cowboy boots, instead of production wardrobe. He apologised and was very gracious about it. But he was anxious to finish and asked, please, please, that I just 'do it', as only Mario can. It was, after all, the last shot for me and I would not have to sit around in my foul-smelling clothes for long. Anxious to please and be perceived as a team player, I smiled and said, 'Sure, what the hell.'

I did my bit and retired to a bale of hay outside the barn to point my nose into the wind to escape the 'Eau de Equus' as best I could. I knew I could not be released until the last shot of that scene had had the gate checked and cleared by the camera crew. 'Hobo' would then do the 'cut to the hero dog' shot, doing much the same kind of rolling around on that floor as I had just done.

The trainer came out to assess the gag* that would be required of his canine star. He took one look at the stable floor and said unequivocally, 'My dog does *not* roll around on that floor.' Poor Mario, ever a man of passionate expression, shot directly through the roof, red-faced with fury. The shoot was brought to a standstill. The scene was crucial. All of this, of course, was relayed to me because...I was to be part of the final compromise, achieved after much heated debate between Mario and the trainer.

Hobo would do the shot where he was to be struck apparently unconscious on the floor of the stable...if *I* would lie down and allow Hobo to put his head on my beloved boots so that he need not lay it on the stable floor. And so, much to my chagrin, that was what we did.

* Stunt or piece of business critical to the story line.

TED JOHNS
Theatre of the barn

During the summer of 1994 I was performing the role of 'Aylmer Clark' in a Blyth Festival production of *He Won't Come In From The Barn*. The play is about Aylmer, a man who doesn't want to give up farming, and features two cows, three pigs, and some chickens. Needless to say, it's a farce.

Aylmer has moved into his barn and is living there. Midway through the play he engages in a heated argument with his son, 'Wayne', who wants to totally rebuild the barn and incidentally kick Aylmer out. At one point we were both downstage centre examining Wayne's financial projections when I noticed an absolutely thunderous audience reaction to lines that were funny, yes, but certainly not *that* funny. People in the front row had eyes like saucers, and great shrieks and howls were rising from the packed house.

One of the cows that normally stood with her backside to the audience had somehow slipped her collar and was loose. In such a situation there are several things to keep in mind. First, this is a large Holstein cow; second, the stage is small; third, cows do not have a reverse gear; fourth, there is a five-foot drop off the front of the stage; and fifth, cows are not noted for their depth perception.

My first objective was to stop Bessie from walking off the stage. I put my fingers in her nose and turned her head upstage, to the vast amusement of an audience of farmers who knew that I would now have to take her on a full hundred and sixty degrees to get her back into her stall. Our lighting man suddenly appeared from the booth, keenly aware that if Bessie chose to lumber straight ahead she could carry most of the set off on her back.

In the end, we did find a rope, did get her turned around, did find her collar and did get her back in her stall. However, Bessie did manage to step on the toe of my rubber boot. She is a very large animal and my toes were blackened for days afterwards. Had she stepped over a few more inches I suspect she would have broken my foot. At the time all this seemed to just add to the hilarity—farmers, I guess, having run into similar predicaments on their own. In any case the incident became a much told tale in our area and merited a minor mention in the *Globe and Mail*, a Toronto newspaper that is widely distributed across Canada.

During a second run of *Barn* in 1995, our Thursday matinee performance seemed particularly ill-fated. First one of our small black banty hens decided she wanted to lay an egg so she fluttered down from her usual perch and began to search for a hiding place. Attempts to catch her caused her to squawk, exciting her rooster friend who began to cackle in protest. The hen was finally removed and the rooster had settled down, and then I noticed that Bessie, the cow, was acting strangely—back humped, tail lifted, eyes staring, not chewing her cud, and repeatedly attempting to lie down and stand up. While maintaining a fairly demanding line of dialogue, I managed to catch a glimpse of a telephone receiver moving to the stage manager's ear.

The veterinarian was present by the curtain call and Bessie's calf was born soon after. It was a bull calf and was in part named after me—Lucky-me C. Billie-Ted. Bessie decided to forgo her evening performance but was in fine form the next day. All this must amount to some kind of theatrical record until such time, I suppose, as we mount another performance of *Barn*.

SARA BOTSFORD
These are supposed to be what?

In the early '80s Sam Groom and I did a Canadian horror film in Montreal. It was called *Rats*, for the huge, steroid-fed rats who were supposedly to take over the city. The producers had decided they didn't want to use puppets. Instead, they used Dachshunds—dressed up in rat costumes. It seemed like there were 50 of these dogs but there were probably only about 25. To wrangle them, they imported a number of very serious dog trainers from L.A., who spent their days lobbing big chunks of food on the ground and blowing whistles and shouting at the poor Dachshunds.

In every single take, one of the dogs would sit down and scratch, or poop in his costume, or roll over. And they barked. Barking rats. Sam and I had to keep a straight face throughout this whole thing and act as if we were terrified of them. It was hilarious. But you couldn't say anything about it. Nope. Not one of these six guys from L.A. ever, once, cracked a smile. It was very serious business for them. We were so hysterical we could hardly function.

The producers did end up substituting some puppet footage for some of the Dachshund footage. The movie's video title is *Deadly Eyes*.

BARRIE BALDARO
Fetch!

Once upon a time, I was shooting a television show in a studio. The scene was a woman's high-rise apartment. A male visitor had arrived and she was to ask him to please pet her beloved dog while she changed her clothes. The gag was that this fellow threw a ball a few feet and the dog would fetch it and bring it back. Then he threw it a bit farther. The dog would retrieve it and bring it back. Then he would, accidentally, throw the ball out the window. The dog was then to jump out the window after the ball, presumably to his unfortunate demise. Bear in mind that this was only a set of a high-rise apartment and 'out the window' was a mere two feet to the studio floor.

The 'professional' dog arrived with his handler at the start of the workday and it took almost the whole day to get to his little part. By then the poor dog was exhausted by the heat and the bright lights and the waiting, not unlike the rest of us, and when the actor threw the ball for the dog to fetch he could barely walk over to get it. He kind of shuffled a few feet, then lay down. The director did his best to inter-cut and make the gag work, to no avail.

Finally, it came time for the dog to jump out the window after the ball. He just sat there. So the actor, out of sheer frustration and his own fatigue, picked the dog up and *threw* him out the window.

MARILYN BOYLE
Theatre 'au naturelle'

I remember in 1962, when Bill Walker was playing 'Harold Hill' in *The Music Man*, the director, Bob Moulton, began each scene with a tableau; everyone entered, then held a pose until the cue. That was a terrible year for mosquitoes. It was a hoot to stand backstage (safely out of the light) and watch the 'statues' breaking their poses briefly to swat mosquitoes. It was like watching a surreal German slap dance.

One night, poor Bill had a moth or mosquito fly into his mouth. The conductor, Eric Wilde, saw it and held the orchestra until Bill swallowed it and could continue.

SUSAN CLARK
Rein Woman

I had been flown by Universal Studios from Toronto, to do *The Virginian*, a western series. It was my first big TV guest spot and my first job under my seven-year contract with Universal. The story in that particular episode was a rip-off of Bette Davis' *Dark Victory.* I was to play a character who was a great horsewoman. I had never been *on* a horse, nor had I ever *planned* to be on a horse.

They gave me an 1890s riding outfit and brought up a beautiful bay horse. After they helped me to mount the horse, they said, 'Hold the reins and walk around. We have a double to do the riding and jumping.' I was so scared that I was shaking. I must have communicated my fear to the horse because it wouldn't stop moving around and shifting us out of the shot. I had no idea how to control it.

In television, because there is not enough time or money to spend a day on one scene, they have to move very quickly. Even with four wranglers holding the legs of this horse, it would move around so much that it would ruin the shot.

They decided to dispense with the horse altogether. Much to my everlasting embarrassment, they put a saddle up on the top of a ladder. I climbed up into this saddle and held on to reins that were shifted gently by a wrangler, Whitey Sacks, who had a cigarette dangling from his mouth as he imitated the movement of a horse's head. He later suggested that if I did not want to humiliate myself in future, he would teach me how to ride.

A year later, he taught me to ride while we were on location doing *Tell Them Willy Boy Was Here* in Palm Springs. Whitey was a cantankerous old wrangler who had ridden polo ponies for Will Rogers in the 1930s. He would take me out on the desert every morning at 5 o'clock before we went to work and teach me. I continued riding with him weekly for five years at the Newhall Ranch—a private stable that had trained all of Roy Rogers' Triggers and many other movie horses. I became good enough that they allowed me to exercise their horses.

By the time I was cast in *Valdez is Coming* with Burt Lancaster I was comfortable enough to do most of my own riding stunts.

LYNDA MASON GREEN
Chimps and Ketchup

I have only on very rare occasions had the opportunity to work with animals. As much as I like animals, I am cautious about those that are trained for the film industry because they are often not to be touched until the trainer allows it, if at all.

On this occasion, we were working with chimpanzees in a particular scene that required the chimps to break out of their cages and attack the keepers and the scientist, me. I had had absolutely no exposure to chimps and had no idea what to expect. We were told that they were well trained and would not hurt us if we did as we were instructed. Fine with me.

On the first take the younger of the two chimps, a male, was to be shot breaking out of the cage and attacking a lab-coated keeper, who was played by one of the trainers. When the 'action' signal came the young chimp became so excited that not only did he charge out of the cage and career wildly around the room but he unloaded his bowels on the trainer in the process. He apparently was in the *early* stages of his training...both kinds. I was not much comforted by this display.

For my part, I was to be pushed violently back against the cages and the chimp inside was to grab my face and tear my skin with its nails. I asked to be introduced to the chimp first so I wouldn't scare her and so she wouldn't scare me either. She seemed extraordinarily intelligent. I was fascinated with her. I was assured again that she, the older of the two chimps, was very well trained and had much experience. We rehearsed the gag which would require me to place her hand on my face and make it look as though she were attacking me and I was trying to stop her. That went fine. We seemed to be under control. So I gave her back to the trainer, feeling pretty confident that we could manage, and went off for the next hour to have my lacerations applied to my face along with some fake blood.

When we all came back, ready to shoot, I was handed the chimp again so she would know me. She whimpered a little when I picked her up. Then she pursed her lips and looked away and back at the trainer. She looked back at me and then tentatively touched my fake scratches very gently once or twice, and sniffed the end of the finger with which she had touched me, each time whimpering softly. I spoke quietly to her but she still seemed uneasy.

Apparently she had seen the scratches and thought that I was hurt and didn't want to touch me where the scratches were. I don't think I am anthropomorphising when I say that I sensed that she was concerned that I was in pain. It was an astonishing moment. I realised that she trusted her sight more than her sense of smell and was confused. We actually had to take her to see someone getting a scratch put on and let her touch my face with a flat hand before she would allow her hand to be drawn across my face for the FX in the scene.

5

Missed Cues, Missed Lines, Mistakes

BENEDICT CAMPBELL
My *Dream*'s nightmare

Joe Ziegler and I were playing 'Lysander' and 'Demetrius' in John Hirsch's production of *A Midsummer Night's Dream* at Stratford. We had been costumed by the great Desmond Heeley in traditional Elizabethan costume. Well, anyone who has ever had to wear 'pumpkin' pants can tell you what a humbling and truly embarrassing outfit that is to wear. Joe and I were no exception, we hated our pumpkin pants (sorry, Desmond) and to make sure nobody had the chance to make fun of us, we sent ourselves up rotten all the time before they could.

We had even invented a little ditty to march around in our pumpkin pants to, which was suitably in the style of John Philip Sousa. We sang it constantly and everywhere, much to the annoyance of our fellow company members.

One particular night during a performance we were singing and marching quietly up and down the halls to our usual theme, when I felt a hand reach through the black curtain by the stage, give me a rather hefty tug and a voice whisper emphatically in my ear, 'You're on!'

On I was, but I had no idea what part of the play we were at and through my terror was finding it difficult even to remember my name. I managed to squeak my way through the scene.

I went looking for Nicholas Pennell and Diego Matamoros who I had so shamelessly left out on the stage with nothing more to say. I found Diego but was unable to catch up with Nicky until the next day in the green room. I shuffled up to Nicky, who was eating his usual breakfast (fried egg and cheese sandwich), and delivered my humblest apologies. He was his ever gracious self and made me feel as if I hadn't put anyone out in the slightest, recounting to me all his past sins regarding failed entrances.

After having a good laugh with him about it, I said, 'So, Nicky, how long did I actually leave you out there? Was it about 10 seconds that felt like 50?' Just so I wasn't let off the hook too easily he flashed me a piercing stare and replied, 'No, it was more like 50 that felt like two fucking hours, dear.'

My ear doesn't often wander from that monitor, even now.

CHARLES COBURN to AMELIA HALL:
'An actor is always fifteen minutes ahead of time!'

GARY FILES
A slip of the mind

Doing *Oh What A Lovely War* in Toronto at the Crest, I was staying at Bill Needles' house.

There's a very odd phenomenon in the minds of some people: somehow the memory of an appointment that must be met is erased if for any reason the appointment is discussed beforehand. Don't ask me why, but on this occasion, I met a friend while I was shopping downtown in the Eaton Centre. He asked me what time the matinee would be on that day. I told him when it was to be and he said, 'Oh lovely. We'll be there.' Somehow, my brain decided that the thing I was supposed to remember to do—be at the theatre for the matinee—was now 'done' because I had talked to someone about it.

I finished my shopping, got on the subway and the trolley, and wended my way toward home. As I stepped off the trolley, someone from the theatre was there. I waved cheerfully, completely oblivious that anything might be amiss, and as I did I could see her mouth one word with, I would say, a certain urgency, '*Ma-tin-ee!*'

The rush was on! I ran across the road and jumped into the truck. When we arrived, I charged full speed through the stage door, I threw my clothes everywhere and pulled on as much of my wardrobe as I could manage as I ran to the wings. Kevin Palmer, our director, was on stage with a book in hand reading my part. I rushed on stage, snatched his book out of his hand, tossed it off stage and continued with the play.

I was completely mortified, appalled that I had been late for the matinee, and apologised profusely to everyone individually.

Eric House, who was also in the play, tried to cheer me up. 'Don't feel bad,' he said. 'I was working at a theatre in Ottawa once. It was a funny, old kind of theatre with a door at the back that led to a fire escape. You could walk around that fire escape catwalk to another door that let you into the balcony of the theatre. Often in rehearsal we would go round to watch the others from there. During a performance, a matinee, I realised that I didn't have anything to do for quite a long time in the play, so I went round to watch the play from the unoccupied balcony...until I heard my cue on stage! But I was not ON stage. I jumped up and ran back along the fire escape walkway in a great panic, heaved at the fire door that led to the backstage area and discovered it had locked itself! I pounded and pounded. No answer. I pounded until finally someone heard me and I was on, to the relief of a very distressed cast who had been ad-libbing like mad for what seemed like hours.'

No matter how disastrous you think things are, actors can always tell you a story of something worse that happened to them. We are bonded by our blunders.

TIMOTHY FINDLEY
Rhino days

There is only one thing worse than missing a performance. In 1961, I was playing in Ionesco's *Rhinoceros* at Toronto's Civic Theatre on Queen Street—and those were my drinking days.

One Saturday morning, I awoke in an alcoholic haze, bleared at the clock—and went into total panic. It was twenty to two—and we had a matinee at two! I called a cab, set a record for getting dressed, and dashed unsteadily down the stairs, out the door and into the waiting taxi. I asked the driver to get me to the theatre faster than a speeding bullet. He complied. We tore through the streets and pulled up at the stage door just as the old City Hall clock began striking the hour. Only, it didn't stop at two. It struck nine times! And that was when I realized that, although I'd been able to see the hands on my bedside clock, I hadn't been able to tell them apart. It hadn't been twenty to two at all—but ten after eight...in the morning.

Home I went—had a stiff drink—and decided the only thing worse than missing a performance is *thinking* you've missed one.

JENNIFER PHIPPS
A cell with no Powys

Sooner or later, we all miss cues. We were doing *Romeo and Juliet* at the old Dominion Theatre where Manitoba Theatre Centre had its first home. Powys Thomas was playing 'Friar Lawrence', John Fraser was playing 'Romeo', and I was the 'Nurse'.

During the scene where Romeo was to meet Friar Lawrence in his cell at the abbey, Romeo and the Nurse were onstage, hidden behind the arras. The curtain rose...there was no Friar Lawrence. Needless to say, the line 'Come forth, Romeo, thou fearful man' couldn't be said. Romeo and Nurse jumped into view and ad-libbed an iambic 'search' but it was finally no good. Friar Powys could not be found. They had to bring the curtain down.

Meanwhile everyone was frantically looking for him. Every room was turned upside down. After a mad search, they found him in a large clothes closet having a nap. He had gone in to rest during the interval and fallen asleep. No searcher had seen or heard him because the closet door was behind an access door. When the access door opened, the closet door closed.

And it seemed that Powys' internal actor's clock had run late.

GREG KRAMER
Laughing all the way to hell

I was playing 'Mephistopheles' in Vancouver TheatreSpace's production of *Faust (Part I)* by Goethe. It was Hallowe'en, 1984. On this night, the Assistant Stage Manager had booked off and sent a substitute in his place.

In my final scene, I had to appear through a trap-door in the stage, the Gates of Hades, to drag 'Faust' back down to Hell. To do this, I needed to be boosted. I heard my cue get closer and closer, but there was no sign of the assistance I needed to get myself hoisted up through the trap-door. In a panic, I ran around backstage looking for help. There was none. Every available soul was up on stage playing the hosts and angels of God for the finale. What's a poor devil to do?

In desperation, I ran out the stage door into the street and, wearing my little devil horns and in full make-up, I appealed to two passers-by, who were no doubt surprised to be petitioned by the Devil for help. But since it was after all Hallowe'en, this sort of thing was to be expected. Luckily for me, they agreed. In a hastily whispered conversation, I gave these two helpful strangers rapid instructions: 'When I say "go", give me a push.' Which they did—on cue—and I made my entrance on time!

Half-way through the scene, while yanking away on Faust's arm, I happened to glance back down at the trap-door which I had just come through. Peeking up through the trap-door at the audience was one of my two temporary helpers who had been hoisted on the shoulders of the other. A look of complete shock was on his face! He'd decided to see for himself what he'd been coerced into doing and was astonished to discover that, yes! he was in a theatre! On stage!

MAGGIE SMITH to DAVID DUNBAR:
'If you do it wrong once you better do it wrong a second time,
so they think you were doing your part.'

DONALD HUGHES
Picking up the rear

In 1988 I was in the Young Company at Stratford with William Hutt playing *King Lear*. The play had been superbly directed by Robin Phillips and we played at the Tom Patterson Theatre, which is the small space. Late in the run the actors weren't quite at the stage of auto pilot but we were having to watch out for that kind of thing.

I was playing 'Oswald' for most of the show but for the opening scene I played the 'Duke of Burgundy'. One of my lines to 'King Lear' began 'Royal Lear, put that portion, which yourself proposed...' There was a young wag in the company from Chicago named Jeff Hutchison. He came up to me one afternoon, just before the opening scene of a matinee.

'Don, you know that line when you say Royal Lear? Don't you ever worry that you will call him Loyal Rear?'

'No, Jeff, I don't ever worry about that.'

'Why don't you do it today, just to get it out of your system?'

'Why don't you just fuck off?' I replied, laughing.

So there I am five minutes later out onstage looking at the regal Mr Hutt and I get to that line and I suddenly, desperately think—which one is it?? Absolutely panic-stricken I open my mouth and say, clear as could be, 'Loyal Rear...' And then I thought—Oh my God, I've just called Bill Hutt, Loyal Rear in front of 550 paying customers! Fortunately I was in such a state of panic at what I had done that I just kept going as if nothing had happened. All I could think was—if you do anything to acknowledge what you just did 550 people are going to *know* they heard what they think they heard. I spent the rest of my time onstage thinking—I can't believe I did that.

Bill finally rose from his throne and said, glaring at me, 'Come, *Noble* Burgundy ...' and we exited. Well, Jeff, the guy who set me up for this, and I laughed hysterically all through our next quick change. As soon as we could talk, Jeff said 'I'm sorry. I'm so sorry. I didn't think you were actually going to *say* it.' At the act break I thought I ought to go to speak to Mr Hutt and apologize.

Bill had his own private dressing room built right next the stage; we called it Bill's hut. I said 'I am so very sorry. That will *never* happen again.' Bill said, 'Oh, that's OK. We've all got one or two of those in our closet. I just about cracked up, though.' The thought of King Lear breaking up had never occurred to me. I thought—well, it's a good thing he didn't, 'cause if he had, I would have been toast!

My slip got around the Festival in about 90 seconds. The show came down in late afternoon and I went up to Loblaw's to pick up some groceries. There I ran into David Brown from the main company. He had just finished his show at the main stage. I said 'You'll never believe what I just did today.' He said 'I already heard about it.'

SUSAN HOGAN
Who's where, and what?

This is the story of the biggest dry I have encountered in my career. Some say that this dry belongs to me but no one really knows who dried.

David McIlwraith, Michael Hogan, Patrick Brymer and I were doing Tom Walmsley's *White Boys* at the Tarragon Theatre in 1982. We were all onstage talking and doing business. I was collating papers, or something. I don't remember what

Michael was doing. Then something happened, we don't know exactly what, and then nothing happened.

There was a long time when no one spoke. This performance was the last preview before the opening and the theatre was packed. Because the dialogue had been really clipping along it wasn't very long before just about everybody had realised there was a problem.

Soon our eyes started shifting around the stage looking for someone with a cue. Nothing happened. Not only did we not know what was next, no one could think of a thing to say. Four professional actors were collectively gone.

Then David McIlwraith left the stage. I collated papers and hummed a tune for another couple of minutes then I walked off stage as well. Trick Brymer never left his seat. He just sat in an armchair staring straight ahead. Michael was doing some business with a swinging door. Nobody knew where we were. Finally Michael came off stage too.

I got on the headset backstage to Larry Farley, our stage manager. 'Larry, we've all gone and we've no idea where we are.' Then we all went back out onstage and waited for something to happen. Then over the loudspeaker, for all the audience to hear, Larry said, 'You're at the bottom of page 43.' The audience just broke up completely. They were falling all over the place. Eventually one of us said, 'So, what do we say and who says it?'

Who was the one who dried in *White Boys*? I can't say who dried because, to this day, we are still arguing about it.

ANGELA GEI
The K-N-E-E, KNEE

Working in small theatres rarely throws me—until this little incident occurred during a performance of *The Woods* by David Mamet with Tom Arnott at Theatre London. It is a wonderful play. Ken Livingstone, who was amazing with actors, was directing.

The Woods is a two-hander* so you are out there a lot, talking. We had the front porch of the cottage and a dock as part of the set that went right out into the audience. That playing area at the end of the dock was about four feet from the audience, which was pretty close. On one occasion, I didn't know that they had put people in wheelchairs into that four-foot space, which meant there would be virtually *no* space between me and the audience for the monologue I would be doing at the end of the dock.

Mamet writes amazing prose. I was always very nervous about getting the words exactly right. I thought I had to be perfect on the lines because the prose was so perfect. I felt I had to learn not only the speech Mamet had written but the subtext as a monologue as well.

---

* A play with only two characters.

So I was doing my best to be perfect and still 'live in the moment', juggling the monologue and the subtext and staying intuitive when I was about to launch into the monologue. I got right to the end of the dock and suddenly all I could see was this person's knee...and literally the knee was inches from my face. It completely threw me. I remember thinking in my head, 'K-N-E-E-, Knee.' That was the only word that came to me. I sat there and *nothing* came to me but that word. 'There's a *knee* right in front of me. I don't know what I'm saying.' I thought I was going to die! So I started to talk...about 'my' (the character's) grandmother, anything I could think of, about the pictures that she'd left me, *anything*. Poor Mamet. I had gone right up and couldn't find the speech.

Through all of this, Tom was sitting there with his feet on the banister on the porch upstage. Anyone who knows Tom Arnott knows that he is brilliant with the lines. If you ever got lost, he was always there to help bail you out, but in this occasion...he wasn't helping. He just sat there and listened to me until I eventually latched onto a familiar word and eventually found my way back on track. So I asked him later, 'What the heck happened?' He said, 'Well, you were on your way, you were still making sense. When you stopped making sense I was going to butt in there but you were all right.'

JACK CRELEY
No retreat

My favourite spoonerism happened when I was working at Vineland with Austin Willis in *Laura*. I was playing 'Mr Lydecker'. My exit line from one scene, spoken with much passion, was, 'I'm going to retreat to a cloister!' One infamous night, what came out was 'I'm going to retroit to a cleester!'

Austin Willis started laughing so hard his trick knees locked in the wrong position so he couldn't get offstage. The two of us just stood there and looked at each other and laughed along with the audience.

WAYNE ROBSON
Rumpel-oops!-kin

The Golden Rule of doing children's theatre is 'You can't fool kids—be honest!' I was performing *Rumpelstiltskin* for Holiday Theatre one Saturday afternoon in Vancouver in '66. The 'Miller's Daughter' (played in this case by Pia Shandel) has three occasions in the play to guess Rump's name. She would of course always get it wrong until her third try, the end of the play. On this day we got near the end of the first try.

'Is it George?'
'No! (cackle, cackle!)'
'Is it Sam?'

'No! (heh, heh, heh)'

'Is it Rum—pel—?'

Instantly, Pia realised she had accidently guessed the correct name and leapt three scenes ahead of herself. Before she could recover and get the rest of the name wrong, the stagehand heard what he thought was his cue, and set off the flash explosion into which I dove—end of play.

We weren't 15 minutes into it by then. Over half the actors had yet to make their first appearances. Nevertheless the curtain came down, the cast did their bows, and the kids and moms came up for autographs. And there was not one complaint about the brevity of the show. On the contrary, we received many compliments on our performances. The only complainers were those actors who didn't get to appear on stage that day.

NOLAN JENNINGS
Fork-ups and Spoonerisms

A number of years ago, I was playing the villain in a melodrama at the Georgetown Play House in P.E.I.

Opening night, I met the heroine's mother on stage. She was played by a very large lady. My line was: 'What cruel fate has brought you here.' Absolutely unaware of what I said, it came out: 'What fuel crate has brought you here.'

GORDON CLAPP
A gutsy lady

I never knew Kate Reid at the height of her powers. She was a giant talent, among the greatest we have ever produced. When I was working with Kate, she had begun to have a problem with her memory.

We were doing the Robert Lowe translation of the *Oresteia*. Kate was playing 'Clytemnestra' but was having a very bad time with the words, especially remembering the names of the characters and places she had to refer to in her speeches. So every time she came to a name she was not sure of her voice would drop off and she would mumble something. So her speeches would sound something like;

'The flame *JUMPED* from <mumble, merble> *TO THE SUMMIT AT* <gerble, merble>.' And so on. She couldn't keep the names straight.

Then once she completely forgot her lines and she turned to the chorus and boldly said, 'SPEAK!...old men!' And we, the poor slobs who were the members of the chorus, just stood there dumbfounded.

She barely made it through opening night. By the end of the second week, Diane D'Aquila was going on for her and continued to do so for three or four nights before Kate came back.

When she did come back, she was letter-perfect and never dropped a line for the rest of the run. It was extraordinary. Despite her illness and all of those fears, she got herself back up on 'the horse'. And she was great.

HEATHER SUMMERHAYES
*Con*stable Dickson

In the 1970s, during the early years of my marriage to Richard McMillan, Rick and I both did our share of children's theatre. At one point, Rick was on tour with Young People's Theatre in a play called *Almighty Voice*. This was performed for middle to senior public school students in various gymnasiums around the province. Rick was playing a Mountie determined to catch the elusive Indian, 'Almighty Voice'.

I remember one performance vividly. In a particular scene, Rick, in hot pursuit of Almighty Voice, and ready to close in, was to bark an order at a subordinate.

'Get my mount ready, Constable Dickson!'

But in his excitement, he instead shouted, 'Get my cunt ready, Mountable Dickson!'

The entire gymnasium full of kids went up in laughter for ten minutes as teachers fainted left and right.

JAN RUBES
Doprdele!

Before I started acting, I was an opera singer. When I came to Canada on the last day of 1948, there was no opera house, so I was teaching tennis up north for a living. Not too long after, an opera manager came to Canada to audition singers for a tour of Guatemala, Costa Rica, and other Central American countries. I sang for him and he said, 'Ya, ya, fine.' He told me we would do six operas and as he rattled off the names I nodded and said that I knew them all. In fact, I knew only one of them and only in Čzech on top of that, but I knew that I had four months to learn them. I didn't think it was a problem. I learned the parts I was to sing and we went off to do this tour.

About midway through the tour we stopped at Costa Rica. The opera house was a magnificent replica of Milan's La Scala right in the middle of San Jose. We were once again an enormous success. The President of Costa Rica was so delighted that he asked that the company stay an extra day or two to do a command performance of *La Traviata*. Of course, you do not say 'No' to a command performance, but this was not one of the operas we were presenting on the tour. Even so, it would not normally be a problem for most opera singers, especially those from The Met, as many of our cast were. Luckily I knew the music, but I had only learned the singing parts in *La Traviata* in Czech.

We had four days to prepare it. We rehearsed and I learned the few sentences that I had to sing solo in Italian, but there was no time for me to learn the endless ensembles, especially the one in the third act when everyone was singing for hours, it seemed. The part is quite basic and repetitive, da, da, da...dum, da,da,da...dum, but there was no way I could learn this long ensemble part in Italian in those few short days...so I got a brilliant idea.

I decided that the audience probably couldn't hear the words very clearly anyway and they were mostly Spanish-speaking, so I decided to use a Czech word that sounded Italian and just repeat it. The word 'doprdele' fitted perfectly into the rhythm, do-pr-del-le, do-pr-del-le. So that was what I did, with great confidence, thinking no one would know the difference. The one problem was that 'doprdele' in Czech means 'up your ass' in English.

As I was singing, everything seemed to be going splendidly, until I looked out at the audience and saw a man in the first row killing himself with laughter. Apparently there *was* one person in the audience who spoke Czech.

After the show, this man came backstage. His name was Benny Benda. He said to me, 'Mr Rubes, that was the funniest...I came to see a cultural event. And just at a very dramatic moment, I hear in Czech, someone bellowing from the stage "Up your ass!"'

We went out for a drink together, had a marvellous time and finally staggered back to my hotel room totally drunk, singing 'Doprdele' at the top of our lungs.

MILES POTTER
Never again

The scene was the National Arts Centre Studio, mid '70s. The play was one of the revivals of *1837* with most of the original cast. Deep into the second act, the rebellion was underway. As the rest of the cast crouched, hunched, or in various ways created scenery, David Fox as old 'Anthony van Egmond' exhorted a dispirited Eric Peterson to return to the fray. As the scene normally went, he reached an emotional climax with, 'Did I ever tell you, lad? I was in the Napoleonic Wars, wounded fourteen times, and never once in the back!' Then, we would break into a rousing song and march on to Montgomery's Tavern.

This night, I suppose Dave's concentration slipped for one crucial second, and as we were all poised to launch into the next moment, he finished the scene with: 'Did I ever tell you, lad, I was in the Napoleonic Wars—wounded fourteen times in the back....

As Eric and the rest of us stared at him in wonder and disbelief, David rose to his full height and with great conviction and commitment, fixed us all with a steely gaze and cried out: '... but never again!' And so we managed to march off to battle with relatively straight faces.

DAVID FERRY
Blowin' the line

I was out at Theatre Calgary in 1976 playing 'Christy Mahon' in a production of *Playboy Of The Western World* directed by Frances Hyland. Mary Haney was playing 'Pegeen Mike'.

There is a scene towards the end of the play where the townsfolk and Pegeen Mike turn on Christy Mahon and put a rope around him. Everyone is on stage jeering at Christy. Pegeen takes a pair of old bellows and heats up an iron in the fire to brand him with, they are that angry at him. Christy has a line, 'Ah, sure, you're blowin' for to torture me!' One night, instead of saying what I was supposed to say I said, with great emotion, 'Ah, sure, you're fixin' for to blow me!'

Well, the townsfolk and poor Mary Haney started to giggle. The laughter gradually became so profound and so deep that they started to leave the stage in groups of three to have a proper laugh offstage and try to get rid of the giggles.

All I could hear whilst I was writhing on the floor acting my bollocks off, were groups of people exiting, laughing, then coming back on stage, like shift work. Finally we made it through the show. The audience found all this hilarious as well. Slip of the tongue or no, we didn't feel too happy about spoiling the end of this remarkable play.

TIMOTHY FINDLEY
The malaprop Malaprop

It was the spring of 1962. I was working at the Central Library Theatre in a season of repertory. We had come to the opening night of the third and final play in the repertoire: Sheridan's *The Rivals*. Already playing Genet's *The Balcony* and N.F. Simpson's *One Way Pendulum*, we were all exhausted.

Rehearsals of *The Rivals* had not gone well. I was playing 'Captain Jack Absolute', and Cosette Lee was 'Mrs Malaprop'—that heavenly woman who muddles her words: 'He was the very pineapple of perfection!'

In Act One, I was waiting in the wings—desperately trying to remember my own first line—when Cosy Lee staggered off into my arms, almost in tears. 'They're not laughing!' she wailed. 'Mrs Malaprop and I didn't get a single laugh!' Later, so I was told, Tommy Hooker, the stage manager, took Cosy aside and quietly informed her that, more than likely due to nervousness, she had been meticulously *correcting* all the malapropisms in her first scene.

DAN MacDONALD
Merry Christmas, Sherlock!

December 25th fell in the middle of rehearsals for the première production of the Alden Nowlan/Walter Learning play, *The Incredible Murder Of Cardinal Tosca*. Theatre New Brunswick had arranged time off for us to fly home, spend Christmas with family, and resume rehearsals a few days later.

On the 24th, we decided to work on Act I until it was time to leave for the airport. I was there, as 'Dr Watson', along with that most perfect 'Sherlock Holmes', Jack Medley. Another Jack (Jack Northmore) played a villainous brute in the piece, and Wenna Shaw was our feisty heroine. That wonderful actors' director, Ted Follows, conducted the rehearsal.

We were, I like to think, all rendered a bit giddy by the season and the anxiety of catching the one possible air connection home that day, so our concentration might not have been as intense as it ought.

It was not yet noon, and Jack N. had just exited, impressing us all with his dangerous potential by bending a heavy poker into near-pretzel shape. Watson comments on this, referring to the damaged poker, and Holmes, who has been examining the bent metal rod, quickly and with apparent ease snaps the poker back to its original shape.

'Good Heavens,' I say, in astonishment, 'That's incredible, Holmes!'

Holmes dismisses his abilities, tut-tutting that it was nothing, a trick. 'Meretricious, Watson!', he says.

I couldn't help myself...'and a very, Merry-tritious to you too, Holmes!'

Rehearsals ended earlier than anticipated.

WAYNE BEST
On Mr T

Mr T was a very interesting guy. Nice guy, did a lot of good stuff for kids but never had any pretensions to being an actor. He was a 'personality' and quite brilliant at exploiting this invention, 'Mr T', made famous in one of the *Rocky* movies.

He was in Toronto as producer and star of an action/mystery series called *T 'n T*. On one episode, we were rehearsing an exchange in the courthouse corridor on the way to the elevator. Apparently Mr T rarely rehearsed for the cameras. So the other actors and the crew rehearsed the lines and camera moves. Then Mr T would come in and the director would run it through just before the cameras were ready to roll.

The exchange went like this:

'OK, you three walk down the hall, you get to the elevator, elevator opens, he says his line, he says his line, you say your line. OK?'

'OK. Yeah. Yeah, I got it. Walk down the corridor, stop for the elevator, elevator door opens, he says his line, he says his line, I say my line. Got it.'

He wanders away muttering these exact instructions over and over again to himself, pointing at the elevator and each actor as he memorises the order of events in the scene.

'Walk down the corridor, stop for the elevator, elevator door opens, he says his line, he says his line, I say my line. OK. Walk down the corridor, stop for the elevator, elevator door opens, he says his line, he says his line, I say my line.'

Camera was ready to roll. We got the 'action' cue and began walking. We get to the elevator, the door opens, the first actor says his line, I say my line and Mr T suddenly blinks, then turns to the director and says with impeccable timing,

'What the fuck's my line?'

Cast and crew including Mr T were pretty much non-functional for the next 10 minutes.

BARBARA GORDON
Canajun, eh?

Some years ago, I was engaged to play the American head of the Iranian-American Center in a movie called *Escape From Iran*, the story of Ken Taylor's heroic efforts to smuggle out some of the Americans caught in Iran during the infamous hostage-taking at the American embassy.

In my career, I have often been asked, 'What is your accent?' or 'Where do you come from?' It had proved to be an advantage on many occasions because it was more difficult to identify me as a Canadian in a time when a lot of the available work was generated from the United States. And in the course of my career, I had learned to be flexible in my speech pattern to accommodate the requirements of the part. Of course, you would *never* utter that commonly identified Canadianism, 'eh?' under any circumstances.

In this scene I, as the American director, was to welcome the hostages to 'home' turf at the Center. Halfway through the first take the director (who was American) called, 'Cut!' and said to me that I should watch the 'ehs' at the end of my sentences. Well, I have been accused of many things in my life but *NEVER* of sounding too Canadian. I chuckled inwardly and resolved to flatten my 'A's and watch my 'oots' and 'aboots'. Since I had never in my life ever said 'eh' at the end of my sentences, it never occurred to me that that was what he meant.

Another take, and the director interrupted a second time...and a third time with infinite patience and the same direction. I was completely confused. He explained that I had tacked on the 'eh' at the end of the sentence and that an American character could not do that. I finally told him that I had never (as an extremely self-aware actress) fallen into that habit and that there must be some mistake.

He smiled sweetly and invited me to listen to the recordings of the previous takes. Sure enough, I heard myself, jolly as all get out, saying, 'Gee, you must be ready for a cuppah cahffee, eh?'...over...and over.

Well, shut me mouth. So much for self-awareness...eh?

BERNARD BEHRENS
The giggle wall

In 1968 at Stratford we did a production of *Midsummer Night's Dream* directed by John Hirsch. I was playing 'Quince', one of the Mechanicals, the town oafs that are planning to put on a play for the 'Duke'. The others in the group were Jimmy Blendick, Eric Donkin, Dougie Rain, Leon Pownall and Ken Welsh. We had been playing this show for months, but for some reason we had endless cast changes which meant endless *re*-rehearsing.

In the final rehearsal before the show on the night two new actors were to go in, Jimmy Blendick came on as 'Lion'. He opened his mouth to speak but instead he started to laugh and couldn't stop.

When I was to say my next line, I started laughing. Then we all got started. I could still get my lines out, but they came out on a wheeze. I sort of squeezed them out. Dougie Rain as 'Bottom' came out for his part of the scene with his prop apple. He started to laugh too, and got so fed up he just threw the apple at somebody and left the stage. We actually fell on the floor. Hirsch started to scream at us, 'Stop this at once. Get on with the rehearsal. These people have to go in tonight.'

These two poor fellows who were taking over that night didn't know what to do. So the stage manager, Thomas Bohdanetzky, just sat on the edge of the stage and read them their cues and told them where to move. The rest of us were on our knees, completely hysterical.

We came off and said to each other, 'Well, we don't know what happened but now it's out of our system.' We came on for the next scene and then the play at the end, and every scene was exactly the same. We couldn't stop laughing. At the end of the rehearsal we got chewed out royally by Hirsch. We went home and felt sure that after a decent dinner we'd come back and be fine for the performance.

The same thing happened for four consecutive performances! We never knew what or why but we just could not stop laughing. It was, in fact, awful. It was exhausting apart from everything else. One dreaded going on.

Then, just as abruptly, it stopped. We came in for the fifth show and it was as if it had never happened.

DAWN GREENHALGH
Tha's all for now

In the second summer season of the theatre in Halifax, one of the plays we did was Tennessee Williams' *The Glass Menagerie*. Diana LeBlanc was 'Laura', George Sperdakos was 'Tom', and I was their mother 'Amanda'. *The Glass Menagerie* is a memory play where Tom has long speeches about his life and the life of those around him.

One Saturday George had a wedding to go to between the matinee and the evening show. He dashed off to the church and then went on briefly to the reception.

On this hot summer's day, not being a drinker he had innocently knocked back some long drinks of spiked punch. By the time he got to the theatre he was barely able to function. Stage management plied him with coffee and he was on his feet when the play began. The curtain went up and George was only needing to be fed the odd line—until he got to his second soliloquy. He said a couple of lines, then abruptly stopped, and sat down on the living room sofa.

'Tha's all for now. My mother'll tell you the rest.'

And promptly fell asleep. We struggled on without him in a frenzy of improvisation until the coffee took hold.

SCOTT WENTWORTH
The last trumpet

We were doing Brent Carver's *Hamlet* at Stratford. I was playing 'Laertes' and Max Helpmann was doing a number of small parts. He was pretty frail by this time, and very content not tackling anything major. He would sit in his dressing room, smoking his cigar and reading the paper.

Max was famous for creative play-writing. When playing the churlish 'Priest' referring to the dead 'Ophelia', he was supposed to say to me, 'No more be done. For charitable prayers shards, flints and pebbles should be thrown on her and she in ground unsanctified should lodge to the last trumpet.' On this night he said, in his marvellous Canadian/Australian accent, 'No more be done. For charitable prayers shards, flints and pennies...should be thrown on her...and she...in ground unsanctified, should lodge to the last supper!' Then he just stared at me as if to say—there you go, make something out of that, smart guy. I looked over to Jimmy Blendick who was playing the King and he had turned upstage. All I could see was his shoulders shaking in mirth.

By the time I met Max he had done it all and seen it all. Theatre was his life. He loved it. Once I overheard a young apprentice in the company say to him, 'I was reading a book about the history of Stratford and, Max, my God, you have played huge roles. How can you stand to play small parts now?' He replied, 'Young man, they'll have to drag me off that stage.'

And that's almost what happened. Towards the end he had been ill for some time with a painful cancer but he kept bouncing back. Finally we were in rehearsal for a new season and he was looking really ill. He was out of rehearsals for five days and then word came that he was dying.

Max stories are the core of Stratford lore, told over and over to succeeding generations of young actors. It would appear he hasn't left the theatre yet.

DOUGLAS CHAMBERLAIN
Anon, anon, and on

Nicky Pennell and I were doing *Two Gentlemen Of Verona* at the Avon Theatre in Stratford. We'd been at it for eight months. In one scene, Nicky and I had about a page and a half of dialogue. One night, I got to the second line and went absolutely blank. But we'd done it for so long that I was into the rhythm of it and I couldn't shut myself up.

I stood onstage and said things like, 'And yet thou, who wither doth the spoon of winds blow? Nights do crown the glory of flowers if lost the rivers. And yet for thou, knowing and yet hence this would come to...'. I did it with all the inflections and everything. I had Nicky Pennell in front of me crying with laughter, the tears were running down his face.

Then, out of the corner of my eyes, I saw the wings filling up with the other actors gesturing, 'Go, Chamberlain. Go!' Robin Phillips was literally on the floor he was laughing so hard. I just couldn't stop myself. I just kept talking nonsense for a page and a half. I was in a deep sweat and just terrified.

Nicky went off but I still had to stay on stage. Then Stephen Russell had to come on. He knocked me out of it and got me back into the show. By the time I came off I was just shaking like a leaf. Nicky was waiting for me.

'For Chrissake, why didn't you shut up?'

'I couldn't, I couldn't.'

'I could have got you out any time. But you wouldn't stop!'

I had friends in the audience who had no idea that I had gone up. They had no idea that I wasn't making any sense. My intention was exactly what I really should have said. I did it with meaningless words but I just *couldn't stop*.

DONALD HARRON
All's well...

Stratford Ontario's thrust stage juts out into the audience and in the early days it was impossible for a prompter to cue you if you forgot your lines. During the first season of the Stratford Shakespearean Festival we did *All's Well That Ends Well* and as 'Bertram' I played a scene with Douglas Campbell as 'Parolles'. When Douglas forgot his lines, which happened more than once, it didn't faze him a bit. He would immediately go into lines from another Shakespearean play, usually *As You Like It*.

This left me standing with egg on my face unable to answer him. I determined to craft a line of 'Shakespearean' verse to reply to him next time it happened. I wrote down the words: 'My dearest cuz, an use-d car, the government thereof.' It made no sense but it did keep the beat of the iambic pentameter. Sure enough, within a couple of weeks Douglas went off *All's Well* and into some other play, I know not what. When he finished his obscure speech and looked at me with a smile on his face, I delivered my home-made, well-rehearsed line. The son of a bitch walked away and left me alone on the stage.

AMELIA HALL
1950, The Canadian Repertory Theatre, and Sam Payne

Sam Payne got the biggest laugh in the production [of *She Stoops to Conquer*] on opening night. It was in the scene outside the Hardcastle house, in the garden, which 'Tony' has deceived his mother into believing is a barren heath frequented by highwaymen. She is hidden behind a tree while Tony talks to 'Mr Hardcastle' who, to Tony's alarm, has come for a stroll in the garden.

There is a deal of repetition of questions in this scene, and it was one of those occasions when Sam was shaky on the words. He dried. The prompter, David, came in quickly with, 'I heard a voice!' But Sam didn't hear David. So Silvio [Narizzano] whispered to Sam, 'I heard a voice!' 'Oh, did you?' replied Sam heartily, ready to improvise for a bit. 'No, no!' whispered Silvio, '*you* heard a voice!' 'Oh,' beamed Sam, turning to the house, '*I heard a voice!*' Roars and applause!

MURRAY KASH
On making a prompt exit

This incident took place many years ago, in the late '30s, at a theatre on Spadina close to Dundas, The Strand. Today, it is the Mandarin Movie Theatre. The Maurice Schwartz Theatre Company of New York came to Toronto for a season of productions. Schwartz was an actor-manager in the tradition of Henry Irving and Donald Wolfit. One of the productions was a Yiddish version of *The Merchant Of Venice* re-written with 'Shylock' as the hero, and 'Portia' the villain. The company consisted of about twelve performers (average age 75), but they decided to hire some spear carriers locally, and that is how I come into this saga.

On the first night, they called in a local man to hold the prompt book, as they had not performed *Merchant* for some time, and were not sure of their lines. This man had never been a prompter, so that instead of waiting for a 'dry' he started reading every line, loud enough that those on stage could hear him. Consequently, Schwartz was hearing his lines before he could say them!

I was playing my spear-carrying role near the prompt corner, when I saw Schwartz edging towards the man holding the book. He hissed out in between his lines, 'Shut up and let me say a word,' whereupon the prompter shut the book and left the theatre, never to be seen again!

DOMINI BLYTHE
Even the curtain calls can getcha

I was playing 'Saint Joan' in Shaw's play at the Walnut Street Theatre in Philadelphia. The next play in the season, *Hobson's Choice*, was to be directed by a friend of mine, so I asked if I could play 'Ada Figgins'. Ada is the extremely simple-minded creature who is engaged to 'Willie Mossop', and the smallest female part in the play. I was dressed in a shapeless, coarsely woven skirt and woollen shawl, and wore heavy wooden clogs on chilblained legs. My tiny headscarf, which concealed my Saint Joan 'crop', had a small piece of frizzy red hair sewn into its front as a fringe. I not only looked terrible but I played the part with an adenoidal cold; I was extremely proud of my transformation from Saint Joan.

The curtain call for this show had to be carefully set up because the play takes place in a house with a lot of furniture. The stage hands would come on and quickly move the furniture back against the doors and windows of the set so that we could take our bows. After the curtain call was finished the furniture had to be moved so that we could get off stage. As I had a tiny part, I was among the first group to take a bow and then move back to make room for the next group of actors to take their bow. When everyone had taken their bows we would move forward together, in a semi-circle of which I was on one end, and take a final company call.

One night, early in the run, we all came forward for the last call and somehow I completely forgot that I had had a tiny part; I did a full, elegant, absolutely inappropriate 'Stratford' curtsey, letting my head droop slowly and swan-like to the ground. As my head went down, the heavy velvet stage curtain fell on it. My head was now outside the curtain and my body was inside the curtain. My headscarf was knocked askew so that the little frizzy red fringe was somewhere around my ear. I was mortified.

The curtain had to come up a little to let me untangle myself. Everyone on stage was in hysterics. The audience was still applauding, which meant we would have another call. I thought, 'I've got to get out of here.' But the exits were all blocked with the stage furniture. So when the curtain came up, what the audience saw was this pathetic twit on her hands and knees crawling under a table, desperately trying to find a way off the set.

I learned a few things about myself that night—one of them was that though there may not be such a thing as a small part, there is certainly such a thing as a small curtsey!

6

Sets and Props: The Nemeses

Theatre Logic: On is in, off is out, up is back, down is front, and, of course, right is left and left is right. A trap doesn't catch anything, a fly doesn't, you can't buy anything with a purchase line, a gridiron has nothing to do with football, a running crew rarely gets anywhere, and strike is work (in fact, a lot of work). But the best thing you can do is break a leg.

Author unknown

BENEDICT CAMPBELL
Centrifugal horse

During a production of *Equus* at the National Arts Centre back in the early '80s I was involved in a frightening accident. As terrifying as it was, the evening ended on a rather humorous note.

The main acting area was on a square revolve raised about two to three inches off the deck. There were audience bleachers on three sides of the acting area and ladders which went up to a lighting grid that hung ominously overhead.

The horse-riding sequences were set on the revolve. To enhance the illusion of galloping, the other men who played horses would grab hold of areas of the revolve and spin it around while I straddled the back of 'Nugget', actor Karl Pruner, who 'galloped'. The revolve started slowly and gradually gathered speed. We were blessed with a very strong bunch of guys, so they could really get the speed up.

This particular evening, I climbed on to Karl's back to do the first 'night ride'. We started off. Everything was going along normally. At the climax of the ride, when we were going at full speed, there was a very violent cracking sound and the bar that Karl used as his balance suddenly snapped. The centrifugal force threw both of us to the floor and then slowly started forcing us outward. All I remember thinking was that there was only one place you could safely be thrown off the revolve and that was down left. Anywhere else was into the bleachers, the lighting grid supports, or the audience proper

As I was about to be thrown off the revolve, I saw Karl fly off before me. His head seem to snap around the lighting grid ladders on stage. I was sure he had broken his neck. I thought he was dead. I was more fortunate and managed to come off the revolve down left. I sat up stunned, thinking how inappropriate it would be for me to finish the scene as if all was normal when my fellow actor was lying dead upstage of me. I proceeded on automatic pilot and was just about to let out my orgasmic shout to signal the end of the act when I noticed one of the corners of the revolve approaching my rib cage at a rather alarming rate. The revolve ran over my ankle and then smashed into my ribs, causing, much to my surprise, very little pain. I was spared a really serious injury by the super-human strength of Charlie Fletcher who grabbed the revolve and pulled it in the opposite direction with all his strength. It hit me hard, but not as hard as it might have done.

I exited in the black-out only to be greeted by Karl who thought that *I* had been seriously hurt. We nervously chatted and laughed our way back to the dressing room. When I took off my clothes to change I realized that I had a blood blister from my shoulder blade all the way down to the bottom of my ribs where the revolve had hit me.

John Wood, the director, came back to see if I was all right and to tell me that he had talked to my mother who was in the audience, and would assure her that everything was okay. (She, of course, had just thought it was a rather wonderful effect.) When he saw my blood blister he felt that it was necessary to have it made up, as he was concerned that the audience would think I had sustained a rather serious injury. It did look pretty bad but I was worried it would get infected with make-up so someone was dispatched to buy a large supply of Clearasil. For the rest of the run instead of taking a rest between acts I dabbed on Clearasil.

The fun was not over for that evening, however. When I finished blinding the horses in the second act, my naked body was put on a bench and covered by David Hemblen (who was playing 'Dysart'). *Every* night David would put my clothes under the bench I was lying on. At the black-out at the end of the play I would reach down, pick up my clothes, and exit to put on my clothes for the curtain call. On this night I reached down and all I could find was my rather skimpy top. I frantically felt around for my pants. No luck. I then thought I'd better just get off the stage because they're going to bring up the lights at any second and there I will be butt naked searching under a bench for my trousers. Even if I got off safely, my pants would still be somewhere on stage leaving me naked from the waist down for the curtain call.

I thought I'd just have to ask Lloyd, the props man, for his pants. Anyone who knows Lloyd (as nice a man as he is) can guess what his response would have been. Fortunately, as I exited, I tripped over something in the dark. It was my pants! I don't think I've ever done a curtain call as enthusiastically as I did that one.

LEN CARIOU
Nothing's gonna harm you

'Sweeney Todd' was a barber who murdered customers. Their bodies were used by the lady, played by Angela Lansbury, in the next-door bake shop to make very popular meat pies. In the play, there was a sequence where Angela Lansbury and I were to go through a trap door and search for a character named 'Toby' who we had discovered was on to our little enterprise. Teaming up to catch him and kill him, we were to come up through a trap door onto a bare stage. The backdrop setting consisted of an eight-ton steel structure that moved up and down, with platforms that would raise and lower. It was designed to indicate an ironworks of the industrial revolution during which Hal Prince had set the play.

During a preview, while Angela and I were searching and singing about Toby, coaxing him to come out, I could hear over the sound of the orchestra a very strange sound from the machinery, a rattling sound that I had never heard before, as it was trying to engage to change position for the next scene. Something was wrong. It had never made a sound like *that* before. Then something caught my eye: the entire ironworks set was slowly descending towards us. Realising that Angela had not seen this, I took her arm as we were singing and edged her downstage out of range of the descending set. Sure enough, the entire thing came all the way down to the deck with a thunder of rattling chains.

The reason that it had come down so slowly was because a safety mechanism had been incorporated into the system should something go wrong. Thankfully we were safely out of harm's way but the conductor, Paul Gemaniani, mesmerised by this ponderously descending set had slowed the tempo of his orchestra so that, ironically, just as the set hit the deck, Angela and I were singing, 'Toby, where are you? Nothing's gonna harm you. Not while I'm around.'

We got off stage, a little giddy and not a little shaken, as we knew that an accident with that ironworks set might have killed us had it not been for the safety system. I was prepared to continue nevertheless, but the show was stopped while they repaired the problem and reset the ironworks backdrop. By then, it was decided that we would do the 'looking for Toby' sequence again. So I went out on stage and spoke to the audience.

'Take two.'

And we continued.

HENRY BECKMAN
Dateline, Atlantic City, summer 1955

My then fiancée Cheryl Maxwell was the producer of an Actors Equity production of the charming musical *School For Husbands*. Opening night would prove to be one for the book and would generate a full complement of cherished moments in a single night!

First, the 'lovers' moon' (part of the set) refused to 'set' so the designer's big hairy arm reached over the top of the scenery and 'goosed' it along.

Then a portion of the set toppled over on a couple of actors who continued with the piece while they braced it back in place.

Later, while the male juvenile was singing his love song to the ingenue while sitting atop an upturned peach basket, it slowly collapsed until his bottom was on the floor with his knees on either side of his ears. He never missed a beat!

By that time, everybody was so rattled it was not surprising that leading man Russ Dearborn 'went up'* in the middle of *his* song. He turned to the audience and exclaimed, 'This is such a cute song, I think you should hear it. I'll be right back.' Whereupon he ran offstage, grabbed the prompt book, came back on and completed the song. As an encore, he flung the prompt book off-stage with a flourish and brought the house down.

The director had been in the lobby eating some candy when he was told of the litany of small disasters. He laughed so hard he swallowed a bon-bon whole and nearly choked.

The next night a fair number of that audience bought tickets to see the show again and were slightly miffed that we'd 'taken out all the fun stuff!'

* Forgot his lines.

NORMAN BROWNING
Susan and the stove

This was opening night some time in the seventies, at the Arts Club production of *Absurd Person Singular* starring Susan Wright, Margaret Bard, and a few others. The show started off with a scene in a kitchen. Susan Wright's character was attempting to kill herself by sticking her head in a gas oven. The curtain came up, Susie stuck her head in the oven and the stove...promptly fell over on top of her! I had never seen the play before and didn't know at first that this was not intended to be part of the action. But we all realised quite quickly, as Susan's little legs were pumping away desperately, that this was *not*, in fact, part of the play.

Margaret Bard, who was about five foot nothing, came on and attempted, in her wisdom, to *pick up* this stove. However she was unable to move either the stove or Susie Wright. Now we had *four* legs thrashing. Of course, the whole audience was going crazy. Finally, a big strapping young man from the audience got up and picked them all up, the stove, Margaret, and Susan...to great applause...and they went on with the play.

TIMOTHY FINDLEY
Snowed

Actors love to hide behind heavy make-up—and directors love special effects. Both can be terrific—if they work. In the early 1950s, I was a member of the International

Players in Kingston, Ontario. Only twenty-one years old, I had to play a man in his forties. To play the greatly old is something of a treat for a young actor. To play the middle-aged is hell on wheels! Take a look around you, sometime, and you will discover what the young actor also discovers. The middle-aged are all pretending to be twenty! How could a person play forty and 'act' his own age?

I opted for deep disguise. Clothes that did not fit. A hat that did somersaults every time I leaned sideways—and a beard that had a life of its own. A life, I discovered, that was not on my person. The beard, it seemed, had some ambition to play out its existence—like the hat—on the floor of the stage. The play, by Robertson Davies, was called *At My Heart's Core*. I wish it was more often performed—though I would suggest abjuring the use of beards. A portrait of Davies himself in the lobby would suffice, since he possessed the beard of beards.

The final indignity occurred on opening night when we came to the last scene in the play. It was to snow. We were all sweltering in a typical Ontario heat-wave, and the soap flakes lying in a sort of hammock up in the flys—the flakes that were supposed to drift lightly down through the light—were all sticking to each other like glue. Every time stage management tried to shake them loose nothing happened. Until, in one appalling moment, they all came down *en masse*. An avalanche of soap poured over Norma Renault, who was playing opposite me.

The ending of the play was meant to be decisive and rather sad. It wasn't.

ANGELA GEI
Lumbered

At Blyth in the second or third year, we were doing a play, *How I Met My Husband*, an adaptation based on an Alice Munro short story. There was still almost no money but this play was I think the first we'd done that needed a real frame set. So they used two by fours nailed together, with real doors in the frames to suggest a kitchen, the bedroom, the front room, the front door and front yard playing areas. It was all very make-shift, very inexpensive, no flats.

Sharon Noble, Deedee Edelstein and I were on stage. We were in the kitchen area on the third platform having a very intense gossip session. Sharon's character was to get up in a fury and leave, slamming the door behind her with all the passion of the moment, vibrating the entire set apparently a bit more than usual. The two by fours begin to fall...slamming all around us with a slow-motion slamming *Bang! Bang! Bang!* as the frames hit the platforms. The whole set fell down around us and in front of us as we sat there stunned. Fortunately nothing fell on anyone in the audience which was in convulsions of laughter...once they figured out no one was hurt.

We were waiting for someone to 'call it', to stop the show, but no one did so we just kept going. In the midst of all of this lumber, it was then *my* turn to exit, leaving Deedee on stage alone. She said her line, my cue, 'Well, I suppose you have to go now too,' which given the circumstances set the audience off again. To which I replied slightly off script, 'Yes, and I can hardly wait.' More laughs. As I left, Deedee called the farm girl who was to come in and help her do the dishes. She looked around, pretty much at a loss. Deedee shrugged, stepped over a two by four, and said, 'Never mind, we'll just wash the lumber in the sink.' End of play.

The audience must have laughed for a solid fifteen minutes.

MELODY RYANE
On doing *Vanities*

We were doing *Vanities* at the Stage West Theatre in Winnipeg, Manitoba. Lorna Patterson was the American star and Mary Long was also in the cast. We had a ridiculously short rehearsal time of only 2 1/2 weeks. It was very high pressure. Opening night, I wanted to stop the show and say to the audience, 'We're so sorry but we are not ready. Why don't you all go home and come back in a week or so?' You get through it and do it nevertheless. But it was sheer terror.

Normally *Vanities* has some wooden blocks that are meant to be stood on as part of the set. Well, they got fancy-schmancy and built these blocks out of Plexiglas. The second night, I got up on one of the blocks, about to launch into the first cheer that opens the show, and I fell through the middle of it. I lost my balance and pitched forward, immediately got up and kept going. As I was doing the cheer, I looked at the other two actresses who were white with shock. I looked down and realised that my legs were gushing blood.

A nurse stood up in the audience and said, 'You have to stop.' She came up on stage and it was decided I should go to the hospital. So Mary and I went to the hospital, both of us in our little wigs and cheerleading costumes, looking...less than normal. And there I got 14 stitches in my right leg. Remarkably, Lorna got up and entertained the audience for the two hours that it took to get me to the hospital and get back to the theatre...and the audience stayed! I came back, probably still numb with shock and we finished the show.

GUY SANVIDO
Door jammed

In 1972 I was in a production of *Last Of The Red Hot Lovers* as 'Barney Cashman' at Edmonton's Citadel Theatre. At the beginning of the act, there was a routine Barney went through as he quietly entered his mother's apartment to set up an encounter with a woman, 'Elaine Navazzio', whom he'd more or less propositioned at his fish restaurant.

After I'd gone through the business of getting everything ready, the doorbell rang. All pumped up I headed for the door. I looked through the spy hole and sure enough there she was. I grasped the handle to open the door, but it wouldn't budge! I tried again, looked through the spy hole again, trying to stay in character, and she was still there. I pulled and pulled. No dice. I turned to the audience and said, 'hard door' with a grin on my face. Finally I gave it one more huge yank and wound up on the seat of my pants halfway across the stage. 'Elaine' entered as I was picking myself up and ad-libbed a sarcastic 'Well, what took you so long.'

It turned out that the actress in question had realised that she'd forgotten a prop *after* she'd rung the doorbell. She couldn't remember if it was important or not, so she had the stage manager run and get it while she held the door knob with both hands and braced one foot against the frame to keep the door shut.

ART HINDLE
Elevator acting

The television show *E.N.G.* was, generally speaking, about a team of people who worked in a network television newsroom, and their professional and personal relationships. It was a drama with some comedy, but mostly quite a serious and realistic show. What was occasionally a little absurd for the actors was dealing with things like the set 'elevator'.

The elevator was not a real elevator, but a box on a concrete floor. It was an elevator door with a round window in it and a black piece of cardboard that would be moved down over the window to create the illusion of the elevator box descending past the window. The tricky part was that in order to maintain the illusion the actor inside would have to slowly bend his or her knees at the same speed as the black piece of paper. Of course, the same thing was required in reverse when you were going up. We would have to do this while looking perfectly natural and not indicating in any way that we might be having trouble keeping our balance or our faces straight.

This usually made most of us feel pretty stupid. It was even more ridiculous if there were several people in the elevator trying desperately to straighten up or crouch down at the same rate. We would come out of the elevator after doing this absurd mime act and start directly into a very serious and intense scene. Of course, chances were pretty good that someone would crack and then we'd all lose it and completely blow the shot.

To this day I think the cast of *E.N.G.* should have received a special Gemini Award for our elevator acting.

SCOTT WENTWORTH
The coconut king

At the Stratford Festival we were doing that 'funny, wacky' play *Richard The Third* with Colm Feore playing the title role. They built an enormous throne, essentially a chair on steps that was moved out onto centre stage on air casters. The scene: newly crowned King Richard sweeps onstage in this huge, kingly cloak edged with vast amounts of ermine. The whole court is with him. He slowly ascends the throne. Every one stands in the gutter around the stage and looks up at him. The music plays and it's terrific.

One day there was no air in the air casters to move the throne out, so somebody just put a chair centre stage. Colm Feore limped out on-stage with most of the company with him. I was waiting backstage to come on, as actors started coming off stage as Richard was imperiously ordering people to go and do things. The minute these actors got off stage they literally fell on the floor in hysterics. I kept to myself, to stay in character, but I couldn't help thinking 'What could be so funny? What unprofessional people!'

On cue, I walked out to greet the King. My eye line had been trained six feet in the air where he should have been. I stood there. I lowered my eyes and I lowered my eyes and I lowered my eyes until finally I saw the King. He was sitting in a regular chair with a head that looked like a coconut with a crown on it buried in ermine. You couldn't see anything but this head peeping out like a cartoon drawing.

I thought, 'I am not going to laugh.' I looked around at the others and they were desperately looking anywhere but at the King or me. I was determined to get through this. I knelt down next to the King and we had our dialogue. He then said 'Rise, Tyrrell, and lend thine ear.' Normally I stood up and walked up the steps and he whispered in my ear. But this time I had to stand up and *bend over again*.

Colm usually whispered something in my ear like 'Pretty good house tonight.' This time he said, 'I look like an asshole, don't I?' And that was it. I just became hysterical. I stood there, centre stage, and laughed. It looked as if the King had told me a joke: 'Rise, Tyrrell, and lend me thine ear. Two Jews, an Arab and a bag of hammers walk into a bar...' It was just absurd.

I made my exit and there was dear Ann Casson, down in the tunnel, about to make her entrance as Richard's mother.

'What's so funny, what's so funny?'

'Look at Colm!' She snuck up to get a look, then came back.

'I can't see him.'

'That's the point!'

TOM WOOD
You never know...

Some years ago I was in the *Pirates of Penzance* at Stratford. They had some clear production ideas about situating it in the twenties, in America, and they had asked me to write a prologue and a couple of scenes as context for the concept.

I came up with the idea of a touring acting company from Britain hired by a small cheap movie studio to do a film of *Pirates*. I wrote a character, a vicious Von Stroheim type director that I played myself, who went around doing silly things like slashing everybody's costumes to make them sexier.

Integral to the design for the unique festival stage was a complete set change. A huge mast on the ship had to be moved at one point and they needed a scene to mask the workings. I came up with one that worked very well and everybody was happy with the show.

One night, the hydraulic equipment that moved the mast wouldn't work. Standing in the tunnel watching the scene to see how it was going, I could see that there was a problem. Backstage, the stage manager announced that the fuse had blown and they didn't know what to do.

Because I'd written some of the show and I knew my character inside and out, I found myself running up onstage without an idea in my head. I thought, I'm playing the director, so I'll just start directing.

'Bring up ze lights!' I said very loudly. They brought up the house lights. I looked at the audience.

'OK. You are all extras now! This side is princes and this side, princesses and ve're gonna film it. And, ve vill sing *Edelweiss*!' Edelweiss?

Then the two guys who played the cameramen came running out and we were absolutely flying by the seat of our pants. I got the audience to start singing,

'Edelweiss,...Edelweiss,...you look happy...to see me.' They were singing and I was ad-libbing like mad.

'More! Bigger!'

All of a sudden the orchestra struck up *Edelweiss*! Many of the company slowly came out on the stage and started to sing it. Then one of the Assistant Stage Managers who was dressed for the change came up and whispered to me that the mast was fixed. I started to have director hysterics.

'You are awful! Ve vant new extras. You're all out of ze picture!'

The house lights went down and we went on with the show.

When I think about it now I don't know where I got the spunk to do it but, as the cameramen came on, as the cast came on and they started improvising, as the orchestra struck up and everyone was singing that gorgeous song, I had tears in my eyes. It was very stirring.

Later I was told about what had happened in the orchestra loft above the stage. At Stratford the musicians don't hear the show itself, but the conductor, in this case Bert Carrier, could hear what was happening on his headset. He suddenly frantically whispered,

'*Edelweiss* in "C"! *Edelweiss* in "C"!'

They thought he'd gone nuts. Gradually they got the picture and joined in.

The rest of the show after that was the hottest one we ever did. At the end of the show they played *Edelweiss* as the trail-out music. It was magic, a highlight of my life.

MERVYN 'BUTCH' BLAKE
The Black Arrow

After the War I was in a play by Robert Louis Stevenson, *The Black Arrow,* with the Young Vic Company. Michel Saint-Denis was the director. I was playing the villain, 'Sir Daniel Brackley'. Tom Brown was the stage manager and he was a wonderfully inventive man.

'Black Arrow' was a pseudonym for a man who was protecting my ward. I, the evil guardian, wanted to do away with the boy so that I could get the estate and all the riches. The Black Arrow knew what the wicked Sir Daniel was up to and he would send in a black arrow as a warning whenever Sir Daniel got up to any shenanigans.

To achieve the effect of the arrow being shot into a room, Tom Brown invented a wonderful contraption, a mousetrap-like mechanism that would spring the arrow shaft into position at the right moment, as if it had just embedded itself in a wall or a piece of furniture or, as was the case at the end when I was to be killed, a body. The effect, coupled with sound, was so good people used to swear they could see the arrow going through the air.

About the middle of the play there was a scene in a chapel when an arrow was to be shot into a table. Of course the table was rigged with one of these mousetrap things. When the arrow was to come in there was a crashing of glass and a snap and the arrow would appear, point 'buried' in the table with a shaft of light on it. In case the spring trap should fail, there was an extra arrow down by the side of the table. If I needed to, I could pick up the other arrow at once and say, 'A message from the Black Arrow.'

At one matinee for children and families, we got to the scene in the chapel when the arrow was to be shot in. We heard the rip, a tinkle of glass, pshoooooo-t, crash! I went to the table and there was *no* arrow. Quickly I grabbed the alternate one, turned to deliver my line, and said, 'A message from the Black Arrow!'

In the meantime, the audience began to laugh. I turned around and there was the arrow quivering there in the table! It was the first time I ever had any presence of mind. I rushed to it and said, 'Another message from the Black Arrow!'

NORMAN BROWNING
Sleuthing

I was in the audience for a marvellous Arts Club production of *Sleuth* starring Owen Foran and David Schurmann. In this Victoria production, there were many crucial special effects and—well—it's unusual if things don't go wrong at some time or another.

In one scene, Owen's character was threatening David's character, 'Milo'. There was a safe that was to blow up, but on one occasion the stage manager forgot to do the effect. Owen bent down, making a gesture to cover the apparent malfunction, desperately trying somehow to *make* the safe blow up, and hoping that someone would twig and find a way to trigger the damned thing from backstage. Nothing happened. Owen finally got up and turned away. At that moment, the stage manager found the button and blew up the safe.

Shortly after this, Owen was to pull a gun on Milo as if to kill him, then suddenly pull the gun away at the highest point of tension, shoot a plate off the shelf instead, then swing again to shoot a pitcher. Unfortunately, as he was pointing at the plate, the *pitcher* unexpectedly blew up as if shot. So he swung the gun quickly over to the pitcher and, of course, the *plate* blew up.

Judging by audience response I suspect the suspense thriller, *Sleuth*, was the best comedy of the season.

ALLAN GRAY
Incredible Murders

I was in a production of *The Incredible Murder Of Cardinal Tosca* along with Norman Browning, Goldie Semple, David Schurmann, and Sven van der Van.

There is at the end of that play a big climactic scene when everyone is killed by pistols. About four guns were supposed to go off. On this occasion, *not one* of the guns worked, including the stage manager's 'effects' gun backstage. We stood there like oafs listening to this pathetic 'click, click, click' going on offstage.

No one knew when or how we were supposed to die. So in, desperation, somebody ended up strangling 'the Cardinal' and the rest were somehow beaten to death.

WILLIAM HUTT
Desperate measures

We opened the permanent theatre at Stratford in 1957 with a production of *Hamlet* starring Chris Plummer. I was playing 'Polonius'. In the famous 'closet scene' where Polonius is accidentally killed by 'Hamlet' there was no arras to hide behind on the Stratford stage, so I was lurking in the shadows behind a pillar upstage, underneath the balcony. Instead of Hamlet running his sword through the curtain as it is usually played, we had worked out the business in this way: Hamlet heard a sound, and put his hand on his sword. As he kept speaking to Gertrude he pulled his sword and, without looking, held it up behind him. At this precise moment I would burst out from behind the pillar as if to intervene and, as these two things would happen simultaneously, I would run accidentally onto his sword and thus he would kill me. It was a very effective piece of business. I died under the balcony and my inert body was out of the way for the rest of the scene.

On this particular night the theatre was incredibly hot and for some reason Chris could not get his sword out of its scabbard. I watched with mounting horror as it became clear that he would be unable to get his sword out in time. Thoughts of all the logistical problems of my dying out on the stage raced through my head. Hamlet and Gertrude would have had to play the rest of the scene tramping back and forth over this dead body and, as the scene ends with Hamlet dragging the dead Polonius off the stage, he would have had to drag me over a step that would have certainly dislodged my wig. Chris was still struggling to remove his sword so I just decided to grab my heart and fall over in a dead faint, as if all the exertion had killed me. After Chris finally managed to extricate his sword he came over to look at the body and poked at me with it as if I were a dead chicken, saying, 'Is it the king?'

Thank God I was in a voluminous costume because I was absolutely screaming with laughter.

GREG KRAMER
Die, Dracula, die!

I was playing 'Renfield' in Arbour Theatre's problematic production of *Dracula* in the summer of 1995 in Peterborough. The rehearsal process had been plagued with set-backs and problems to such an extent that come opening night, we still hadn't rehearsed the final scene. We did not know how we were going to kill 'Dracula' and had only superficially agreed upon a plan.

When the time arrived, as it was bound to do, there was one of the most awkward moments I have ever experienced on stage. Everyone seemed to be moving in a soup of molasses, trying to remember what to do next. We had decided and somehow managed to kill 'Dracula' in *e-x-t-r-e-m-e s-l-o-w m-o-t-i-o-n*, the only weapon left in our arsenal of theatrical tricks. I thrust my silver teaspoon (which I had been using for eating flies) under Dracula's armpit with grand panache. Others came forward and tossed a big, black cloth over his head. Van Helsing (played by Ellen-Ray Hennessy) then gave Dracula the final send-off, an extra twist of the spoon which was supposed to be in his heart. Only it wasn't. It was in my hand, held victoriously aloft for all to see. To the audience, it must have looked as if Van Helsing was giving Dracula's nipple a good tweak to send him off into the next world!

The poor Prince of Darkness staggered, moaned, and careened around the stage, eventually expiring behind a tombstone while the rest of us looked on in shock, trying desperately not to giggle. Silence. The beast was, finally, dead. At that moment, with uncanny timing an ambulance went down the street outside the theatre, its siren wailing through the auditorium as the lights slowly faded on the scene.

RICHARD MONETTE
On stage fright

I was in Toronto doing the final preview for *Nothing Sacred*, the George F. Walker play. There is a duelling scene with pistols where my character was to be shot and then roll down a slope. We had just got the pistols a day or two before we were to open and I had said, 'Do you have a back-up for this?' They said, 'Oh no. This will work. This'll work. Don't worry.' And we tried. *Bang! Bang! Bang!* They worked perfectly. Nonetheless I said, 'Look, I've worked with guns. The guns never work.' But such was their confidence in these guns, there would be no back-up.

I'd been having anxieties and dizzy spells that made me go in and out. But anxieties come with the actor's job, you continue on. Finally we open and we're out there. We get to the penultimate scene of the play and I'm on top of the set which is like a huge mountain and I'm waiting for this guy to shoot me, after which I'm to roll down the hill. He pulls the gun...*NOTHING happens...NOTHING*. And I hear myself at the top of the hill saying, 'Shoot, shoot, shoot, shooot, *Shooooot!*' under my breath. And I start to get one of these anxiety attacks. Finally somebody offstage takes a piece of wood or a chair and bangs a pipe. Clang! So I fall to my knees and I roll down.

I got off stage and my heart was pounding so extremely that I thought I was dying of a heart attack. Domini Blythe, a friend of mine, was in the audience and when she came backstage after, I said, 'Domini, I've got to go to emergency. I think I'm really sick. I think something's happened to me.' She said, 'Darling, I'll take you right over.' And that is what we did.

As it happened I did not have a heart attack at all but the incident shook me so badly that I did not appear on stage for many years after that.

MICHAEL MILLAR
Corpsing the corpse

I was once in an Agatha Christie play. Much like many mystery thrillers, at one point a blackout occurs, an unseen character enters and threatens the other characters, and a couple of shots ring out. In this one, the character who entered in the dark is found face down on the floor with a gun in his hand, dead!

On our first preview, the blackout happened, the character entered and threatened everyone as rehearsed, but the shots *didn't ring out!* The actor playing the 'victim-to-be', his first performance in any play, was supposed to fire the gun but, as he was about to, it fell apart! Someone had not closed it properly after loading the blanks, and it seemed our actor had forgot to check his prop. We all heard the gun fall in pieces onto the carpet. Not knowing what else to do, the actor just decided to 'die' anyway, which he did. The whole mystery was based on who might have shot this 'stranger' but *no shots had been fired.* Of course, we all knew we were in for one of those wonderful theatrical 'moments' when the lights went on.

Now we were a tight group who all loved theatrical anecdotes and ironically, not long before we had all just been talking and laughing about stage deaths gone wrong. The funniest had been the one where someone was supposed to be shot and wasn't. The situation on that occasion had been apparently saved by a quick-thinking actor who yelled out, 'Poisoned, by God!'

When the lights came back on to our own little dilemma, it was difficult to spot a straight face; even the 'dead' one had apparently died smiling. I looked over at the actor who had told that anecdote and saw his grinning countenance grin even wider as he strode confidently over to the corpse, the pronouncement of 'a divine poisoning' seconds from becoming a reality. But I realised at the same time that my character had the most 'shoot', 'shot', 'gun' references to say in the play, so I beat him to the body, bent over, picked up the main part of the gun, looked at him knowingly and said:

"Hmmm...silencer!"

Had the cast not been trying so hard not to laugh, we might have got away with it. As it was...well...we didn't.

JERRY WASSERMAN
'The Man' unarmed

In May 1975 I got my first big break in the professional theatre. I was cast in the
role of 'The Man', another psycho murderer, in what would be the première production of Tom Walmsley's first play, *The Workingman*, a contemporary Canadian
play with multiple plot twists, and the kind of proto-Tarantino sex and violence
scenario for which Walmsley quickly became notorious in the Canadian theatre.
Pam Hawthorn directed.

On opening night, I had to make my entrance onstage into a shabby sixth-floor
apartment, first pretending to be a cop and interrogating the two young men and a
woman who were there to make a porno film. I took one of the men (played by
Wayne Robson) into the offstage kitchen, then there was the sound of a shot and I
re-entered holding a smoking revolver. I would then proceed to terrorize the other
two, sexually threatening the woman (played by Kayla Armstrong) and demanding,
in a hypnotic monologue, that the man (Robb Smith) make the choice my father
was once forced to make by an invading stranger. The scene was wholly dependent
on the audience buying the idea that the young man and woman believed that 'The
Man' had really shot and killed their friend in the kitchen, and that he would not
hesitate to shoot them as well. I of course had to be convincingly psychopathological.

Fighting back opening-night first-professional-lead-role nerves, I made my
entrance, took Wayne Robson offstage, and shot off the blank cartridge. Then as we
had rehearsed, I cracked open the gun to pop out the spent shell so that the rotated
barrel would show a full shell when I re-entered five seconds later. But somehow the
shell got jammed a little way out of the barrel. I couldn't get it out or push it back
in, and I *couldn't close the gun!* It was open at the middle, so that if I held the handle
normally, with my finger on the trigger, the barrel would hang limply, ridiculously,
unthreateningly down.

My life flashed before my eyes. I considered the following options: 1) I could
just refuse to enter—turn around, walk out the stage door, leave town and never
have to face anyone I knew ever again; 2) I could throw myself on the mercy of the
audience, step onstage and say 'Excuse me, but I've got a terrible problem here,'
show them the gun, and ask if we might start over again; 3) or I could leave the
broken gun offstage and enter holding out my trigger finger as if it were the gun
barrel, with my thumb erect, like a kid playing cops and robbers, and somehow
hope that the audience wouldn't notice. This idea truly did go through my mind.
Instead I chose option 4.

I made my entrance in character and played the scene as if nothing were
wrong, holding the gun not by the handle with my finger on the trigger as I would
normally, but with my hand unnaturally wrapped around the gun's middle to keep
it, as much as possible, from revealing itself as open, jammed, and totally useless as
a weapon. The key to making this plan work, I knew, was to be so *intense*, so
focused, so weird and dangerous and mesmerizing that the audience wouldn't really
even see the gun, or if they did, wouldn't care that it was non-functional. I knew the

other actors would play the scene through, no matter what, so I just concentrated on being as real and as scary as I could be.

It worked. I got through the scene and through the play. No one laughed. There was no mention of what could have been the worst debacle in what surely would have been my brief professional career. I felt for the first time that I was a real actor.

ELLEN-RAY HENNESSY
Enter with no legs

In the early '90s, Tom McCamus and I were in a two-hander, a play called *Writing With Our Feet*, written by Dave Carley, at the Factory Theatre. Tom played a man who lived in a garage and couldn't leave it because he was agoraphobic. I played his sister and a number of other characters. One of them, a cousin named 'Alphonse-Annette', was an alcoholic whose legs had been cut off because she got dead drunk one day and fell asleep on the train tracks. She motored around in an electrically controlled wheelchair. In the play, she arrives at the garage, pissed to the eyeballs with what she thinks will be the next million-dollar invention, spray-on condoms.

I used a real motor-controlled wheelchair, covered with flags and beer labels, with bags everywhere containing all my props. I could pop wheelies and buzz around but I was concerned about what would happen if the motor didn't work. They said not to worry, it was a professional wheelchair and it wouldn't not work. Right. There was no crew for this show, only a lone stage manager running the show from a booth up above the audience.

I had very quick costume changes because I played so many characters. One night, as I hurriedly change from the old aunt to Alphonse-Annette, I jump into the wheelchair, cramp myself up so I look like I have no legs, throw a blanket over myself, push the joystick and nothing. Dead.

This character has been spoken about over and over all night. This character has no legs. Now this character has no wheelchair. How do you make an entrance on stage with no legs? I start to freak out. Tom's coming to the end of his monologue and I'm offstage improvising in a French accent, stalling for time, trying like mad to figure out what to do. By now, Tom knows that something is up but he can't help me because the whole play is about how he can't leave the garage. There is no one but me backstage. While I am talking, and believe me I have no idea what I said, I suddenly spy a small wooden dolly for moving furniture.

I get onto the dolly, cover my legs with the blanket and wheel myself out, with my hands, onto the stage. Now I'm a midget as well. I'm hysterical at this point, beyond any moment of truth or honesty. I am laughing my head off. Tom is facing upstage because he can't even look at me. Then I realise that, in my desperation, I have come onstage with none of the necessary props, none of the condom stuff, all of which were in the side pocket of my wheelchair. The nightmare continues.

Improvising like mad, talking away, I wheel myself, on the dolly, offstage to get the props. I come back on with the necessary stuff and, finally, get the scene back on some kind of track. The audience is howling. I finish the scene. It's time for me to exit. I back the dolly up, and the tassels on the blanket have become tangled up in the wheels. I'm jammed. I can't exit.

Now, I can't get *off*. I started improvising again. It was the longest goodbye in the world. It was so insane that it was obvious it had to stop. Finally Tom just picked up the entire dolly with me on it and carried me off stage. I lost ten pounds that night. I was so hysterical I had no idea what I was saying. Tom was crying, he was laughing so hard. As for the wheelchair, all I could think of was the person who had to use it for real.

I asked people in the audience about it afterwards and no one knew. They thought it was supposed to be like that. What a life!

BRENDA SHUTTLEWORTH
'Hello?'

The Hollow, by Agatha Christie, was directed by Stephen Hare at Pleiades Theatre in Calgary. The theatre combines both professional and non-professional actors. The show was fraught with mishaps, one of which involved 'Uncle Henry', played by Phillip Whyte.

In Act Two, my character has a phone conversation with her boss. No one else is on stage. Uncle Henry is supposed to answer the phone, then call for me, at which point I come into the room and take my call. At one performance Uncle Henry turned in such a way that our lovely vintage 1950s black phone fell from its table and smashed on the floor. Hearing the clatter but not my cue, I decided to open the door, whereupon I realized that the phone was shattered into tiny fragments, with brightly coloured spiral wires in a big clump on the floor. The only thing still intact was the receiver since it was still in Uncle Henry's hand. I started off nonetheless. 'Is it for me?' Uncle Henry, wide-eyed, nodded and smiled, but no words came out. I asked, 'Is it still working?' 'Oh, yes,' said Uncle Henry. I replied 'How extraordinary!' Then, I took the receiver, scooped up pieces of vintage black phone, placed them on the table in a heap, asked my 'boss' if she was still there, apologized to her for the big bang and resumed the play.

I don't know what I'd have done if he'd said, 'No.'

NICHOLAS RICE
Country fresh ear

My most bizarre theatre mishap occurred ten summers ago in Lindsay in *Return of the Curse of the Mummy's Revenge*.

I was playing weird Dr Finklestein, who at one point goes stark raving nuts. 'Can't you give him something to calm him down? Here, Doc, here's a sedative.' In rehearsal we had used chewable Vitamin C, which in each run-through I dutifully ate. Then just before our cue-to-cue, we did a run, and some of the pill caught in my throat. I coughed, not seriously, but enough to draw focus.

The late Jimmy Saar was directing, and he'd also written the show, so he knew just what worked comedically. In his notes he said I should find new business for the pills—anything but eating them. Fine. So next time, I wore it in my eye like a monocle. The time after that, I put it down my pants. Classy stuff. Then came the dress-preview.

The scene arrived, and I thought I might stick the pill in my ear. At the same time, I noticed that it wasn't Vitamin C this time, but a Tic-Tac mint. That's fine, into my ear it went and I got a nice little laugh.

At the interval, I went to take the mint out, but...I couldn't. The harder I tried, the deeper it went, and soon it pressed painfully into my eardrum. I had no choice but to do Act Two with one ear totally blocked.

Immediately afterwards, I went to Kawartha General. The conversation in Emergency went like this:

'What's the matter with you?'

'I have a Tic-Tac in my ear.'

'How did it get there?'

'I put it there.'

'Oh.'

The doctors probed unsuccessfully. Finally they brought out a hydraulic device, they stuck it in my ear, turned it on, and the Tic-Tac came out with an icy whoosh.

The show came and went, but I returned to Lindsay over several years, and the Tic-Tac became part of local lore. Techies I'd never met would come rushing over, gesturing at my ear and asking, 'Are you the guy...?'

RATCH WALLACE
On Shake'spear' carrying

It was in 1969, during either the opening night or the preview of a production of *Hamlet,* I made my debut on the Stratford stage. The production was directed by John Hirsch and starred Kenneth Welsh as 'Hamlet', Leo Ciceri as 'Claudius', Angela Wood as 'Gertrude' and Neil Dainard as 'Laertes'. Jason Robards III, John Coutts and I were all spear carriers.

Among many of my jobs as a guard in the castle, was one particular moment in Act IV, Scene V: the triumphant return of Laertes with the Danes behind him proclaiming that he 'shall be King!' Jason, John, and I were to rush on stage to be part of the last line of defence for Claudius and Gertrude before Laertes and the mob invaded the castle.

In the interests of theatrical excitement, John Hirsch had created backstage the effect of a noisy rabble breaking down the castle gates with the combined efforts of stagehands shouting and beating blocks of wood with sledgehammers and the angry voices of the mob about to go on stage waving clubs and torches to proclaim Laertes. It was a war zone back there.

The three of us stood ready in the midst of the clamour with our eight-foot, steel-tipped spears levelled for our charge on to the stage at the cue. At the height of the pounding and yelling, the stage hand on the backstage balcony above us dropped the large brass platter he had been pounding. It crashed to the ground beside me, startling John Coutts, the guard on my right. At that very moment, the mob yelled in guttural unison, 'The gates are broke!' and pushed forwards toward the stage. John must have been disoriented because he did not open up as rehearsed to allow me to pass on stage. Instead he clipped me in the shoulder while prematurely closing his spear. At the same time, his extended left leg caught my right leg, launching me headlong onto the stage. I catapulted, still clutching my spear, past the balcony columns and a stupefied Claudius, and landed, nose first, two steps into the walkway between the audience and the stage!

I looked up to 2000 pairs of startled eyes staring down at me in stunned silence. The hush was deafening. As I struggled to recover, I reached out to retrieve my trusty spear. It was not beside me...in fact, it was nowhere near me. I turned to face the frozen tableau of actors which were the court and realised to my horror that my spear was sticking straight out of the main stage like a giant dart twanging in a dartboard.

There was nothing to do but try to get it out, so I dutifully charged up to retrieve the offending instrument. It would not budge. I grabbed it again and pulled...nothing! Inspired by the King's raised eyebrows, I lunged at the thing and rocked it back and forth like a man possessed. The spear stayed fast in the stage. The audience exhaled audibly. I leapt on the handle of that spear one last time and ran madly about in circles until I heard the explosion of snapping steel and splintered stage floor inlay as the spear came free. I jumped into my rehearsed position with the blunted spear at my side, my body shaking, sweat pouring from my brow, and assumed my guard's stance. The audience broke into thunderous applause, as I prayed the play would just go on as if nothing had happened, which it did...around the gaping hole of pale splintered wood in the middle of the charcoal grey stage. I stood throughout the scene imagining myself skewered on my own spear, roasting nicely as the cast looked on with satisfaction.

To my amazement I was not fired and later John Hirsch's only comment was, 'Ratch, you must try to have a little more control...'

GARY FILES
Lamp-wasted

We were touring *Butley* in British Columbia when we came to a theatre in Campbell River that was built some time in the '20s. In the show, there were two practical or 'live' goose-necked lamps. At the very beginning of the scene, I had to take one lamp and transfer it to another desk. Then I was to pick up the other lamp and transfer it back to the first desk. At some point I had to have both lamps in my hands as I did this exchange.

The wiring in this particular theatre was, of course, also quite old and, as it would soon be apparent, left something to be desired in electrical grounding. As I picked up the second lamp, now holding both live lamps in my hands, I could instantly feel the current connect through me. If I'd had a bulb in my mouth, I have no doubt it would have lit up. There I was buzzing numbly, unable to drop either one of them because my fingers were paralysed. All I could think to do was bang them together, which I did. *WHACK!* There was a huge *BANG!* and a huge blue flash. I was blown upstage as the lamps fell to the ground. The audience gasped. But I seemed to be all right, if a little tingly. So I pulled myself, slightly singed, to my feet and said, 'That fucking caretaker!', stumbled off stage and yelled to the rest of the cast not to touch the lamps.

Then we continued with the play.

Strangely, the physical shock of it, so to speak, really didn't hit me until intermission when I was trying to have a cup of tea and I couldn't manage the cup.

THOMAS HAUFF
Light the light

At the New Theatre, now called the Annex Theatre, in Toronto, we were opening a new play by Larry Fineberg called *Human Remains,* directed by Stephen Katz. When this anecdote happened we were into the third preview before the opening.

The stage setting was the inside of a dark barn. In the course of the play it had been firmly established that we were at least five minutes from the outhouse or the car and there were no buildings around. There was no place we could believably go for any help. The lights weren't supposed to go on in this barn until my character lit a kerosene lantern.

The cue to light the lantern came. I reached my hand into my pocket for the matches but there were no matches! There weren't any matches in any of my other pockets either. I asked all the other actors if they had any matches and they didn't. We did a mad scramble around the stage and there were no matches on the set. By this point my brain was frozen. And we couldn't, believably, go anywhere to get any.

I was kneeling on the front of the stage just about to say, 'Look, I'm really sorry but we can't go on 'til someone gives us some matches,' when two packs of cigarettes came flying out of the balcony to land right at my knees. One came from Larry Fineberg and one was from Stephen Katz. I opened up a pack and there was a box of matches inside!

When the lights finally came up and found us in this supposedly freezing cold barn, all our hair was plastered to our faces with sweat.

GARY FILES
Stage nerves

Louis Del Grande and I were 'Oscar' and 'Felix' respectively in a production of *The Odd Couple* many years ago.

What most people don't realise about Louis is that, despite his apparently casual and often comedic approach to acting, he is a very nervous actor. He literally shakes from nervous anxiety and his palms get clammy. He was afraid he'd forget his lines if he looked another actor in the eye, so he always looked just to the side when he was on stage. None of this is particularly unusual. For their entire careers some of the best actors throw up every time they are to go onstage. Louis shook.

At one point in the play Louis, as Oscar, had to light a cigar. Louis is not a smoker but the cigar was a crucial part of the character. Every night it was a bit of a problem, most often in trying to get the cellophane off. On one particular night, the little tag pulled off without breaking the cellophane. The more Louis tried to get that thing open the more it seemed to fight him. Of course, this made Louis even more nervous. Finally, in a burst of frustration, he broke it open and broke the cigar into shredded pieces at the same time. It looked as if it had exploded. Poor Louis still had to light what was left of the cigar, so he broke off as much as he could, stuck it in his mouth, and reached for the matches.

Lighting matches on stage can be tricky at the best of times but Louis, because he shook so much, had needed special wood matches that would burst into flame almost the moment they were struck. They were not safety matches, and they had given him lots of them in case there was a dud or he broke one in his nervousness. Louis, already pretty rattled by the unplanned struggle with the cigar, reached for the box of matches. Somehow it flipped up and matches flew everywhere. The tricky thing was that you could not step on them because they would ignite at the slightest amount of friction, giving the unsuspecting a hot foot. Every single match *had* to be picked up. Louis was apoplectic. So there we all were, continuing with our lines and the scene while we helped him pick up the matches. We were in hysterics. The audience had begun by now to titter and laugh. Finally, we found all of the matches, handed them to Louis and continued with the scene, all the while thinking that surely he would not try to light the cigar *again*. Not to be.

Finally he got a match lit and determinedly placed it to the frayed end of the broken cigar. Phwaahh, phwaahh, he pulled on the cigar. Smoke *billowed* around him...but it *wouldn't light*. Bits of the frayed end of the cigar lit briefly and burned as they wafted across the stage and fell on the floor. We stamped at still burning bits as they landed or tried to catch them before the set caught fire or something drifted out into the audience. Still he could not get it lit. There was Louis...phwah, phwah, phwah, almost hyperventilating trying to light this thing and we had completely lost it. We could not speak. The audience was howling.

It took quite some time before we could continue with the play. But it was, after all, a comedy.

7

Dressing the Part

SHIRLEY DOUGLAS
The great Desmond Heeley

I had never worked with Desmond Heeley but I had heard of him for years and years. He was to be the designer for the Stratford production of *Phaedra*.

Suddenly this 'creature' came into my life. I had never met anyone like him before or since. If I never work with him again, my experience with him will be one of the great moments in my life.

Desmond is a genius, one of the five great designers of the world. What takes place in that room when you go for what is supposed to be a first costume fitting is amazing. Desmond pulls out great bolts of fabric. It is a very rarefied atmosphere. There is silence, no talking, no sound but the sound of shifting cloth and breathing. His concentration is riveted on the material as he starts to pin and to arrange and design on you as you stand there. And the scissors come out and he starts to cut. The designer in my experience is rarely the cutter. Desmond did all of his own cutting.

When he finished this costume for me, I loved it. It was fabulous. I wore it for the first dress rehearsal. The next day he phoned me and said, 'I am so upset. I feel so terrible to do this to you on your day off. But I realised when I saw you on stage last night that your costume doesn't work. I very seldom make a mistake like this but I have made it. I have spoken to the management and we are going to make you a new one.' We had less than 48 hours before opening night curtain.

No one would ever have dared say a word to Desmond Heeley, or to ever question his designs. He was a legend even then. Brian Bedford, who was directing, would never have said a thing to him. It was Desmond who said that it wasn't right. When I asked him what was wrong with it, he said simply that when he saw us all on stage, I did not look as if I belonged to the rest of the royal family. As soon as he said it, I realised that he was absolutely right.

In he went and pulled together bits from here and there and buckets of black silk out of the basement. At one point, I saw him rushing with a big packet of ivy with big red berries on it, holly I guess it was. He came running in with it, measured here and there, and rushed away again. I couldn't imagine what he would do with it. What he did was steam-iron them flat and then gild them. He used this holly as the basis for an enormous breastplate.

The final effect was stunning. I felt elevated by this creation that I knew a genius had conjured for me. I can't tell you what it does to you and the energy it gives to your performance. It makes you want to be worthy of the costume. It was truly one of the greatest costumes that I had ever worn.

TONY VAN BRIDGE
Toga tact

The technical dress rehearsal of the Stratford Festival's *Julius Caesar, circa* 1955, provided its tensions and aggravations. Remember that in those days, a technical rehearsal was held just two days before the opening performance: it was yet some time before the cushioning effect of previews. So tempers flared a little, and actors forgot lines they knew perfectly well and looked for justification. One such actor had enormous trouble with his toga. No matter how much he tried for dignity, that bedevilled sheet found ways to frustrate him. The toga has always been a notoriously difficult garment to wear. It could even have been responsible for the decline, if not the fall, of the Roman Empire.

Following the rehearsal, the actor spotted the head of wardrobe himself with the offending toga over his arm. 'Where are you going with my toga?' The H of W gave him a withering look. 'I'm going to make it fool-proof,' he said, and—there is no other phrase for it—*swep'* out.

I'm not sure that the actor in question deserved such a scathing retort, but it demonstrates the polite cold war that is ever-present between actors and their costume departments. Since it is a cold war, their differences usually remain gently unexpressed, or are phrased in those colourful and insincere terms of endearment that fly around theatres like confetti.

'Darling, it's a beautiful costume, absolutely your very best, but it is a tiny bit tight under the arms,' really means 'I can't breathe in these filthy rags, you idiot!' Or: 'Precious, it's quite, quite beautiful; perhaps we could tone down that red just a smidge,' can be translated as 'If you think I'm going to be seen in these vile colours you must be mad, you silly bitch.' Or from the other side of the battlefield: 'I've pulled it in a little bit at the waist, to emphasise that wonderful walk you have,' obviously means 'If you will insist on playing juveniles at your age, I have to do something about that pot-belly, don't I?'

KENNETH WICKES
Forever young

I was in a production of Arthur Miller's *Death Of A Salesman* at the Neptune Theatre in Halifax in the early 1970s with Sandy Webster and Ken Pogue. It was a very good show. I was playing Bernard, the 'boy' next door. I was forty at the time. Never mind. I got a good review from Herbie Whittaker.

One night during the run I was leaving the dressing room to make an entrance on stage when I discovered that the zip to my fly was broken, and I had only minutes to go before I was on.

The problem was that when I got out there I had to sit on a desk facing the audience with my legs all akimbo so I couldn't really manage with an open fly. The ASM grabbed a needle and some thread, got down on her knees and sewed it closed. She had forgotten to get scissors to cut the thread, so in, shall I say, the heat of the moment, she leaned forward and bit the thread off with her teeth.

Several young bloods, waiting to go onstage, lined up behind me and said 'I'm next! I'm next!'

ROBIN GAMMELL
Draft

An enormous disadvantage of the tent at Stratford in those early days, was that it got very hot in the summer. It was deadly, not only for the audience which, of course, had to be reasonably comfortable or they just wouldn't come, but also for the actors who were often in heavy costumes.

They improvised an air conditioner of sorts: a huge cage filled with dry ice, behind the tent, and an enormous industrial fan to draw the cooled air into the tent up through the voms.*

I was a member of the chorus, a supplicant in *Oedipus*. The production was fantastic. Tanya Moiseiwitsch designed marvellous costumes and masks. The chorus all had nut-brown masks and robes that were made from heavy, solid-looking material which was in some cases actually upholstery material. In the summer, these heavy, hot costumes were deadly so we often did not wear anything under them.

As well, in self-defence, we would often 'adjust' our blocking, which normally had us crouching in the gutter area around the stage when 'Jocasta' or 'Oedipus' were on stage. Instead, whenever possible, we found ways to creatively, aesthetically cringe and contort our way backwards into the voms where we could lift up the costumes to cool our sweltering bodies for a few moments. Of course, if you were making an entrance through one of the voms when the chorus was in this position, you got a rather startling view of bare bums.

The chorus was regularly reprimanded by stage manager Jack Marigold for changing the blocking. I don't think he much cared about who saw our bums.

* Tunnels leading from beneath the audience seating to the gutter, the area surrounding the main stage.

ARABY LOCKHART
A stitch in time

In one of the early seasons of the Straw Hat Players we did a play called *Papa Is All*, a story about Amish folk with Donald Davis playing the tyrannical father. The big scene is built around a quilting frame. Here the key information slips in and tilts the whole plot to its conclusion. It was a tense scene and I noted a restlessness in the audience right after it started. The more the restlessness grew, the more intense we became. The audience started to titter. Something like this had never happened before. I was appalled at the insensitivity of that audience. What had started them off?

I found out as I got up to make the exit the script required. I couldn't budge. I had sewed myself to the quilting frame and the audience had watched me do it! Now, a quilting frame is a heavy 12 ft. x 12 ft. rectangle of wood, the door frame a mere 3 x 6! I couldn't take the frame off with me and one look at the startled faces of fellow thespians indicated they had no more idea than I had of what to do. Fortunately I was not an expert sewer. With much tugging I pulled myself free, ripping the front of my dress as I did so. With as much dignity as I could muster I made my exit in tatters amid roars of laughter.

JACK MEDLEY
Through the looking glass

Sometime in the seventies, I played the Red Queen in *Through The Looking Glass* at Manitoba Theatre Centre. It was a magnificent set. The stage was covered in black mylar and strips of black mylar and lace hung everywhere, forests of it.

During my first entrance my footsteps would come over a loudspeaker from a long distance, then I would pick up the pacing of the footsteps the audience was hearing as I entered. I was to come across the back of the stage and *sweep* regally through the black mylar and lace.

The costume was magnificent. The design was inspired by Queen Mary, the dowager Queen who died in the late fifties. It had an eight-foot circular velvet train, a crown that was at least a foot tall, and an enormous sceptre. I was laced into a corset which went from just below my neck to my hips and made it impossible to bend. As a consequence, I couldn't look down very easily, and I couldn't sit down at all. They provided a leaning board to rest on offstage while I was in costume.

Opening night, we had an invited audience and we were full to the rafters. I made my entrance...I came sweeping on and...suddenly my feet went right out from under me and I fell head first. It knocked the breath out of me. The crown crashed down and the sceptre clattered in another direction. Someone had left a cable about knee high where my entrance was and I went flat on my face.

Well, the first words out of my mouth, in front of this full house, *for a children's show* were, 'What the fuck!' The audience was dead silent. But what was worse was that I couldn't get up. I couldn't move. I must have looked like some great velvet turtle flailing away, completely helpless on the stage. The next thing I knew, a dozen gremlins, who normally move the set around (they had money in those days) came running from every direction to lift me up. So there I was being lifted up bodily and finally plunked on my feet.

Of course, we shut the curtain and had to start over again. To this day I don't know how I pulled myself together enough to make another entrance as the regal Red Queen. But you do, somehow.

TODD WAITE
Man of Mantilla

I was playing 'Luc' in The Belfry's English language première of Michel Marc Bouchard's *Orphan Muses* and Glynis Leyshon, the Artistic Director of The Belfry was playing my sister. I was to play this part dressed in my mother's Spanish dress and mantilla.

This particular scene was normally very tense, still, and serious. At one point Glynis was to give me a good shove away from the door to prevent me from leaving. I am 6' 4" and the fabulous Ms Leyshon is, well, not. I had always felt quite secure that her little push could be no match for my masculine bulk. Well, wrooooong!

One day, she somehow flew at me just as my weight shifted from one foot to the other. Not only did I fall completely backward, but I slid the entire width of the raked stage on my slippery silk mantilla, until my head arrived abruptly against the opposite side wall with a 'bonk'. At this point, both my extravagant diamond earrings popped off and as I tried to get up, my lace mantilla flew of its own volition to another part of the stage. Of course we both corpsed.

Glynis has directed me three times since then, and I always do *exactly* as she tells me!

PAM HYATT
A helping hand

It was 1968, May, at the Royal Alexandra Theatre. *A Festival Of Carols* was the final offering in Theatre Toronto's first season. Richard Digby Day directed. The play, written by a Scarborough resident, was theatre-of-the-absurd genre.

Act III's set, on the highly raked stage which [Artistic Director Clifford] Williams demanded for all plays, revealed a towering, Alice-in-Wonderland-ish, judge's bench upstage, slightly left of centre, upon which Hugh Webster perched in a curly-locked, white judge's wig and judicial robes. Down right was a small, vertically barred prisoner's cage in which Eric House stood, clad in classic black and white striped garb, a similarly striped pillbox atop his character's forlorn head. And angled from mid to down left was the empty jury box.

As Act III began, the rest of the cast—John Colicos, Richard Monette, Colin Fox, Chris Wiggins, Barb Hamilton, Anna Cameron, myself, and a zillion others—had to burst through the upstage centre door, chattering like cocktail party schmoozers, and descend to the jury box to take, inevitably, our seats.

I played Lola, mistress to John Colicos' character. My costume, designed by Clayton Shields, was a skintight, sleeveless, floor-length gown in shocking pink and silver with a large diamond-shaped aperture revealing most of my midriff: pointy (false, of course) bosoms out 'til tomorrow, and a wig of silver and pink which Marie Antoinette would have envied, reaching toward the gods. The make-up via Clayton's clever hand was in a balletic Firebird style. But it was the shoes that were killers!—three-inch heels, pinchy pointy toes, hot pink, very *Vogue*-ish Italian. The combination of skintight dress and teetering heels restricted my 'stride' to mere inches and a mincing geisha-type of walk.

One particular night, our cue came for that third act mêlée entrance. On we came, chatterboxing gaily. I somehow neglected, however, to adapt myself to the steep incline of Williams' raked stage. Momentum took over. I careened downhill, flipped off the stage and *into the lap of a startled front row patron!* The audience went berserk, as did the entire cast. Astonishingly, neither I nor that kind man suffered any injuries.

Of course, the problem, once I righted myself, was how in God's name to get myself back on stage in that outfit. Eventually, when we'd all finished corpsing, two men took my outstretched hands and pulled me up while my new lap friend pushed my nether regions from behind. I minced over to the jury box, took a bow, and settled into my appointed place.

MONICA PARKER
Polka?...anyone?

I was about twenty, in the early days of Second City in Toronto, when that amazing cast was pulling together the TV show. We were all hanging out together, all friends, John Candy, Dan Aykroyd, Rick Moranis, Marty Short, Catherine O'Hara and everyone. I was also originally going to be part of the TV show.

One day my agent called to say that I had an audition for an American TV show that would be shooting in Toronto. It was *The Bobby Vinton Show,* which meant nothing to me but it *was* an American series, so I thought this was pretty good. They hired me. I was over the moon! I remember running back to the Firehall and telling Marty, Danny and everyone, 'I just got an American series!'

Well, away I went. I thought I was on my way now for sure. When I showed up on set the first day. I was introduced to the line producer Alan Thicke, later of *Growing Pains* fame, and the Exec Producer Chris Beard. I had been told that I was going to be doing sketches and gags and this and that as part of a sketch company.

My first day on set, I was handed a helmet with horns, like a Valkyrie headdress, with long yellow braids attached to it, a pair of oversized platypus shoes and a polka-dot dress with padding. Apparently, they thought I wasn't big enough. It was my job, wearing this costume, to polka out the guest stars for each show. Then they would read an insulting fat joke from a cue card and I would not be seen again for the rest of the show. That was to be my only part in the show each week. During one show, I polka-ed out Don Rickles and he said, 'Hey kid. Whadidya do, swallow a stove?' Once I polka-ed out all of the Spinners (a pop group) at one time. It was the single most devastating job I ever had.

My whole career I had avoided doing fat jokes and being the 'butt' of them because that kind of stereotyping is just a very bad place to go. Now all my studying, my years of working had come to this. I was so humiliated. I hated it.

One time a guest, Phyllis Diller, didn't show up. Jessica Walters was not at all happy to be working with me when she expected to be doing the sketch with Ms Diller. Nevertheless, I ended up doing all her lines including her trade-mark 'Hah!' laugh. What made it worse was that I was funny in this dreadful sketch. Ms Walters was furious.

At the end of the season I quit. But when the show got picked up, they phoned me and asked me to come back. I said, 'No, I hate this. I can't come back.' They said, 'No, no, no. We didn't know how talented you are. Please. We'll give you anything you want.' I didn't know it at the time, naïve me, but the show had been picked up 'as is', which meant that the cast had to be as it was in the first season. They promised me more money and more sketches. They begged me to come back and eventually, stupid me, I said, OK.

But when we got back to doing the show, nothing had changed. Same deal; they threw in a couple of horrible sketches. It was awful. I was dying. So I quit in the middle of the season because I felt they had not honoured their contract with me. I went off to Hawaii. Next thing I knew, I got a phone call in Hawaii from John Candy who had known the whole miserable story.

'Monica, you are not going to believe this. I just got a call from *The Bobby Vinton Show*. They want me to wear your pig-tails and your dress and be you.'

He turned it down.

MARTIN SHORT
Grimley lives

'Ed Grimley' came from a revue that was in progress when I joined *SCTV*, called *The Wizard of Ossington*. There was a piece called 'Sexist'; its premise was two people [a man and a woman] applying for one job. I played the guy—a role originally done by John Candy—and he is a moron. The woman is very, very qualified, overly qualified. The employer goes through our education, employment history, and at the end says, 'I can't choose, you people are so evenly qualified.' She says, 'This is outrageous.' The employer says, 'Of course, maybe if you arm wrestle.' We arm wrestle. I win. She storms out with a diatribe against male chauvinism. The employer says, 'What's her problem?' I say, 'Maybe she's having her period.'

I started to call this character Ed Grimley. I based him on a few people I knew. I was doing the piece again with Robin Duke and Peter Aykroyd and I remember one time I looked at Robin who was downstage. I kind of bared my teeth by accident. The audience laughed. My tendency when the audience laughs is to freeze and figure out what I've done later. So the teeth-baring became part of the character.

I also started to grease my hair a little bit to give a bad look. I remember Peter laughing one night and saying, 'It keeps getting higher every time you do this.' So as a joke I came out with it completely up and that got a laugh. I felt, well okay, I'll keep it in. And Ed Grimley just kind of evolved.

LEN CARIOU
APPLAUSE all around

The first original musical that I did on Broadway was *Applause* with Lauren Bacall, which was, of course, based on the film *All About Eve*. This was in 1969.

I was playing the boyfriend, 'the director', and the first song of the show was a love song, a ballad, that I was to sing to Betty Bacall downstage, close to the audience. There I was, singing my heart out in my best boy baritone, when I got the feeling somehow that something was wrong. I continued to sing, looking into Bacall's eyes, trying to sell this song, when we both heard a kind of 'twittering' from the front rows. Finally I looked toward the sound and I saw these women whispering and pointing towards me. I looked down and realised that my fly was open and part of the tail of my white shirt was sticking stiffly out the gap like a flag. I'm sure the double take I did, did nothing to quell their mirth.

Of course I had to continue singing this romantic love ballad...flying at half mast, while I tried at the same time to turn upstage and discreetly zip myself up. At that moment Betty looked down, realised what had happened, and lost it. She started laughing, then I was laughing, and a wave of laughter spread through the audience.

At that point we gave up the idea of recovering the romantic mood of the scene.

AMELIA HALL
1947 Canadian Art Theatre with Joy Thompson

One of our most popular productions was *Dirty Work At The Cross Roads,* and it was in this play that I had a most embarrassing accident. The Haskell Opera House boasted a roll-drop curtain. At the end of one scene I stepped forward onto the apron of the stage as this curtain rolled down behind me. Then, while the set was being changed, I entertained the audience with my soul-stirring rendition of Marie Dressler's song, 'Heaven Will Protect the Working Girl'. As I got to the end: 'You can keep your upper classes, Take back your demitasses, For Heaven will protect the working girl!' I gestured triumphantly and swept off the stage through the downright wings; making a swift turn I nipped back onto the stage behind the roll-curtain to start the following scene. Somebody handed me my hat, and, as I was putting it on, the curtain started to roll up.

Now, I was standing with my back to the curtain, and as it began to ascend, the hem of my long cotton dress caught in the roll, and the curtain wasn't the only thing that started to go up! Because it was summer I was wearing under the costume only the briefest of panties and a bra. As the audience shrieked its merriment, I saw my whole future flash before me and wondered what would become of me. Would I go right up with the curtain and hang like a skinned rabbit? Or would my gown be ripped from me? Or would my body be horribly broken? These questions were never to be answered, because someone had climbed up to the man on the curtain perched on his platform above the stage, and suddenly with a crash the curtain, and my skirt, came down. Five seconds to marshal my wits, and the curtain was up again. Somewhat breathless but bold, I declaimed my opening line, 'How strange it all seems,' and the dear audience had the grace to applaud.

SEANA MCKENNA
Not the movies

Having fallen off the Blyth Festival stage on my very first professional opening night and having spent the second act of *This Foreign Land* in the Clinton Hospital's emergency ward getting eight stitches for my slightly 'concussed' head, I thought I had paid my dues early for opening night mishaps. I was to learn that the theatre gods insist on their occasional titles.

In 1983, it was opening night of *Tartuffe* at the Stratford Festival and my first season on the Main Stage, in formidable company. A beautiful Victorian design by Tanya Moiseiwitsch. Douglas Campbell and Brian Bedford had just left the stage, and I was entering as 'Mariane' for my scene with Pat Galloway as 'Dorine'. In the scene, she finally convinces me to stand up for myself and refuse an intended marriage with the *cri de coeur*: 'Not Tartuffe!'

As I said this line with all the force I could muster in my corset, I felt something pop and give. I immediately clutched my skirts, not knowing what was slipping, my overskirt or my underskirt. Instead of running into Dorine's arms for comfort, I waddled, never releasing my grip on my skirts. I could sense the audience's unease, either with my strange posture or with the excessive lace creeping out from under my simple overskirt. It seemed my petticoat had come undone and was now beginning to trail below my feet.

Finally I saw a moment when I could do something! As Andrew Gillies, playing 'Valère', made his first entrance, I sidled upstage towards a console. I thought that I could let the petticoat drop and quietly kick it under the table. Andrew looked askew at me, thinking it odd that I had waited until opening to change the blocking and upstage him. On his first line, inquiring if the news about a marriage to Tartuffe was true, I unclenched my right hand. I heard the petticoat drop, a muffled 'boomph, boomph'. On my next line, 'I find that Father does have such a match in mind,' I stepped out of it, leaving a heap of cotton centre stage. Andrew's backward-leaping double take was almost worth the aggravation that petticoat had caused me.

We carried on, as if losing one's slip was a normal occurrence in everyday Victorian life. In fact, some audience members thought it was intentional—perhaps part of a strange Victorian courting ritual in which you remove a piece of clothing with each visit from your fiancé.

Later I awaited the director's response with some anxiety. Outside on the terrace that night, amidst the festivities I got it. The late John Hirsch shrugged, and said to me, in his truly inimitable fashion: 'What do they want? It's live theatre...these things happen. If you don't want surprises—go to the movies.'

LESLEY BALLANTYNE
Hung up

I was one of the dancers and also did some small roles in the village scenes in a production of *Hans Christian Andersen* at Young People's Theatre in 1979.

After the umpteenth quick change of the show, Valerie Moore, Anne Wootten, and I were now three villagers who had been directed to 'gossip' with each other in the scene. Russell Kilde was to come over and offer us some 'pies' from his rack and then continue on his way.

Unknowingly, I had been dragging around the stage a wire coat hanger caught on my petticoat. Russell alerted me to the fact, *sotto voce* of course, with this now classic line:

'Excuse me, Miss, but I think you've lost your IUD!'

MARIAM BERNSTEIN
The shimmer of satin

In 1988, I was playing 'Hermia' in Neptune Theatre's production of *A Midsummer Night's Dream*, sharing a dressing room with the actresses playing 'Titania' and 'Helena'. Titania (Caroline Yaeger) was costumed in a dark, skin-tight body suit with a shimmery full skirt made of shredded metallic fabric. One night, after playing 'Hippolyta's' opening scene, Caroline changed into her Titania outfit, and left the dressing room. She did not realise that she had brushed against my personal clothes that I customarily draped on my chair, and my white bra hooked onto the fabric of her skirt.

She ended up on stage with her 'Oberon', proudly exclaiming 'The fairy land buys *not* the child of me!' A swish of her skirt, and all of a sudden, smack in the centre of the *black* platform, was a satiny white bra. There was a moment of shock, during which the two follow-spot operators, noticing an unidentified white article on stage, focused their spots on the offending article to facilitate identification.

Fortunately, Oberon had the presence of mind to add a large cape flourish to his speech, during which he kicked the bra off the platform, under the set. At intermission, the actors came to the green room, asking, along with the technicians, whose bra was on stage and how it got there. I was mortified to learn later that it was indeed mine own undergarment.

CORINNE CONLEY
At the Mountain Playhouse

In 1951 the imaginative and energetic Joy Thompson opened the Mountain Playhouse in the charming ski chalet with bar and restaurant atop Mount Royal in Montreal.

Arriving by horse-drawn caleche or on foot (you had to park your car at the foot of the mountain) added to the aura of occasion on those balmy summer nights, and the laughter that rocked the 200-seat theatre was enough to spoil an actor's expectation of audience response forever.

That was certainly true the night we opened *Voice Of The Turtle*. As I came on for my curtain call my contact lens popped out. As the curtain closed, I beseeched the cast to look for it. When the curtain opened again, the audience was greeted by a line of actors bowing in the opposite direction!

SONJA SMITS
O spite! O hell!

At the Manitoba Theatre Centre in the late '70s I was appearing in *Midsummer Night's Dream* directed by Arif Hasnain. The very physical fights were choreographed by R.H. Thomson.

Kate Trotter, 'Hermia' and I, 'Helena' were wearing long, luscious Grecian-style wigs. My own hair was under a wig sock and bobby-pinned very close to my head.

During a scene in the forest with the lovers, Jim Mezon and Ric Reid, I was lying on the ground in the middle of the stage. The boys each took an arm to pull me up, but Jim Mezon had his foot firmly planted on my hair. The boys pulled and I resisted as I felt my wig being pulled off my head. The boys won out, pulling me up to a standing position, absolutely bobby-pin bald headed, with my wig looking very much like a dead rat, lying in the middle of the stage. I felt as though I had been suddenly stripped naked in front of the audience.

I proceeded with the scene (my fellow actors later informed me) with my arms tightly wrapped around my body, in a semi-crouched position, and very cross indeed. Fortunately, my next line was, 'Oh spite! O hell! I see you are all bent to set against me for your merriment!'

The wig, once it made it off the stage, passed like a football from one actor to the next, and was never seen again.

TOM WOOD
Hair suit

Susan Wright, Michael Ball, and I were doing *The Alchemist* at The Citadel Theatre. I was very young, a couple of years out of university and here I was, working with these wonderful actors in a very complicated play. It was set in Klondike days. Susan had a beehive hair-do like Miss Kitty in *Gunsmoke,* low cleavage, the dance hall girl.

The scene was very convoluted. There was a word that drove Susan's character crazy. She would talk Michael's character into saying it, then she'd go nuts so she wouldn't have to sleep with him. I was dressed as a Mountie, and had to run around and try to catch Susan when she went insane.

We had staged a chase that ended with me grabbing her; she would duck under my arm and go the other way. One night I went to grab her. She went the other way and I looked at her and she looked very different. I realised that I was looking at her wearing a little nylon cap with all the bobby pins through it. I lifted up my arm and her wig was hanging from the buttons on my jacket.

We just collapsed on the floor. We couldn't walk. Susan kept saying under her breath, 'I'm peeing myself. I'm peeing myself.' We crawled off the stage and left Michael Ball on the stage to finish the scene by himself. We just rolled around on the floor backstage, screaming and laughing hysterically.

DARYL SHUTTLEWORTH
Suspended

It was closing night at the Piggery Theatre, North Hatley, Quebec. In the final scene of Raymond Storey's thriller, *Angel of Death,* my character 'Jamie' who is supposedly dead, arrives and confronts his half sister 'Alice', played by Helen Taylor. He relates horrible tales of front line combat; how he was pursued by an angel through the trenches; how he went AWOL; how he has been living in the attic for several months (going slightly loopy in the process).

Jamie has killed 'Walter', played by Brian Dooley, and stuffed his body in her closet. Frightened, Alice runs for the window to call for help. Jamie catches her by the waist and restrains her. He reveals a revolver and puts it to her head. The father enters, then a woman, played by Ruth Dahan, appears from the attic (where Jamie has left her for dead). Jamie—confused and tired by months of torment—imagines her to be the angel of death. Jamie turns the gun on himself and kills himself, falling in a heap on the floor. Alice is left holding Jamie. Her last line is: 'So much blood...so much blood.'

For two weeks in mid-summer, that's the way the scene unfolded, to great effect. However, the final performance was marred by a sagging pair of suspenders and an off-stage revolver.

From the very first performance, my suspenders should have been replaced. They continually slid off my shoulders. I should have asked for a new pair, but this was a summer theatre, and I thought, heck, it's a character thing...Jamie can't afford a new pair of suspenders. So, I let the suspenders slide off my shoulders and worked it into my performance.

Now, the gun. For safety reasons, it was determined that the revolver would be fired from backstage by our stage technician. When this gun was fired it let off a god-awful *BOOM* and scared the pants off the audience. Perfect for a thriller.

On closing night Helen ran to the window to call for help. I ran to catch her. As I started forward I noticed that my suspender was sliding down. I decided to free myself of it and in one quick motion I cast it aside, with great panache, in an arcing loop upstage. That worked well, very effective. Unfortunately, this nifty piece of athleticism was performed next to a three-foot bedpost on the downstage corner of the bed. As I catapulted forward toward Helen my peripheral vision caught sight of the looping suspender heading toward the bedpost but I was not absolutely sure I'd seen it go over. One step further and I was sure. My momentum came to a halt and the entire bed, which was perched on a riser, jerked forward. The audience gasped. My suspender was a ragged mess, but it was holding firm, and I couldn't get to Helen without retreating to untangle myself. The audience laughed. Helen had reached the window and was frantically trying to open it. Hearing the gales of laughter, Helen looked back and slyly moved close enough so that I could pull her to me. We moved in a backwards fashion to the bedpost where I tried to unhook myself. The audience continued to laugh. With no fear of being heard, I quickly told Helen what had happened and continued to free myself. Needless to say, the conclusion of *Angel of Death* was going to lack a certain terrifying quality with two actors tied to a bedpost and the audience laughing. I decided to take a little break (after I freed myself from the bedpost) to allow us all to compose ourselves. When the laughter subsided we got on with the rest of the scene.

Everything was fine until I had to fire the fake gun. I pointed the gun to my chest, pulled the trigger and...NO BOOM. Great! I'm standing downstage centre with a gun pointed at my chest, surrounded by three actors...waiting. I heard an anemic click from backstage. Still no BOOM. We waited. Offstage, several frantic clicks fired in quick succession, followed by an oath from the technician. Evidently our 'real' gun was not going to fire and we were on our own.

Think quick. What to do?

I had to die—that was certain—but how? My first thought—I swear to God—was to pull two tiny needles out of my shirt pocket and stab my eyes. No! Too Greek! Maybe I could hit myself in the head with the gun. No! Too stupid. After what seemed an eternity I decided to have a quasi-heart-attack. I clutched at my chest, I wheezed and coughed and then I fell to the ground. Halfway to the floor I was thinking that I would ring our technician's neck, but by the time I hit the floor (facing upstage of course) I was laughing. A pause ensued. Helen sputtered and cried her final line:

'So much...so much...ahhhhh!'

Our director, Perry Schneiderman, who had seen this stellar piece of work, met us in the lobby for a drink. After a toast, he turned to me with a straight face and said, 'You planned that, didn't you?'

RICHARD CURNOCK
The hat trick

I was in an 18th-century play that Stratford did in 1982, directed by Derek Goldby. At the end of the production John Broome had choreographed a dance around huge candle sconces with dozens of real lighted candles. Some of the actors were dancing and some standing at the side. I was wearing a huge plumed hat. I made my move and could smell something burning. I turned to the person beside me and said 'Something's burning.' She said 'It's your hat.' So I took it off and jumped all over it to put it out.

This was the first night and a lot of people came round to see us. I was saying to everyone, 'What about my hat! Did you see it catch fire and see me jump on it and put it out?' To a one they said 'No. No. Didn't notice a thing.'

ARLENE MEADOWS
The kitchen fire

The 1965 opera season was in full swing. The COC [Canadian Opera Company] had engaged me to sing both 'Herodias' in *Salome* and 'Maddelena' in *Rigoletto*. Both scores were difficult but maybe the Herodias a little more so and thus I had missed some of the rehearsals for *Rigoletto*. I felt a little as if I was living the performer's nightmare, trying to remember scores and staging from both productions.

Finally we opened with *Rigoletto*. In the scene when the tenor turns me in a great embrace, my eye caught the light of the lit candles—and then as he bent me over the kitchen table, my wig flipped back behind me. At that moment, my heart told me something was wrong! What I did not know was that the wig had flipped back into one of the candles and caught fire.

The next thing I knew the tenor was tearing a flimsy, flaming blouse from my body and people in the audience were screaming. A few more were running to the stage.

Once I was cognizant of what had happened, I hugged the tenor and said, 'Thank you. You saved my life!' He responded with affected boredom, 'Oh, my darling, it was nothing. I have been in the theatre for so long that it is my home— and to me, this was a kitchen fire!'

They tell me that this incident is why the COC no longer uses real flames on candles anywhere on stage.

DEAN REGAN
Travellin' shoes

I grew up in Vancouver in the late '50s, and as a young dancer of 18 one of the places I auditioned for work was California. I got my first dancing job at a nightclub in Los Angeles, the Moulin Rouge, and it sat up to 1,000 people at tables. It was Vegas in Los Angeles without the gambling, a place for people to go and see the stars.

The show I went into there was a jungle epic with a hundred dancers, four elephants, and horses, not to mention the actors and singers. Each show was made up of segments of specially written material. They were huge, impressive productions. The jungle show had an English colonel and a girl who was captured by the natives and tortured while we did African dances around her. In an *Oklahoma* type show we had pink boots and hats for the girls and blue boots and hats for the boys. We even had about 50 coloured pigeons that would fly from the lighting booth on to the stage. To match our costumes they were spray-painted pink and blue—something not permitted today because the pigeons used to die from the paint. We had to have people planted around with brooms to clean up after the animals and collect the expiring pigeons.

The whole thing had to be really well organized and under quite a lot of control. There were floors of dressing rooms, and our dance boots and shoes had to be specially made for us in New York. We all knew how much they cost because we had to look after them. After a while, looking to move along in my career, I auditioned and got a job in Las Vegas as a featured dancer in a hotel there, owned and operated by the same management who owned the Moulin Rouge.

This show was called *Newcomers of '28* and featured Buster Keaton, Rudy Vallee, and Paul Whiteman and his Orchestra. I gave my notice to the Moulin Rouge. It was OK by them, and they hired a replacement who rehearsed in the daytime. The only requirement was that I had to buy my shoes and my boots. After all, they'd been specially made for me. That made sense, so I paid them $85 for the boots and $35 for the shoes.

I was still working at night and I noticed that my shoes and boots were being used by the replacement when he rehearsed in the day. I asked about it and they told me that it was just temporary, as they had ordered his pairs but they hadn't yet come from New York. I was starting to get the idea that this was a scam.

Well, I had a plan. My final night, as I finished each number, I packed up my shoes and my boots in my bag. As I was leaving I was met at the top of the stairs by the line captain, Flo Young. She was a gorgeous redhead, tough as hell. She asked me where my shoes and boots were. I told her they were mine. I had paid for them and I was taking them with me. She told me that they would hold my cheque and that they wanted those shoes. Nothing doing, I said, and I went home to my apartment.

A few minutes after midnight there was a knock on my door. I opened the door to two very rough-looking gentlemen. I knew perfectly well who they were and what they could do to me if they didn't get what they wanted.

'We'd like to have the shoes and the boots.'

I gave them to them. It wasn't worth a broken leg or a broken arm. I guess it wasn't so much the money to them as an issue of not being done in by a kid. A few dollars poorer, I happily went off to my new job—working for the same people, somewhere else.

On BEATRICE LILLIE

As the [First World] war accelerated, male performers were going off to battle and Charlot [a theatrical producer of the day] found that Bea, with her five-foot-three trim figure and youthful look, was a natural to appear as a male impersonator. With expensive wigs to cover Bea's beautiful and full long hair, she made an attractive soldier boy or boulevardier.

'I suppose I should have been more careful. As it was, male impersonating just simply sneaked up on me,' Bea remembered. 'Almost before I knew it, I was wearing a tuxedo "with an air"!'

In one case it was an air of naïveté. Jack Buchanan jokingly referred to her impersonations by asking on which side she dressed. Bea quickly pointed out the location of her dressing room in the theatre.

8

Bare Bods and Bodily Functions

FRANK MOORE
Hairtofore

I was among the original Toronto cast of the Canadian production of the '60s Broadway hit, *Hair,* at the Royal Alexandra Theatre. *Hair* was famous for its then radical politics and its innovative presentation. It was notorious, of course, for the nude scene.

We were, with few exceptions, a bunch of Canadian kids with little or no experience of many of the issues dealt with in the show. The privilege of growing up in Canada precluded any real understanding of what it meant to face being drafted, for instance. And none of us, to my knowledge, had attended The Gypsy Rose Lee School Of Public Streaking. Personally I was still embarrassed to be seen wearing Bermuda shorts.

We didn't arrive at the point where we were about to 'let it all hang out', without prior conditioning. To help us march in step toward the inevitable formation of that pubescent parade, we were given some 'indoctrinational' encouragement.

Part of a regular rehearsal day would be given over to a self-consciously casual discussion of body parts. Breasts, for example; their importance in the overall scheme of things had been drastically overestimated, it was proposed. They were, in fact, no different than elbows. Similarly, penises were described as direct descendants of knee-caps. Well, not being complete idiots, we knew we were expected to conclude that we needn't feel shy about displaying mere elbows and knee-caps.

An appetizer of this sort was usually followed by a main course of 'touching exercises' designed to further reduce whatever resistance remained towards doffing our duds. You would be quite correct in assuming that what took place was exceedingly innocent.

And so opening night was upon us. Let me take you back to when 'The Moon Was In The Seventh House' and it was 'Easy To Be Hard' as we all 'Let The Sunshine In'. At the end of the first act, the character 'Claude' was in a quandary over whether he should burn his draft card to protest the war in Vietnam, as all his friends had just done, or honour his commitment to his country by going to war. As he voiced this inner conflict in the song, *Where Do I Go?* all other members of the 'tribe' sang choral accompaniment while placing an enormous scrim or blanket over the entire stage. Openings had been cut into the scrim at appropriate intervals and fastened shut with Velcro. At a certain point in the song, we eased ourselves under the scrim, seemingly in a state of cosmic calm.

Once underneath, however, we became demented divestors, madly tearing at our skin-tight costumes which were by then drenched with sweat, and seemed bonded to our bodies. Moreover, because of the improvisational nature of this section of the show, you never knew where you would end up under that scrim. For that inaugural undress, I found myself right at the front of the stage. My life didn't pass before my eyes exactly, but I did experience what is known in political circles as 'Doctrine Reversal Syndrome'.

Management never officially forced anyone to perform the nude scene. They didn't have to. Peer pressure ensured that most of us would conform. Theoretically, one could opt out from time to time. On opening night under that scrim, I wrestled with a dilemma. Despite my conditioning, three things became crystal clear: 1) I didn't believe breasts were in the least like elbows; 2) I felt incredibly protective towards my 'knee-cap'; and 3) standing up naked in front of hundreds of people who were more than fully dressed suddenly struck me as totally irrational.

'Not tonight. Maybe tomorrow, if I end up in the back row,' I told myself. And, under the mistaken impression that we were to stand up and sing whether we actually stripped or not, I burst forth from my Velcro vagina, a lone psychedelic newborn clothed in all my tie-dyed glory, surrounded by a stage full of completely naked people.

Any words I might use to describe how foolish I felt would have to be considered euphemistic. Mind you, I wasn't the only one who opted out or suffered from procedural confusion that night, so there had obviously been gaps in the instructions. But the others at least had had the good sense to stay under the scrim.

RICHARD DONAT
Hosanna, Hosanna

Maggie Thomas and I had been living together for a couple of years but weren't yet married. Her Welsh parents were very dubious about Maggie's considering marrying an actor. They thought I was a bit of a scoundrel and a cad. Maggie and I had gone together to New York while Richard Monette and I opened in the Michel Tremblay play, *Hosanna*. She thought it would be a great idea for her parents to meet me while I was working on Broadway.

Her parents knew about the homosexual subject matter of the play, and Maggie was going to prepare them for the graphic details after they had arrived. The night her mum and her banker dad came to New York, her mum retired early, and her dad decided to take a stroll. Their hotel was just down the street from the theatre where *Hosanna* was playing. He saw the marquee with my name on it. It was 10:30, the show was still on, and as there was no one about he just walked into the theatre. We were at the very end of act two, and Richard and I were almost naked.

The first sight my future wife's father had of me, I was in the altogether, embracing a naked man onstage on Broadway.

WAYNE ROBSON
Broken covenant

I was performing the role of Lenny Bruce in the bio-play *Lenny*, directed by Richard Ouzounian, at the Vancouver East Cultural Centre in early '74. The role is taxing, very physical and emotional, and by the end of each performance it was all I could do to maintain my concentration.

In the final scene, Lenny 'shoots up' and is then carried, 'dead' and completely naked, to centre stage where a final salute to his life takes place. It was a moment of great emotion for me, made all the more difficult by my having to lie there starkers, holding my breath, as if dead.

One night I lay there, exposed to the world, as the final drum roll announced the approaching end. The lights started to dim slowly. Suddenly from the audience, a loud female voice exclaimed in evident astonishment, 'He's not Jewish!'

JENNIFER DALE
Tourist attractions

In an episode of *E.N.G.* I played the love interest for 'Mike', the character that Art Hindle played in the series. And inevitably there was a bedroom scene.

We were working in the beautiful round bedroom at Casa Loma, the same one that had been used in *Love and Larceny* by CBC a few years before as the honeymoon suite. We had just finished the love scene and the crew was about to break for lunch. Art and I decided to hang out in the bed until everyone had moved off. We were having a quiet conversation, with obviously not very much on, until eventually we realised the entire crew had left for lunch.

In the film business a bedroom scene is generally a slightly more carefully protected circumstance, a 'closed set' which usually works with a pared-down or 'essential' crew. We felt that we had no reason to be concerned for our privacy. What we did not realise was that the production assistant assigned to keep people from wandering onto an active or 'hot' set had also gone to lunch.

We lay there talking for about 10 minutes. Suddenly a whole group of Japanese tourists entered the 'closed' set *en masse*, stopped at the foot of the bed, and stood clicking cameras and pointing at us.

They must have thought that we were part of the tour.

BRUCE GREENWOOD
Chopped

Standing naked in the wings before an entrance can be unnerving. It bears an uncanny similarity to nightmares I've had about just that: suddenly finding myself in front of an audience with my penis hanging out. But it is possible to convince yourself it's a 'great entrance', step out into the lights and take some satisfaction from the gasps and mutterings out there in the house. I thought I might feel less insecure if I chose to approach it that way.

We were doing *Bent* at the Arts Club in Vancouver and eight shows a week found me strolling out there and swinging it in Allan Gray's face. In the scene, we would have a short chat, then I'd exit to the bathroom, put on a robe and re-enter. We would continue to talk until there was a crashing at the door as two brown-shirt goons demanded to be let in. As they came through the door I would run into the bathroom with them tearing through the apartment in pursuit.

Once in the bathroom I'd stuff my cheeks with blood-bags and squirt a cup or so of blood on my leg as they smashed down the door and fired a gun and I screamed. I'd come staggering back in, only a step ahead of them. They'd grab me by the hair, drag me down stage centre, yank back my head, and draw a huge blood-filled knife across my throat whereupon I'd vomit blood impressively all over the stage. Then I'd pitch forward onto my face and expire as a curtain with a massive iron bar in it slammed down in front of me, providing the backdrop for the next scene. In full drag Alex Diakun would enter stage right singing a torch song as the curtain shimmered.

One night, the scene plays as usual; the goons burst through the door, and I scream as the brownshirts barrel into the bathroom after me and fire the shot. So far so good. But my robe has come open. The belt is loose and dragging. I don't see it falling around my legs. I don't notice until much too late that my feet are tied together.

I'm in motion but my feet are going nowhere. As my face is sailing toward the floor it becomes clear that my hands are still at my sides and they're not going to break my fall. The only things that come between me and the floor are my forehead and my penis which, out of sheer terror, has swung upward and laid itself across the chopping block of my pelvic bone.

The pain is shocking and I'm convinced that I've pinched it off. I stagger to my feet and lurch two feet over my mark before being brought to my knees by my scene partners. All I can think is that the audience is witnessing the most awful accident in the history of theatre, and that my dick is somewhere upstage.

I did still have to die and I'm sure on this night it was convincing because I wanted to. I pitched forward and the curtain came down. On my neck. The curtain was down but my head was still on-stage. Now Alex comes out and sings a couple of bars of his song. I have two choices: I can let my bloody head lie in his nightclub till the next black-out, or I can suddenly come to life. So as the crowd watches, I wrestle insanely with the bar in the curtain and finally yank my head back into the dark. I feel for the worst.

Miraculously, I'm intact. I let go an agonized sigh of relief that can probably be heard by the guy in the back row. I do a kind of two-legged sumo crab walk back to the dressing room and stand shaking at my make-up table with my injuries on a towel, all the while describing to the rest of the cast what has happened in a choking whisper.

To this day bathrobes disturb me and I rarely run when I'm naked.

JAMES B. DOUGLAS
M.A.S.H.

M.A.S.H. was a wild Robert Altman film. We knew, at the time we were shooting it, that this film was going to be something special. I played 'Colonel Merrill'.

I remember shooting a scene where Colonel Merrill was in bed with a Japanese geisha. The central characters (played by Eliot Gould and Donald Sutherland) were trying to blackmail him. A continuous scene, it was shot with me in a flesh-coloured jock strap to make me appear nude. They had cast a Japanese go-go dancer as 'the girl'. She had never acted before, and was very shy about taking her clothes off.

Altman, who is always improvising, stopped the shoot and came over to me. 'James, this girl is obviously very shy. We'll have two cameras running. I want you to initiate all the action.' So away we went. I got her into the bed, out of the bed, under the covers, out of her kimono, and all the while Donald Sutherland was doing the funniest ad-libs.

In the final film, Altman turned the scene into flash photos, a brilliant way to cover the obvious fact that I was initiating all the action. Film buffs will see that the photo flashes were part of a continuing shot because in the last flash blood is dripping down my face. One of those geisha spears in the young woman's hair gashed my forehead. Still have the scar. My colonel's medal.

ALAN PEARCE
Warm spoons

Some of us started a theatre in Vancouver in the late '30s in a second floor walk-up space called the Community Playhouse. We were a professional company. One of the shows we did was Clare Boothe's *Kiss the Boys Goodbye*. It was a well-written show, a fictionalised account of the search for Scarlett O'Hara. I played a part patterned after a big name newspaper man and Aileen Seaton, a very delicate little thing, was playing the lead.

On the other hand, the second female lead was a rather robust creature. At one point during the show she came running on clutching something in her arms. One time she stopped too abruptly for what she was wearing. One of her boobs popped out! She couldn't do anything. Her hands were occupied. It was one of those things that was much worse for her than anybody else.

I got up to shield her from the audience and very delicately replaced her boob into the kind of halter thing she was wearing. I suddenly thought—this sure is a time that a couple of warm spoons would've come in handy!

JOHN DEVORSKI
Whatever Lola wants

In the mid '80s, I was cast as 'Young Joe' in a production of *Damn Yankees* at the now defunct Cambridge Motor Dinner Theatre. The seductive 'Lola' was being played by a wonderful actress named Geraldine Farrell.

We had been doing the show for months and in the course of working together, had often found ourselves accidentally and deliberately cracking each other up on stage. On some nights it was a challenge to get through our scenes without corpsing.

In one of our scenes together, Lola tries to seduce Young Joe so that he will renege on his bargain and the 'Devil' will have his soul. She has a spectacularly sexy number, the famous 'Whatever Lola Wants, Lola Gets' in the team locker room. She sings and dances in a skimpy two-piece costume consisting of a bustier and dance pants over sheer pantyhose.

On one fateful night, Lola came out in her little Spanish outfit to do her big number in the locker room. Things were going fine. However when she got part where she was to tear off her Spanish skirt she revealed rather more than was intended. She had forgotten to put on the dance pants! She continued, unaware that she was dancing with nothing on her lower half but pantyhose.

The audience of course screamed. I burst into hysterical laughter, but she still did not take any notice. She continued with the number assuming, as I found out later, that the audience was reacting to me for some reason and that I was once again trying to crack her up. The audience just went crazy and I was laughing so hard that I was crying...and there was no way that she would look at me so I could somehow signal her. She continued blissfully unaware until she got to the part where she would grab onto the lockers and shake her derrière at the audience. She felt 'a little draft', looked down, screamed, and ran off stage.

I had completely lost it by then and there was nothing to do but sit there laughing, crying, gasping along with the audience. Finally, a gutsy Gerry came back out with her dance pants *on,* sang the last line of the song and took her bow...to more howls of laughter and huge applause.

Of course, everything she said for the rest of the show was coloured by her earlier 'display' and again brought the house down. That night Lola did a little extra to 'get what she wanted...'. I doubt the members of the audience will *ever* forget that show; certainly the incident has become legend on the cabaret and music theatre circuit.

MARCIA DIAMOND
Seeing red

The New Play Society did a production of Morley Callaghan's play *To Tell The Truth* in 1949 at the Museum Theatre in Toronto. This production had a cast list which is fun to read now: Herbert Gott, Beth Lockerbie, E.M. Margolese, Murray Chercover (later to be involved with CFTO TV), Don Harron, Mavor Moore, Alfie Scopp, John Sullivan (later to become Sean Sullivan), Lloyd Bochner, Donald Davis, Diane Foster, Gerry Sarracini, and Marie Lyle. Larry McCance who did the set went on to be President of ACTRA.

The show was such a success that we transferred to the Royal Alexandra Theatre. We were all just thrilled to death because no Canadian play had ever been there before. They offered us ten dollars per day as a kind of *per diem*. We took this experience very seriously and subsequently worked extremely earnestly.

In the play was a scene where Lloyd Bochner and Don Harron were playing characters vying for the attention of Diane Foster's character. In the action, Lloyd was to tear off Diane's red silk blouse and leave her standing there in her sexy undies. The blouse had been fixed to rip away easily which it usually did. One performance Lloyd got particularly excited in his acting and got carried away. He managed to somehow get hold of Diane's bra as well and rip everything off!

There was a huge gasp from the audience. I was standing in the wings waiting to make my entrance. We were all shocked. Lloyd got red, red, red in the face, looked at her and walked right off the stage. Don had the presence of mind to run in front of her so she could somewhat compose herself and get her blouse back on.

It became the story around town. I even remember an article in *Maclean's Magazine* that wrote up the incident and spoke of Diane's 'piquant breasts'. Imagine, in 1949!

BERNARD BRADEN
The cover-up

[Braden was 'Mitch' in London's 1947 production of A Streetcar Named Desire. *'Stanley' was Bonar Colleano and 'Blanche' was Vivien Leigh.]*

During the last week of Vivien's tenure as Blanche, I was in my dressing room, waiting to go on for the last scene of the play. In the previous scene Blanche and Stanley were alone in the apartment, Stella having been taken off to hospital to have her baby. Stanley had made an overture to Blanche who'd broken a bottle and threatened to twist the broken end in his face. He'd disarmed her and thrown her across the table before carrying her to the bed as the curtain fell.

Bonar suddenly appeared in my dressing room, white-faced (which wasn't easy for him), and said, 'Have you got a drink, for Christ's sake?' I handed him a bottle of whiskey and, as I went to get a glass, watched him take a hefty swig from the bottle.

'What's the matter?'

'You don't know what happened out there.'

'What happened out there?'

'You know when I throw her over the table in those two bright follow spots?'

'Yeah.'

'One breast came right out.'

'Jesus! What did you do?'

'Well, I had both arms around her, what could I do? I put my mouth over it.'

IAN DEAKIN
Horn of...not quite enough

I'm standing on stage, everyone turns to look at me (it's obviously my turn to speak), and I'm wearing no shoes. Despite the fact that I haven't a clue what to say next, or who my fellow actors are, it's the shoes that cause me horrific embarrassment. I stand riveted to the spot, terrified, and then I wake up. My actor's nightmare, but it pales in comparison to the real thing.

At Neptune Theatre in 1972 I was performing in an adaptation of Fellini's *Satyricon*. My wardrobe consisted of a loin cloth. At an invited dress rehearsal of a studio production, during the banquet scene my loin cloth dropped off! In hope that no one would notice, I quickly dashed behind a cornucopia bursting with vegetables. Unfortunately it was to no avail. The stage design was in the round and the Horn of Plenty provided coverage on only one side.

ALLAN GRAY
Mother always told you

We were working in Vancouver at the Playhouse. An actor who has since gone to L.A. was playing the 'Chocolate Soldier' in *Arms And The Man*. He was costumed in period soldier's uniform, including tight, cream-coloured pants that were seamed straight around the crotch from front waistband to the back waistband. At one point he bent over and the seam split completely open.

This might have been embarrassing enough if he had been wearing underwear but he wasn't. So when the seam burst, out popped the 'family jewels'. Naturally, the audience went completely crazy.

Fortunately there were two pillows on the settee. He grabbed them both, and continued the entire scene holding them strategically in place, one in front and one in back. The audience probably never heard a word he said, they were laughing so hysterically.

SUSAN MCLENNAN
Star turn

My very first 'professional gig' was as the photo-double to the star of a made-for-television movie. I was hired to spend six weeks on the set. At the end, I was delighted to be invited to the black-tie première screening of the film. I had—and I knew it—the most perfect dress for the occasion. It was a dress a wealthy friend had had made for me to wear at her wedding. It was salmon silk, accented with antique lace and it snapped up demurely on an angle across the front.

The big day came, and I was nervous, but excited, as the hour listed on the invitation drew nearer. By the time I left for the theatre, every hair, every eyelash—

everything—was in its rightful place. Once there, I took off my coat. All eyes turned, and I even heard a gasp or two. I'd expected a little bit of notice, but this was beyond my wildest dreams. I strode through the crowd to my appointed seat, feeling eyes upon me every step of the way, feeling them still long after I had sat down.

Finally, the woman in front of me, who had been busily conferring with her husband, turned around and tapped me on the knee.

'Excuse me, dear.' I waited for the ensuing compliment. 'But did you know that your left breast is hanging outside of your dress?'

I didn't dare look down. I didn't dare do anything. I stared at her blankly for a moment, and then nodded vehemently.

'Yes, thank you. Yes...yes, thank you, I did.'

I waited the excruciating hours, that I'm sure were only seconds, for the lights to go down, so I could verify the situation and put my breast back inside my dress.

Without a doubt, I have never, ever made a more memorable entrance.

HEATHER SUMMERHAYES
My first 'moment'

In the autumn of 1974 I had been accepted at the St Lawrence Centre as an apprentice. Upon graduating from theatre school I would finally make my professional debut as an Actress!

The first production of that season was Robertson Davies' *Wu Feng*, a play about a 15th century band of young Formosan revolutionaries. Although I had no speaking lines, I was given what I called 'a moment'; Neil Munro, who played our fearless leader, was to jump from a high platform, strip me of my outer garments in a symbolic tearing off of the 'old ways', at which point I was to be lifted on the shoulders of two strong men and paraded across the stage before the village elders. This would signal the start of a frenzied dance by the young revolutionaries, who would likewise and symbolically throw off their overcoats.

Opening night! My family was in the audience. My pride and excitement were almost unbearable as I carefully applied Texas dirt backstage, covering my face, legs, and arms. I climbed into my gauzy 15th-century undergarments. I wrapped myself in the outer quilted jacket, constructed to break away at the mere touch of Neil Munro's fingers. It had all been scrupulously rehearsed, and I was ready, as they say, for my 'close-up'.

I hit the stage with exhilaration. Goddammit, I was *acting!* But so was Neil Munro. He jumped down from his perch and with a flourish, tore at my costume. The two strong men picked me up on their shoulders and carried me across the stage, past Alan Scarfe and Lubomir Mykytiuk, setting me down in front of Gerald Parkes.

Gerry's face bore a peculiar smile. My eyes fell to the place on my body where Gerry was staring. I was Texas dirt to the bottom of my neck, but gleaming white the rest of the way to my waist, my breasts bobbing gloriously for all to see!

The frenzied revolutionary dance began. I was determined to show Leon Major how professional I could be, so, naked as I was, I did not run from the stage. Instead, I watched Gerry and Lubomir grin as I tried to cover myself with the scrap of costume that I had left and joined the dance.

This occurred at least three more times during the run. Thinking Neil might be taking slight advantage of me, I naïvely went to Leon Major, my director, to ask how to handle the situation. His advice?

'Make-up to the waist.'

RUSSELL ROBERTS
Damn the decorum

In the summer of 1981, I was in an eight-person production of Shaw's *Saint Joan* for Northern Light Theatre in Edmonton. We performed in a tent with the audience sitting on a grassy hill. We all played numerous characters and our basic costumes were modern three-piece grey wool suits.

One stifling hot afternoon, in one of the longer soporific exposition passages with Christopher Gaze waxing eloquent on the problem of 'Joan', we were experiencing one of those times when actors sometimes go on automatic. Chris just went on...and on. That is until one explosive outburst, when the plate of his front teeth flew out of his mouth! We watched with stunned rapture as they arced, like slow motion, tumbling, twisting, falling until, with lizard-like deftness, he scooped them up and dropped them into his pocket!

All was still; the audience poised, actors resolutely not looking at each other for fear of what might happen if we did, biting lips and flaring our nostrils. A universal giggle was mounting, but we mastered it, reined it in, and subdued it. Then, when he was finished his speech, with a flourish, Chris plonked his plate of chompers back in his mouth!

Paul Gross was the first to go. Then feeling Ric Read's shoulder shaking next to mine, I followed, as did Alan Lysell, Michael Murdoch *and* the audience. A happy, inclusive giggle ensued between audience and actors, quite decorous and accepted.

And then there was Wally.

The wonderful, wacky Wally McSween is sadly no longer with us but he had the most enviable, horse-like knack of dozing while standing up. Consequently, he had missed the previous shenanigans! Roused from his slumber by this unusual hum of mirth he blankly stared around trying to discern the cause of this humour. Finding no obvious culprit, he deduced it must be himself. With the reverence befitting the Archbishop character he was playing, he solemnly lowered his head and checked his flies!

This was the funniest thing seen in years. Hanging on to one another we just turned upstage and howled. A good five minutes was added to the performance, and the audience along with the actors experienced one of those golden moments of theatre.

MARILYN GARDNER
The hag with the gag

Richard Hogan and I were doing 'The Scottish Play' [Macbeth] together. Directors often leave the character of 'Hecate' out but in this production she was in and was being played by Dick. I was one of the three witches cowering under him as he called down fire and brimstone.

There we were looking up at him, aghast. Thank God, our backs were to the audience. As he was passionately and ferociously going on and on, his plate dropped out of his mouth. The entire plate of front teeth and two side teeth fell on the stage and bounced what seemed like four or five times.

The three of us went, completely. We couldn't have spoken properly but fortunately the roles called for speaking in 'strange tongues' so we got out the rest of the scene. We were hysterical.

BARRY FLATMAN
Romancing Ann-Margret

In a Movie of the Week directed by Alan Alda I was to play one of Ann-Margret's suitors, a one-day part. I was really looking forward to it. I was going to be working with two Hollywood legends in a very intimate and private scene. The part called for a dashing, good-looking, cool dude. I got into the hair and make-up trailer and they went to town getting me just right. I was given a nice tan and my hair was perfect. I was to meet Ann-Margret in about five minutes. I did a last check in the mirror and saw that my nose hair needed trimming. There were going to be a lot of close-ups so this was a little something that had to be dealt with.

I always carry a special 'actor's bag' in which I carry everything I might ever need to be prepared to shoot. I have a wonderful little pair of curved scissors that do a great job on my nose hairs without any danger of cutting myself. For some reason, they weren't in my bag. So I quickly borrowed a pair from the make-up lady's counter. These were beautiful, razor sharp, high steel German scissors. She offered to do it for me but no, I was going to be fine. Snip. I cut right through the front of my nose.

I bled like a pig. We had 15 minutes before shooting was to start. First off, they had to try to stop the bleeding. I had rags and Kleenexes all over my face, and in walked Ann-Margret to say hello.

'Oh, hi. I'b your lover.'

I felt like an idiot. She is the most wonderful person. You meet her and the next minute you would go to war for her. And here's this bleeding oaf in front of her.

Finally we got the bleeding stopped. All over the wound they put a type of make-up, called mellow yellow, that covers the problem but disappears on camera. On camera I would look like I had a normal nose. In reality I had a big yellow blob caked all over the end of it. My self-confidence level was in the toilet.

In the scene we were sitting in a restaurant having a romantic, candle-lit dinner. This is the kind of scene that requires a relaxed, casual approach. I was sweating buckets. And she was a devil. Every five minutes she would just look at the end of my nose and twinkle her eyes. It turned out OK but it was not my idea of romancing the gorgeous and wonderful Ann-Margret.

KERRIE KEANE
At sea with a pilot

We were shooting a television pilot, *Dirty Work*, and had been out all day on a sailboat off Santa Monica. As the afternoon came around and we began to lose the light, we hardly noticed that the fog had rolled in over us. We had been sitting on the deck, dutifully staying out of the way while the crew worked in a very limited space. When they were ready to shoot, I jumped up, not realising that the fog had made the deck surface icy slick. I slipped, lost my balance and fell, apparently hitting my head so hard that I was knocked out cold.

The next thing I remember, I was on a coast guard boat with the sirens wailing. A paramedic was leaning over me, saying, 'Hello, hello. Kerrie? Can you hear me? Who is the President of the United States?' Apparently all I said to the guy was, 'No, no. I'm Canadian...'

The crew fell apart laughing. I wanted to say that if he wanted to know if I was conscious and functional, he had to ask me who was Prime Minister, but I didn't get that far.

I spent the rest of that shoot with mellow yellow covering a huge bruise on my forehead and my hair strategically and artfully placed over that. Amazingly I got some of my best reviews from that show, so I have decided that the secret to doing my best work is to be knocked unconscious.

MARIE HÉLÈNE FONTAINE
Cure for cotton mouth

Some ten years ago, in Toronto at the French theatre, Théâtre du Petit Bonheur, I was playing 'Mirandoline' in *La Locandiera*. Pierre Colain was directing.

Mirandoline was a woman, an innkeeper, who was very aware of her sexuality. She had 'big legs', shall we say, and she liked to have them wrapped around one of her many lovers. René Lemieux was playing 'Fabrizio', a servant who was madly in love with Mirandoline even though she ignored him.

Mirandoline's opening monologue of the play is perhaps ten minutes long. During this speech, this strong, ambitious woman reveals what she wants out of life. It is very intense and impassioned. All of her cards are on the table.

It was opening night. I was very nervous. And on top of that I could see in the audience the lover with whom I had recently broken up. And as I continued through this huge monologue, my mouth began to dry up as if I had two boxes of crackers and peanut butter in it. As I tried to get through the monologue, I would turn upstage as if I was taking some Miles Davis moment, and I would try to bite my lips, my tongue, anything to get blood or saliva or something into my mouth. I couldn't do it. I couldn't speak. My voice sounded like sandpaper. I was desperate. The audience started to shift and mutter. Suddenly I got an idea. With the last of what was left of my vocal chords, I called for Fabrizio the servant.

Poor René responded from back stage, 'Oui Madame?' I called him into the room on stage and he entered as Fabrizio, completely dazed and confused because he is not supposed to be on at that point. All I remember is this dear, innocent, panic-stricken face staring at me as I demand that he come over to me. Then I kissed him, hard and deep. My tongue must have touched his kidneys, I'm sure. And bless him, he let me do it for as long as it took to get some saliva in my mouth. Finally I released him, sent him off to the kitchen completely stunned, and continued with the monologue.

René told me later that he was so dry himself after that kiss, that he went back-stage and drank a gallon of water.

ELIZABETH SHEPHERD
Acting dead

I was in London, England doing a play called *Les Parents Terribles* at the Orange Tree Theatre, directed by Derek Goldby. I was mum, 'Yvonne', and at one point in the play I asked my son to come and cuddle in bed with me. While I hoiked myself over in the bed with my hands to make room for him, I accidentally dislocated my right thumb. I got through the scene and through the rest of the play until the end when Yvonne died.

I was lying on the bed acting dead, and the actor playing my husband was acting being upset so earnestly that he was *squeezing* my injured hand! He squeezed so hard that the corpse could barely prevent itself from screaming!

BRIAN GEORGE
Holding the tableau

We opened a student production of *Dracula* in my University of Toronto days with a rather Victorian tableau of the entire cast on stage. I stood behind the girl who was playing my wife, my hands on her shoulders as if I was posing for a formal photograph. We had to hold this tableau for what seemed like ages while the audience filtered in. Of course, it was imperative that we all remain dead still or the effect would be spoiled. Sometimes this was more difficult than others.

I have, shall I say, a rather long 'distinctive' nose. It has always plagued me with hay fever. As the audience filed in, I began to realise that I had that nasty telltale tingle in my nose that came with the early stages of my hay fever. My nose began to run. As I stood stock still I could feel a thin trickle slowly drain towards my upper lip. I thought, oh no! What do I do? Do I wipe my nose and break tableau, or hope I can sniff it back? So I started to quietly inhale very deeply. Not enough. Then I tried a few short, I hoped innocuous, sniffs. But it was at that stage where the mucus is very clear and watery and the sniffs didn't work. The trickle continued, but I was determined *not* to break the pose. The mucus reached the tip of my nose, formed a drip, and slowly, slowly started to elongate into a clear, wet, shiny hanging thread.

At this point, the audience had suspected nothing was amiss. I was desperate to get rid of this embarrassing drip somehow without breaking the tableau, so I thought I would try to blow at it out of my mouth and hopefully send it off to the side somehow. The girl sitting in the chair in front of me had by then figured that there was a problem and that she could be 'in the line of fire' if something were to drop. She hissed at me, '*Do* something!' All I could do was apologise to her again and again. I was in agony.

Meanwhile, this drooly bit of mucus was getting longer. I began to sway, I hoped, imperceptibly, thinking maybe I could swing it off. The audience had, by that time, noticed this shiny thread swinging like some grotesque pendulum from the tip of my nose. They were mesmerized, staring. I prayed for the lights to go down.

Finally, the drip released and dropped with a quiet 'plip' on the girl's shoulder, much to her profound disgust. I was mortified.

Only *then*...did the lights go to black.

It was the most humiliating moment I have ever had on stage.

MONICA PARKER
Mr Hoppy-kins

I was hired to be in the movie, *The Road To Wellville,* directed by Alan Parker Jr. I was so excited. Here I was going to North Carolina to do a movie with *the* Anthony Hopkins, Best-Actor-Oscar-for-*Silence of the Lambs*-Anthony Hopkins!, and on top of that...Bridget Fonda, Matthew Broderick, Dana Carvey, John Neville, John Cusak and on and on...It was endless. We were to be on location, staying and also shooting in the spooky hotel that prompted Stephen King to write *The Shining,* Mohawk Mountain House.

My first day on set, I was sick as a dog. I had been up all night with a 103°F fever and the last thing I wanted was to have anyone know I was ill. I went straight to the set nurse and said, 'Just give me something, anything that makes me OK.' So there I was, dead tired, nearly delirious with fever, pumped up on all these drugs, doing this weird movie in this strange, gothic hotel. I was really 'out to lunch'.

I was playing an Englishwoman so of course I had to do the accent. During my close-up Anthony Hopkins walked onto the set. All I could think of was that I was about to work with one of the greatest actors alive, *and I have a fever!* I know I am completely out of it on these drugs and I have to do this accent. *He'll see right through me.*

Every brain cell I had left was instantly concentrating on saving my butt. I just had to *do it!* And it's even harder when someone is watching. Whatever I did, I got through it and I was about to leave. As I made my way off set, someone stopped me, turned me around and introduced me to Sir Tony. He said to me, 'Oh, it is lovely to meet another Brit.' In my own voice I said, 'Thank you. Thank you very much.' He said, slightly surprised, 'You're not from Britain?' So I explained that yes, I was born in Scotland but raised in Canada and that I didn't consider myself British anymore. He smiled and said, 'I lost money on you.'

So the movie came out, and God love him, Sir Tony had chosen to play the vegetarian Dr John Kellogg as an American rabbit. He wore those weird bunny teeth, and he talked and moved like a rabbit. I'm in the only movie in film history in which Anthony Hopkins has been bad. Hard to believe.

Matthew Broderick quipped, 'I was so hoping to be in a movie with the *English* Anthony Hopkins.'

TRISH O'REILLY
The actor's friend

Actors share many things in the course of working and playing together. One of the things they share, unfortunately, is germs. Passing a truly vicious cold around may be one of the deeper bonding experiences available to a cast, but I for one could live without it.

It's not so much that I mind reeling around the stage and bouncing off the scenery with a high fever. What I really hate is that little tickle in the back of the throat that won't go away. I don't think there is anything more horrible (short of dying) than to be seized onstage with an uncontrollable coughing fit.

One of my very first professional jobs was *The Pinchpenny Phantom of the Opera* at Cullen Dinner Theatre. When we began rehearsals, Tony Hamill, who was playing the theatre manager, 'Gaston', was already ill with bronchitis that turned into bronchial pneumonia. He staggered through it all, managing to get well without taking any time off, but in the process he just about lived on a throat lozenge medication called 'Fisherman's Friend'. He always had one in his mouth and shoved it in his cheek to speak. If he had to sing, he'd pop it out and stick it somewhere on the set. The two by fours on the back of the flats were covered with his sticky little gifts.

As 'Pristine', the beautiful (but stupid) aspiring opera singer who is Gaston's love interest, I had to really kiss someone for the first time in my life. I was feeling terribly shy about performing such an intimate gesture with this virtual stranger, and as well was fighting my fear of imaginary 'boy germs'—never mind the very real germs flying around. The pungent aroma of Fisherman's Friend did not add to my enthusiasm. However, I managed to stay calm—and, for a while, healthy—and eventually came to enjoy those kisses. Very much, indeed!

Six weeks later, at the end of the run, it was my turn to get the bug. The cough began as a tickle, progressed to a rasp, and soon I was hacking away in earnest. For some reason, I always seemed to have a coughing fit during my little soliloquy scene in the 'dressing room'. It was torture. I would be alone on stage, desperately coughing and choking with no one else out there to fill the time with a clever ad lib. The stage manager finally offered to put a glass of water on the counter as part of the pre-set—just in case. But it got so bad that the water didn't help. On one particular day, my throat seized up, my eyes watered, I tried to speak, then just as I lunged for the water, I saw it—a Fisherman's Friend, six weeks old, covered in dust and well-ripened pneumonia germs, a beautiful, blessed Fisherman's Friend.

I had that sucker in my mouth before you could say 'streptococci'. And thank God for it because it got me through the scene.

I was grateful to Tony for a lot of things on that production—for being kind and supportive and loads of fun to work with when I was a nervous beginner. But I don't think I was ever more grateful to him than I was at the moment when I saw that precious lozenge!

SHARON NOBLE
On flying from the flu

There was a time in 1980 when I was working at Stage West Regina in a murder mystery entitled *Busybody* with the late Nancy Culp as the star. The flu had ravaged the cast, felling Nancy Culp and sending her back to Los Angeles for treatment. Judy Leigh Johnson, already in the cast, was moved into the lead role of 'the busybody charwoman' on practically a moment's notice. A local performer was moved into Judy's role and the show went on...except we were all suffering from the flu.

I, in particular, had been having laryngitis and severe coughing spells. One night, I found myself with an overwhelming urge to cough in that particular moment which comes to all murder mysteries, the revelation scene. The police officer, played by John Swindells, was accusing each of us in turn. Finally Judy, as the charwoman, embarked on a long monologue which pointed to each of us in turn, the end of which was to unmask me as the murderer.

Sitting very still, clenching my stomach muscles, I *tried* not to cough, but large tears were rolling down my face and I knew that I would explode any minute. I calculated the duration of Judy's speech and put a plan into action. Judy's face took on a pallor of confusion and anxiety when I unexpectedly stood up *and left the stage*. Of course, she had *no* idea what was happening!

I ran full bore to the dressing room, coughed my lungs to tatters, then ran to the rear door by which a novice actor playing a young police officer was waiting his entrance. Judy was about to wind down her monologue...and I had somehow to get back on stage.

The young actor was astonished to see me beside him. I whispered to him to take me strongly by the arm and shove me ahead of him, as if he had found me trying to leave and was forcing me back into the room. He was puzzled but agreed. A moment later I was upstage centre. Judy wiped sweat of panic from her brow and, back in charge, pointed her finger accusingly at me. Sweet applause erupted from an audience who never knew anything had gone amiss.

RALPH ENDERSBY
Danger on the set

One might think runaway horses, speeding dog sleds, and two-shots shared with bears, moose, and rattlesnakes might be career hazards. But in fact, an approaching love scene presented what I feared would be a life-threatening situation.

On a peaceful evening at a farm in northern Ontario, during the shooting of the feature film *Homer*, our busy, efficient cast and crew were informed that a local cat, found dead on the farm the day before, had tested positive for rabies. It was essential for anyone who had been scratched or bitten by the animal to undergo a painful series of injections directly into the stomach—with a very long needle. Fortunately, I had never met the creature but my fellow performer, Trudy Young, was about to face those nine, terrifying needles.

That's where *my* problem began. Trudy and I were scheduled to share romantic moments in selected scenes the following morning. I was concerned that I might have to kiss a rabid actress.

The minute I arrived home that evening, I called my doctor and then a veterinarian, inquiring about my chances of getting rabies from kissing a girl who could have rabies. Their questions were difficult to answer.

'How passionate would the kiss be?'

Naturally, this was not up to Trudy or me, it was up to John Trent, our director, and many years in the business had taught me to take direction seriously.

'Will saliva be exchanged?'

Again I wavered, unable to answer. It was not something I could plan. Finally after a few additional questions I got the answer I was looking for from the vet.

'There's a two-week incubation period, so enjoy yourself.'

I only had to hope that John didn't reschedule the scene to the end of the picture. As it happened, the scene was shot as originally scheduled and both Trudy and I survived.

BARRIE BALDERO
La, la, la

I was playing 'Sir Toby Belch' in Shakespeare's *Twelfth Night* at the Bastion Theatre in Victoria. I had gone out for dinner one night with Stan Lesk, the actor who was playing 'Feste'. We got to the theatre and started the show.

As we progressed Stan began to feel ill and we deduced that he must have eaten some bad fish. We got to the scene where 'Malvolio' chastises all the low characters for carousing so noisily and drunkenly. All four of us had intertwining lines and had to sing some Shakespearean four-part madrigal.

Suddenly Stan left the stage, but he didn't get completely off. He collapsed behind a flat of scenery. The three remaining actors had to carry on trying to say all the lines, his as well. When we got to the four-part madrigal we would sing our part la, la, la, then Stan, from behind the set, would throw up.

So the song became, 'La, la, la (barf). La, la, la (barf).'

It would have been hysterically funny if we hadn't been so worried about poor Stan.

DEREK McGRATH
That little something extra

I was playing 'Linus' in *You're a Good Man, Charlie Brown*. Grant Cowan was 'Snoopy' and Blaine Parker played 'Charlie Brown'.

At the end of the show each night we would do a very quiet, gentle, moody, soft-summer-night kind of number around the song, *Happiness is...* The cast were at various parts of the stage on oversized playground equipment, blocks and so on, painted in primary colours. 'Patty' and I, as Linus, were on a teeter-totter which was hollow to make it light enough for the stage crew to move easily. During this number, Snoopy would say, 'I like to lie up here on my doghouse and listen to the sounds of the night. But something seems to be missing.' Then he'd howl at the moon and say, 'In my opinion, that was just what was missing.'

On this particular night, Patty and I were on the teeter-totter as usual. Grant said his line about lying up on his doghouse listening. At the precise moment when he was about to howl, Patty let go with a flatulent emission that was not only amplified by the hollowness of the teeter-totter we were sitting on, but was picked up by the on-stage mikes as well. The effect was quite spectacular.

The audience started to laugh. Grant, with impeccable timing, skipped his howl and instead, continued his last line.

'In my opinion, that was just what was missing.'

We all completely fell apart.

NICHOLAS RICE
Unclenched

Gerry Salsberg was 'Oscar' and I was playing 'Felix' in *The Odd Couple* up at the Leah Posluns [Toronto] in 1991. We were doing the scene in Act One where all the poker pals have left and Felix and Oscar are alone in the apartment for the first time. Felix is going crazy—whining, crying, carrying on. Oscar is just kind of watching, trying to calm Felix down. As he begins to settle down, the moment comes for Felix to clear his sinuses.

In rehearsal, I had given this a lot of thought. How could I do something, some action or make some noise which plausibly could clear the sinuses? I came up with a kind of diaphragmatic push and a vocal roar.

The scene was going fine, as it usually did. But on this one night, I had eaten perhaps a bit too much in the cafeteria, and instead of a vocal roar, it was my other lower orifice which sounded—loudly and horribly. If my sinuses were not clear, something else definitely was. This was embarrassing enough but what really rankled and still makes me wince all these years later, was not so much the fart *per se*, as the fact that it was simply out of character for Felix. He is said to have 'clenched hair', so presumably everything else is clenched. Farts are just not part of his life. I shouldn't have done it.

Appropriately enough, I rushed upstage to open the window to let in some air. If I'd really been thinking, I would have rushed into the kitchen, found Felix's ever-present aerosol air freshener and conscientiously sprayed the room.

As I turned from the window, I had caught Gerry's eye. This was possibly the only time I'd ever seen him corpse, even slightly. I could hear the quaver in his voice and see the flicker in his eye. Instinctively, we both sniffed the air. Sure enough, the fart was more than mere sound—it was truly making its presence felt. Tears welled up in Gerry's eyes.

What was more, we could hear a slight stirring in the audience. I realised with horror that they'd heard! I could only hope that that was all. We barely regained our poise and finished the act, but the incident would not pass without comment from the rest of the cast who had also heard it, loud and clear, over the dressing-room speakers.

MICHAEL IRONSIDE
Technical difficulties

I was doing a CBC radio drama some years back, a courtroom drama as I recall. The cast included Gordon Pinsent and Barbara Hamilton and six or seven other actors. This was my first time doing radio.

These were taped sessions but, compared to shooting television or movies, the segments that were taped were very long. Even Gordon, a veteran radio performer, was getting a little antsy and asked if we could take a break. The director said that, yes, we would take a break but that he wanted to just get through this last sequence. Gordon was standing beside me and he turned to me, smiled and winked and said quietly, 'It's time for a little "technical difficulty".'

They started the tape again and we continued and as we got to one line of Gordon's, he 'broke wind' just as he said his line. It came out as the quietest little 'pffffdt!'. You could see the guys in the booth looking confused as they began checking dials and settings on their board. It was all I could do to control myself. Gordon showed no expression whatsoever. We started again. And on *exactly* the same line, Gordon let go with a 'pffffdt' again. Hands went up to headsets. We could see people in the booth with their heads together. Somebody shrugged. Finally someone came out and announced that we would have to take a little break because of a 'technical problem'. Apparently they thought maybe there was some kind of static feedback in the system.

Gordon leaned over to me and said, '*That's* method acting.'

GORDON PINSENT
Working with a farteur

[The concluding episode for the 1996 season of the television series Due South *brought together two lifelong actors and colleagues, Gordon Pinsent and Leslie Nielsen. This episode was written by one of the stars of the series, Paul Gross. It concerned two aged Mounties who used to be friends. It was a great comic opportunity for all concerned. Nielsen is fond of a little fart machine that he carries around in his pocket. He often uses this machine to great comic effect in his work (and his life) and this episode of* Due South *was no exception.]*

We were on the set rehearsing a scene where Leslie's character was to bend over to pick up his walking stick, stand up, and fart. I then had a line to Paul, 'You should be glad you're not on a stakeout with him in a tiny cabin in the dead of winter.' We rehearsed it a couple of times and I was finding it very hard not to laugh because I can get the giggles. I went to the director, George Bloomfield, and said, 'Look, if you want a proper line reading on this maybe you should shoot the scene in two parts, so you can get my reaction in a separate take.' He said sure and then didn't/couldn't. So after struggling through a couple of rehearsals I turned to Leslie and said, 'Could you do me a really big favour and don't do the fart in the actual scene? If you do the fart, I won't get past this moment, I'll die. They will be taking me away. Just give me one take without the fart.'

Leslie was amenable. He said, 'All right, Gordon, I won't fart.' We came on to the set for the take. We did the shot. He didn't fart, but I still couldn't do it! I waited, to leave a space for the fart, because I knew they would have to put the fart sound in later. The truth was, the fart had become part of the timing of the dialogue. It was the stupidest silence I have ever been through. I could still hear the fart *in my head.* I got the line out, but barely.

A whole lifetime working as an actor and I end up being straight man for a fart.

ROBERT GOULET
Even princes and kings

Richard Burton and I shared many stories and laughs over the years. We worked together in the original Broadway production of the musical *Camelot.* In that 1960 production Richard was 'King Arthur', Julie Andrews was 'Guinevere' and I was 'Lancelot'. As life would have it, I did a national tour of a revival of that show in 1993, as King Arthur. I had many reasons to think back to our time together. I had very good reason to recall one of his stories in particular.

When he was a young actor with the Royal Shakespeare Company, Richard was playing 'Prince Hal' in *Henry The Fourth Part 1* at Stratford-on-Avon, a town not far from Wales. His brothers had come to visit him and they spent the day in the pubs. He got to the theatre just in time to put on his make-up, pull on his tights, put on his chain mail, his armour, his capes, strap on his broadsword, and step on to the stage.

'Bobby,' he said to me, 'it's a small theatre and people are rather close to you. I didn't have time to have a pee before I got dressed. But I wasn't worried because, you know what it's like when you're on stage and you have to pee, the adrenalin sets in and you don't have that feeling any more. Well, the feeling didn't go away for the entire first act. Now, I'm the last one off the stage at the end of the first act and the first one on at the beginning of the second act and we only had a ten-minute intermission. I had no time to go all the way to my dressing room, take off my armour, my chain mail, my tights, pee, and put them all back on again so I stood in the wings and smoked rather heavily.

'Ten minutes into the next act and playing a scene with Michael Redgrave who was playing "Hotspur", he delivered the line, "If I mistake not, thou art Prince Hal." At this point I was to turn to him and start a fight. As I turned, I started to pee—like Vesuvius erupting. I felt like it was going twenty feet straight out. I was deeply embarrassed because my *brothers* were all there watching! Finally, with a Herculean effort I was able to stop the flow. I pulled out my broadsword, made a great lunge for Redgrave, and broke the broadsword off at the hilt. Desperately, I picked him up with my shoulder and sent him flying through a backdrop. As he was going through the air I heard him say "Mind my balls!" Backstage afterwards, he said "I did think you were perspiring rather heavily, dear boy, you left large wet footprints on the stage."'

During my tour as King Arthur, all these years later, I had to have an operation for prostate cancer. I had been told that I might be incontinent for up to two or three years after the operation! I was, naturally, somewhat worried because I only had three weeks off before I had to go back onstage as King Arthur—*in tights*!

The operation was a success, thank God, but I was increasingly troubled about how I would manage onstage. I asked my doctor to remove the post-operative catheter early, a few days before I had to go back to work, so that I could see how my body would behave. He said 'No. I wanted you to take six weeks off, you wouldn't do it, so the answer is, "No".' Well, there was nothing I could do. The doctor removed the catheter the night before I had to return to work and gave me a great big diaper to wear to bed that night.

I was expecting a waterfall. My dear wife was very brave for I thought we'd be swimming, but things were pretty well under control. I had to use the men's room a couple of times during the night, but I didn't experience any incontinence.

The next night, three weeks from the day of the operation, I was back onstage in my tights. As Richard's story was very much on my mind, I wore half a Depends and three pairs of jockey shorts with the tights over top. I must have looked formidable. When I stood on top of a mound on the set, people in the front rows could look up my tunic and see my formidability.

My first song had gone well and I was into my second song, *Camelot*, when my Guinevere, Patricia Keyes, and I were alone on stage. Now, when you sing a high note you've got to push with your body. As I hit one, I felt a splurt. I said to myself, still singing, 'Was this a big splurt or a little splurt? Did they see it? Did they not see it? Should I be angry? Should I smile?' I thought to myself it was too late to be angry. If they saw it, they saw it. There was nothing I could do about it.

So I finished the scene, and as I walked off stage with Guinevere, I said, 'Pat, in that last song, on the high note, did you see the twinkle in my eye?' And she said 'Yes. And when I saw the twinkle in your eye, I knew there was a tinkle down your thigh.'

GILLES SAVARD
Making the Seine in Paris

We were doing a Spanish play in one of the many theatres that were along the Boulevard de la Péripherie, a road that encircles Paris and marks the beginning of the suburbs.

I was fresh out of film school in Paris. This play was set in the 17th century, a three-act, full scale production. I played a young prince who wanted to kill the king so he could ascend the throne. In the first act, we were drinking many toasts as we hatched the plot. Every time there was a toast we had to toss back the entire contents of the glass, so we had told the 'page' who was to pour our drinks, just to give us a small amount. However one night, a substitute playing the page kept filling our drinks to the top.

Between acts, I had just barely enough time to change my costume before I had to be back on stage, lying in my bed as the curtain opened. The audience was not to know whether I, the prince, was in some kind of coma or if I had been killed. I lay there unmoving and as the curtain opened I realised...*that I had to pee!* My toes were curling. I began to feel as if I would explode, and I realised that I had to get up, have a duel with the villain, and lose. He was to take my dagger and kill me under my arm, and the blood was to flow. I figured that in action I would forget all about my urge, but as I got up, it got worse.

I could not stop it. I got up, lifted my sword and peed. I could see it going wheeeee...away from me. To make it worse, I was wearing pale green satin pants which were changing colour on the side where the pee was. A circle of wet formed on the carpet below me.

I was mortified. I thought I would just die. I just walked off stage in the middle of the scene. The director was there and he said, 'What are you doing!?' I said, 'I just peed.' He said, 'So what. Get out there.' So I grabbed my cape, went back out on stage and finished the fight with the cape draped over the side with the pee stain.

MONICA PARKER
Enter laughing, exit...as best you can

I was doing *Luv* at The Press Theatre in St Catharines with Don 'Ditch' Dickinson. He would drive us to the theatre from Toronto every day because I was having anxiety attacks about suspension bridges, big bridges of any kind. I couldn't cross them without completely losing it. My palms would get sweaty and I would just panic. When we came to the Burlington Skyway, he would say to me, 'OK, get down on the floor.' And I would. We'd cross the bridge, get to the other side, and I would get up in the seat again. During our run this went on every day. What a guy. He was truly a mensch about it. We kind of bonded during that show partly because of that and because nobody could make me laugh like Ditch could.

Night after night while we were doing the show, he would make me laugh, and night after night I would laugh so hard that I would have to force myself to control my bladder. One night, I remember, I just couldn't stop. I remember just...peeing. Laughing and peeing. I was so mortified. I sat down on the edge of the stage and tried to wipe up with my dress so that when I stood up there wouldn't be a puddle on the stage. Of course, the absurdity of this made me laugh even more.

DAVID SCHURMANN
Not on the prop list

We did Edward Albee's *Who's Afraid of Virginia Woolf?* for the Persephone Theatre's second season. I was playing 'George', Janet Wright was playing 'Martha', Susan Wright 'Honey', and Terry Waterhouse 'Nick'.

We were doing the last dress and technical rehearsal before we opened, and we had reached the thick of the hysteria between George and Martha at the end of the play. Janet, as Martha, was absolutely enraged, at the height of her fury. Suddenly Susan started to laugh. Everyone clearly lost their concentration. Eventually Susan, as the very demure Honey, was turned upstage with her butt in the air, actually hanging over the back of the couch in convulsions of laughter!

Now, this was the final rehearsal of a very serious play and I was furious. When we sat down to get notes from the director at the end of the show, I stood up to make a little speech and let them know just how unprofessional I thought they all were, especially Susan.

'But, David, didn't you see it?'

'See what?'

'For God's sake, it was right there on the stage.'

'What? That little piece of wood or whatever it was?'

'Piece of wood? You idiot! That was Janet's tampon.'

Going for a sense of the ribald character she was playing, Janet had decided to do the rehearsal that night without the benefit of underwear.

9

De Tours and De Cold Tours

DOUGLAS CAMPBELL
The Canadian Players

We toured works by many of the great and classical playwrights, Shakespeare, Shaw, Ibsen and so on through many towns and cities in Canada, north and south. When we set out in 1954, we really had no idea what we were up against. We would go out for maybe five or six weeks, come back exhausted, then come back and go out again for another five or six weeks. The roads to North Bay, Sudbury, Timmins and Cochrane, places further north and so on, were pretty primitive. There was no Trans-Canada Highway in those days.

There were I think eight or nine of us. Norm Freeman and Jack Hutt were the front of house manager and stage manager. They would go on ahead and set everything up. The company were myself and my wife, Ann Casson, Bill Hutt, Bruno Gerussi, John Gardner, Roly Hewgill, Willy Needles and Franny Hyland. We all received $100 a week and out of that we paid our own gas, food, and accommodations, but you could find a motel room in those days for about $4 a night. The only place to eat in most of these towns was the local Chinese food restaurant. I think we all lived on scrambled egg most of the time. We had almost nothing in terms of props and sets with us. We had one small van with a few flats and costumes and that was about it. The rest of us would jump in our cars and get to the next town on our own.

On one occasion, in the dead of winter in January, we were invited to do a special engagement in Moosonee by a gentleman, Colonel Reynolds, who owned the railway that serviced the northern Ontario towns. There was a tuberculosis sanatorium up there on Moose Factory Island, mainly for the native population. The Canadian Players performance of Shaw's *Saint Joan* was to be a very big event for the hospital staff and the local inhabitants. We would be there for four days.

Ann and I travelled in Colonel Reynold's private rail car which was like being in another world, a standard of luxury and style that has long since gone. I remember even the toilets were heated. The others were in one of the attached cars having, I think, much more fun than we were, but we could not refuse his generosity. When we arrived, there was a handbill advertising the show at the station which said that

The Canadian Players would be playing at eight o'clock in the evening or 'one hour after the arrival of the train'. I wish I had kept that bill.

The 'theatre', a Quonset hut, was absolutely packed with people, mostly hospital staff, doctors, nurses, and some other local people. The Inuit and Cree women and children sat right down front. The men, for whom there was no room in the Quonset, stood outside in the minus 40 degree weather, wrapped up in their parkas and watching through the windows for the entire performance. We didn't finish until about 1 o'clock in the morning.

Immediately after the show, we were ushered out and onto snow buses to attend a cocktail party at the hospital on the island. Ann and I were the last to come out to where the last bus was waiting. I remember it was a bright, bright moonlit night, cold and cracklingly still. As we were about to board, we heard a soft hissing noise like a snake, shhhhhhhh, which got louder and louder until suddenly out of the trees quite close to us came an Indian on a sled with four dogs. You could hear nothing, not the sound of the dogs or any other movement but the hissing of the runners on the snow. It was just magical, a stunning sight, just extraordinary. I will never forget it.

It was an enormous occasion and of course, nobody went to bed that night. We partied all night. We were there for the four days and at the end, we all got back on the train and continued to party all the way back to Cochrane. The booze flowed from everywhere. I hardly remember when we slept at all that trip. It was quite a time.

WILLIAM NEEDLES
Quonset hut theatre

A lot of exciting things happened on the first tour of the Canadian Players, beginning in Ottawa, where it seemed the whole world had gathered for the opening of *Saint Joan*.

It was amazing the impact that show had in spite of or, perhaps, because it was so simply done. We had some chairs and tables and some crosses we wore over business suits. We had six spotlights. Everything could be packed into a Bell Telephone truck that followed the cars we were in. We had a terrific cast: William Hutt, Douglas Campbell, Bruno Gerussi, Ann Casson was 'Joan', Tony van Bridge, myself, Roland Hewgill. It was an all-star cast. We went all over the States and Canada.

Colonel Reynolds was the President of the Ontario Northland Railroad at the time and it ran a train twice a week from Cochrane to Moosonee. In honour of the occasion of our visit he had tacked his private car on the back of the train and we were entertained in it. The train stopped all along the way. A woman would wave and the train would stop and she would give the driver a note that said, 'Please pick up a spool of thread for me and stop on your way down to drop it off.' It was the delivery chain of the area. You passed through frozen tundra all the way up.

The night we played Moosonee it was 40 below outside. We set up in a Quonset hut. Some Eskimos and the Indians were standing outside the hut, scratching the hoarfrost off the window glass to see what we were doing. There was no more room inside. Well, *Saint Joan* is a good three hours, if not longer. Bruno [Gerussi] kept turning to me and saying, 'They're still out there. They're still standing there. It's forty below out there.' They were as intrigued as the audience inside the hut. They couldn't hear anything or see anything but they watched for the entire performance.

When we were getting to the Epilogue I said to Dougie Campbell [both director and actor in the play], 'Let's cut the Epilogue. They must be freezing.' 'Nonsense. We're not cutting a word, not a word.' Afterwards six priests who had been up around the Churchill area came backstage with the tears streaming down their face and said, 'It's the first time we have heard English spoken in ten years. It was so wonderful. We had such a marvellous time.' Douglas said to me, 'You see? You never know.'

Then they took us over to the TB sanatorium and we toured that at about 3 a.m. We were worried that we would wake the children and they told us, 'Oh, no. They'll love it!' So we toured the whole place. We came back on sledges across the ice with the moon shining so brilliantly it was like daylight. The smoke from the houses was going straight up in the air, that's how cold it was. They stayed up with us all night. We didn't go to bed at all. They put us on the train at about 8 o'clock and away we went. That experience was really magical.

MARK BRESLIN
The worst 'Tour Story' ever

Back in '79, before there were Yuk Yuks clubs across the country, we used to send a group of comedians out west to play the local clubs in the area. These tours would be booked by a prominent music agency who were well meaning, but not too aware of the delicacy of comedy performance. As a result, the gigs were wildly uneven, ranging from beautiful theatres, jazz clubs, and college campuses to biker bars and strip clubs.

Our first tour took us to a nasty little club in Calgary which was a strip club by day and a heavy metal venue by night. Yuk Yuks was the opening act. On this occasion, we did not get a lot of laughs. We were nonetheless confident that we would redeem ourselves the next night, the second of our three-night contract. We retired to the hotel's 'fabulously appointed' suites.

At 3:00 a.m. there was a pounding at the hotel room door. I was summoned to the manager's office, where I was told that the group was not funny and that we had to clear out of the rooms into the -30°F Calgary night *immediately, now!* I waved our three-night contract in his face, at which point he reached into the drawer of his desk, pulled out a large gun, pointed it in my face, cocked the hammer, and told me that *that* was *his* contract.

We were out of our rooms by 3:20 a.m.

On to Vancouver, where we were playing a major rock venue in the 'burbs'. Somehow we were mistakenly advertised as a male strip show. The audience was full of 'lady' bikers who were primed, but not for comedy. When I came out to introduce our comic line-up, they made it clear that I was somewhat short of their expectations. One of them marched up on stage and knocked me out cold. I woke up in a hospital, to hear that the 'ladies' broke the place up and police were called.

We continued on to Victoria, which I thought would be an oasis of peace and quiet after the hell we'd been through, only to discover that our hotel was directly across from an all-night sawmill.

SHAWN ALEX THOMPSON
Landing in the Cuckoo's Nest

Shows that are taken out to entertain our armed forces are *big*, like a Bob Hope variety thing. In this case I was the host and comedy guy. There was a magician and a ventriloquist. Shirley Eikhard sang and there was a troop of dancers.

We did a show in Alert Bay which is 200 miles from the North Pole and, I believe, the most northerly inhabited spot in the world. It's basically an army base where they send bad Canadian army guys. Almost all these soldiers were there because they had done something wrong somewhere else.

We had flown seven hours from Goose Bay on the floor of a Hercules army transport plane with all our equipment piled inside. We lost a propeller on the way so we had to land in Thule, Greenland to get a new prop. That took three days. We were stuck in this frigid American Airforce base that had one thing, a little room filled with slot machines. Otherwise the place was a barren white wasteland. In true American style, there was a casino in Thule, Greenland.

Flying was difficult because there was a whiteout so we had to wait. Finally they felt there was a window of opportunity and we took off. I thought it would be neat to sit in the cockpit and enjoy the opportunity to see the terrain as we took off and landed. I sat behind the pilot and they let me wear headphones. I was pretty excited remembering a similar experience flying into Tel Aviv. Alert was not Tel Aviv. For a start this was the season of twenty-four-hour-a-day darkness. All I saw out the window was blizzard. The pilots couldn't fly on instruments because of the magnetic north. They started to talk in technical lingo that translated meant, we can't see a bloody thing. And they thought *they* were worried.

We suddenly landed on not a runway but a sheet of ice with two guys and a couple of flashlights. We were in the middle of nowhere. The Commander took us to the gymnasium where we were to put on the show. He actually introduced himself by saying, 'The men don't care about your show. They just want the mail.'

We did the show and the commander was right. They could have cared less. No laughs. No nothing. They basically wanted to kill all of the male performers and get at the dancers. We spent the entire two hours fending off these guys who would simply wander backstage at will and make beelines for the dancers. It was like *One Flew Over The Cuckoo's Nest*. At night we were very worried, especially about the women. They had to post guards for us. One guy wanted to kill me for something I supposedly said. The soldiers wanted to trade secrets with us about what they really do at the base so we would let them see one of the girls! It was just nuts.

DOUGLAS CAMPBELL
Flying into Saskatoon

When, during a Canadian Players tour, we got on the plane to leave Cold Lake, it was so cold, it took hours to heat up the motors of the plane before they would turn over. Finally they got the plane into the air and flying toward Saskatoon, which was our next date. Max Helpmann and I were sitting up at the front with the pilots. The rest of the company was at the back cabin.

As we approached, we flew right into a blizzard that was blowing through Saskatoon. You couldn't see anything at all. There was a terrific wind blowing, maybe 30 knots, buffeting the plane around quite roughly, and the drifts were well above ten feet. On top of that, the radio had gone out, so we were absolutely on our own. Now these pilots were used to flying in all kinds of conditions, but I could see even they were worried a little bit. They said to us, 'If you see anything that looks like an airstrip, let us know, will you?'

Finally we saw something that looked like a place to land but down closer they realised that it was a road and not an airstrip. At the last minute, we pulled up and continued on until we found the lights for the strip. We came in at a terrific speed, almost take-off speed, because I don't think the pilot thought he was going to make it and he wanted to be able to pull out again. It was impossible see the ground because of the blowing snow and drifting. We hit the ground like a piledriver.

They got us down safely, but we overshot the runway. In order to get back they had to rev the engine and sort of 'hedgehop' the plane over the drifts. They really knew what they were about, those fellows, though they were a little pale when we finally landed. When we got off the plane the wind chill felt like 70 degrees below zero, and we still had to unload the sets and put them into the bus ourselves. I've never been so cold in my life.

Of course, neither Max nor I, nor any of the rest of the cast, really had much idea of how dangerous that flight was at the time. Ignorance is bliss. It's only now I realise how close we were to disaster.

JEAN-LOUIS ROUX
Montreal to Stratford

Towards the end of April 1956, and after arduous negotiation, about ten members of the Théâtre du Nouveau Monde left Montreal en route to Stratford to participate in what has become the celebrated Shakespearean Festival. After our initial acceptance, the thought of this 'exile' made a few of us very apprehensive. A decision was made, mainly by the Gascon-Roux-Hoffmann trio [Jean Gascon, M. Roux and Guy Hoffmann] to go back on our agreement. When we shared this with [artistic director] Michael Langham he could only express his feelings with 'Oh! What a blow! ...What a terrible blow!...' I have to admit that our attitude was slightly dishonest.

It was March, I think, and the rehearsals were set to start in May. In the silence that followed that very British exclamation we played our winning hand: the actors of the Théâtre du Nouveau Monde would go to Stratford only on the condition that they would perform one of their own shows in French. Michael accepted right away. We were trapped and forced into 'exile' to Stratford for the next few months.

That is how the Avon cinema in Stratford was annexed by the Festival for the first time. We performed Molière's *Les Trois Farces* there. It was an enormous success! During the last performance, some of the Stratford regulars were surprised to see Christopher Plummer in the role of one of 'Sganarelle's' relatives in the farce of the same name. We were privileged to share the stage with our colleague who worked tirelessly at polishing his French accent. A meagre audience attended our few performances but the reviewers in both the local and Toronto papers gave us raves.

It was the last year of Stratford's original tent theatre. The rehearsals started off in a Siberian cold, forcing us to work all bundled up in our coats and scarves (with even our hands tucked warmly away in gloves). Nonetheless, we were warmed by a neophytic fervour. We had become cogs in a remarkably well-organised machine. Work schedules, rehearsal timetables, everything was planned in advance and followed to a tee. Since we were in the habit of not deciding what we were going to do the next day until the night before, this was truly a revelation for us, especially when it became apparent that this discipline didn't in any way hinder our creativity. On the contrary. For our anglophone counterparts, we incarnated what, over and above the strict observances of schedules and discipline, a little fantasy, freedom, and imagination could bring. A fruitful exchange.

At Stratford, we also discovered the incredible disrespect the English have for their Shakespeare. We were dumbfounded by the way they played with the order of scenes, cut passages deemed too obscure, or modernised certain outdated terms. Michael Langham éven allowed 'Henry V', as he walked about the night before the battle of Agincourt, to recite part of 'Richard II's' prayer. At that time, we French didn't dare change an iota of our classics. We were stunned by such gymnastics.

The critics were very favourable towards us. However I am glad none were present for an exceptional matinee performance of *Henry V* some time after our opening night. Stratford's apron stage allowed for spectacular entrances and exits through the theatre, either by way of the tunnels at stage level or by the risers in the back. Thus, before the famous battle of Agincourt, the French *gentilshommes* would rush forward from these tunnels in their brilliant accoutrements, brandishing banners in one hand, swords in the other, striding up the aisles shouting out their war cries before disappearing high up and out the theatre's exit doors: 'Montjoye! Orleans! Saint Denis!' That afternoon, in the rush of the assault, I tripped and found myself on all fours, striking my shins against the edge of the concrete stairs. I picked up my sword and banner, which had nearly poked out spectators' eyes both to my right and my left, and struggled to continue my ascent. My war cries, though, turned to the most traditional of Québécois curses as I hobbled up the aisle.

CLAUDE BEDE
The last Canadian Players tour

One of the last stops on our tour of *Julius Caesar* was to be Port aux Basques, Newfoundland. We had performed in Corner Brook in a lovely country club, a beautiful log cabin lodge, with a roaring fire in a stone fireplace. They had warned us of a terrible drive ahead of us on the new but unpaved road to Port aux Basques. 'There's nothing there.'

We set out early in the morning. I was driving one of the cars and with me were Henry Ramer, Nancy Kerr, and Anna Reiser. As we drove along the winding road the scenery just got more and more beautiful, all these gorgeous outcroppings of rock. By sundown we came over the crest of a hill and saw this astounding sight. Before us lay the ocean, a Mediterranean blue without a ripple. Above was a huge, brilliant orange sun just hanging in the cloudless pale blue sky. On one side was an enormous barren black stone mountain with the lacy configuration of snow flowing down one side. The picture was perfect. It was a vision of such breathtaking beauty. All stark and right there. I'll never forget it.

It was growing dark so we carried on to the town. The hotel we were to stay at was not yet completed. They had laid boards over the ground so we could enter it. All the local dignitaries were on hand to greet us. Exactly the correct number of rooms had been prepared for us as if the hotel was completed. Right down to the soap and towels.

We were welcomed by the Anglican minister who had arranged our visit and who asked if we would mind staying after our performance in case one or two members of the audience might like to chat with us. We were happy to oblige. The performance went off well, and the entire audience stayed for the chat.

CLAUDE BEDE
Two boards and a passion

Those coast-to-coast tours of the Canadian Players were unforgettable. There were hardly any theatres, you know. We just had to find whatever stage we could. We performed in every kind of hall and church basement. There was no Canada Council. When we got low on funds our manager, Dennis Sweeting, would put in a call to Lady Eaton and she would send a cheque to bail us out. It has been wonderful to go back over the years and see all the theatres and theatre centres that have been built. And I am always touched when people tell me, 'I discovered the theatre when you came through with the Canadian Players.'

The last National Tour was filled with adventures. We were touring Shakespeare's *Julius Caesar*. On one leg of the tour we were to leave The Pas in Manitoba to fly to Lynn Lake, well above the tree line. There were no roads in to Lynn Lake at that time. We set out in two small planes, one for the actors and one for the sets, costumes, and lights. We flew over the tundra and the clouds were all around us. When we landed, we were greeted by a Mountie in full red coat and furs with his dog standing beside him. He informed us that the airport was now closed because there was a snowstorm coming. We said no, no, you can't. We are expecting our other plane with all our equipment. He told us that they had already contacted the plane and instructed it to turn back.

There we were, in this far north mining town to give a show with no sets, no costumes, and no lights. We went straight to the dance hall where we were to perform and the stage manager went into gear. He took down the one spotlight and repositioned it. We lashed the tables together to make a stage. The curtains became the togas. Actresses were sewing and actors making swords out of wood and tin foil. Remarkably we gave an acceptable show to the rapt audience of natives and miners.

DOUGLAS E. HUGHES
Don't worry

In 1985 I was doing a touring production of *Alligator Pie* out of Winnipeg with Actors' Showcase, now called Manitoba Theatre for Young People. We were touring most of the province and by mid-December we found ourselves way up north at this place called South Indian Lake. How they could call anything so far north 'south' is beyond me. It was right across the lake from Leaf Rapids where we had to play the following Monday. A ferry crosses the lake in the summertime but obviously it wasn't running in December. As well, it was very early in the season for the 'winter road'—the lake freezes over and they just drive across the lake, but that doesn't officially open until the middle of January.

Our itinerary had it that we would fly from Thompson to South Indian Lake, then fly back to Thompson, pick up the van and drive to Leaf Rapids. We flew into South Indian Lake on this old DC3 with our set and costumes strapped in on one side of the plane and us strapped in on the other.

We had the time of our lives at the wonderful school there. Everyone was just so delighted to have someone from out of town come to visit. We had a great weekend. They drove us to the airport and the plane wasn't there. It turned out they had to deliver a freezer to some place in the Territories, an interesting concept in itself. So we had no plane and no way to get back to Thompson. The stage manager began to work out some way to get us to Leaf Rapids.

Like all good stage managers he talked to the natives. He discovered that it had been unusually cold that winter and a fellow named Angus who had a 4x4 truck had already been driving the winter road for two weeks. If we could just get our set, our costumes, our luggage, and ourselves on that truck, he could drive the four of us across. Now, we're all thinking, does our contract cover this, or our insurance, or...? But there was no other way so Angus pulls up in his 4x4. We didn't believe it would all fit in and we didn't want to think about the weight of it. We got everything in. We had the set right up against the back of our heads. All he had to do was put on the brakes suddenly and we were dead.

Just as we were about to pull away, one of Angus' kids ran over to us and said, 'There's a crack in the ice. And it's not a story,' and then he ran away! Angus assured us we would be fine. 'Don't worry. Don't worry.' So off we went. Sure enough, about halfway across the ice, there was this great big huge crack right across the lake, a fissure, with great big chunks of ice sticking up out of the lake. Angus' plan was to drive around the crack staying close to land. Don't worry. Don't worry.

As we were whipping across the lake we could see a pickup truck coming towards us from the other side. Except, they apparently couldn't see the crack. We watched as the other vehicle fell right into it. We drove over and there were these guys watching as their truck started to slowly make its way into the lake, like the *Titanic*. Angus, of course, had to stop and have a smoke and have a chat while people tried, with snowmobiles and chains and whatnot, to pull this thing out. When he was satisfied that all that could be done was being done he climbed back into the truck. We were, of course, imagining ourselves and our set and our costumes also sinking like the *Titanic*. But Angus got us around the crack and all the way to Leaf Rapids. We did our show and man, did we sleep that night!

TONY VAN BRIDGE
Delirium trembles

[It should be noted here that Mr van Bridge elected to play 'Othello' with a shaved head and 'dark brown make-up over the whole lot.']

The tensions of the *Othello* tours were relieved here and there by moments of the ridiculous. I remember a matinee in Timmins, Ontario, where the lack of backstage facilities made it more convenient to don make-up and costume back at the hotel. All small North American hotels have their complement of silent, motionless men who spend their lives sitting unblinking in the foyers. They seem doomed to an eternity of immobility as, hardly breathing, they stare across the hallways, waiting presumably for their own personal Godots. The small group thus employed at that Timmins hotel, in all probability, have not yet recovered from the sight of a white-robed bald Moor, bejewelled and ear-ringed, walking across their world and into a waiting taxi. Perhaps they thought this was the Godot they had waited for, and they now sit, lost in an even deeper limbo, awaiting his return.

In Brandon, Manitoba, we performed the play in an old movie house which had no stage at all. Boards from a portable boxing ring were laid across the front seats, providing an acting area about as solid as a trampoline. It might have felt a bit more secure if they had given us the ropes as well.

Since there was no stage, it must follow as the night the day that there were no dressing rooms. At the very back of the cinema was a door that opened directly onto a dark alley. On the other side of the alley was another door that let us into the side of the local Woolworth's. There—among the costume jewellery, pencil sharpeners, two-for-the-price-of-one bras, and bags of jelly babies—we made up and put on our costumes, slipping briefly into the night as we crossed the black alley to the back door of the cinema. Following one quick change I all but ran into a solitary gentleman weaving an uncertain path to the lighted main street, clutching a brown paper bag by the neck. I am willing to bet that he did not buy another paper bag for a month.

JOHN NEVILLE to TOM WOOD:
'Any good actor's bags are always packed.'

JAN RUBES
Apologies to Elliot Lake

The Canadian Opera Company tours across the country pre-dated the existence of a performers association in Canada. Those tours were gruelling. We never had a day off. We were always travelling from one-night stand to one-night stand. We would check in after a day travelling on the bus, eat quickly before the show, perform a matinee or evening show, sometimes both, greet people at the reception after the show, then back to the hotel for a few precious hours sleep before we would have to get up and get back on the bus, sometimes by 5:00 a.m. After months of this, year after year, in all kinds of weather winter and summer, we would be exhausted. Eventually the performers got their act together and became active in forming an association, Canadian Actors' Equity, to establish rules of employment and conditions for touring. Finally, we would actually have a day off once each week during which we were not supposed to either perform, attend receptions, or travel.

We were doing a very difficult Mozart opera, *Così Fan Tutte*. We finished our sixth performance of that week at the International Falls across from Elliot Lake. Even though the union rules now stated that we were to have a day off, we all voted to travel during the day off so that we could arrive at the next town and have two nights in one hotel. We would then have a full day to rest, do laundry, relax and be refreshed for the next performance.

Of course, by the end of the week the company was very tired and 'itchy' so we arranged to have a big, juicy chocolate cake and some beer and scotch brought on the bus for, I believe, baritone Vic Braun's birthday party. We had no performance that night so we felt free to indulge. And we certainly did. It was a very happy, singing bus that arrived in Elliot Lake at about 5:00 p.m. We staggered off the bus, completely drunk and smeared with chocolate cake, and into our respective hotels. Those of us who could still walk, went to do some shopping. As we were checking out our purchases, we saw a poster for the Canadian Opera Company advertising our performance in Elliot Lake...*on that very night!*

We ran back to the hotel and asked the manager if he was aware of this error in the booking schedule. He called the committee and indeed, we were to perform that night. Someone somewhere had slipped up on the dates.

The company was obviously in no shape to perform. Two of our members were completely unconscious, but it was impossible to cancel the show. We had no choice. In the end, some of us switched parts and modified others. I have no idea how we got through that performance but it must have been a *Così Fan Tutte* like no other.

DAVID BOLT
What accident?

The time was late fall 1968 and the place was Saskatchewan. Of course, Saskatchewan is also an idea: The Canadian West, which is why I bought a Stetson hat. Nobody in Saskatchewan wears such a hat, except for a few guys from Alberta and the occasional actor from Toronto.

I was working for the Globe Theatre out of Regina. There were two school companies, one touring shows for grades 0–6, and the other touring the high school show. We would meet up occasionally and put on the adult play, Brecht's *The Good Woman Of Setzuan* which is about a young woman's survival in hard times. The farmers out there understood every word of it.

I was in the little kids' show along with Stephen Markle, Terry Tweed, and Veronique LeFlaguais. Stephen is now a prominent director in the U.S., Veronique is a darling of the Quebec media, and Terry is president of CAEA as well as being a pretty sharp director. But then we were all in a show about a nice wizard, a bad scientist, and a smart kid. I forget the title. Markle and I used to liven it up by doing star imitations, like Christopher Lee and Peter Cushing, which the kids enjoyed.

The winter of '68–'69 turned out be one of the worst on record. But we didn't know that on a certain December morning in Saskatoon.

We got into the Volkswagen van—you know the kind, a Baader-Meinhoff Gang special—and headed off for the little town of Vanscoy. I was driving. A cold wind was blowing across the flat land. The road was freezing over and we started to drift. No problem. I was able to correct the drift for about half a mile. And then, just as I twigged that the road wasn't slippery at all, the left front tire was flat, we hit a pothole and flipped. No fooling. We sailed right up in the air and landed on the roof. And even though we were upside down we could tell from the skyline that we were looking through the front window back at Saskatoon.

I was still sitting because I'd been able to hold on to the steering wheel. And my Stetson was still on. But the others were in a jumble, covered with props and luggage. One by one we got out. The van was a write-off, upside down and squashed and everything smelling of gasoline. I tried to stay in control, being the driver. But I was nowhere as cool as Markle, who looked at his watch and said, 'My Timex takes a licking and...' you know the rest. Terry gave the impression that it would take a much, much more serious crash to upset her, but Veronique went berserk, crying and all the rest.

Some teachers from the school happened by and picked us up along with the gasoline-smelling costumes. Needless to say, the show went on. Afterwards, we reported the crash to the RCMP, who were very nice and believed me when I said that no alcohol was involved.

But that night our nerves began to unravel. I phoned my wife in Regina and said 'Don't worry about the accident. Everybody is all right.' She said, 'What accident?' Markle had a temperature of 104°F. Terry was in the beverage room in a precarious state of solitary stoicism. But Veronique was just fine. She had freaked out right away and got it all over with.

RENÉ LEMIEUX
Welcome to the Hoey Hotel

During the Children's Theatre tour across Canada, we were missionaries of French Canadian theatre. Because we were subsidised by the governments, we had to play every town and hamlet that had two people who spoke French living there. One of these towns was Hoey, in Northern Saskatchewan. We must have been less than ten miles from the border of the Northwest Territories. It was winter, very cold and blowing snow.

We arrived in Hoey, population 167, at about 9 p.m. at night. We would be performing at the local school the next morning, then from there we would pack it all up, travel to another town, set up and perform again that same afternoon. After the second show, we would travel to the next venue and stay in a hotel in the town where we would be doing the next morning's performance. It was a gruelling schedule.

So we checked into the Hoey Hotel, a whitewashed, dilapidated, two-storey clapboard shack that was so old it was probably built during the gold rush. It had only five rooms to rent. One was occupied by a permanent resident, an eighty-year-old Indian, another was occupied by the owners, a young couple with a three-month-old baby, and the other three rooms were booked to accommodate all seven of us for the night. There was a double bed in each room, which meant the assistant stage manager slept on the floor.

By the time we arrived we had been travelling on the bus for several hours and we were hungry and very tired. We were desperate to have some dinner but the lady who owned the hotel, who was also the cook, said that the kitchen was closed. There were no other restaurants in town and the nearest town with another place to eat was twenty-five miles away. We begged her to cook us something. Finally she relented. The 'dining room' was a corridor with six stools at the counter. Out of her freezer, she pulled hamburgers and hamburger buns and cheese and threw them on the grill frozen. The result was the mushiest burnt hamburger I have ever had. It was disgusting.

The bedrooms were so small, the doors would not open halfway before they slammed against the end of the beds. We had to go through the door sideways to get in. There were no private showers and only one bathroom, boasting an ancient bathtub with no showerhead. It was so cold, the soap was frozen to the soap dish. Hot water was out of the question so we were not able to bathe that night either.

Four of us decided to bundle ourselves up and huddle in one room, smoking and playing cards. We smoked until the room was so dense with it we couldn't see the cards anymore. We had to open a window because we couldn't breathe. The storm window was one that swung out from the bottom and could be propped open with a stick. Unfortunately, it was frozen shut. We pounded on the bottom of the window and hoped that the ice would be jarred off. What we didn't know was that the hinges that should have been holding the window to the frame were no longer there. When we jarred it open the whole window fell off the side of the building into the snow. Now there was no storm window on an already freezing room.

By that time, we were getting pretty giddy. We started laughing so hard that we hardly knew what we were doing. We started to jump on the bed and boom! the bed frame broke and the mattress fell in. We finally fell asleep, all four of us on the broken bed.

As we were leaving we picked up a package of matches advertising the Hoey Hotel. It said, 'The Hoey Hotel makes all the difference' as if it was The Ritz. For some reason we thought that was very funny.

GERALDINE FARRELL
In the Yukon

Klondike Days is a revue set in the gold rush days of Dawson City. I played 'Diamond Tooth Gertie', a saloon owner of the period, who became famous for a diamond that was set in her front tooth. It is still the wild west up there today. The sign on the ticket booth asked the patrons to please check their knives and guns with the manager...and they meant it. Poker chips in Dawson are currency everywhere but the bank.

The town also had its share of rugged individualists and eccentric characters. I had met a young miner, who said he had someone with him who wanted to meet me. I was in my saloon costume, a very flamboyant gown, hair up, feathers, the whole thing. He introduced me to this scrungy looking guy with a big scar right across his face. He looked like someone I would pass on the street in Toronto, sleeping beside a shopping cart that contained everything he owned. He made some kind of sound that didn't quite qualify as speech. He said, 'Hi ya. Hi. Um—howerrrrrrya. Doin'.' I could barely understand him. My friend explained that the gentleman with the scar had spent years in the bush and had lost some of his social skills. Dawson City, with a population of maybe 2000 people, was a big city to him and he really didn't like it much. He told me that this guy was one of the richest men in the Yukon. He had one of the most productive gold claims in the area. Apparently he just wanted to meet Diamond Tooth Gert.

Later during the run, another fellow came in drunk. He was so drunk he could hardly stand. It turned out that he had a good reason to celebrate because he had stumbled across one of the largest nuggets to have been found up there in years... I know that because he spoke to me as he was standing at the bar, 'Hey! Ya wanna see somethin'?' Silly me, I said, 'Sure.' He pulled this massive nugget out of his pocket! It was huge. It must have been 2 or 3 ounces, almost the size of a golf ball, but I have no idea what it was worth. He waved it at me and stuck it back in his pocket. He did that all night long to everyone who passed him.

Just to be up there is astonishing. The landscape is monumental and the sky is almost navy blue. One of the most spectacular sights I have ever seen in my life happened toward the end of the season. We were on one of the mountains where people go on the night of the summer solstice to celebrate the day the sun never sets. There was the Midnight Dome and, I think, King Solomon's Dome. We were up on one of these domes very late at night toward the end of the summer when the darkness had started to come back. On one side of us the sun was setting in spectacular colours, on the other side the crescent moon was rising in a blue/black sky, and in the middle above us were the northern lights. It was unbelievable, just breathtaking. The Yukon was definitely an adventure.

CHRIS WIGGINS
On working in the frozen North

One of the earliest of the Canadian black and white TV series was *The RCMP* series in the '50s. I was playing a bush pilot who was downed. We were up north in February doing an episode near Great Whale River, at that time part of the DEW Line and considered a big 'city' with 260 families.

In those days many people still lived in traditional houses. The igloo is a house, the iglooglik is the icehouse. Stairs had to be cut down into 18 feet of snow to get to the doors which were buried completely. They were insulated beautifully under there.

The cast and crew were in survival outfits. It was very cold. I tried once to ask or gesture somehow to one Inuit lady for permission to go down into her iglooglik to get warm. I was trying to say, 'Could I go into this shallow topped tent?' She had no idea what I was saying and was falling down laughing at me as I struggled to communicate with her. Apparently I'm a great comedian with the Inuit.

I asked a local RCMP fellow if he could give me a phrase to help explain to her and ask her if I could go inside her house. He said, 'Well, you don't have to.' I told him that I felt I had to ask for permission.

'No, you really don't. There is no word for "private" in their language. They really have no concept of privacy. As cold as it is outside, there is no reason why you can't go in if you can find the door. You can go in anywhere you want. It is their way. Even if they are in bed making love together, just wave and smile. It doesn't matter. They are very different about these things. I promise you.' He continued, 'We can't put signs up on the dangerous installations to keep them out for their own safety because they do not understand the idea that there is a place that they are not allowed to go. All we can do is make it impossible to get near those installations.'

He suggested that I give them cigarettes or anything I had in exchange and that they would be perfectly happy to allow me to come into the house.

A tiny woman was cutting wood that was piled up against itself in a teepee shape presumably so that they could find it in the deep snow. She was taking it down and stuffing it in the stove. She did this all day long. I was still not sure, but I followed her. I sat on the edge of a sleeping platform that was covered in marvellous furs. And across the corner of the house was a string of mukluks that had been recently chewed to make them soft, a tin of Ovaltine, and a picture of Elvis Presley. I wished I'd had my camera.

I must have fallen asleep in the warmth of this amazing room under the snow. I woke up not quite knowing where I was, surrounded by the most wonderful little faces staring at me. These adorable children in pixie-like helmets and furred tops, eyes wide open, were daring each other to touch my beard. It was the first time they had seen a white man with yellow hair and a ginger beard. I'll never forget waking up to that ring of little faces.

LARRY HOROWITZ
The Frobisher Bay gig

About fifteen years ago, I was sent by my manager, Mark Breslin, to perform in Frobisher Bay. To me, anything north of York Mills qualifies as tundra. I find out Frobisher Bay is *200 miles north* of the province of Quebec...and not even on the actual official continent!

I flew up on a transport plane of some kind with chickens clucking and oranges rolling up and down the aisle. It took about 20 hours to fly a circuitous route over all those places, like Resolute Bay, where we dropped parachutes (supplies) and everything, to get to Frobisher Bay.

It was very 'frontier' up there. People were walking around with guns slung over their shoulders. The place I was working in was called the Komotek Inn. It was a big prefabricated igloo that had a restaurant which had a deep freeze and some kitchen components and a little bar. It was *the* restaurant in Frobisher Bay.

I was a big star to these people because I had been on *The Bob McLean Show* on CBC television or Elwood Glover's *Luncheon Date*, one of those shows. I guess all they got up there at the time was CBC television.

At a big festival there called 'Tunik Time', they had walrus roping and seal races and they had a new fire engine. They drove this fire engine down the middle of the downtown street with people lining both sides cheering as the ladder extended. I waved at all these people from the top of the ladder.

The fire chief demonstrated his new asbestos outfit. All the kids were surrounding him as he poured gasoline on his pants and prepared to set them on fire. What he didn't know was that gas fumes had crept up the pant legs. So when he lit the fire, the pants exploded...the whole back of his pants blew out and he was thrown across the street. I told him that I would love to have the pants as a souvenir.

I did the show. The audience was mostly aboriginal people...and the Mounties who had raided their homes that day looking for illegal liquor. Rifles were stacked up at the door.

'Good evening, ladies and gentlemen. We got a great show for you, so I really hope you folks can really get "Inuit".'

I don't know why I thought this was funny. I'm doing my regular set, jokes about the subway, ya know, and Studio 54 and everything. They have *no* idea what I'm talking about. I get *no* laughs. It was a horrible engagement.

I had to stay there three nights even though I was performing for just two nights because that was when the cargo plane came to pick me up. There was a hotel. I saw it there but they didn't put me in the hotel. For the several days that I was there, they put me in this little corrugated tool shack. It had to be a hundred below, but this was where I stayed. The wind would blow under the door and the whole thing would rattle and I would hear animals howling outside at night. There was a whole caribou carcass on the porch of the shack next to me and at night I would hear growling.

'...RRRrr...RRR...grrrrwwl...rahwll...rrlll...'

The next morning I went out and half the carcass had been eaten. These wild *things* were right outside my door!

My third night, I'm wandering around. I'm not having a good time, so I take a walk out on the bay, the frozen bay. And I'm walking, I'm walking and all of a sudden this snowmobile pulls up behind me. It's a guy with a rifle slung across his chest. He says something to me in a gravelly voice.

'Get on.'

'What?'

'Get on.'

'Why?'

'The dogs...' and he gestures toward the ice, 'The dogs...!'

It sounded pretty ominous, so I got on the snowmobile...with this stranger...with a rifle! He took me back to shore.

It turns out wolves had cross-bred with domestic dogs and produced some kind of insane mutant offspring that kills people, carries babies off onto the ice, and everything. Apparently I almost got eaten by those wild wolf/dogs.

For entertainment, these folks would put torches into the snow and stand up on the cliff, beside the torches, with their guns. The wild dogs would come in towards the torches and they'd shoot them. This is how they'd spend the evening.

I finally got a telephone operator on one of the few phones in town and called Toronto. I told my manager, Mark Breslin, my life was in danger. I told him that the wolves were trying to eat me and he just laughed and laughed.

The last day of the job, I was so sick of staying in the shack that I went to the airport. It was a little tiny building with a chair and clock. I sat there for over thirty hours reading the VD posters on the wall that the children from the local high school had done...out of crayon. There were pictures of men and women walking together and big X's across them and other pictures of them apart from each other. I brought some of these posters home with me, along with the pair of asbestos pants with the bottom blown out of them...my keepsakes from Frobisher Bay.

I never got paid for that engagement. Not a cent. To this day I still hope that I will run into the guy who hired me so I can get some money from him.

CLARK JOHNSON
Arctic antics

I was in New York, starving, in theatre school again at the Actor's Lab. Mike Cavanaugh, a buddy of mine who does special effects, was offered a British mini series in Frobisher Bay. At the time I had no money, only three weeks left in theatre school, and a one-year-old daughter in Canada. When he offered me a four-month job helping him do special effects, I told him, 'Get me a ticket. I'm on the plane.'

I had never been north of St Clair Avenue in Toronto at that point. It was March, but it was eighty degrees Fahrenheit in New York when we got on that plane. I took almost no luggage. I wasn't really thinking. We flew to Montreal, then Fort Chimo and I began to notice there were no trees below us any more. When we got off the plane in Fro' Bay, it was fifty degrees below zero Fahrenheit with the wind chill. I was in my jeans jacket.

We got into town and I looked around and thought that this was what the American west must have been like. It was pretty rough. Everybody had guns. The 'hotel' was made of construction trailers lashed together with a bar in the middle. Coffee was $5.

So we started work. In March, it was still almost constantly dark. We were heading into eleven hellish weeks of cold, blowing flour-like snow. We stayed drunk most of the time. By the end, it would be constant daylight and still too damned cold. Most of the shooting was done on the ice on Fro' Bay itself. It was hard work. Everything froze. And there was one other complication.

This bay has the highest tides in the world after the Bay of Fundy. If you don't get off the ice by a certain time, you can't get off until next morning. At the change of tide a ribbon of water opens up between you and the land. If you don't beat the ribbon, you have to hope you have enough gas to keep you warm in the truck for the night or that they send someone in a kayak to come and get you.

Even though we knew we had to get off, every night it was a race to get through the ribbon before it got too deep. We'd drive hard with the doors of the truck open because you never knew when you were driving across the beginning stage of this rising water whether or not you'd hit a dip and fill up the cab. One night, we were heading back with about eighty feet of water in front of us. I said, 'OK, boys. We're going through,' and I gunned it. We skipped across a little bit of water and the cab started to fill up, but we kept going and somehow we made it to the beach. We were jubilant. We went nuts, jumpin' around and hollerin'.

We kept going, still movin' pretty hard, straight for the hotel to have our usual eight, nine, ten drinks. As I hit the brakes in the parking lot, I learned a valuable lesson. Salt water, cold, and brakes don't go together. I put my foot down...nothing happened. I couldn't stop. By the time I could take this in, we were up on the hotel porch and the front half of the truck was through the plywood and *in* the hotel. The guys all jumped out and went to the bar. I backed out and parked the truck and went in to join them. I passed the manager on the way in, said, 'Sorry,' and kept going. He shook his head. He was not happy.

The Mounties came. Not because of the hotel damage but because we were playing pick-up-truck chicken out in the parking lot. (By then, the brakes had dried out.) We were completely bombed and pretty wild.

'You know boys, the locals are really getting pissed off that you southerners come up here doing anything you want. We gotta run you in.'

We understood. We'd gone too far so we were going to spend the night in the hoosegow. Mostly, though, we worried that we would miss our call in the morning and the production would be pissed off at us.

We walked into the Mountie shop for booking, and the first thing I saw was a disco light. I thought, 'What the hell is that?' I looked over and there was a jar of pickled eggs on the counter. The Mounties had their own full bar...*in the station!*

We spent the rest of the night drinking with these guys and finally slept in the cells. Before we crashed, they asked us what time we had to be into work so they could wake us up and get us out in time. It was like we were all 'Otis', sleeping it off in the Mayberry jail.

ROBERT ITO
Inuit ladies

The Atlantis production of *Trial at Fortitude Bay* up at Frobisher Bay had originally cast an Inuit man to play this part, but apparently he got sick so they flew me in at the last minute.

They were very concerned that I would not look right because my heritage is Japanese and most of the rest of the cast were real Inuit. So they made me up with a thin moustache and darkened my skin tone a little. I changed my facial expression and tried to imitate the squint that elder Inuit men have from decades of protecting their eyes from reflection and blowing snow. They also have a very specific walk, they call it 'sliding feet', that took some practice. When you walk on snow, you learn to keep your legs further apart and to distribute your weight as evenly as possible. You do not lift your feet off the ground much and you tend not to take big strides. I watched a lot of documentary footage for hours to try to get it right and our translators, Ellysipee and Davidee, worked with me on some Inuktitut words and the accent.

The morning that I walked on set in full wardrobe, seal-skin parka and boots, the set was full of people who were native to the area. This was the test. I wondered how they would react, and whether they would accept me. All the Inuit ladies looked at me and started to mutter among themselves. Apparently, they were confused because they knew every man in all of the villages in the area and they didn't recognise me. Then they walked over to me and started to feel my arms and legs for some reason. I learned later that they were trying to figure out how strong I was. Physical strength is extremely important to them. It is the difference between life and death in the north and they had no inhibitions about touching a strange man to access his 'worth'. It was their way.

They spoke to me in Inuktitut and English assuming I understood both. I explained that I was from Los Angeles and that I did not speak their language. They decided that I was an Inuit who had gone south, got soft, and lost the language. Finally someone told them that I was Japanese and not Inuit at all. They laughed and laughed. They thought it was a big joke on them. They were wonderful people and they gave me a lot of confidence that I could make the part believable.

In more general terms, just being there among the Inuit was a fascinating experience. I learned a great deal about their philosophy and their value systems. They have a very long tradition of keeping an oral history through storytelling. At one point, I heard the women telling hunting stories which described how the men of the village would hunt and kill a huge whale from very small seal-skin kayaks. Another story told of the 'huge hairy beasts' that they hunted in ancient times. The huge hairy beasts were mastodons! Remains of these beasts have been actually found in this area by archaeologists. That is how old their oral traditions are.

I made many new friends on that shoot. We found that we had much in common and I came away with a feeling of enormous respect for a culture that is in danger of disappearing.

WILLIAM WHITEHEAD
Drugs on tour

A theatrical bus tour hits different people in different ways.

In the winter of 1958, a Canadian Players tour took its actors, stage management, costumes, and sets by bus from St John's to Victoria—and up almost into the Arctic. There would be long hours on the bus and then difficult set-ups in school auditoriums, always on the second or third floor with no elevators, or in movie houses whose immovable screens left about four feet of stage on which to play *Romeo and Juliet* or *Pygmalion*. And never enough time to relax.

Each time we arrived in a new town, one member of the company would be dispatched with a shopping list detailing the personal needs of everyone else, while the rest of us started to get the set and ourselves ready for the next performance.

One afternoon, Deborah Cass, who was playing 'Juliet's Nurse', returned from her shopping foray with a marvellous re-enactment of the local druggist's reaction when she asked for six bottles of his strongest laxative and then, consulting her list, added, 'Do you have anything for diarrhoea?'

DENISE FERGUSSON
How to get here from there

As a Canadian actress working in theatres from coast to coast, I have come to know my country well. Where else could you work in a theatre that housed permanent companies that spoke totally different languages? At the National Arts Centre in Ottawa we used to have parties with the French company. By two o'clock in the morning we didn't know *what* language we were speaking.

It was when I travelled all the way to Japan that I got to see my country from an outside perspective. I had the very great privilege of going on a tour of Japan as 'Marilla' in *Anne of Green Gables*. I really had no idea. I thought we were just the little Charlottetown company going to Japan. We were actually launching the great Canada '91 celebrations! We met members of the Royal Family. People lined up around the block to get tickets. It was startling how the Japanese people felt about Canada and Canadian culture. I had no idea the respect they held for us and what we do.

Les Grands Ballets Canadiens were there. The Orford Quartet, the Winnipeg Symphony Orchestra were there. It was an amazing experience and I was so proud to be part of it. We toured around seven cities and then came back to Tokyo. The final night of the tour, the orchestra played *Oh Canada* at the curtain call and they all had little Canadian flags on their instruments. Little flags on the violin bows and trombones. There was confetti flying and streamers. I cried like a baby. It was astonishing and wonderful and I felt *really* Canadian.

SHAWN ALEX THOMPSON
Culture shot

I like doing variety shows for the Canadian Armed Forces. They can be a great audience. One time we took a huge show to Cyprus when the Green Line between Turkey and Greece was being patrolled for the UN by Canadian and Australian troops. The Green Line was a three-mile stretch along the island that no one but UN forces could enter. At some points the Turks and Greeks were only a few feet from each other with their guns pointed into each other's faces, ready to shoot at any moment. A few days before we arrived, there had apparently been an incident in which a Greek guard had shot a Turkish guard and killed him. It was an accident but it caused a huge uproar. So everyone was on edge when we got there.

The hotel which had been a beautiful five-star place had been badly shelled and was now being used as the Canadian barracks. We played for two nights in the cavernous, shelled-out hotel ballroom. In an effort to be diplomatic, the Canadian Commander invited the Turkish General for one night and the Greek Commander for another. The first show was on the 23rd of December and the Turkish commander had accepted the invitation.

They had not told us there was anything we could or couldn't do, so we just did the show as rehearsed. 'Hello! How are you? Welcome to the show. Anybody from out of town?' I gave the usual top-of-the-show greeting. One of the gags in my comedy act involved a revolver-type BB gun. I would tell the audience how they were going to love the show and then, I would pull out the gun. In North America it always got a laugh.

But in Cyprus the Canadian and Turkish commanders were sitting in the front row. I wasn't up to speed on the history of the troubles there, I just did my bit. At the point where I revealed the gun there was a laugh from the Canadian soldiers, and then the audience went deathly quiet. Carrying on, I noticed the Canadian commander and the Turkish commander hustling out of the room. We went on with the show but it died. The show just died. I had somehow put a pall over the entire two-hour show. All the performers came backstage asking, 'What's wrong? What are we doing? What happened?'

Protocol had allowed the Turkish commander to bring a number of armed body-guards into the Green Zone, a fact that had not been shared with us. When I had pulled out my gun and done my little Canadian jokes the Turkish commander's body-guards, none of whom spoke English, stood up in seven different places in the room, cocked their weapons and were ready to kill me. The seriousness of the situation was not lost on the soldiers in the audience. That's why they didn't feel like laughing. The bodyguards must have heard the first laughter and realised that it wasn't an incident. Nonetheless, the Canadian commander felt it was prudent to leave.

It was explained to us later that if you are a bodyguard for the Turkish com-mander and he dies, you die. I was probably waving the gun in his direction. Near death in the lights.

GEORGE SPERDAKOS
Se offendendo

A production of *Hamlet,* mounted by the great Sir Robert Atkins for Regent's Park, was invited to represent England at the Festival of Baalbec in Lebanon. It was being held at the Temple of Bacchus and the company, of which I was one, was thrilled.

This was 1956, the year of Suez. I had been to Baalbec on my own the year before, as a tourist with my knapsack, so I knew what a fabulous place it was. I was so looking forward to returning as an 'artiste' in a robust part such as 'Laertes', but I had to swallow my youthful hopes and make the best of the five small roles I'd been given. In Beirut the Arabs couldn't pronounce all these Anglo Saxon names but they could say my name perfectly. There I was with this great Mediteranean name and my black hair and dark colouring and they treated me like one of their own.

The temple was absolutely fantastic. It was very exciting, rehearsing and getting ready to do the show there. On opening night when we looked out into the audi-ence, we could hardly believe our eyes! There was so much obvious wealth sitting out there, all the sheikhs and their mistresses and their wives, all in their elaborate outfits. We were out of doors but the perfume was creating an indescribable aroma.

The production finally got to the 'Yorick' scene with the grave-diggers of whom I was one, specifically grave-digger #2. I didn't have a hell of a lot to say so I had created this business, all rehearsed, with a bunch of grapes. I ate the grapes and lis-tened to my fellow actor, grave-digger #1. He talked and I nodded and listened and spat out the grape seeds.

Three or four minutes into the scene I suddenly felt something grabbing me under the arms. Two huge bodyguards had come up on the stage. They hoisted me into the air and carried me off the stage! I was acting. I was in my part. I didn't know what was happening. The first grave-digger had no idea what was going on. The play stopped.

I was in a state of shock. This just didn't happen, people coming onto the stage in the middle of the play. No one knew what the hell to do. Apparently they thought that I was insulting their sheikhs by spitting at them. Atkins had to come up on stage and explain, through an interpreter, that it was part of what is known as 'business' and it was not intended to insult anyone by any means, we were terribly sorry and all the rest. There was much gnashing of teeth, flashing of angry eyes, and guttural exclamations that didn't need an interpreter to translate. The glitterati took a twenty-minute break for some yoghurt and black coffee, then we finished the play.

The production was being reviewed and the next day, when the papers came out, it was me they singled out! They praised my 'astonishing versatility playing a multiplicity of roles'. One critic even wished me 'a flourishing career and a long and prosperous life'. Hardly mentioned were all the rest of the sterling company.

The other actors were magnanimous about my overnight *succès d'estime*, but Sir Robert was in a state of shock. Back in Beirut, ashen and hyperventilating, he confronted me just before I was feted by the President of the country! I relish, to this day, the heightened irony of it all and the glorious memories of that magnificent place.

LINDA THORSON
An *Avengers* adventure

Many, many years ago when I was doing *The Avengers* with Patrick Macnee, we were invited to appear in the *Circus Krona* in Munich. Part of the deal included joining the Magic Circle as we were to take over Houdini's act for one week as a publicity campaign to launch *The Avengers* in Germany. At the weekend, I was invited to a ski lodge in the mountains and was offered as my skiing instructor, Heinz, who was to my eyes the most gorgeous creature on two feet...or two skis as was the case.

I had purchased a fabulously expensive ski outfit just for this outing and had been loaned all of the equipment. As my first lesson proceeded, I tried to keep smiling through my frustration. I was hopelessly inept but determined to keep Heinz's attention and admiration for my tenacity if nothing else. We had been up the mountain for hours, Heinz, me and four others who were also taking a lesson, when I realized how desperately I needed a lav.

Well, I don't know what other people do but as a seasoned jogger, I was quite used to nipping behind a tree. By this time, I was bursting. So as Heinz switched his attention to another learner, I side-stepped my way up a hill and behind a large evergreen. Once I had finally unbuttoned and unzipped my hideously complicated new outfit, I only had a split second to squat, skis crossed in front, and experience blissful relief. But this was short-lived, as I watched with growing horror the tips of my skis UNcross...AND POINT DOWNHILL!

Before I could say 'Jack Robinson', I was gaining speed. Unable to pull a single scrap of magic out of my ski hat, I sailed past the beauteous Heinz, ski suit around my ankles and a steaming streak marking my trail, almost knocking him to the ground. Unable to stand or stop, half dead with em-bare-ass-ment, I finally slowed to a halt in front of the cabin, went inside, packed my bags and left for home.

I have never been on a ski hill since.

RENÉ LEMIEUX
From Russia with love

The children's theatre company that I had been touring with for many years, on one occasion toured in Europe, to Switzerland, France, Russia, all over. We were doing *Gulliver's Travels* in French. I played the part of 'Gulliver'. In that adaptation, he was a clown.

Gulliver visits different countries, and between these scenes he delivers long monologues, five altogether including the conclusion. One day during rehearsal the director said, 'Why don't you do the monologues in Russian?' I do not speak Russian, but for three months I studied with a coach and I learned these speeches phonetically in Russian. I can still remember a part of the final speech that speaks of Gulliver's enormous sadness. It was a very moving speech.

When we got to Russia, I was very nervous. I hoped that I could be understood. The Russians have a great passion for art, poetry, and the theatre, and they were very anxious to see theatre from other countries. Young and old, with their children and on their own, packed the theatre. They knew it was a children's show, a French Canadian production, performed in French which was not a language that they spoke or understood, generally speaking, but it did not stop them.

They did not understand the French part, but it was all very colourful and active so it was interesting nonetheless. When I opened my mouth and spoke Russian, I could see their eyes widen. They were so surprised that I was speaking in their own language, that for a few moments on stage it felt as if they reached out to me and embraced me as if they were many who had become one.

At the end they were so generous. They gave us a dozen bouquets of flowers and many curtain calls. It was very exciting. The only small problem was that afterwards people would come backstage and speak to me in Russian. All I could do was repeat my lines until one of the translators came to my rescue.

Later on the tour, a translator from Georgia (in the USSR) suggested that since we were to tour to Georgia, I should learn the final monologue in Georgian. Georgian is as different from Russian as French is from Italian, and we only had two days before we played in Georgia. For the next two days, they coached me as we walked through museums and ate meals, while we travelled on buses, everywhere, every waking moment. I finally learned it.

In Georgia we did the show in a mammoth theatre with three balconies filled with four thousand people. I did the first four monologues as I had rehearsed, in Russian. Then for the last monologue I began to speak in Georgian.

After only the first few words, the entire audience, all four thousand stood and began to clap and scream and stamp their feet. There were tears, cheers, and ovations, a huge emotional outburst that I had never experienced before or since from any audience.

JAN RUBES
Canadian accent

[As we transcribed Jan's story from taped interview, an element that is crucial to the story—Jan's natural speaking patterns—could not be included. Having been born and lived most of his life in what was then known as Czechoslovakia, Jan has a very distinctive trace of his homeland in his voice.]

We were on the tour for the Canadian Opera Company for eighteen years, mostly in the United States and Canada. In that time, we sang mostly the same operas which we came to know so well we could sing them in our sleep. One of the problems with tours, especially one-night stands, is boredom on the bus. Fortunately, the manager of our touring company was an avid poker player. So the back of the bus was changed into a nice little gambling parlour with green shades and a table. We would go to the table at 9:00 a.m. as soon as we got on the bus. It made the tours bearable and certainly enhanced my income.

On one occasion, we were leaving Owensboro in Kentucky at 7:30 a.m. to make a matinee performance in Paducah. By 10:00 a.m., I thought I was getting a severe case of stomach gas. The pain got so bad that I had to stop playing poker. The manager knew that if Jan stopped playing poker there was something definitely wrong. Just the month before, one of the members of the company had nearly ruptured his appendix so it was decided that it was best not to take any chances. At the first blue 'H' sign the bus turned aside to a town called Princeton, in the hills of Kentucky, and I was dropped off. The company, of course, still had obligations to perform the matinee further on.

At the check-in, I couldn't understand the people, what they were saying. Their accent was so strong I had difficulty recognising English words. Eventually, I understood that I was required to sign for my belongings before they could be put in safe-keeping. They must have thought me very strange as they counted about $213 in loose change that I'd had in my pocket from the poker game. The doctor finally diagnosed me as having a kidney stone and said that I would have to remain under observation. They gave me painkillers and put me in a room. I was very tired by then and looked forward to some rest.

These people all seemed to want to talk to me. I assumed that they must be interested because I was an opera singer and not a local person. I supposed that was perhaps a novelty. Soon the room was full of people, patients pulling I.V. stands, nurses coming in to talk to me, everyone in the hospital seemed to be in my room. Finally I said to a black nurse, 'Oh please, could you please...Why are all these people coming in here?' She explained, in her deep Kentucky drawl, 'Oh, Mr Rubes. Honey, you just keep on talkin'. This's the first time these people *ever* heard a Canadian accent.'

10

Bigwigs and Legends

MAURY CHAYKIN
On making a good impression

In 1983, I was living in New York City. I was asked to meet Paul Newman at his residence, for a film that he was directing called *Harry and Son*. At that time, he was living in a hotel in the upper west side overlooking Central Park. I decided to use, probably for the first time, deep breathing exercises to relax myself, not only for the audition itself but for the experience of meeting Paul Newman. I think I overdid it, because I was hyperventilating and about to faint as the casting person ushered me into the room. Paul Newman was sitting cross-legged on the floor. He said, 'Sit down.' I was very happy to do so. I kind of collapsed to the floor and he said, 'Isn't this neat?'

I did the audition. It went very well. He got very excited and when we were done he said, 'Thank you very, very much.' He was very sweet and enthusiastic. And I left feeling pretty great. I almost floated down the hall.

Later that evening, my agent told me that Paul loved the audition and wanted me to attend a brunch on the next Sunday at his apartment. This did not mean that I had the job. This was to get together and have a reading of the script with several other people that Paul had really liked.

Sunday came. I was very excited. Several actors that I recognised were there: Rob Lowe and other familiar faces. I came into this lovely gathering with a beautiful brunch buffet prepared, tables beautifully set, overlooking the park. There was a woman there who seemed to be acting as host.

Now I had always been a little vague on what Joanne Woodward looked like so I naturally assumed this woman was her. She welcomed us and explained what would be happening. At that point we all sat down to brunch. On one side of me was Rob Lowe and on my left was a middle-aged lady to whom I had not been introduced. We began to chat. In the midst of our conversation, I politely introduced myself, 'By the way, my name is Maury Chaykin. What's yours?' She said flatly, 'Joanne. My name...is Joanne.' She was not amused.

I figured I'd blown it right there. She never said another word to me for the rest of the brunch. But she did dart me a couple of very sharp looks. I thought, 'What the hell, I made a mistake.' To my amazement, Newman cast me.

A month later, we were rehearsing at an armory in the Bronx. Joanne, of course, was in the picture as well. Robby Benson was the young male lead. We were twelve or fourteen people sitting around a table in the middle of this armory. And once again, Joanne was sitting next to me. I cheerfully said, 'Hi, Joanne,' hoping she had forgiven and/or forgotten. She looked at me and made no reply. Apparently she had done neither.

I didn't have a very big part so I flipped through the script to get an idea of when I would have to talk, because I really had to pee badly. If I was not needed for a while I could just take a quick break. I discovered that I was not on for six or seven pages, so it looked like I had a good opportunity.

There was one washroom in the place, no male and female, just one toilet in a little room. I got in there and was doing my business when I heard Paul Newman say, 'OK. We're going to skip these pages and jump ahead'...to my scenes! I was in midstream...and so startled by this that I missed the bowl and peed all over the seat, all over the toilet and the floor. I struggled to get myself pulled together, barely getting my fly up and I ran back to the table. But I was in such a hurry, I left the bathroom in a mess. As I got back to the table, who was getting up to go to the bathroom...Joanne.

COLIN FOX
The Tunnel Repertory Company

At the end of a job interview in New York with director Rob Cohen, as I headed for the door, casting director Marjorie Simkin reminded Rob of 'the two questions'. I turned back, puzzled. Rob said, 'Oh yeah, Colin—two things: can you swim, and are you afraid of rats?' As this massive project moved into gear, it became apparent that those were no idle questions.

Throughout the filming in Rome of *Daylight,* over a period of 4½ months, every member of the crew and cast including its star Sylvester Stallone, Claire Bloom who played my wife, and I, was subjected to fire, smoke effects, explosions, flares followed by water, water by the lake-full plus, you guessed it, rats! Two thousand hand-reared rats from England, descendants of the furry stars of *Indiana Jones* along with their own rat wranglers!—all elements of a story of survival of drivers and passengers trapped under the Hudson River in the Manhattan Tunnel. The tunnel's interior was replicated in exacting detail on the back lot of Cinecitta south of Rome in a quarter-mile-long structure that could be set ablaze, doused, flooded, then drained on command. Its road-bed was littered with American cars and trucks specially imported for the purpose of becoming charred wrecks on the road-bed of hell.

After initial weeks of read-throughs, rehearsals, fittings, and underwater swimming lessons with the British stunt team, Stallone arrived via private jet outside Rome.

My first meeting with 'Sly' was on the already charred tunnel set where my fellow actors and I were assembled for another day of reacting to cataclysmic events. First impressions:

a) Stallone is not all that short. He's simply not tall, of average height and superbly proportioned.

b) He's actually a shy person. The entourage, the cigar, the boisterous clubhouse humour masks a quieter, astute, intelligent man, a Stallone who writes and rewrites scripts, watches his director, cinematographer, and fellow actors, and has been known to suddenly reveal the tough street-smart fighter from Philly and fire any of the above.

c) Stallone the trapped icon—who can't go shopping or dining without presidential-scale arrangements beforehand: encapsuled, bodyguarded, with little hope of spontaneity.

However, once we're all in the daily grind of making the movie, crew and production staff numbering 150, including 20 different nationalities, with English and Italian spoken in tandem, Sly becomes what he really prefers to be: an actor doing his job.

Gradually the banter reserved for his entourage (trainer, bodyguards, make-up, wardrobe, stunt double, producer—all his own staff) shifted to include us. He likes sending himself up, and making jokes and being sent up, within the prescribed limits of making fun of the capo!

His co-star Amy Brennerman, Claire Bloom, Vigo Mortensen, Jay Saunders, all of us, became known as the 'tunnel repertory company'. Director Rob Cohen had purposely cast actors who could not only act but improvise in situations that no scriptwriters could possibly predict—usually crisis situations where the survivors had to learn to work as a team or perish. Stallone became part of that team.

After one very emotional scene between Stallone and a character who will have to be left to die, Rob Cohen came up to Sly afterwards. 'Congratulations, you've just graduated from being a super star to an actor.' Stallone was not in the least offended. 'Yeah! That's what I'm doing from now on. No more fucking Rambo!'

Claire Bloom, raised in the rich tradition of British stage and cinema (she made her film debut at 16 with Charlie Chaplin in *Limelight*) looked for a while like a tourist who had taken a wrong turn in Miami, but she soldiered on with the rest of us. We had the same wardrobe for 4½ months (the film's time span was 20 hours) and we were soaked to the skin sometimes three times a day.

Thank God for Rome! The gruelling film days were easily forgotten as my wife Carol and I explored the Eternal City, shopped in Campo dei Fiore and stayed in an apartment in a Renaissance palazzo on Piazza Navona in the heart of historic Rome. When you've lived like royalty, with your own car and driver (Francesco and the Mercedes), you know what Cinderella felt like at 12:01 when it's all over.

Back in Canada, *Daylight* not to be released for months, you hit the bricks and audition for scraps left by our L.A. friends when they shoot in Toronto. Talk about it all turning into a pumpkin!

But you did it. You've played in the majors. The only Canadian in the cast. The trick is to find that elusive fairy godmother, and do it again.

KERRIE KEANE
Married to Vanessa Redgrave

In the movie *Second Serve,* based on the life of transsexual tennis player Renée Richards, Vanessa Redgrave played the lead role. I played the woman that he had married before he had had the sex change operation that made him a woman. Vanessa played him before and after the operation which meant effectively that I was married to Vanessa Redgrave.

It was absolutely fabulous working with her. She was very passionate about world politics and so interesting to talk with.

The day I arrived for my make-up test before the shoot began, I was sent to one of the enormous sound stages at the studio. No one was there. I asked the guard where everyone was. He told me that they were at lunch and would be back soon, so I went back in. There was a series of make-up mirrors with the light bulbs around them over on the stage and beside them were chairs. As I walked over, I noticed a very tall man, sitting in one of the chairs. I went over and as I sat down...*she* turned. It was Vanessa!

'Kerrie, what do you think?'

It was stunning. I had really thought that she was a man.

'You know what I've done, don't you. We have spent all morning trying to get this look with wigs and so on, but it just wasn't working. So they all went to lunch and I've cut my own hair.'

And she had, just like a man's. Only then did I realise that indeed there was hair all around the chair. She was willing to do whatever it took to get it right, even though she knew that the producers would probably have a fit when they saw her.

RICHARD DONAT
On Henry Fonda

I played Henry Fonda's son in *City on Fire*, a disaster film shot in Montreal. I spent a lot of time chatting with him on the set. He was very aimiable. We used to talk about fishing and gardening because he was a big gardener. I always imagined going to Hollywood, going over to his place, and knocking on the door to see his garden. I felt I could have done that, but sadly I never did.

One day I asked him, 'Do you ever get nervous before going on stage?' He replied 'No, no, never. Never have. My friends call me neurotic. But it's my friends who are puking behind the scenery. I'm standing there so excited I can hardly wait to get on. And they call me neurotic!'

DONALD DAVIS
Dear lady, Kate

I had the distinct honour of working with the great Katharine Hepburn in the summer of 1960 at Stratford Connecticut Festival, or as we used to say, Stratford on the Housatonic. The artistic director, Jack Landau, invited me to come and meet Miss Hepburn while I was performing *Krapp's Last Tape* by Samuel Beckett in New York.

Unbeknownst to me, Jack had proposed to Miss Hepburn that I should play 'Orsino' in *Twelfth Night* and 'Enobarbus' in *Antony and Cleopatra*. He had also brought her to see *Krapp's Last Tape*. He called me up and asked if I would like to come to tea with him and meet Katharine Hepburn. I said *yes*, of course. I would be delighted. I thought perhaps I was going to read for her or something but it turned out that she had loved my work and was only concerned that I wasn't tall enough for her!

When I arrived she marched over to me and there was I, six foot one, and there was she, five foot six, and there was no question any longer about my height. We sat down and had some tea. She was a close friend and associate of Robert Helpmann whose brother Max was married at the time to my sister, Barbara Chilcott. We drank our tea, exchanged anecdotes about Bobbie Helpmann, and got along famously.

Katharine Hepburn turned out to be a very energetic lady. She came to rehearsals with every line learned. She used to get very impatient with people who were learning on the spot, as a lot of us do.

Miss Hepburn was also very much aware of aspects of her appearance that she found unflattering. She felt her neck was scrawny. She also disliked her hands. She and the director and the costume designer set *Twelfth Night* in the Regency period, naval officers at Brighton, and all that. Miss Hepburn had to dress in naval uniform as she was playing 'Viola' who disguises herself as a man. All our naval costumes had very high collars with stocks on them. As well, the sleeves of our jackets come down to a point over the tops of our hands so that really all that was visible from the audience was our fingers. We even had padding over our hips to accommodate Miss Hepburn's general silhouette. We were all adapted to her appearance.

She and I got along very well. Kate was very fond of taking an elderly outboard out into the mouth of the Housatonic river and ploughing through the weeds looking for birds and wildlife. As I'm fond of doing the same thing, I would go out with her and we would spend hours of a morning puttering around the river. The dear lady is also very allergic to sunshine and was always swathed in scarves and sunshade hats.

At the final performance of the season I found, on my dressing table, a charming little watercolour drawing of the weeds and egrets we would see on our boat rides together. Miss Hepburn is quite a gifted amateur artist. She had written on it 'To Don Orsino Enobarbus Davis from your friend, Kate Viola Cleopatra. Don't forget your friend.' Signed Kate. It was an extraordinary summer for me. One that I have, indeed, not forgotten.

DONALD HARRON
Kate at five

Meanwhile, back on the Housatonic, *The Merchant of Venice* was being directed officially by Jack Landau but in fact by Kate Hepburn, who had even managed to wrap
the designer, Reuben TerArutunian the Intractable, around her little finger. The only
thing that bothered me was 'Portia's' tendency to shed copious tears. Guthrie had
taught me that this was the audience's job, not the actor's.

In *Final Dress*, [John] Houseman says that Spencer Tracy tried but failed to visit
his leading lady in Stratford that summer, but I am convinced that he did manage a
secret weekend. Kate had told me her *real* beau was coming (she rarely mentioned
him by name) and he must have because from that time on she never shed another
tear. Evidently there was one man from whom Miss Hepburn would take direction.

I tried to conceal my anxiety over the difference in our ages, but she could see
right through me and said sweetly, 'Donald, don't you worry. When you choose that
casket and turn to kiss me, I shall be five years old.' She looked radiant in her
costume and sure enough, when I turned to 'claim her with a loving kiss' she was
hopping about with girlish glee.

First-string theatre critics, demi-gods in those days, liked nothing better than
ripping film stars to shreds every time they dared to tread the boards. She bore it
much more cheerfully than most. Walter Kerr complained that 'Miss Hepburn jiggles
up and down with the impatient ecstasy of a woman of six.' He was only a year off.

MARTHA GIBSON
On Jane Mallett

At Theatre Passe Muraille we were doing *Ghosts,* a three-character play about a
married couple and a psychiatrist, written by Larry Fineberg. Louis Del Grande
directed a cast including Neil Vipond, me, and Jane Mallet.

Jane Mallet, a legend in Canadian theatre, was at that time in her early 70s. She
had not been on stage for many, many years because she had been raising her family,
but she was remembered as a fabulous actress. There was something of the same
feeling, that same mystique that had surrounded the extraordinary Laurette Taylor
in New York.

Laurette Taylor was a famous American actress who created the part of
'Amanda' in *The Glass Menagerie*. She was a legendary actress in her time. No one
could explain what she was like on stage. You had to see her to understand her
impact on an audience. Even after seeing her, she defied analysis. It was said that in
rehearsals, she never learned her lines and everyone thought she was awful until she
opened with an audience. And when she did, she was brilliant.

We started rehearsals around Christmastime and I remember thinking, 'My
God, how could people have talked about her that way. This woman is very sweet
but has no talent at all.' Jane was incapable of concentrating during a rehearsal. She
could never run a scene from beginning to end, but would side-track into stories.

She never seemed to know her lines, changed her business every day, could never get my character's name right, wandered all over the stage with no apparent memory of the blocking. She had, it seemed, completely lost it. She seemed to have absolutely no nervousness about the upcoming opening night and was oblivious to the idea of being on stage. I, on the other hand, was very nervous.

One day as we were sitting together she said to me, 'You know, Martha, I am just one of those actresses that can't rehearse. But watch me on opening night.' I asked what she meant. She said, 'It's all going to come to me on opening night and I will know exactly what I'm doing. You watch. And I will be able to repeat it every night after that. That's how I work, I learn from the audience.' I was convinced that we were in big trouble.

Sure enough, on opening night, she was absolutely dynamite, completely and totally in control of her play, her dialogue, her action, her character. She was so focused on you when you played opposite her, that it was as if an angel was carrying you around the stage. It was almost as if she was psychically linked. It was an amazing experience, almost a metaphysical thing.

The safest I have ever felt on stage is when I was there with her. She made us feel as if there was nothing we could not do. We could do no wrong, and that no matter what happened that was different (and occasionally she still changed things) it would all be perfectly wonderful. We had total trust in her.

The love that poured from the audience for her washed over us. She had a gift for bringing an audience into focus so that they became one single entity. Neil and I knew that she was the focus of this play, and that there was nothing that we could do but get on the ride and enjoy it. We knew we were in the presence of genius.

RICHARD CURNOCK
The sandwich gag

I performed with Dame Maggie Smith at Stratford in *Hay Fever*. I was playing 'Richard Grethem', one of the visitors to this grand house and Maggie was 'Judith Bliss' the eccentric hostess. Maggie was such an inventive actress. The action at the end of the first act is general chaos. Among the set dressings was a cake stand with several layers of sandwiches on it. One night Maggie got a laugh as she reached for one of the sandwiches. Instead of going on with her lines, she built and built the laugh by opening all the sandwiches, one by one, to see what was in them. She could have gone on for ten minutes. The audience was hysterical. All the rest of us just waited and watched in unabashed admiration.

BRUCE GRAY
I've been around, you know

My scene with Robert Redford and Kate Nelligan in the feature film *Up Close and Personal* was to be shot in a very posh Hollywood restaurant called 'Rex'. Unfortunately, Kate had hurt her back and couldn't shoot that day. To keep to the schedule, the director gave some of her lines to my character and some to some other characters. They also moved the scene from a shot of us standing at a bar to sitting at a dining table instead. They needed a couple of extras (or 'atmosphere' as they prefer to be called) to fill out the table of executives so they put this guy down in the seat beside me.

This person was a mess. His clothes didn't fit and he had his greasy hair parted from just over his ear all the way over to the other side to cover his bald spot.

I was thinking 'Now don't be grand about this. Just include him.' So I leaned over and explained to him what was happening.

'Look, we're vice-presidents of the television network in this scene and we're going to be ad-libbing about the business. We want you to know what's going on so you can be engaged in this dialogue as well.' He looked at me.

'Have you read the script?'

'Yes, yes. Several times. Now, why don't you be...'

'Executive producer.'

'No, no. You can't do that. There are no executive producers at this table. I'm a vice president and he's a vice president so you should be maybe...'

Then Robert Redford walked by the table.

'Hi, Ed.' I turned to the extra in amazement.

'You know Robert Redford?'

'Yeah, like I said, I'm the executive producer of this movie.'

Well, he was incredibly good-natured about everything and a very informative fellow. He is the agent to Tom Brokaw and Connie Chung and a host of other big news people. He was Jessica Savitch's agent, her story being the very story we were filming. He regaled us with stories.

At the fourth chair of our table the assistant director placed another 'extra'. Having gotten wise, I thought I'd just ask this fellow who he was. He turned out to be Steve Kaplan, the head of ABC news!

Twelve hours flew by like 12 minutes. He was the most fascinating man I have ever met. He had spent the weekend before with Castro and was off to Iran the next week. Redford came up to the table to ask if Kaplan could help him get an introduction to the Dalai Lama.

At one point something buzzed and Mr Kaplan reached into his pocket and pulled out this thing the size of a credit card. It turned out to be a phone. Bill Clinton was calling to invite him and his wife over for the weekend! I've never been beside anyone who talked to the President of the United States on a credit card.

He said to me that I must be thrilled to be in this movie with Robert Redford. I said 'Oh, yeah, yeah. But he's just an actor. Now, YOU...'

DEREK McGRATH
The Zen gunfighter

I was doing an 'HBOnly' movie called *Draw*. I was playing 'Reggie Bell', the kind of guy who would hide under the bed, shoot you in the back, and then brag about it. He was a seedy, cheesy, weasely little guy. I had big scenes with Kirk Douglas and James Coburn, shoot-outs with both of them. Kirk Douglas was very kind, but friendliness didn't come naturally for him. Once he invited me into his trailer and then didn't say a word to me. I didn't know what to say to start a conversation. I couldn't very well say, 'So...what do you do?' It was kind of embarrassing so finally I left.

James Coburn on the other hand is a huge personality, a big man with a shock of white hair and a big cigar. He is a very charming man and, interestingly, a Zen Buddhist. He has very bad arthritis in his hands but it doesn't affect his ability to shoot straight. The character he was playing was a legendary but alcoholic sheriff, hired to replace the town's deceased sheriff and to bring in the man who had killed him, gunslinger 'Handsome Harry Holland', played by Kirk Douglas.

In one scene, I, as Reggie Bell, had discovered that this famous sheriff was a drunk and went to his room to taunt him. I pulled a gun on him, then pulled the cork out of his whiskey bottle with my teeth, spat it out and poured the liquor on the floor saying, 'Go on...Lick it up.' James Coburn was supposed to reach under the bed for his gun, fire it and blow my gun out of my hand.

Coburn's gun was loaded with blanks but the blanks were over-loaded, so the blast actually hit me, knocking the gun out of my hand. If you see that movie and you see me react, it is *not acting*. It hurt! I had a thousand blood blisters on that hand afterwards. But what was so amazing was that James Coburn, with an arthritic hand, had reached under the bed, turned and fired in one beautiful, fluid motion and fired *accurately*, hitting me in the hand. He had had no reason to be concerned for accuracy because I was not supposed to be hit at all. In someone else's hands that gun blast could have done a great deal of damage.

I came away from that picture with real admiration for James Coburn. And I'll never forget this one small gesture. I had admired a black Playboy Jazz Festival hat that had been given to him by Bill Cosby. I never said anything to him, but I think he must have known somehow. On the last day of shooting, we were sharing a limo. He took the hat off, tossed it over to me, and said, 'Hey kid, take care of this for me, will you?'

LYNDA MASON GREEN
On day-player hell

Day players, for those who do not know, are actors who work on a project for one day, possibly two. Established actors call them 'cameos'...and are paid better.

It is quite difficult to come onto a set that is working at a pace and manage to fit into the rhythm quickly. And since you are only on for the day, the leading player and/or star also will often 'feel you out' to decide whether he or she will have to work 'around' you or work 'with' you. This process is very quick. When you are young and inexperienced, you may not even know that it has happened. Such was the case on a picture that was finally to be released as '*Highpoint*', directed by Peter Carter and starring Richard Harris.

When I was in my twenties, late one night I got a call to do a day on this picture. They needed me the next day and since this was before fax machines, the production office read my lines, and no one else's, to me over the phone. I never saw a script. This was like sending a batter up to the plate with a popsicle stick. What was worse was my scene was to be with Richard Harris! I was going to do a scene with 'King Arthur'!

I was to play a model who discovers Mr Harris' character stuck on a ledge of a tall building, trying to escape the bad guys. As one of the models, all of whom were in various stages of undress (naturally), I spent my day on set rather embarrassingly dressed in a pair of bikini underwear with a man's shirt tied around my top like an apron...and that was all.

We rehearsed the scene and while final adjustments were being done for sound and lights, Mr Harris decided to exercise his well-known Irish wit on me.

'So darlin', are ya married?'

'No.'

'Do ya fool around?'

In my little brain, I had always associated 'fooling around' with 'cheating on one's spouse' and my response came out of that thought process. I quipped back at him.

'Maybe...if I was married.'

A roar went up from the crew. Everyone seemed to be repeating something to one another and the number of guys who were collapsing with hysterics multiplied. I finally figured out that the bodypack mike on Mr Harris had been on, and the crew had been hanging out at the sound cart, eavesdropping.

Mr Harris pretended not to have heard what I had said or to understand what all the hilarity was about. Nonetheless, and very much to his credit, he flattered me by inviting me to improvise the scene with him.

MAVOR MOORE
Was I too young or too frank?

In 1940 Katharine Cornell came to Toronto when she was about forty, playing 'Juliet' in a touring production of Shakespeare's *Romeo and Juliet*. I was about twenty at the time and for me she *was* Juliet. She was absolutely sensational. She didn't try to do it with make-up, or try to make herself look young. She just played the spirit of the character.

It was a superb cast. (All of these people young, at the time, remember.) Basil Rathbone as 'Romeo', Brian Aherne as 'Mercutio' and a very young American actor called Orson Welles played 'Tybalt'. Welles was made up quite extravagantly like a cat. His hair was combed up into two ears and he had a long mustachio that was like cat's whiskers. He overplayed it like mad, quite out of keeping with the rest of the cast but he made an impression.

A year or two later, I was a radio features producer at the CBC, the youngest producer they had, and I was to produce a series called *Nazi Eyes on Canada*, a melodrama about what the Germans were going to do to Canadians. Welles had come up to star in one episode. Frank Willis was the producer of the series and I was the director.

At a reception held for Welles upon his arrival I was introduced to him as his director. In trying to make friendly conversation, I said to him, 'Mr Welles, the last time I saw you was as Tybalt in *Romeo and Juliet*.' He said, in a very disparaging tone, 'Ah, yeah. What a production!' I replied, 'I thought the production was pretty good. I just thought you were a bit outrageous in it. However I did have a professor, at the time, who thought, like you, that the production was lousy but that you were marvellous.' Welles, with an absolutely straight face and not a drop of amusement, said, 'Well, the professor was right.' The consequence of that was that he 'declined to act' under so young a director. I was barely 23, he was 26. But he wouldn't work with me so Frank Willis took over the direction and I took on an acting role opposite Welles.

It was a fascinating experience. Travelling with him at the time was a secretary called Miss World. Her principal job was to keep him supplied with magic tricks, card tricks, and bangles and ropes (which he played with all the time), and to deliver messages.

I remember one occasion when Miss World interrupted a rehearsal by rushing up on stage breathlessly saying 'Oh, Mr Welles, Mr Welles. Miss del Rio is on the line from Hollywood.' Orson turned away from the microphone and said, in that distinctive voice of his, 'Oh, God. Tell her I love her.' He waved her away, turned up the collar of the cloak he always wore, and went right back into the scene.

PAUL SOLES
Curtain cough

I had the distinct pleasure of being in a production of *Macbeth* with Glenda Jackson and Christopher Plummer. We ended up on Broadway after several cast changes and out-of-town stops. One amusing night in Baltimore, we were playing in a concrete theatre centre built in the late sixties. This particular night everybody in the audience was coughing and I mean everybody. The sound ricocheted off the concrete, driving the acting company a little crazy, especially during the dramatic moments.

Now, these were two great performances from these two stars. I used to stand in the wings and watch them get better and better and richer and richer and, always, surprising. I was playing the 'Doctor' so I was out onstage during Lady M.'s mad scene. Jackson chilled me every night. She was absolutely unpredictable, including the curtain call she gave this particular night.

We had all had our bows, with the exception of the stars. Glenda swept onstage in her red velvet gown and from the instant she was visible she coughed. And she didn't stop coughing until the curtain came down. It was beautiful.

TONY RUBES
On *Yentl* and Barbra

The movie *Yentl*, directed by and starring Barbra Streisand as 'Yentl', shot its village sequences at a location about an hour outside of Prague. An English actor and I played young Yeshiva students walking through the village market place discussing books as 'Yentl' followed us. It was basically a one-day shoot for us but we had been going out to the location every day for two weeks and had not been required on camera as yet. Barbra was directing and had been rewriting a lot of the dialogue herself, so we were behind.

Finally, on a moment's break, Barbra came by and asked us if we were ready to do the scene. We said, sure. So she asked us to run it through for her. We did that. But after a week of sitting around with nothing else to do but work on our little scene, every word had become huge and weighted and the delivery was 'Shakespearean'. She did not react well.

'Oh no. No, no. You've got to tone it way down. And I don't like those lines anyway.'

This was a great relief because we didn't really understand them ourselves, which made our overblown delivery even more embarrassing. So we sat down in front of the Winnebago and the three of us rewrote the whole scene. She took our suggestions often and it was probably the most fun we'd had on the shoot up until that time.

So we shot it. We walked through the market with Barbra as 'Yentl' following us and eavesdropping on the conversation. The scene went well and that was a wrap for us.

We were waiting at the edge of set for the shuttle bus back to Prague. As we stood there, we thought it would be nice to get a picture of us with Barbra as a memento of the shoot. But she was busy in the trailer dealing with wigs and so on, so we thought better of asking. One of the veteran English actresses, Miriam Margolis, came by and said she would take care of it for us. She walked about half-way to the trailer and she yelled at Barbra to come out and get a picture taken 'with the boys'. Barbra leaned back and looked out the window and indicated that she couldn't leave at that moment. We decided to let it pass.

Later, as we were waiting for the shuttle, looking like a couple of lost puppies, we saw Barbra go by us on the dirt road in her chauffeur-driven green Mercedes. We waved, she waved back and continued on along the road. They turned left up at the corner and drove out of sight. Minutes later, we saw this same Mercedes driving, in reverse, back to that corner, back around the corner, and, still in reverse, all the way to where we had been standing. The window came down and Barbra stuck out her head.

'You guys want to take those pictures now?'

I pulled out the camera and she jumped out of the car. We took a few shots each of me, then my friend, with Barbra looking as we were the best of pals. We thanked her, she jumped back into the car and drove off. She was wonderful.

SEAN MULCAHY
The best telegram ever

At the Citadel Theatre, Edmonton, 1970, I was sharing a dressing room with Paul Kligman. Paul was playing Shakespeare's *Othello*, I was 'Iago' and the show was directed by Henry Comer. Prior to the first run of the show, Paul and I were quite worried, facing a full house for the first time, when a cable arrived from Johnny Wayne, one half of Wayne and Shuster, and an old friend and colleague of Paul's. It said:

'Dear Paul, don't forget to wait for the laughs.'

He laughed and then I laughed and the show went off like a charm. It was a huge success for which they were scalping tickets, in Edmonton, for Shakespeare!

MONICA PARKER
Advice from a veteran

When I was working in Toronto on a picture called *Improper Channels*, starring Alan Arkin and Mariette Hartley, in the course of conversation with Alan one day I asked him if he had any advice for me. I had been planning to move to the United States, specifically California, and was happy to have some guidance from someone who had lived and worked there in L.A.

He nodded sagely and said, 'Yeah...I do.' I said, 'Oh, great. Well, what is it?' He paused for a minute to consider what he would say, and continued, 'Pay attention,' he said. 'This is really important.' I waited. Finally, he said, 'Never work with Shelley Winters.'

That was it.

YANK AZMAN
Gilda-ed beginnings

In 1973 or thereabouts, I was doing a show at Toronto's Global Village Theatre. The girl selling tickets in the box office had just come back from a trip to Florida. On the way back through New York City, she had seen a musical that she thought was wonderful. The same show was about to begin re-casting for a Toronto run.

She got up a little song (*Zippi dee doo da*, I think), worked on it, and tried it out in a local bar. Finally, she auditioned and got the part.

The show was *Godspell*, and the box office girl was Gilda Radner.

GORDON CLAPP
Lincoln?

Brian Dennehy cracked me up with this story, as an illustration of how 'full of it' actors can be.

He had been somewhere shooting the 'Oppenheimer' movie, I forget the title it was released under. He and Barnard Hughes and a few other people were out to dinner at a restaurant. They were regaling each other with stories rather loudly and generally enjoying their meal and having a good time when a gentleman walked up to Brian Dennehy.

'Lincoln?'

'Lincoln! Hell no. I've never played Lincoln. I've played Grant. Do I look like a Lincoln, to you? Barney here has played Lincoln somewhere. And Joe over here might have...didn't you play Lincoln in the States?'

'No. Do you *drive* a Lincoln. The car park is closing now.'

DAN MacDONALD
Call me 'Douglas'

The Canadian Players attracted the best of Stratford's backstage and on-stage talents: designers, directors, costume and set builders, wig makers and, of course, the most talented actors available—people like Douglas Rain, Max Helpmann, Kate Reid, Ann Casson, and the subject of this anecdote, the redoubtable Douglas Campbell.

I have always referred to that great, rumbling bear of our theatre, Douglas Campbell, as 'Douglas', never 'Doug' or 'Dougie'. I've heard others use those diminutives (whether to his face or not I don't recall) but I have not; not since he bellowed, 'Stop calling me "Mister"! We're all actors here. My name is "Douglas".' I did what I was told, and 'Douglas' it has been during three pleasant decades of knowing the man.

There were other reasons for abiding by his admonition, among them: 1) an insecurity that this roiling pacifist might actually break my bones; 2) *any* MacDonald might find it more pleasant to mouth his first, rather than last name; 3) he was a force on the Canadian scene as leading actor/director at Stratford, plus he was my company manager on a Canadian Players' tour; 4) he was hugely talented, experienced, congenial, and eager to pass on his knowledge to us, the younger performers and finally, 5) he had informed us one night that he disliked 'Dougie' or 'Doug'. He considered them creeping, disrespectful Americanisms.

'Don't call me "Dougie"!', he boomed out over post-performance drinks in a hotel room one night, 'I *hate* "Dougie"! My name is "Douglas"!'

Then, with a roaring laugh he added, '*And I hate that too!*'

LISA LANGLOIS
On location with Tony Curtis

I was working on *It Rained All Night the Day I Left*, a film which at the time boasted the largest budget ever for a Canadian film, five million dollars. Since it was 1979 and we were shooting in Israel, the film also carried war insurance.

Tony Curtis starred in the film. As he sat in the El Al waiting room, Moshe Dyan walked by, saw him and then did an about face. He walked by Tony again, hesitated, and then finally bent down face to face with Tony and asked, 'Are you Tony Curtis?' Tony looked Moshe squarely in the eye-patch and replied, 'Are you Moshe Dyan?' Moshe exclaimed, 'I love your movies!' and Tony retorted, 'I love your wars!'

And later in the shoot...

Since we were filming in the desert, Bedouins would sometimes stumble upon our shoot. One group of Bedouins encountered Tony as he was sitting on a horse wearing a cowboy hat. 'Are you John Wayne?' one of them asked shyly. And Tony said, 'No, I'm his son.'

They were very happy.

I, on the other hand, was not recognised. However another Bedouin, presumably looking for another wife, offered the production manager three camels and two horses in exchange for me. Female horses to boot! I was touched.

WILLIAM HUTT and DOUGLAS CAMPBELL, snarling
affectionately to one another backstage:
Campbell: 'You can't play the great classical roles with knock knees!'
Hutt: 'Can't play the great roles with no sense of humour!'

MERVYN 'BUTCH' BLAKE
Advice from Bernard Shaw

Very early on in 1930, when I was at the Royal Academy of Dramatic Art, we were doing George Bernard Shaw's *You Never Can Tell*. A well-known actor was directing it, Ivor Bernard I think it was. We were in the middle of rehearsing when the director said, 'Well, today we are going to have a very, very important visitor coming. I can't tell you who it is. But I hope you will be on your best behaviour. Oh, Mr Blake, would you run down to the registrar's office and get me my trunk copy. I've forgotten it like a silly idiot. And hurry up, because this visitor will be here soon.'

I had to go down to the registrar's office at the front of the building, right down the wonderful grand stairs of the front of RADA. As I was pelting down the stairs I bumped into an old man who was coming up the stairs. I said, 'I'm frightfully, frightfully sorry. I've got to get something from the office and I'm in a terrible hurry.' He chortled, 'Ho, ho, ho.' And I rushed on down to do my errand. When I came back up I discovered, to my chagrin, that I had bumped into Bernard Shaw! When he was introduced to us, he said to me, 'So you're the young man who's in such a hurry to get down the stairs of life. You must be careful of those who are coming up to the top, especially those who are a little older than you.' It was great fun because he was laughing all the time.

Then he proceeded to direct us and show how every part was done, rather broadly we thought. He was awfully nice to us. Finally we said good-bye and then he disappeared. Ivor Bernard said, 'Mr Shaw is a wonderful writer, but he's a bloody awful actor. Don't do a damned thing that he told you. You do what I tell you.'

On BEATRICE LILLIE
Royal Subjects

The show was called *Spring Party* and they did three a day many times for the Eighth Army from Gibraltar to Cairo. They performed for General Montgomery in Tripoli and for General Eisenhower in Algiers.

'In Tunis, at one of the shows,' Bea said, 'the flies were so terrible they gave me some netting around my bed. I waited until all the flies were in and then I got out of bed and had a good night's sleep!' In a room which she shared with Dorothy Dickson, she found a rat drinking from a leaking tap in the sink.

In Tunis Bea was downed by dysentery and confined to her bed, forcing her to miss a party given in honour of King George VI. Then His Majesty was laid low by the same malady. Later, during a garden party at Buckingham Palace, Bea was presented to His Majesty. She voiced her disappointment at missing the Tunis party and gave the reason for her absence. H.M. commiserated with her, stating his problems with the same disease. The King excused himself and Bea was surrounded by her friends eager to know what she and the monarch talked about. 'Diarrhoea!' cooed Bea.

PAUL SOLES
In the shadow of greatness

In my starting-out days in London, Ontario I worked at a radio station doing a Saturday afternoon early phone interview program. Among the subjects we covered were the Arts. I had a great respect for Charles Laughton, who was the best reader of the English language at that time and who was coming through London with his one-man show of readings. What a break!

He'd been booked into the Grand Theatre by its manager, a ripe old character named Ken Baskette. Ken was to arrange for us to do an interview with the great man. I was to call Mr Laughton at his hotel the afternoon of his performance. Came the appointed time, I made the call and asked for Mr Laughton. The operator told me that he had left strict instructions that he was not to be disturbed. 'He has a performance tonight.' I said, smooth as butter, 'Yes, I know. It's all been arranged by Ken Baskette so you can put me through.' And she did.

The gravel voice answered. 'Hello.'

'Ah, Mr Laughton, this is Paul Soles at CFPL. I've called up about the interview that Ken Baskette has arranged.'

'*What?* No one told me. You have awakened me from the first sleep I have had in three days!'

I was in my mid twenties, in absolute awe of this person and, at that moment, I felt about an inch high. He went on to blast Ken Baskette and me and everything else. Then he cooled down and decided we could, indeed, go ahead for eight or ten minutes. An hour later the interview ended. He was an immensely generous person.

I went to see the show that night and I went back at the intermission to pay my respects. I opened the stage door and there he was! Lit in silhouette by the light of the little bulb over the call board, he was sitting on, and overflowing, one of those metal ice-cream-parlour chairs. He had an open briefcase, a bottle of VO sitting in it, and his head in his hands. He was looking at the call board. There he was, the same man who had just held the entire audience in thrall, with a tiny little glass of scotch, sitting all by himself.

I introduced myself and he blustered for a moment then beamed a big smile, looked backstage and up into the loft and said, 'Beautiful theatre this, isn't it? Do you know it's known all over the world? Lovely theatre.' A moment I treasure.

AMELIA HALL
Canadian Repertory Theatre days

While Dora [Clarke] and I had been going quietly mad in the office those first two weeks [of the company's existence], we had had a visit from a Montreal actor. I had never worked with him, but I knew of his work in Montreal. After twenty minutes I asked him if he would mind returning in an hour, when I would be free to continue the interview. After he had left I looked at Dora, 'Well?' She laughed. I continued, 'Since your impression is the same as mine, I'll take him for a walk when he comes back and set him straight.'

He came back, and we walked along Sussex Street.

'Since you came to Ottawa for the purpose of asking me for a job, why did you behave in the office as if you had come to ask me for a date?'

'Bruce told me that was the way to get around you.'

'Bruce must have been pulling your leg. It's not very flattering to me to suggest that I am so desperate for male attention that I have to pay a man a salary to receive it!'

He agreed.

'And furthermore, I don't care much what you and I feel about one another as a man and a woman, just so long as you do your work well. Now, I don't think you are a character actor, and since you'll probably play only young men, I won't be able to put you on stage every week. I can give you a job if you can do some work in the office when you aren't acting. Can you?'

He could. And that was how young William Shatner came to the CRT, as actor and promotion assistant.

RICHARD MONETTE
The duelling Hamlets

I played 'Hamlet' for the first time at the age of nineteen at the Crest Theatre. We played, very successfully, to more than 50,000 people. But interestingly ours was not the only *Hamlet* playing in Toronto at the time. Richard Burton was performing in that title role at the O'Keefe Centre. Of course, they knew about us as well.

I had to go and see his 'Hamlet'. And on the night I saw it, when he got to the soliloquy when he was to say, 'Plucks off my beard and blows it in my face? Tweaks me by the nose? Who does me this? hah!' he said, 'Plucks off my nose, blows it in my face...' and then...he...started...to...sort of...lose...contro-wl...and he just...went to Welsh. 'rl...djnuhnuhnuh...' And finally recovered. Quite amazing. But this was *Richard Burton*! No doubt most of the audience either didn't know or didn't care.

When I met him after the show, he was very gracious to me. He asked me if we had left in all the soliloquies.

'No, we had a time constraint.'

'My friend Allan Badell is going to cut out all the soliloquies when he plays it and I told him you can't do that, it's all plot. They're all plot. You can't cut them.'

Elizabeth Taylor was there as well. She shook my hand as we were introduced. She had a tiny little hand. When she shook mine she grabbed it so firmly that it was painful. She was absolutely stunningly beautiful, very petite. Of course, when you meet very famous or important people you become schizophrenic. I saw this little person, and she *was* very small, tiny, but because I had only seen her in movies, to me she had a head that was forty feet wide. And those violet eyes! They truly *were* violet! Stunning!

That night the Premier of Ontario was in the audience and they had been asked to meet him.

'You know, Richard, I don't think that I will go. You go ahead.'

'I think you'd better come.' Then she turned to me.

'You know I can't do anything right. If I sit out in the audience they complain that I'm distracting from the play. If I *don't* sit out in the audience they complain that they won't sell tickets if I'm not there. I never do anything right.'

CHRISTOPHER PLUMMER
Memories of Sir John

A champion of faux pas called 'Sir John'
At shocking his friends truly shone
Not intending to sting
He would say the wrong thing
And wonder why they'd all upped and gone!

Most of the theatre cognoscenti and a large slice of the public know that apart from being one of the greatest verse speakers of our century, John Gielgud is notoriously guilty of literally thousands of delicately mistimed and hilariously embarrassing faux pas, boners, bloopers, goofs, gaffes...call them what you will, which, by now, have all helped make up the rich legendary fabric of theatrical history.

Example A: After Richard Burton's *Hamlet*, outside his dressing room, about to take Burton to supper...'I'll wait for you out here dear boy, 'til you're better...I mean...ready.'

Example B: The late George Rose told me this exchange between Sir John and himself while Sir John was directing him as the ghost in *Hamlet*.

Sir John: Could you hold the skull a little higher so we can all see it?

G.R.:   Yes, of course.

Sir John (*nonsequitorially*): By the way, did you see Paul Scofield's 'Lear'?

G.R: Yes.

Sir John: What did you think of it?

G.R.:   I much preferred yours in '52.

Sir John (*blushing*): Mine? My Lear? Did you see it?

G.R.:   I was in it.

Sir John: What?

G.R.:   I was in it.

Sir John: Oh...What did you play?

G.R.:   Oswald.

Sir John: Of course you did. And how very good you were too!

Everyone who knows John, of course, is pleasantly aware that there is not a malicious or bitchy streak in his entire make-up. I have worked with him on several films and can gladly add my 'tuppence' to the thousands of actors who have already donated theirs that he is the kindest, most modest, and the least selfish of performers ever to grace our profession.

These qualities have surely contributed to the healthy and elegant manner by which he has reached his exalted age. He still strides rapidly forth, ram-rod straight while, one by one, his contemporaries fall by the wayside.

Back in 1961, I didn't know him so well. I was a great and distant admirer, and I knew most of the funny anecdotes but that was all. We were both members of the Royal Shakespeare Company that season. And what a season! The youthful members ranged from Geraldine McEwan, Dorothy Tutin to Judi Dench and a young glorious Vanessa Redgrave...Ian Bannen, Ian Richardson to Ian Holm, Roy Dotrice, Colin Blakely...You name 'em! Collectively, they would become the very spine of English drama for the next 30 years. To add to the illustrious roster... the 'older' guard...Dame Peggy Ashcroft, Dame Edith Evans and, of course, Sir John. Some company! And I had garnered all the plum roles on the program...'Richard III', 'Benedict', 'Henry II' in *Becket*! I...a COLONIAL...fresh from the crass New World, had come to take the wind out of their sails, beat 'em at their own game, show the Brits how to do what they do best! I was pretty cocky and insufferable, I tell ya!

One day I passed Sir John in the corridor waiting to rehearse his 'Othello' in the room I, as 'Richard', had just vacated. He was leaning with casual grace against the wall, an elegant scarf in loose folds about his neck, a hat tilted at a studied jaunty angle, looking for all the world like a stylish blade from the Restoration. With the loudest and gruffest of North American cat calls, I whooped out my grating greeting of recognition, condescendingly slapped the great man on the back (a slap which far more resembled a football tackle or a jab from Mike Tyson), patronizingly inquired as to what I seemed to infer was the dubious condition of his health, and from some Olympian height (some height north of Medicine Hat) wished him the best of much needed luck as if he were appearing in some minor church basement presentation down the street. As I passed, I heard him quietly adjust his clothes back to their original splendour and in a voice so gentle, warm, and compassionate, beautifully modulated, and not without the slightest hint of edge, I heard him say, 'Ah, Christopher...and how are *you*, in your own small way?'

I would like to think it was one of his bloopers, but I don't hold out much hope.

JACK CRELEY
A really good job

Sean Connery was in Toronto doing Shakespeare's *Macbeth* for CBC Television in the early '60s. This was when he was married to Diane Cilento and they were starting a family. At dinner at David's [Smith] and my place he was talking about his career.

'I've been offered a really good job at Lloyd's of London. So I'm going to give this acting thing another couple of months to see if anything happens and if not then I'm going to take the job. I've got to get something with more security.'

He got back to England and within two weeks the Broccoli brothers had phoned him to do 'James Bond'. He was that close to giving it up.

JOHN NEVILLE
Velveteen bloopers

When I arrived at the Neptune, the theatre was running a deficit as is usually the case. They were interested at that time in building a new theatre. I suggested that we should try to get the audience up again and get out of the red before we started such an enormous project. After two or three years, we were again in the black. Nonetheless I hesitated on the new theatre for quite a long while. Finally, they got a group of local citizens together and there seemed to be a very positive feeling going for the project. Of course, I joined them.

There was a wretched Conservative government at the time. The Minister of Social Services, Edmund Morris, was an ex-mayor of Halifax, a fearful, dreadful creature. About the time I began campaigning for money with the rest of this group to finance the building of a new theatre, this quote, from Edmund Morris, appeared in the Halifax papers in August 1986:

'John Neville. He's only an actor. That is all he is, with a gold ring in his ear asking us for $12 million so he can put on a pair of velveteen bloomers and run around the stage. We are not the Philistines he says we are.'

We have had it framed and keep it over our lavatory. It has provided many a laugh for guests making use of the facilities.

SHIRLEY DOUGLAS
The 'mothers' meet

Roberta Maxwell and I had been performing in a stage production of *Agnes of God* at the Bathurst Street Theatre in Toronto in 1984. One night after the performance, someone came rushing backstage and said that Anne Bancroft wanted to see us. She and Jane Fonda were in town shooting the movie version of *Agnes of God* at the time.

When this marvellous actress came in, although I had never met her, she gave me a hug, told me what she thought of the show in a few sentences, and then sat down and said, 'Now I need to talk to you. Listening to the play tonight, I realise that they've cut key lines from the film script. I need to get these lines back to make the "Mother Superior" work.' We talked for about an hour. She would ask what I had done in specific parts of the play, and we looked at the script and worked through it as her assistant took notes.

I understood very well her coming to talk to me. I have asked other actresses for advice when I have needed it for preparing roles, especially if they have performed them themselves. Every time their insights have helped me enormously and their humour even more.

These connections are among the things I value most about being an actress.

JACK CRELEY
Fuck off, Creley!

Jack Palance was a classmate of mine when I was studying acting and we have remained close friends ever since. He was sleeping one night and his phone rang. A voice said 'Mr Palance? This is Joan Crawford speaking.' Palance said 'Fuck off, Creley. It's three o'clock in the morning.' The telephone rang again and the voice said 'This really is Joan Crawford.' And Palance said, 'Creley, I'm going to kill you if you don't get off the phone. I'm trying to sleep!'

Apparently, Joan Crawford was looking for a sexy leading man for some movie she was doing. She'd been told that Jack Palance was a good choice, and that if she phoned him in the middle of the night, she would hear just how sexy he sounded!

MICHAEL IRONSIDE
My Sir Alec Guinness story

I think it was in 1984 that I did *Jo Jo Dancer* for Richard Pryor's Indigo Company and Columbia Pictures. It was my first job after I got to L.A. I must have been about 34. At one point, after the picture was over, I had to go to Columbia Pictures to look at some publicity prints. I went with my daughter who was at that time 11 or 12. As we were walking through the halls, a smallish elderly man walked by. Watching him, I realised that he was Sir Alec Guinness. I was so in awe of him, I ran face first into a door that was ajar in the hallway, landed on my ass, and split my lip. As I was lying on the floor, I heard someone say, 'May I help you, please?' It was him! reaching to help me up. I said, 'Don't touch me. Don't touch me,' and pulled away, almost crawled away. Somehow I got up and ran down the hall and hid around the corner.

This, of course, scared my daughter. She ran after me and found me tucked in behind a Xerox machine in the corner. 'Daddy, are you all right?' I said, 'Do you know who that is?' She said she didn't. 'That's Alec Guinness...Sir Alec Guinness.' She still didn't know. 'Obe wan Kenobe' [from *Star Wars*]. She said, 'I'll be back' and she turned and took off down the hall. I look around the corner and there she was chatting away with Sir Alec Guinness. I couldn't come out of my corner.

JACK CRELEY
Don't hog the guests

There used to be drinking, play-hard times in Toronto. Whenever anybody came to town, David Smith and I would have a party for them. I bet thousands of people have been through this house. We used to give parties where David and I had gone to bed and there were still people here the next morning sitting talking!

We threw a party for Richard Burton's cast of *Hamlet* (he himself was in Montreal marrying Elizabeth Taylor), where we consumed 124 dozen snails with our bread and salad.

Vivien Leigh came to one of our after-theatre parties. There were supposed to be about a dozen people. Word had gotten out that Vivien Leigh was coming to our place, and far too many people brought suitcases full of liquor. When I saw her coming up the stairs, I was so overcome, I ran and hid in the den. Somebody else had to go and get her sable coat.

Vivien apparently had a wonderful time in spite of the fact that she was monopolised for hours by a certain young actor. I knew how to deal with that. I just 'accidentally on purpose' spilled red wine in his lap so he would move on. And he did.

DONALD HARRON
Kents

[Re Mr Harron's performance as the 'Paperboy' in the West End production of A Streetcar Named Desire*]*

I was sent upstairs to a cubbyhole, henceforth my dressing room, to prepare for my London stage debut. The scene went well, except that the audience laughed when 'Blanche' called me a 'young prince out of the *Arabian Nights*'. Miss Leigh was offended by this reaction. She began muttering under her breath, and at first I thought she was sending me out for cigarettes. Then I realised it was not 'Kents! Kents!' but something much more obscene on her exquisite lips.

MARION GILSENAN
A book and its cover

Recently I was cast in a production of *A Little Night Music*. This was something new for me as it is a musical and singing is not my strong suit. Nonetheless I did it, had a six-minute solo number, and had an absolutely wonderful time. It was a joyous piece and the happiest of casts, just a delight. I realised with a twinge of regret that I had probably missed many wonderful experiences because I had abruptly resolved at the age of twelve to stick to straight theatre.

As a child in southern England I studied at a theatre school, and at twelve I was blonde and already becoming very curvaceous. I thought myself quite the little local star. On one occasion, I was asked, along with other young talents, to perform for a local charity concert.

On the night, I realised that I knew most of the other performers. There was, however, one new girl, a rather plain skinny girl. Her hair was in boring braids and her name was as plain as her appearance. I paid little attention.

After the resounding success of my performance, still basking in the applause I went down into the audience to watch the rest of the show from the back of the auditorium.

The unfamiliar 'plain Jane' appeared shy and awkward on the stage as the pianist played the introduction. Then she *sang!* I nearly fell over with astonishment. Who could have guessed that a twelve-year-old girl could come across with such power, such purity and absolute joy as she sang. The entire audience was dumb-struck. I promptly abandoned any ambitions that I might have had for a musical career. 'Leave the musical stardom to her,' I thought, checking the program.

The girl's name was Julie Andrews.

AL WAXMAN
On Lee Marvin

I was trying to produce a picture during the days when the federal government write-off structure made it quite easy to raise money. Among the first things you needed was a major star to say in writing that he/she would do the picture, and you were off. It's a lot harder now. I had had a couple of scripts developed. One was a western and one was a story about a mining town that was written by Gordon Pinsent (it was produced years later by Gordon himself as *John and the Missus*). I began to shop them around and some people in Hollywood were interested, so I headed to L.A.

A friend of a friend of mine managed to help me get the scripts to Lee Marvin who had just won his Oscar for *Cat Ballou*. He liked them both very much. Lee was just starting to shoot *The Iceman Cometh* for American Film Theatre so he asked me to wait and call him when he'd finished the shoot. He explained that he really couldn't think of anything else when he was focused on work. 'I'm monosyllabic,' he said. So I came back down to meet him a few weeks later.

When I got there, I talked to his agent, Myer Mishkin, a very famous agent. He said to me, 'Look kid, forget this. I know Lee likes the script. I know he likes you, but it's not gonna happen.' I asked why not? All the stars who appeared in American Film Theatre worked for a fraction of their normal fees for the rare opportunity to do a high quality theatrical piece on film. Mishkin had not made much on the deal.

He said to me, 'I'm talking to you. You're some hick kid from Canada. I'm lookin' at ten percent of "if, come, maybe". I can't let Lee do this.'

I finally talked to Lee and he said the same thing, that he couldn't do it. He was loyal to his agent of 22 years. He said to me, 'Look, kid, I'm sorry I can't do it but I can't say "no" to you just like that. Both your scripts are really interesting. Why don't you come out to my house for dinner?"

Now in those days I couldn't afford a hotel, so I'd stayed at Stephen Young's house. Nor could I afford to rent a car, and in L.A., it is virtually impossible to get around without one. I asked where he lived, feeling a little worried about getting there. He said he was in Malibu Colony which was almost 45 minutes drive, and impossible for me. I explained my situation and to my surprise, he offered to come and pick me up.

Stephen's house was on Palm Street or Palm Drive, something like that. Lee agreed to pick me up on the corner of the street. I did not know at the time that there are several streets with similar names in L.A. I stood there waiting and waiting, thinking that maybe I was dealing with some 'movie star' who didn't mind standing me up. The fact was that this dear man had gone to every variation of 'Palm Drive' on the map before he finally got to me. Finally he picked me up and we drove out to his house.

It was fairly common knowledge then that Lee Marvin was a drinker. I realised as our dinner progressed, that he had had only two drinks during the entire evening. It impressed me a great deal that he would take such care to stay sober. I found him sensitive and thoughtful, and it was a very pleasant evening. It was a simple meal with him and his wife. He handed me his Oscar to look at and later we walked on the beach and talked.

When it came time to go home, I felt that I couldn't ask him to take me all the way back into town, but he insisted. And as we were driving back he said to me, 'I know you are going to make it. I don't know how you are going to make it, because I don't know how anyone makes it. No one does. There is no pattern for success. You'll make it your own way."

Maybe it was just a kind thing to say to someone who was struggling, but it was something that meant a lot to me at that moment. The very fact that someone well established would say something so generous and insightful has stayed with me to this day.

TONY VAN BRIDGE
How d'you do, Ma'am

At the end of one performance in Edinburgh during the Stratford Festival tour of *Henry V* in 1955, I was quietly engaged in removing my costume and make-up and had, in fact, divested myself of all clothing but my underpants. There was a knock at the door, which was immediately flung open by Michael Langham [artistic director of the Stratford Festival]. Standing beside him, framed in the doorway, was the Queen's aunt, the Princess Royal.

For the merest second or two, we stared at each other; but I had no time to be covered even with confusion before Michael Langham ended the interview by shutting the door. Short as the meeting was, time did one of its little tricks. I was able to notice first, that Michael apologized to *me,* and second, that the Princess's smile and composure never wavered. As to whether the incident was ever referred to in Royal circles—whether royal children were ever regaled with tales of the time that Auntie met the naked actor—will never be known. Of course, there had been an announcement that Her Royal Highness would be coming backstage, but somehow I missed it. *How* remains a mystery.

TEDDE MOORE
An actress, Ma'am

I was invited to a dinner for the Queen on one of her state visits. I had tried to avoid being in her path during the post-dinner walkabout, hoping instead to bat my lashes at that famous rogue Prince Philip. There were male 'pushers', I don't know what else to call them, who corralled the guests and pushed us where they thought we should be. I was talking with friends when I turned to find the Queen standing in front of me. She extended her hand and spoke to me very kindly.

'And, what do you do?'

'I'm an actress, ma'am,' I answered in a suddenly teeny voice.

Unable to hear me, she leaned closer into me.

'I beg your pardon?'

I was overcome by an unfamiliar shyness. I couldn't believe the apparent instant loss of all my voice training. I resolved to rescue myself. In a voice that was now suddenly incredibly loud, I barked (there is no other word for it):

'I'm an actress.'

She was completely astonished. The volume of my voice caused her to rear her head back. Her eyes popped wide open. It was actually very funny but I was so shocked at what I'd done that laughing was the last thing on my mind. I wanted the floor to open up and swallow me.

She passed right on and left me to ponder my reality: I had just yelled at the Queen.

WANDA CANNON
Who *can* talk to her?

The wonderful Kimble Hall and I were part of a gala presentation for the Queen, directed by Norman Campbell, at Roy Thompson Hall. We did our little show and were all to meet the Queen afterwards. I hadn't realised how her presence would affect me until she walked in to the backstage area of the theatre. I am sure that I saw an aura around her. I'm not into Royalty and all that goes along with it, but I swear that I saw a light around her body. It was extraordinary.

When it was our time to meet her, I suddenly became very nervous. I wanted to say something to her that would be unusual, that she would find humorous and interesting. Something she had never heard before. We'd had all the rules explained and we were dutifully waiting in a line.

Then it was my turn to greet her. She came along to me and said, 'And, is this all you do?' I was absolutely dumbfounded. I didn't know how to reply to that. So I said, 'Uh. No.'

And I couldn't think of one more single word to say to her. She looked at me and realised that nothing more would be forthcoming and walked on to Kim Hall who was standing beside me. I was in a state of shock.

I listened to Kim and he was exactly the opposite. He gave her his entire résumé! The woman couldn't leave. He was just compelled to tell her everything he had ever done in his whole life. After she had wrenched herself away he turned to me and said, 'Did you hear that!'

'Yes, Kim, I did.' Then Philip came up to me and I felt much more relaxed talking to him. He and I had a very nice little moment's chat before he moved on to Kim. And if Kim didn't do the exact same thing again to the Prince!

Both of us just stood there in a state of complete disbelief at how we'd reacted. We were experienced professionals. How could this happen?

11

Audiences and Fans

MERVYN 'BUTCH' BLAKE
Little 'cups of tea'

We were doing a matinee performance of *Henry IV* at the main stage at Stratford. Jason Robards was playing 'Hotspur' and Max Helpmann was 'King Henry IV'. There is a scene in which 'Hotspur' has all his troops on the stage and is suddenly attacked by King Henry. There follows an enormous fight choreographed by Douglas Campbell.

As Hotspur was talking to his men, Henry and his troops were to enter from the doors at the back of the auditorium. They'd use all the aisles, gradually creeping toward the stage in the dark. Just when they were to confront each other, Henry was to stand up and shout, 'Charge!'

Coming down the middle aisle as one of 'Falstaff's' men, I passed two little elderly ladies, two little 'cups of tea' as we used to call them. There was a great tense pause before the fight was to begin. Just at that moment, one of the ladies said to her friend, who must have been somewhat deaf, 'Aggie, I've never been in a fight before. Have you?' And the other one said, 'No, dear, I'm so excited!' It resounded all over the theatre.

Suddenly Max Helpmann yelled, 'Charge!' But we were all laughing so hard, we completely lost our staging. Everything was at sixes and sevens, and our carefully choreographed battle became a complete bit of nonsense. By then, the audience was howling as well. Finally someone said the right cue and we managed somehow to get off the stage.

BARBARA HAMILTON
Spring Thaw at Stratford

One year *Spring Thaw* played the main stage at Stratford. As we arrived to set up for our show, we were treated as if we were defiling the altar of The Bard by putting on an unimportant satirical revue. This unimportant little revue happened to be the most successful theatrical enterprise in Canada at the time.

Stratford players have many weeks to rehearse their exits and entrances from the dark tunnels leading to the stage. We had only just arrived that afternoon and by the time we were set up, we had about an hour to rehearse...and the lights were *on!* When we opened that night, Douglas Campbell and Bruno Gerussi stood at the end of the darkened tunnels with small flashlights.

On one black-out exit, I tripped and lost my shoe going down the stairs to the tunnel. I cursed like a drunken sailor. My language was shocking but it was dark and for some reason I figured that if the audience couldn't see me, they couldn't hear me! On my next entrance, however, the dearest, sweetest, most adorable little white-haired lady handed me my shoe and said that she knew it was mine because she had recognized my voice in the dark.

LEN BIRMAN to ANNA REISER and TEDDE MOORE
in a telegram for a particularly painful opening night:
'Remember, smiling or gritting the teeth
looks much the same from the front.'

IAN DEAKIN
The man with no face

My debut at Stratford was in *The Alchemist*, which director John Neville had cheekily set in the old west. During one performance, the late great Susan Wright and Tom Wood came off stage. She looked at me in wide-eyed wonder.

'There's a man out there with no face.'

'What!'

'Take a look—no face.'

The first chance I got, I broke the fourth wall. She was right. A bald-headed gentleman had fallen asleep with his chin resting on his chest. All we could see from the stage was a smooth, ovoid, flesh-coloured shape where a face should have been.

RICHARD WAUGH
Close encounter

In the season of 1988 the Shaw Festival presented the J.B. Priestley mystery *Dangerous Corner*. It is an amazingly forward-thinking play for its time. A spiral of dirty little secrets leads to the disillusion and suicide of one of the main characters. I played 'Gordon Whitehouse'. I was 24 years old and it was the largest and best role I had yet had.

At the climax of act two Gordon had a long and emotional speech in which he confesses to his homosexuality. The other characters in the play, played by Keith Knight, Sharry Flett, Peter Hutt, Tracy Ferenz, and Wendy Noel, stood upstage of me, suitably horrified. The director, Tony van Bridge, had placed me about six inches from the front row of the George Theatre.

One night, as I finished my speech, tears in my eyes, feeling the moment, an older woman in the second row said to her companion in a voice audible to the entire house:

'He's not very good, is he?'

I was mortified. I turned my face upstage only to see my fellow actors in various stages of hysterics. By the time the curtain fell, everyone had their backs turned to the audience.

LOUIS NEGIN
Audience participation

We did a play in Montreal at the Saidye Bronfman Centre called *Family Business* in which I played the sensitive son. The Bronfman theatre is very intimate, and the matinees of this show often attracted a lot of little old ladies. At the end of the show my character had a long, quietly emotional speech about my mother dying in a car crash. It was intense and meant to be very moving.

During one performance, just at this point, I heard a woman speak out to her friend, in a very loud voice.

'Er iz kayn faygele?' Literally translated this means, 'He's a bird?' In Yiddish, however, this word is used to describe an Oscar Wilde type character.

Onstage, I kept doing my speech, trying to rescue what was left of the atmosphere. The conversation from the audience continued.

'Ney. Er iz nisht kayn faygele. Er iz kayn momma's boychik!'

Back and forth they argued at full voice. I just started to laugh. The rest of the company was laughing. The stage was rocking. Oh, no. This wasn't the end.

'Are you ready to go? I want to miss the traffic. Come, we'll go now.'

'You don't want to see the end?'

'Naa, I've seen already. Let's go.'

And they did.

GRAHAM GREENE
And those aren't sweet lips!

Towards the end of the run of Tomson Highway's play *Dry Lips Oughta Move to Kapuskasing* at the Royal Alexandra Theatre in Toronto, we found ourselves feeling a bit flat. We'd been playing the show for quite a while and you can lose that performing edge.

One night, waiting in the wings for the play to start, we heard this woman, sitting somewhere around third row centre, chatting away to her friend at the top of her voice. She was saying how wonderful this was going to be and what a great experience her friend was going to have. She talked about the difficulty she had getting the tickets for this particular performance, how long she had to wait and how lucky they were to sit so close to the stage. 'The show was fabulous. The cast was magnificent.' She was beside herself with delight. We got pretty cheered up by this and were ready to go out and give her a great show.

The house lights went to half. Then went dark. The show began. A single spot-light came up on Gary Farmer's bottom, as he lay on the couch. And we heard this voice say flatly and loudly, 'Hey! This isn't *Les Miz*!' I honestly don't remember much of what happened after that.

ROSEMARY DUNSMORE
Too much dog doo-doo

A matinee crowd is often older than an evening audience. That shift brings its own adventures. It is not uncommon to have an audience member take ill during those performances and require assistance. 'Is there a doctor in the house?' may sound like an old joke but the reality is far from it. As an actor you must carry on as graciously as possible for the sake of the rest of the audience. Sometimes, as well, the elders of our communities are a very different audience by virtue of their social expectations.

I was doing a one-woman show at the Saidye Bronfman Centre in 1984 playing a woman who was very free and easy with her language. In the play I told a long story that had to do with dog excrement. I was to address the monologue as if I was speaking to someone in the audience, and I had to say the words 'dog shit' quite a number of times. As I was getting more than half way through this particular speech I heard an elderly lady say loudly, 'If she says "shit" one more time, I'm leaving!' I could hear this and I *knew* that I would have to say 'shit' again. I talked on, blah, blah, blah...and, again, I said 'shit'. Sure enough, up she got with her companion in tow.

The Saidye Bronfman is a very wide theatre and if you are sitting in the middle it takes forever to work your way to an aisle. So for the next seeming eternity all I could see was this elderly couple clambering over everyone, bumping and shifting people as they made their way out.

After that I stopped wearing contact lenses on stage so I could never again see the audience.

WAYNE BEST
The Oy Vey corral

Ron Lea, Winston Reckart, Kate Trotter, and myself as 'Billy' performed *The Life and Times of Billy The Kid* at the Saidye Bronfman Centre, the Jewish community centre in Montreal, sometime in the '80s. That season included Pinter's *Betrayal, Hedda Gabler*, and a play on *Spinoza*, none of which are light fare. I think when people saw the title of our show, they expected to see some cute 'John Wayne' sort of entertainment. This was not the case.

Michael Ondaatje's script certainly was not light entertainment. Parts of it were quite graphic and very esoteric. 'Billy's' long and infamous speech after he has been captured is a perfect example. His arms and legs are tied and as he's riding across the desert, his hat falls off. The sun beats down on him, driving him temporarily mad. He hallucinates that the sun turns into a pair of hands, reaches down into his scalp, and plucks the hairs out one by one. The hands peel back the skin of his scalp and reach into his body and, in graphic anatomical detail, Billy describes what they are reaching down through. It continues for five pages until one hand reaches the penis, pulls it up through the body, through the top of the head and jerks it off. By the time I finished this speech each night, I would be completely exhausted, collapsed under the belly of the horse, heaving like a bellows.

On this particular night, we played to an audience of maybe seven people. The echo of my own voice in the near-empty theatre was deafening but the silence that followed that speech seemed even louder. In that chasm of nothingness, with impeccable timing, an elderly Jewish lady who had been munching on her candy in the front row throughout this speech, blurted out a pained 'Oyyyyyy vey!'

We had T-shirts made up quoting our new-found subtitle for the show, 'Gunfight at the "Oy vey" Corral'.

ALLAN GRAY
Bent

In 1982 we were doing the remount of *Bent,* a play about the Nazi persecution and imprisonment of homosexuals, at the Vancouver Playhouse.

It was a packed house, a matinee. John Moffat, God rest his beautiful soul, and I were doing the sex scene in Act 2 in Dachau. In this scene, the characters are to stand at opposite sides of the stage facing forward, rigidly at attention. They are told that if they move, the guards will shoot them. Though they can't see or touch each other, they talk each other into orgasm as an act of defiance. The dialogue is very intense, very graphic, 'Can you feel my mouth...' and 'Can you feel my cock...', etc. At the best of times, this is a difficult scene to do, but we were up there trying to work ourselves into orgasm for a matinee audience full of church ladies.

The Playhouse has doors at the side of the auditorium and a ramp that comes up from that side to the stage. In the middle of this intense, erotic dialogue, I saw out of the corner of my eye a woman in a bright red suit come through these doors, walk up the ramp and onto the stage. I had no idea who she was but had no choice but to continue with the scene. 'Can you feel my...' whatever, this and that and so on. She didn't bat an eye. Instead she stood in front of us and addressed this audience of 670 people, completely ignoring the fact that there is a play in progress, and said, 'Excuse me. Is this where the auditions for the opera are?' At this point, the stage manager, with his headset still on came running on stage, grabbed this woman by the scruff of the neck and dragged her off stage.

Of course, the audience started to laugh. Meanwhile, John Moffat, who had been doing most of the talking during all of this hadn't put his contacts in and *didn't know* that this had happened because she had spoken at the same time that he had spoken his lines. We couldn't address each other during the scene, we were too far away to whisper, and we couldn't look at each other so there was no way I could let him know until afterwards when we came off after the curtain call. All he knew was that the audience had started to laugh at a very inappropriate time.

John was very disturbed and confused. He said to me, 'Why did we lose the audience like that? Why were they laughing?' I said, 'Didn't you know...?' So...I told him.

I don't know what kind of auditions this woman was used to but I have never been to one where there was a packed audience, not to mention the fact that we had no piano.

HEATHER SUMMERHAYES
The invisible man

One night I went to see my friend Peter Dvorsky in performance at the St Lawrence Centre, where he was co-starring in a production of *Born Yesterday* with Jimmy Blendick and Fiona Reid.

At the top of the second act, the lights came up, Jimmy Blendick made his entrance, and began a brief monologue, pacing up and down the stage. At that moment, a man suddenly jumped up from behind the sofa at centre stage, looked at Jimmy and said,

'You can't see me!'

Jimmy came to a dead stop and stared. The strange man repeated it again.

'You can't see me!'

The entire audience stopped breathing. We knew something was not right.

'What the hell are you doing? We're trying to do a play here!'

'You can't see me!' said the man again, and began to prance around the stage. It was surreal. Jimmy turned out front and shouted to the back of the house in a plaintive voice,

'Help?...Stage management? Stage management?'

Just then, Peter Dvorsky, who knew nothing of what was happening on-stage, made his entrance. He looked at Jimmy, they both looked at the man, and Peter looked back at Jimmy. Jimmy shrugged, and without a word, they both began to chase the man, who kept insisting that no one could see him.

It was pure theatre! We in the audience leaned forward on the edge of our seats, too fascinated to laugh, though the impulse was there. Eventually, stage management did show up and eject the stranger, leaving Jimmy and Peter to stagger about on the stage, giggling. They made three hysterical attempts to get back on track in the scene before they finally made it, to much enthusiastic applause.

IAN DEAKIN
On Manitoba Theatre Centre's *Equus*, 1975

In the final riveting scene of *Equus*, the boy relives his first 'roll in the hay' under the watchful eyes of his beloved horses. The scene involves the nudity of both actors playing the young lovers. As Zoe Alexander and I peel off, I notice a couple in row C stand up and start to exit, much to the annoyance of the other patrons. Len Cariou, as the psychiatrist 'Dysart', begins asking his probing questions.

'What did you do?'

Lying on top of Zoe, facing the departing couple, it required some degree of concentration to remember my lines.

'I put it in her.'

The couple, who were by then at the back of the theatre, opened the doors to the auditorium and as they prepared to leave the building, turned to deliver their parting shot.

'Why don't you put it in the horse?'

You could have heard a stirrup drop. It was all I could do to restrain 'Nugget' (one of the horses, played by Robin Ward) and the rest of the team of boys from the Royal Winnipeg Ballet from trampling them to death in the parking lot.

BARRIE BALDARO
Madame Butterfly's revenge

It was 1966. CBC was looking for a low budget summer replacement comedy show. Terry Kyne came up with a show that would have just two performers, Paul Soles and myself, and four gorgeous models. The writing was zany, a precursor of *Laugh-In* and *Monty Python*. One of the sketches was based on *Madame Butterfly*.

I was dressed as 'Madame Butterfly' in full geisha costume and Paul was 'Pinkerton'. The music from the opera was to play in the background while we were shooting on a real pier at Toronto Harbour that was to substitute for Tokyo Harbour. We were later to lay in a voice-over of Madame Butterfly's thoughts as she looked out over the harbour. Something like, 'If I could only get my hands on that perfidious Pinkerton. The bastard has run away like a coward and I will never see him again.'

Butterfly bemoans her situation and her anger at Pinkerton for leaving her in the lurch. Suddenly, lo and behold, from around a building beside the pier, appears a character in the costume of an 1880s American naval officer, 'Pinkerton'. He begins to run romantically in slow motion towards me with open arms. And Madame Butterfly's thought narration is, 'Oh! Can it be? Can it be Pinkerton?' He gets closer and closer and I remain stock-still as he bounds toward me, the lost lover returning. However, it is not the romantic reunion expected. When 'Pinkerton' reaches 'Madame', she karate-chops him around the face and neck and body and throws him into the harbour.

So we finished the rehearsal and had a half-hour break for coffee in our trailers. In the interim, a Japanese freighter tied up by the pier where we were to shoot. The Japanese saw the television equipment and were curious. Then I appeared in geisha costume with full make-up and wig. One by one the entire crew of about thirty from cabin boy to captain came up on deck. They hugged the rails and talked back and forth, pointing and waving very animatedly. To our amazement, all thirty of them produced cameras and began snapping and clicking away so fast that it almost sounded like rain.

We decided to get on with our work. The music was turned on, which they of course recognised. As we began to shoot, Terry, like any good director, took advantage of the unexpected presence of the Japanese ship by starting his shot on their flag and pulling down to me in the foreground. Someone waved a cue to Paul Soles and the entire crew on the ship deck pivoted as one, all thirty sailors, to see him appear in costume at the end of the pier. As if by cosmic revelation, it dawned on them that this was Pinkerton and that I was Madame Butterfly. They became very excited. Paul began to run toward me. He got up to me and as rehearsed, I karate-chopped him and threw him into the harbour.

The Japanese crew exploded! They went mad! They yelled 'Banzai! Banzai!' and jumped up and down and absolutely went wild. They loved it. Finally, after a hundred years, retribution!

DAVE BROADFOOT
'The lake it is said never gives up her dead'

I was booked to perform at the Independent Loggers Association annual banquet at a hotel that must remain nameless...the Stockman Hotel in downtown Kamloops. No need for it to be nameless forever. Some banquets are preceded by an open bar reception that might last as long as an hour or, at the very most, an hour and a half. The Independent Loggers' open bar reception lasted for three days. My introduction was handled by the inebriated banquet organiser, the man who had hired me.

'All right, gentlemen ... Here he is ... Gordonnnnnn Lightfoot!'

It was not a good beginning.

I could tell right away, the loggers were puzzled by my lack of guitar and by the absence of back-up musicians. None of them had ever seen Gordon Lightfoot in person so they didn't know he's much, much older than I am. Not knowing what else to do, I plunged into my first joke which was about the father of the Minister of Finance, Paul Martin senior:

'Mr Martin was campaigning across the country at the time capital punishment was about to be abolished. When he arrived in Kingston, there was nobody downtown. He became frantic wondering where he was going to get an audience. He found out everybody had gone out to witness the last hanging in history. He rushed out to the penitentiary. Arrived there just in time to hear the "hangperson" say to the hangee, "Do you have any last words?" The hangee said, "No, I don't." Paul Martin said to the hangperson, "Since we have a crowd here and this gentleman doesn't wish to speak, might I take the opportunity?" The hangperson turned to the condemned man. "Well, what do you think?" The man said, "Sure, let him speak, but hang me first!"'

The problem was...the loggers were waiting to hear me sing *The Edmund Fitzgerald* and they didn't realise I was doing jokes. One of them sitting in the front row jumped up and shouted defiantly,

'OK, Lightfoot, you brought up the hanging business. Are you saying we should be using the rope?'

'Only if it's between two consenting adults.'

Then, he called me an asshole. I replied, 'That means we can speak as equals.'

At that point, things got out of hand. Fist fights broke out throughout the audience. Then, all of a sudden, a man about the size of two glued-together juke boxes, got up out of the audience, *came up on to the stage*, made his way over to me, put his arm around me like a vice and said very, very loudly:

'You're going to sing now!'

Speaking as quickly as I could, I tried to explain. 'No, no, no, I'm not Gordon Lightfoot. Gordon is a singer. I'm Dave *Broad*foot. I don't sing. It's all been a mis ... Auuuughh!'

Immediately...as his knee made contact with my groin...a miracle took place. A Gordon Lightfoot song, in Gordon Lightfoot's voice, came from my throat. It was not very loud but quite heart-rending. Meanwhile, the rest of my body slowly limped its way off the stage backwards. Luckily, earlier in the day, I had acted very professionally and memorised the location of the fire escape.

GARY FILES
On losing the audience

We were doing one of those dreadful plays from the '70s that manage to incorporate a four-letter word into every line. It was supposed to be an ultra realistic social comment about 'real' life. It was unrelenting. Through the entire thing there was barely a word that did not have to do with an orifice or a bodily function.

One night, we peeked out at the audience and there sat a handful of nuns and, we were told, their charges from a home for the 'mentally challenged'. These people were the entire audience. We couldn't help wonder if they had had any idea what the play was like.

We started the play. I can only assume that when it became apparent that there would be no letting up on the obscenities that we were required to spew, the nuns rose and took their charges out of the theatre. We looked out...and the entire audience was gone. We didn't quite know what to do. None of us had had an entire audience leave before. It was startling. Undaunted, we finished the show and called it a dress rehearsal.

IS MORE?
An actor, killed early in *Richard* III and on his way home at first intermission,
encountered a lady of strong accent in need of directions.
As it became clear that she had been at the performance,
the actor asked why she had left early. Exclaiming 'Is more?',
she went dashing back to the theatre,
bowling over front-of-house staff in her path.

MARILYN LIGHTSTONE
Theatre manners

It was 1967 and I was appearing in my first season at Stratford as 'Iras', attendant to Cleopatra, in *Antony and Cleopatra*. This production was directed by Michael Langham and starred Christopher Plummer and Zoe Caldwell.

Part of the Festival season was devoted to school matinees. To this day, I cannot understand why the powers that be thought that this play about mature angst would be suitable for an audience of youngsters but this was one of their choices.

On this particular afternoon we were waging an uphill battle with a very rowdy group. It was very difficult to concentrate and they were being so disruptive one wonders what, if anything, they were getting out of the experience. I don't know how the actors playing the more substantial parts managed but they struggled valiantly on.

We had made it to Cleopatra's death scene where Iras poisons herself with the asp and dies. Thereupon Cleopatra was to apply the asp to herself saying, 'Dost thou not see my baby at my breast?' I waited for Cleopatra's lines but I heard nothing, silence. Since I had 'died' first as directed and was lying face down, I was of course, unable to move a muscle, so I did not know what was happening. Then I heard the sound of Ms Caldwell's costume as she got up from her throne and walked slowly to the front of the stage.

I could *feel* her looking at the audience and then I heard her say very firmly and plainly, something to this effect:

'Your behaviour is extremely inappropriate and totally unacceptable. You now have two choices. Either you will sit quietly or we will consider the play finished immediately.'

Needless to say there was, finally, complete silence. After a brief pause we heard an adult voice from the audience.

'Miss Caldwell, please accept our apologies and please continue.'

Without missing a *beat* she went right back into her dying speech and we finished the play.

Something very powerful happens when an actor steps out of character to address an audience directly. I'll never forget it. Most importantly, I feel that it was, without doubt, the right thing to do. This was, after all, intended as a learning experience for these young people, and surely part of educating an audience is to let them know what is acceptable and what is not.

MARY JOLLIFFE on reservations
A farmer came up to the ticket booth at the Stratford Festival Theatre.
The attendant asked him which show he would like to see.
He replied, 'Just want a pair of tickets.
Don't much matter as long as it comes
between hay'n and harvest'n.'

AILEEN TAYLOR-SMITH
On artistic merit

In my time as Artistic Director of the Huron Country Playhouse, I had one or two occasions with audience members that were...unexpected.

In the first year of my tenure, we presented *Private Lives*, a production of which I was extremely proud. Watching from the back of the house one evening, I saw two people who were apparently in search of an exit. I assumed that one of them must be ill, so I quickly hurried over in the semi-darkness and asked, 'Is there anything wrong?' intending to offer my assistance.

'There certainly is. I'm bored to death!'

TEDDE MOORE
The mavens

I was attending a performance of Shakespeare's *Macbeth* at the O'Keefe Centre in Toronto. It starred Christopher Plummer and Glenda Jackson as well as Stephen Markle and Paul Soles. As I was walking up that long aisle at the O'Keefe to go out at intermission, I passed a yuppie couple still in their aisle seats. The woman was saying in bored voice 'Well, I don't know. She's so over the top.' Her companion said, with all the condescension he could muster, 'My dear, this *is* Shakespeare. It's *supposed* to be over the top.'

PAT ARMSTRONG
As 'Fritz'

In *Frankenstein* at Alberta Theatre Projects, I (a tiny female) appeared as 'Fritz', the male servant. Overheard opening night in the men's washroom, 'What do you think of it so far?' 'Pretty good. I really like the little guy.' 'That's not a guy, it's Pat Armstrong—a woman.' 'Oh. Well, I like him anyway.'

DOUGLAS CHAMBERLAIN
Wrong Theatre

I was leaving the mainstage theatre at Stratford just as the cannon was going off before a matinee when I overheard one female patron say to her companion, 'I *told* you we were at the wrong theatre. We want the Merry Fucking Wives of Windsor!'

DONALD HARRON
Yer Alex Gwinnuss

I overheard this as a member of the founding company of the Stratford Festival. A tent had to be specially built for the first season. The newly poured cement that would form the basis of the seating had finally hardened during a rare dry spell, and rehearsals were being held on the actual stage. There was no tent to cover it yet, so I sat on the brow of the hill to watch Alec Guinness rehearse his opening monologue as 'Richard III'. A couple of local residents sat nearby. They couldn't catch the words, because Guinness rehearsed in a whisper, but they could see him limping around and gesturing, with the peculiar spastic gait he had adopted for the cripple-who-would-be-king.

'That'd be yer Alex Gwinnuss, yer movie man,' said one old codger to the other. 'What's he doin' now?'

'He's practisin' on the platferm fer the concert they're gonna give.'

'I can't hear a blame word he's sayin'.'

'Oh, he's finished gittin' off all his words by heart. Now he's workin' up his gestures.'

RICHARD MONETTE
Bagels and a Danish

I remember when I was a young man of 19, doing my first 'Hamlet' at the Crest Theatre in Toronto, I was asked to address some residents of a Jewish home for the aged, who had come to see the production, after a show. So I talked to them and at the end of the discussion, an old gentleman came up to me and said, 'Listen, when you get back to Denmark, would you give my regards to my brother?'

The man who was doing public relations then, a friend of mine called Bennet Solway, thought this was hilarious and told the story at another fund raiser for the home for the aged. One lovely elderly woman responded, 'Isn't that silly of that man! Didn't he know Denmark was a large country?'

PETER MacNEILL
Petey Weety

In recent years I have been involved in a number of Movie of the Week television shows, and have made a lot of new friends, one of whom is an assistant director by the name of Megan.

I was taken by her friendly and often irreverent manner. She always had a yarn to spin or a joke to tell, most of them off colour! She took no one and nothing seriously except her work. She must have felt a certain fondness for me, as well, as she started calling me 'Petey Weety'! As this was coming from Megan, I did not complain. No doubt there were a lot more damaging names she could have called me.

On one of these movies she started in the early morning and kept it up all day. 'Petey Weety, you're wanted on set' or 'Petey Weety, make-up is ready for you.' Finally came the call 'Petey Weety...that's a wrap!' Trudging back to my dressing room in the Honey Wagon, I was stopped by an elderly female extra who inquired earnestly, 'Mr Weety, may I have your autograph?'

ANGELA GEI
The birth of the Blyth Summer Theatre

In the cast of the first season of Blyth there were three men and I was the only woman. Straight out of theatre school, I was to play all of the female parts, and the three men played everyone and everything else including a stove. During that first season, we did *Mostly In Clover*, a series of scenes based on a book written by Harry Boyle about farmers in that region of Ontario and directed by James Roy and Steve Thorne.

As part of the process of establishing a theatre company in what is essentially a farming community, we had to integrate ourselves into the community, in effect, prove that we were not 'city folk' or at least that we weren't 'outsiders'. So every free lunch hour, between rehearsals, we would go to have lunch with all the different ministers and reverends and priests in the area. After we'd eaten, I would go off into the kitchen with the women and do the dishes while the boys would talk in the living room. I had to do it. It was expected and I *had* to prove myself and gain their acceptance.

Later that same summer, during rehearsals of *Mostly In Clover*, we visited one of the local farmers who had been the model for one of the characters in the Passe Muraille's *The Farm Show*. We would sit down to lunch and listen to all the stories.

A city-bred person, I had never been on a working farm before, so this was great research for me. I would sit there quietly and not say too much. As I listened, I became aware that this man's wife was staring at me, also not saying much. She watched me for a long time, until finally it was time to leave. We said our 'Thank yous' but as I started out the door I heard a sharp, clear woman's voice say, 'Hey, you!'

I looked up and I saw her throw something at me. I just barely caught it.

'You want to portray us?...You'd better learn how to use this.'

I looked at it. It was her apron. It became the apron I would use for the show. I will never forget that. That moment was more important for me, in many ways, than the hours I spent in rehearsals.

ART HINDLE
Everyone's a critic

I was working on a recent version of the film *Invasion of the Body Snatchers,* which starred Donald Sutherland. We were shooting down in the Tenderloin District of San Francisco. Kevin McCarthy was echoing the role he played in the original black and white version, as the character who threw himself onto the windshield of the car driven by Donald Sutherland, screaming, 'They're coming! They're coming!' It was a very small bit, a kind of tip of the hat to the original film version.

We were all standing around together between takes, waiting for the next shot to be ready when a bum, a real guy, not an extra, came lurching over to us. He asked in a slurred voice what we were shooting. Kevin McCarthy, who at this point was dressed in his costume, which was pretty ragged and filthy, not unlike the clothing the bum was wearing, told him that they were shooting *Invasion of the Body Snatchers.* The derelict squinted at him and said, 'Dned dey did dat?' Kevin said politely that yes, they had done it before but that they were doing it again. The guy looked directly at Kevin McCarthy with suspicion and said, 'The firzd one waz bedder.'

And he walked away.

JAMES B. DOUGLAS
The deviation

There was a gala opening night at The Mountain Playhouse in Montreal for a production of *The Long, The Short and The Tall* in which I was starring. I had a terrible cold. In spite of the fact that in the role of 'Bamforth' you can get away with snarly, snotty speech, I was not in top form.

The very distinguished looking British High Commissioner came to the elegant reception after the performance, bedecked with all his medals. There was a receiving line. When he came to me he said,

'Ah, yes. Bamforth. I enjoyed your performance immensely!'

'Thank you, but I'm sorry you couldn't see my full performance because I have this terrible cold. Unfortunately, Sir, I have a tendency to get colds because I have a deviated septum.'

Without missing a beat he said, 'Oh, dear boy! How the devil do you shit?'

To this day I don't know if he was serious or had a twinkle in his eye.

FRANK SHUSTER
Youse guys

In between performances at the Confederation Centre in Charlottetown, Prince Edward Island, John Wayne and I were strolling down the street. A small boy recognized us and said 'Are you Wayne and Shuster?' We said, yes, indeed we were, the boy exclaimed, 'Youse guys are so comical, it ain't even funny!'

GRANT COWAN
The dog actor

My sister came to Chicago to see me in *You're a Good Man, Charlie Brown* in which I played 'Snoopy', Charles Shultz' esoteric beagle. She really wanted to go shopping at Saks Fifth Avenue, so we went over and were wandering around this posh, posh store, looking and looking. So, too, were two very grand ladies, beautifully coiffed, wearing Gucci shoes and Pucci outfits. We saw them and they saw us and as we passed each other one of them barked at me!

'Ruff, ruff!'

I looked over. Then the other one said, 'See, I told you it was him.'

Then they just walked away. Apparently they didn't want to lower themselves to *talk* to a 'dog actor' but they did make an acknowledgement with this elegant little bark!

HARVEY ATKIN
Innocent faces

Playing a cop means you must always look neat. When I was working on the TV series *Cagney and Lacey* I had the wardrobe department sew a crotch strap to the front and back of my uniform shirt so I could keep the shirt neatly tucked into my pants.

Being a producer means you must find ways to publicize your program and the producers of *Cagney and Lacey* were no different. They often offered people roles as extras on the show or tours of the set for charity prize purposes.

One day I was just a little late for a call to set. I found myself behind a flat waiting to make my entrance, hurriedly adjusting my crotch strap. At this exact moment a young girls' school tour rounded the corner. There I was, a well-known-to-TV-audiences cop, with my hand deep in my flies. Frantically yanking at my shirt, while I looked over into thirty innocent faces.

PAT ARMSTRONG
Tiny Tim?

It was 1960, and I was with the Nottingham Repertory Theatre having just left drama school (Bristol Old Vic). The little boy rehearsing 'Tiny Tim' was ill. I replaced him as I am quite a petite woman and have often played children. At the end of one performance, a mother brought her child backstage. I was in my dressing room wearing the basic black of the times, a chic sack dress and spike heels, a pale, white face, and scarlet lips. I was smoking a cigarette and sipping on a sherry.

'Mommy, Mommy!' the child shrieked and sobbed, 'Tiny Tim is a girl!'

DAVID DUNBAR
Dick Durban

Being the star player in any season has its good points and bad. I was the leading man in a season of summer stock some years back and I had some smashing roles. A critic for some regional paper gave me glowing review after glowing review. It became a little embarrassing. Then came the review for the opening night of *The Boy Friend*. The critic wrote paragraphs and paragraphs about how swell I was. 'Destined for stardom!' There was my picture smiling away in the paper. The full bit.

At the end of all the raves I read, 'This young man, obviously destined for stardom, calls himself Dick Durban.' Aside from the fact that he got my name wrong, which was at once ironic and hysterical, this did not bode well for me with the company. It wasn't long before they were calling me Deanna Durbin. Then some kind soul started to call me Dick Durban, which became Dickie. It quite stuck.

DONALD HARRON
Idiot reviews

One summer at Dora Mavor Moore's little barn beside her house in Toronto, the Village Players did an obscure comedy of Federico García Lorca's called *The Shoemaker's Prodigious Wife*. I was cast as an eight-year-old boy (I was an ungainly twenty-two at the time) and succeeded in getting the best review of my career. The program neglected to mention that I was playing an eight-year-old and Rose MacDonald in the *Toronto Telegram* wrote 'Donald Harron was perfect as the idiot.'

RICHARD MONETTE
My first 'Hamlet'

I had been in Toronto doing a television show for CBC, *First Love* by Turgenev, when I was first asked to audition for *Hamlet*. I was nineteen at the time. It was originally supposed to be Bruno Gerussi as 'Hamlet' with John Hirsch directing but one or the other of them dropped out. The management—Murray Davis—went with Marigold Charlesworth and Jean Roberts as co-directors. I thought that I was auditioning for the role of 'Laertes' or 'Horatio'. When they offered me 'Hamlet', of course, I knew it was an overwhelming and intimidating prospect. But I thought that if they had seen something in me that suited their vision, I would have to do it. I just couldn't refuse.

One of the results of that *Hamlet* was a review which is now famous. The first paragraph began, 'If you happen to be Richard Monette...stop reading right here...' It was *not* a very complimentary notice.

It was, however, very bracing for the career ahead.

BENEDICT CAMPBELL
Bus stopped

During the run of *Troilus and Cressida* at the National Arts Centre in Ottawa, I was walking along the street one day at rush hour, making my way through a very large group of people who were huddled around a bus stop, waiting to get back to the suburbs. Many dour faces. Just as I had passed, I heard a voice bark out from behind me.

'Hey, Troilus. Hey! Troilus!'

I stopped in my tracks without turning around.

'Yeah, you. Troilus.'

I turned around slowly, sensing something ominous. I remember the man's voice more than his look, a high-pitched, piercing, nasal Ottawa Valley accent that drew my attention more than the words he spoke. I smiled.

'Hey! You're "Troilus", right? From *Troilus and Cressida* over at the theatre there, eh?'

I played the humble artiste to a tee, complete with downcast head and shuffling heels. In fact, I was totally unaccustomed to being stopped in the street like that and was a little embarrassed.

'Ah yes, yes I am.'

'Yeah, I thought so. Yep. You're "Troilus" in *Troilus and Cressida*.'

We stared at each other not saying anything. He was nodding sagely and I stood red-faced trying to think of something to say. We stood there looking at each other, with everyone at the bus stop looking at us to see what 'piece of action' would be next in this hiccup in their routine. Finally against all my better judgement I asked that question that should never be asked when you are not sure of the response.

'Well, how did you enjoy it? Did you like it?'

Without a moment's hesitation, he replied with all the confidence of a farmer looking at storm clouds.

'Oh no. Noooo! Didn't like it at all. Nope. No.'

'Oh.... Well.... ah.... I'm sorry to hear that.'

He responded as if I had contradicted what he had just said.

'Oh, no, no, no. NO! No I didn't like it at all. No, No.'

Why I didn't cut my losses and run I'll never know, but as our show was being insulted in front of all these strangers, potential paying customers, I thought it was only right that I express my allegiance to both the production and the company.

'Well, I'm sorry you didn't like it, but there are quite a lot of people who have liked it.'

'Well, I didn't like it at all.'

By this time, I could hear the faint giggles coming from the crowd standing around. I took one final stab at positive publicity.

'I'm sorry you didn't enjoy it, but you're one of the few. People have been telling me how much they enjoyed it and I understand the papers were very favourable towards us as well.'

'No, no, I just didn't like it at all.' He went to move away from me and then, summing me up with one final glance,

'No....and you weren't very good either.'

This was too much for the bus waiting group and they finally just let out unabashed guffaws at my expense. I grabbed my tail, placed it firmly between my legs, and shuffled off into the sunset.

12

Fame and Fortune

JOHN NEVILLE
Coming to the New World

Very early in 1972, I was invited by the great Jean Roberts to come to the National Arts Centre in Canada for the first time. She was the head of the English Theatre Company in those lovely days when there was an English company and a French company under the same roof. It was quite wonderful.

I was to direct *The Rivals* by Sheridan. I felt that this would be quite a challenge because the play was designed for a proscenium stage and she wanted it done in the Studio space. When I arrived from England, I was introduced to an extraordinary, top-notch Canadian cast: Tony van Bridge, Mary Savidge, Gerard Parkes, Douglas Chamberlain, Tom Wood, Pamela Brook and many others. It was an incredible cast. I was quite nervous and said so. I remember saying to the cast at the beginning, 'If anyone in this cast is not nervous, they should leave now.'

We had a wonderful time with the play and this terrific cast, and I completely fell in love with Canada. For me, this was to be a four-week job before I returned to Britain. At that time, I had quite a substantial career there and, of course, my wife and six young children. Instead, I phoned my wife to tell her that I loved it here so much that I wanted to bring the family to Canada permanently. Which was what we did.

After *The Rivals*, I was asked to be in *Mrs Warren's Profession,* for Jean once again. Then I was invited to direct an opera at the National Arts Centre. From there I was invited to play in *Hedda Gabler* in Winnipeg with Martha Henry, Douglas Rain and Roland Hewgill. And while in Winnipeg, I was asked to succeed Sean Mulcahy as Artistic Director at The Citadel in Edmonton, which I did for six wonderful years. From there, I went on to Halifax for five years as Artistic Director of the Neptune Theatre. I had a marvellous time, all very heady stuff.

It was during my time in Edmonton that I became a citizen of Canada.

In the course of these early years, I was interviewed several times, but one in particular I remember. It was a long interview conducted by a young man at the CBC in, I think, Toronto, who was fiercely nationalistic. I was given a pretty thoroughly bad time in this interview because I was not born here. He wanted to know why I was here, what the hell did I think I was doing, and so on. His questioning had a very aggressively nationalistic slant. It was not very pleasant. At the time, I was probably too shocked and too shy to say, 'Look, I've fallen in love with Canada and if Canada wants me to stay, I am delighted to do that.' I wanted to explain to him that I had uprooted my entire family to do that because I had felt so strongly.

It was a half-hour interview and the people in the control room were looking a little concerned for me. At the end of the interview, as an addendum that seemed to be laden with innuendo, he asked me why I wore an earring in one ear. The truth was that I had begun wearing one earring as a sailor in the navy during the war. It was a slight affectation, I suppose, that was a throwback to the buccaneer days. I had never seen anyone but a sailor wearing one earring even in Britain. But because the interview had been so uncomfortable I did not explain this to him. Instead I answered without a pause and with a straight face, 'Because I thought *two* earrings would have been effeminate.'

The control room crew went berserk laughing.

As a final ironic note, I found out by accident some time later that this interviewer was not in fact a Canadian, but an American draft dodger. It was the one thing I might have complimented him on.

IAN D. CLARKE to BARBARA WORTHY:
'At the end of any gig always have the equivalent
of one week's salary in the bank.'

JACK CRELEY
Destiny

After studying acting in Los Angeles with Maria Ouspenskaya, I made my way to New York where I studied at the New School with Erwin Piscator. Among my classmates there were Jack Palance, Bea Arthur, Harry Belafonte, Tony Curtis, Elaine Stritch, Tony Franciosa, and Rod Steiger.

One night, after classes, Tony Curtis, Belafonte, and I went out on the town together. We were the Three Musketeers, the chums, the three pretty boys about town. As I made my way home alone some kids pulled me into a doorway and beat my face with a lead pipe. At age 24 I decided to become a character actor. Everyone in New York was feeling so sorry for me and my bashed-in face, I accepted an offer to work at the Mountain Playhouse, in Montreal, for Joy Thompson.

After my seasons at the Playhouse, I came to Toronto. Soon, while my friends in New York were waiting around to do one American Playhouse a year, I was doing five major cBc television roles at the same time. Eventually I even stopped carrying my return bus ticket in my pocket.

BARRY MORSE
The Fugitive story

In the late fifties I got some television parts in American television shows like *The Twilight Zone, The Outer Limits, The New Breed,* and *The Untouchables.* I played a variety of sometimes hilariously contrasting characters, none American. It was my versatility that apparently caught the attention of the television producer, Quinn Martin.

He got in touch with me when I had arrived in L.A. at the conclusion of the national tour of Harold Pinter's *The Caretaker.* Quinn told me he was preparing a new series in which there was a recurring role that he would like me to play. He didn't tell me anything about it. He just sent along a script that I duly read. It was all about a middle-America doctor, Richard Kimble, who was unjustly convicted of murdering his wife and was on the run. I was offered the role of 'Lieutenant Philip Gerard', the dogged policeman who pursued him and was bent upon his recapture. It seemed to me an updating of Victor Hugo's classic novel *Les Miserables.*

Although I didn't quite see why Quinn had thought of me for this rather conventional American type cop, I went along to lunch with him. He wanted to go a lot further with the character than what was presently in the script. He wanted the cop to be pathologically obsessive. Despite the fact that there had never been an instance where a non-American actor had played such a typically American character on an American series, he thought it would work.

We shot the pilot in Tucson, Arizona. I had never met David Janssen, the actor who was to play the doctor, though I was familiar with his work from his previous series *Richard Diamond.* A piece of trivia few people know: Diamond had a Girl Friday, whom the audience never completely saw. Those beautiful legs were played by the then beginner Mary Tyler Moore.

While waiting for the crew to get set up, David and I were wandering along some side street, chatting away and getting to know each other. He asked me, in that dark brown voice of his, what I thought about the show. I had not much encouraging to say since all the trade people that I had spoken to about the idea were convinced that it could never possibly succeed. The 'experts' were concerned that the thing didn't have an ending. 'How can you have a series that no one knows how it will end?' they said.

We shot the pilot and had the preview showings and Quinn told me that the audience-response reports were extremely good, 'They just loved David, and they just *hated* you!' That was exactly what he had wanted. The more they hated my character, the more they could love David's character. This was very brave of Quinn. In those days it was unthinkable that a leading character in a big series should be antipathetic because the advertisers didn't think people would buy their goods.

David was doubtful that the show would have much success. He had done several pilots in the course of his career that had come to nothing. I was on a flat salary but David bemoaned the fact that they were unable to pay him his full price so they'd had to give him 'a piece of it'. I always remember what he said next, 'Of course, we all know what 10% of nothin' is.'

JACK CRELEY
All gravy

Once, David Smith and I accidentally nearly bankrupted the Chez Paris restaurant in Toronto. The Chez Paris was the after-work hangout for folks in the business. Of course, in those days everybody knew each other. Everyone would gather at about 11 o'clock and stay until it closed at 1 a.m., drinking and eating expensive food.

One time David and I were on a save-money campaign so we ordered restaurant bread and gravy. They didn't know what to charge us. I think it ended up being twenty cents. Then Austin (Willis) and Kate (Reid) came in and said 'That looks really good. Let's have that.'

In the end there was this huge group of actors coming in for weeks for their drinks and eating bread and gravy when, previously, they had been ordering dishes like lobster thermidor.

AL WAXMAN
Barney's Beanery

I left law school in Toronto to study acting at the Neighborhood Playhouse School of the Theatre in New York City in the late '50s. After struggling along, working as an usher and living in a cold-water walk-up, I decided to try my luck in Hollywood. I was new in town and I needed a job, so a friend of mine introduced me to Barney, the owner of Barney's Beanery on Santa Monica near La Cienega. It was even then a famous hang-out where out-of-work actors would get a cheap lunch and big-time actors would come slumming in the evening. Scotch was $.45 and rye was $.35.

The funny thing was that you almost needed a résumé to get a job there. My friend told Barney that I had been cooking for the Hilton in New York and I nodded, 'Oh yeah. Sure.' I didn't know how to cook. I still don't know how to cook. But I got the job.

It was really a Mexican open kitchen, strictly short-order hash-house/beanery fare. You were cooking mostly on a grill with a U-shaped counter all around you where people sat. And you were *on* all the time that you were working because you were also the 'entertainment'. A good short-order cook would have the fries and the eggs going and still be bantering with the customers and the other guys who were working there. It was a lot of fun...but I got fired after five weeks. I got caught 'over-portioning'.

We had hamburgers that were stacked with wax paper between them. When I saw an out-of-work actor walk in, I would take three of these burgers and mash them together into one giant hamburger. Food would be hanging over the side of the plate. The plate would be overflowing with this huge burger and as many fries as I could get on there. He'd take the hamburger, cut it in half, and take the other half home for later.

Barney caught me and that was the end of my cooking career.

DAMIR ANDREI
A gentleman of substance

We get little respect in the 'real' world. Like most actors I had already learned to walk a precarious line with the truth when representing myself to financial institutions. Opening a bank account, it was always better to be a substitute teacher, which I also was, than an actor.

I must have been giddy with hubris in the fall of 1981, when I went down to National Trust to apply for a mortgage. They were having a quarter-point-off sale (mortgage rates were 18%!) so there was quite a wait to get an application form. I patiently lined up for forty minutes before I eventually got to the head of the line. A bored bank clerk was handing out the mortgage applications. 'What do you do, sir?' she asked while fishing for a form from a huge box. Seized with some misapprehension of my own normalcy, I snappily replied, 'I'm an actor.'

A flash of unmistakable alarm crossed her face. The form hovered between us. I took one end of it but she held on to the other. 'Really, sir,' she said, 'it's a sale. There are all these...*people* here...' I think I briefly wondered if telling her I was a director as well, would make a difference or provoke outright laughter. I realised that we were both actually tugging at the form and that the line behind me was suddenly quiet and interested. Forty minutes I'd waited!

'This is unbelievable!' I sputtered, 'You know nothing about me except what I do and you won't even let me fill out your lousy application?'

She looked at me with a puzzled, kindly smile, as if I was a recalcitrant kid, who, any minute now, would realise how unreasonable he was being.

'But sir,...OK, sure, you can fill out an application.' She let go of the form.

'And then you'll throw it in the garbage?' I said, crumpling it up. She smiled charmingly in acknowledgement. I'd finally understood the real world.

I went home in a funk and listened to my messages. My agent had called and I had a commercial audition the next day. It seemed National Trust was looking for a spokesman and the casting people thought I might be perfect. The character description said, 'Corporate—with a sense of humour'. Oh, what fantasies of revenge went through my head. Then I called my agent and reminded him that I still had a Bank of Montreal spot on the air.

I got my mortgage through a mortgage broker eventually. And recently I was to note that National Trust has had terrible profit figures for a decade now. The hex worked.

SHAWN ALEX THOMPSON
A guiding light

When my career took off, around 1985, it took off in all directions at once. Quite by accident I landed a part in the American network daytime television program, *The Guiding Light*. The problem was twofold. I was a Canadian citizen with no work permit to work in the States, and my career break north of the border happened at the same time! Yeah, yeah, I know, it's tough all over but here is my tale.

I had been doing the TV show *Switchback,* a live hour-long show, a kind of *Letterman* for teens on Sunday mornings. I wrote that show as well as performed it and I loved it and was very committed to it. I certainly didn't want to give it up. CBC were not going to pay for me to work in New York and *The Guiding Light* wanted me to quit the show in Canada, so they weren't going to pay for it either. The deal was I had to pay for my own airline ticket.

I did *Switchback* for the entire year and a half I was also doing *Guiding Light*. I had to fly back and forth between New York and Toronto every weekend. That year I did 250-odd hours of television. I was probably the only person with two shows running simultaneously in two different countries. I was totally burnt out when the two gigs were finished. I was only being paid $550 per episode of *Switchback* and there were immigration and tax problems that took exactly seventeen weeks to sort out so they held my pay at *The Guiding Light* until they could legally pay me.

I was the star of an American soap and I had $550 a week to live on in New York. Here's the catch: my plane ticket and taxis back and forth to the airport cost $550. For seventeen weeks I was making more money than I have ever seen in my life but I had no money. Up to that moment, I was a mostly unemployed actor, ergo I didn't have a credit card. My dad helped me out by giving me use of his. This was before the days of cash machines but I could use the card to pay for my flea-bag hotel and restaurants.

Here's the story, all true: It was Friday night in New York. We'd finished *The Guiding Light* for that week. I'm to fly to Toronto in the morning. I've got my ticket and enough money to take a cab to the airport. A group of us went out to Studio 54 for a party. I left to go home about 4:30 in the morning. (Ah, youth.) To save cash I decided to walk home; it was only about eight blocks. I got mugged. This huge man in about seven coats pushed me into an alcove waving this little gun. I had forty-five dollars in my wallet. I gave him the money.

I'm alive. I walk back to my crusty $44 a night room. I go to bed grateful that I had survived and that he had thrown the wallet on the ground with my lonely credit card in it. I get up in the morning to fly back to Toronto and I realise that I have no money to get to the airport. But I can get a cash advance at the hotel desk. I know because I watch commercials. I go to the lobby of the Mansfield Hotel, this dive on 44th Street, and the guy behind the desk looks at me as if I was from outer space. Money for a piece of plastic? How did he know I didn't steal it, etc. It is, by now, pissing rain. The desk guy suggested a car service. I started calling car services and they just laughed. There was a torrential rainstorm happening. I had to catch this plane.

Then I remembered that when I had first come to New York I had taken a bus in from the airport for four dollars. I ran back up to my room and went through every pocket and bag and came up with about $4.50. Eureka. The depot is about six blocks away. I figure, what the hell, I'll walk. In the pouring rain. With all my bags. I slog off to the depot and arrive soaked like a drowned rat. I go to the ticket booth. The ticket price has gone up to six bucks.

I went through all my bags to see if I'd missed anything. I hadn't. I was short a buck fifty. I was in New York. I was on a soap opera making thousands of dollars a week, appearing on national television on two shows in two countries. I begged at the bus depot for an hour and a half for a dollar fifty. There I was with all the other homeless people begging. In half an hour I got a dollar! Four people gave me a quarter. Do you think I could get that next fifty cents? I tried and tried. An hour went by and I was getting desperate. I could see the irony in all this. I realised I would laugh about it one day but that last hour was fairly high stress. Finally, some exceptionally lost individual, who may have been a beggar himself, who could barely speak English, opened his hand full of change and let me pick out what I needed. I got my ticket and flew to Toronto.

LEN DONCHEFF
Boy, oh boy!

Some years ago I was cast as Willy Loman in a production of *Death Of A Salesman*. The cast included a young Art Hindle playing 'Happy', Irene Hogan as 'Linda', George Murray as 'Charlie' and Peter McConnell as 'Biff'.

In those days, a parking ticket was $2. I happened to live in a house on a street in downtown Toronto that had no parking space available. Consequently, I had accumulated a stack big enough (probably about $135 worth, a lot of money to me then) to prompt the local police to send out a cadet to haul me off to the station.

It was about 6 p.m. I was heading off to the theatre for the second show and I had no money to pay the fine, so there was no point in a trip to the station. I noticed that this young guy was a cadet so I said to him, 'Can you stop me if I just keep on going?' He said, 'No.' So I kept on going. On Monday, I phoned the City Hall or whatever and explained to them what I intended to do about the unpaid tickets. I intended to turn myself in. They said that would be all right.

In those days you could pay the tickets or spend a couple of days in jail and your record would be cleared of the debt. But if you showed up on Friday night, Friday would count as a full day. They would have to let you out on Saturday morning because they could not keep you over the weekend, beyond the allotted two days. That way I could clear the tickets and not have to miss a show on Saturday night.

I went on to do the rest of the week's performances. When Friday again rolled around I was at home between the matinee and the evening show to have dinner with the lady with whom I shared the house. On matinee days I normally kept my 'Willy Loman' wardrobe on between shows. As I left for the theatre at about 6 p.m. for my 7:30 p.m. performance, the same young cadet showed up at the door demanding that I come to the police station to pay the tickets. This time he had brought along a couple of policemen. We, neither of us, had that kind of money, so I explained to my lady friend what was happening and asked her to call the theatre and tell the director to send someone down with the money right away or I would not make the performance.

Peter McConnell was an ex-cop, so he knew where to go and what to do. I was taken to the station. I tried to explain my circumstances and told them I had called City Hall but they, the cops, were not interested. I was sentenced and put in a holding cell until they could arrange to transfer me to the Don Jail. All I could do was wait and hope that Peter showed up in time. I watched the clock and watched the clock. He wasn't there, didn't come. I figured he was in traffic or had trouble getting together the money. I thought I was going to miss the performance and force them to cancel, a disastrous loss of revenue on our busiest night of the week.

Finally a cop came in and called my name. I leapt up and said, 'That's me!' assuming that I have been bailed out. But no. They were all set to take me to the Don Jail, so off we go in a squad car.

Now these guys *knew* that I was about to explode because I was so worried about making the show. But apparently, they felt that this was a good time for them to take a look at some real estate one of them was considering buying somewhere over in the Leaside area, miles north and east of the Don Jail where they *could* have dropped me off first. They toured around and toured around, toured around a little more and finally got me back to the Don at about 7:20 p.m. Curtain is at 7:30 p.m. What's more...the theatre was in the west end of the city.

Peter, thankfully, figured out where I was being taken and was waiting for us at the Don. He bailed me out, we leapt into the car and floored it across town to the theatre. I got out of the car to make my entrance from the lobby while he drove around back, parked the car, sprinted into the theatre, up the stairs and tucked himself into the second tier of the set to play the sleeping Biff before the lights went up. By then, I had caught my breath just enough to make my entrance. I trudged down the aisle through the audience, up to the stage, dropped my suitcases, and began the scene with the dialogue that at that moment had taken on another level of meaning:

Willy: Boy-O-boy.
Linda: Willy? Is that you?
Willy: Yes. I came back.
Linda: Did anything happen?
Willy: No...Nothing happened.
...and we continued.

MICHAEL IRONSIDE
The fall-back

When I was a young man, before I became an actor, I was a roofer in Toronto, working occasionally for my brother-in-law's business. To this day, even after some

65 films and a couple of hundred hours of TV, I still wake up terrified that someone will realise that I don't belong in the film business and that I'm really just a roofer from the east end.

Vic Armstrong is a famous stuntman in Los Angeles. He doubled for Harrison Ford for years, did the stunt co-ordination on Bond movies and the *Indiana Jones* pictures, to name only a couple. I met him on *Tai Pan* in China and again when I was doing *Total Recall* in Mexico. We were on that film for six months. Vic had designed the stunts and the fight sequences so he, his stunt crew, and I became close friends.

I was playing the guy who is trying to track down the character played by Arnold Schwartzeneggar. During the climax of the film, we have a fight-to-the-death scene in which my arms get cut off by an elevator. Arnold then holds up the ampu- tated lower arms and says, 'See you at the pah-ty' as he throws them down. I pre- sumably had fallen to my death.

To accomplish the stunt, a cast was made of my arms and a rig was designed so that these copies of my arms would be what was cut off. In order to get myself into this rig, I had to climb about 30 feet up a ladder.

I have had about eight surgeries on my knee since 1969 trying to repair an old high school football injury. Occasionally when I am doing a lot of running, as I did on *Total Recall,* it hurts. I try not to let it interfere with work, but on this day as I was climbing up the ladder, my leg gave out on me a little and I stumbled. I never- theless climbed up and got myself into the rigging. We did the shot and I came down again as they reset for a second take. There had been some technical difficulty. When I got back down the ladder, Vic asked me if there was something wrong.

'Yeah, but it's OK.'

'No, you. Are *you* all right?'

Apparently even through my make-up, he had seen me go white from the pain. I told him about my knee.

'I can't climb the ladders any more. I'll never be able to roof again.'

This was still a worry. If acting didn't work out, I had thought I could always go back to roofing, but this bad knee meant that that was no longer possible. It made me feel like I was working without a net.

Vic thought it was hilarious that one of the leads of a huge feature film who had been working in the film business for years was worried that he would never be able to *roof* again! He still tells this story, which is a little embarrassing. But amazingly, that's how deep-seated the insecurity is, and the feeling stays with me. I guess I'll have to make a go of this acting thing.

ANTHONY BEKENN
On different realities

In the same year, 1970, that I became a student at University of British Columbia, I saw a film that made a huge impression on me. It was *Who's Afraid Of Virginia Woolf* with Richard Burton and Elizabeth Taylor. It also starred Sandy Dennis and George

Segal, and proved to be an Oscar-winning performance for Ms Dennis that year.

Eighteen years later, I was to work with Sandy Dennis in the female version of *The Odd Couple*. What a fun experience that was! Having seen her in many films—one of my favourites was *The Out-Of-Towners*—I expected that same quirky, mousy personality. Quirky she definitely was, but hardly mousy. The rest was pure persona. She had a wicked sense of humour both on the stage and off!

During the run of the play, the Oscar telecast was showing on our day off, so I invited a few people over to watch the show. I was on the couch next to Sandy when the award for best supporting actress was presented, the category in which she had won almost twenty years earlier. I asked her about how it had felt to win her Oscar. She said only that Mike Nichols had picked it up for her.

For the first time, it hit me that all that stuff up on the TV screen, 'winning an Oscar' and so on, was *tangible*...because someone who had won was sitting beside me on my second-hand couch in the east end of Toronto. I think I realised for the first time that it could happen to any actor, no matter where you came from. But winning such awards did *not* mean that you wouldn't once again, years down the road, be sitting on a second-hand couch in east end Toronto.

It was an interesting revelation about our lives as actors and the nature of success and fame. But what a journey!

PAUL MacLEOD
Reality bites

It was an incredible opportunity, a chance to work with important television producers from Toronto. I was to play the interviewer on a commercial, for a well-known cold medication, to be shot in Lunenburg, Nova Scotia.

On set, I checked everyone out. Bud, the copywriter, for instance. A veteran wordsmith, Bud could persuade millions to buy product. Next, Peter, the producer: this brilliant, highly paid American had a flare for gripping stories, mostly about bloody battles with his wife before the divorce. Then I met Pam, the sound technician. She was from Prince Edward Island, so I assumed she'd be all right. I invited her out for a drink and suggested a drive to Blue Rocks. She thought Blue Rocks was the name of a bar. On the way, she forced me to stand in a graveyard while she took photos of me amongst the statues. I feigned a headache and returned to the hotel.

Next morning I finally encountered the star of the commercial, Sherrie M. She was a stunning blonde with a delightful personality. The only drawback was that she was eight months pregnant and looked it. The crew guessed she'd have twins. Everyone turned to the producer to solve the problem. First, he tried to hide her behind some lobster pots but they weren't big enough. Then he suggested the product logo be placed across her stomach in the editing process. Finally, Sherrie was covered in a yellow slicker, which worked wonders.

She did a couple of takes. I expected to see the whole town on the wharf to witness this important event. Only a couple of old salts showed up. One of them asked the star if she had any samples of the beer she was selling—any kind would do. He was told politely to shove off. He retaliated by firing up his chainsaw during takes. He got his beer.

Finally, I was called on set. At last my chance to shine on national TV. And before the home-town crowd. Only, the two old salts had gone home.

MICHAEL IRONSIDE
Real money

My first big break in the film business was when I was hired for a small part in David Cronenberg's *Scanners*. It was initially a very small part, two days' shoot. David came to me after the first day and said that the script was going through some changes and that the part was going to be a little larger. Well, great! And as it evolved, the part ended up being effectively the antagonist lead. However my contract, for whatever reason, was never altered or re-negotiated to reflect that. I was still on a 'daily' contract at daily rates.

We shot in Montreal up until Christmas of 1979. I remember we were wrapping up and Jennifer O'Neill, the female star, and her husband at that time asked me if I wanted to go to dinner. I thought that was great. Montreal was a long way from home for me. It was an adventure, because I'd really never been anywhere before.

We went to a very fancy restaurant, and in the course of the conversation Jennifer asked me what I was buying the crew for Christmas. I was so green, I had no idea what she was talking about.

'What do you mean? I'm trying to steal my wardrobe.' (I had had a wedding to go to at Christmas and I didn't own a suit.)

'What do you mean, you're trying to steal your wardrobe?'

'I'm making eight (thousand dollars) and change on this picture.' She looked dumbfounded.

'Canadian?'

'Yes.'

'A week?'

'No, for the whole picture.'

At that her husband started choking on his chicken. He apologised as they both became red in the face from embarrassment.

'I'm so sorry.'

'Why?'

'Because it's not very much money.'

So I asked how much she was making.

'Seventy thousand a week, American.'

I clicked that off in my head and realised that she was making upwards of $350,000 American. There was an pregnant lull in the conversation.

'My God. I'm so embarrassed. Is there anything I can do?'

'Yeah. You can pay for dinner and I'll have another drink if you don't mind.'

I had been hanging around in the film business in Canada for a few years, and that was my first inkling that you could actually make a living as an actor.

JEAN LECLERC
What is famous?

As young actors, most of us trained for the theatre. If we made some money on the side doing TV, or whatever, then this was good but the primary focus was our stage work. I went from doing stage in Canada to star on Broadway in *Dracula* and this seemed to me the way things should be. It was great fun, a wonderful experience. I got fantastic reviews and we sold out for two years. Sometimes, I would come out of the stage door after a performance and there would be twenty or twenty-five people standing there, waiting for me! I thought, 'This is what fame is all about. This is wonderful.' Success in my field.

I moved to California. Shortly after, I received a call to come to New York and audition for the part of 'Jeremy Hunter' in a daytime series called *All My Children*. They sent this description of the character along with the script: tall, blond, all American with British background. I called my agent and said, 'Have you seen me lately?' He replied, 'Don't pay any attention to that. They really want someone who could play a character who would be believable as an ex-monk from Tibet and at the same time an ex-mercenary.' It was pretty funny.

I flew to New York figuring, what did I have to lose. When I arrived to do the audition there were wall-to-wall tall, blond, *Gentleman's Quarterly* guys. I mean, wall to wall. I said to myself, 'Oh, Lord. What am I doing here?' After the audition I flew right back to Los Angeles because I wasn't going to wait around for a decision when I felt certain that I was not going to get the part; it was too far fetched.

Two days later I was called back to New York, this time to screen test with Susan Lucci. I was so remote from the daytime TV world that I had no idea who she was. I got the part. I signed a three-year contract thinking that if I lasted two months there that would be great. I just had no idea what this world was about. When I went to work I found out that this program I was on was reaching twenty-three million people a day! It was unbelievable to me.

As it turned out, the relationship between my character and Susan Lucci, this huge star of daytime TV, was an enormous success. And I thought I had been famous when 25 people waited for me at the stage door! A week after my character, Jeremy, went on the air I decided to go out for lunch. Outside the studio the taxis stopped. The buses stopped. All these people were screaming, 'Jeremy! Jeremy!' Then the letters started, hundreds and hundreds of them, marriage proposals, the whole thing. I was stunned. I went on to do *All My Children* for twelve and a half wonderful years.

A daytime TV series is, without any doubt, the most difficult thing for an actor to do. It is an art form in itself with its plusses and its minuses. A prime time series, on any network, will take five to ten days to shoot an episode of one hour's length.

In daytime TV we do the same service in twelve hours. And we repeat that five days a week. It is a never-ending experience about keeping the energy level up and the story line connected from one episode to the next. We would come in at seven in the morning and never left 'til eight or nine at night. We shot, on average, forty pages a day, delivering five shows at the end of the week. There is no hiatus. It goes all year round. We would have guest stars who would come on for a few shows and say, 'My God! How do you do this?'

I believe daytime TV is the best possible school. It is an imperfect art form. It becomes repetitious. How many damsels in distress can you save? How many tears can you shed on yourself? But small miracles happen every day on those sound stages. It's amazing what they do. When you know how to do this kind of work, I feel you can do anything.

TONY ROSATO
On *Saturday Night Live*

My family immigrated to Ottawa from rural Italy when I was 8 years old. My father became ill, went back to Italy alone and died a few years later. My mother, who did not speak English well, worked two jobs her whole life, sometimes as a migrant field hand with me in tow, to provide the two of us with one room with a hot plate. I grew up with little or no supervision mostly in the streets on my own. Whenever I could I would duck into a movie house and spend hours there. It was a long road from that movie house to the *Saturday Night Live* stage.

The three years that I spent on *Saturday Night Live* were fabulous. I was one of several of Second City's *SCTV* troupe who were scouted for *SNL* shortly after the original 'Not Ready for Prime Time' cast had dispersed. The cast that I joined on *SNL* included Eddie Murphy, Joe Piscopo, Christine Ebersol, Tim Kasarinski, Robin Duke, Brian Doyle Murray, and Laurie Metcalf. And during the season, Bill Murray, Chevy Chase, John Belushi, Robin Williams and other alumni people came by often to contribute.

It was awesome to be meeting and working with these people. Joe Flaherty had shown his friend, John Belushi, a video of the impressions I had done of John while I was still at *SCTV* and he loved them. Partly because of that, everyone seemed to be heralding me as 'the next John Belushi' including John himself. When Robin Duke and I arrived in New York, he and Dan Aykroyd went out of their way to greet us and take us out on the town, talk about the show, and help us acclimatize. Later John made a point of introducing me to his agent, Bernie Brillstein and asked that he take me on. Bernie represents me to this day.

It took until the end of the first season for me to understand just how important this show was. It was the highest rated comedy show in television, with a significant influence in American pop culture. Its rock and roll style of satire reflected the conscience and pulse of a generation of Americans that would be the next to come into power. I was meeting and working with icons of our time, politicians, poets, writers, thinkers, musicians, idols, stars. I mean, what do you say to Mick

Jagger? or William Burroughs? or Truman Capote? Above and beyond all that, they handed me this amazing chunk of money each week and my own limo.

At the age of twenty-four, maybe I should have found all of this overwhelming. Instead I felt totally ready for it. I had a huge appetite for experiencing life's banquet and here it was, laid out before me. I felt as if I were standing on a surfboard on top of a huge wave and all I wanted to do was *ride it*. It was pretty exciting and, at the same time, I had no idea what I was doing there.

Tim Kasarinski and I were the only two cast members who were also part of the writing team. I think you have to be very evolved to write great satire. You have to be able to transcend the social perspective that we all live with day to day. Ultimately the way you comment on life and society becomes a reflection of transcendant insight. To do that you have to have had time, time to have lived.

I only realize in retrospect that I was much too young. I was a good insinctive clown, a cute face with a few good comedy licks. I was not really experienced enough in life to understand or be able to write and execute truly sharp satire.

I also had no idea how much I had taken on in terms of sheer workload. Though both *SCTV* and *SNL* had similar audiences and both involved sketch comedy with political and social targets, there were big differences in their execution. On *SCTV* we had had seven months to write the shows in an easy, compassionate, unconditionally loving atmosphere of 'family' members where ideas were allowed to grow and be nurtured into workable premises. We had the luxury of several days to tape and then more time to hone it in the edit. All of that preparation and care showed in the quality of the final result.

In sharp contrast, *SNL* was big, national, network and *live!* The environment and logistics were much more complicated. The original *SNL* had been successful because it was effectively a bunch of rebellious brats screaming at their parents...to an audience of 40 million people. Our cast was expected to revive that original success. But the instincts and behaviour patterns that made us good were not appropriate to dealing politically within a corporate structure. In addition, we would have only 2½ days to write 90 minutes of material, often for performers we did not know well. We rehearsed briefly, then the show was shot, ragged edges and all, live to air with a studio audience! That's the way it was done, every week.

As with *SCTV*, I wanted deeply, passionately to do the best work of my life for this show. I loved doing it, being there, the energy, the creativity, everything. Even at the height of the insanity, I would sit in my room and think 'God , I'm so lucky to be here'. But never having had much 'parental' interference in my own life, either personally or professionally, I had no idea how to handle my parent/bosses. That and the responsibility of the writing work-load on top of being a performer added up to crushing pressure. The only thing that kept us awake enough to get the work done was cocaine. That was the only reason that we used it. But it was a recipe for disaster.

One evening became a turning point for me. I was sitting in a room with Terry Southern, who wrote *Dr Strangelove,* Michael Donohue, the head writer at *SNL,* John Belushi, Bill (William) Burroughs, and later, Peter Sellers. We all sat there drinking scotch and/or doing whatever else was around, discussing life, art, culture, philosophy, politics—late into the evening. I was in awe of these people. They had so much to say. There I was, one of them, accepted by them. It was a complex bond of kindred spirits. We had all had similar childhoods and much in common in our early years. I felt very lucky to be among them and at the same time I felt suddenly very small and insignificant. I realised that I had very little to contribute to the conversation simply because I had not lived long enough. It spelled the beginning of the end for me.

Over the next few months I began to rebel. I created arguments on issues that were valid on one level but I reacted, almost deliberately, out of proportion. I became an asshole to work with because I wanted to leave the show and I didn't know how. All of this was aggravated by my cocaine abuse. Eventually, during the contract renewal period, the producers invited me back...with conditions that I 'behave myself'. I reacted badly to that, insulted a few key people in a heated phone conversation and refused to apologize, so they released me. I was finally free. I stopped doing the drugs and haven't done them since.

Shortly after that I went out to Los Angeles and almost immediately landed a part in a sit-com that was a remake of John Cleese's *Fawlty Towers* and starred Bea Arthur. I really didn't have much time to reflect on what I might have given up by leaving *SNL* until after that show had ended. I have no idea how my life might have been different had I stayed. In the end, I'm happy to be doing what I love to do and I will always feel deeply grateful for the experience I had on both *SCTV* and *SNL*.

BEATRICE LILLIE
On M. LeFevre's mother

Guy LeFevre, a Canadian-born actor, singer, and composer featured in the show [one of Charlot's *Revues* in which Beatrice Lillie was also starring] was being kept by an older woman who was very wealthy and harboured a haughty and decidedly jaundiced view of actors. One day the lady arrived backstage after a performance to pick up her beloved and was confronted by a newly hired young call boy.

When the lady imperiously informed the lad that she was there for Mr LeFevre, the eager-to-please child raced to the bottom of the stairs and shrieked, 'Mr LeFevre! Your mother's waiting for you!'

Bea and [fellow actress] Odette [overhearing this exchange] slammed their doors simultaneously shut and collapsed in tears in laughter.

ERNIE COOMBS
Stepping out

Being recognised in public is something we showbiz personalities become accustomed to. Actually we dote on it, don't we?

Usually there is the moment of recognition, then the gasp of awe, followed by a gush of adulation. My response to this is a beneficent smile as I modestly assume a benign manner in order to put my worshipper at ease. Then I wait for the gush.

But there are exceptions. One Christmas season my wife and I spent a weekend at a small resort in the Muskoka region. There was a dance that Saturday night, attended by local folk as well as resort guests. As we were doing our fancy two step, Lyn and I bumped against another couple. As we stopped to apologize, I saw 'that look' come over the couple's faces. I assumed my Famous-but-Modest stance, only to hear the guy exclaim, 'Mr Dressup! What the fuck are you doing here?'

SARAH POLLEY
All grown up and on a date

When I was seven years old, I did my first job, playing 'Ramona' in a children's series by the same name. For that show, I had to have about eight inches cut off my hair, and it was dyed red about three times before the colour would take. The series was only ten episodes but it was a lot of fun and I'm told it was quite popular. In one or two cases people told us that it had actually encouraged kids who saw the show to read the Beverly Cleary books on which it was based. So I was really proud of the show.

Ten years later, I was on a date with a guy, a boyfriend. We're sitting in this restaurant and this waiter comes up and looks at me funny and says, 'Are you "Ramona"?' I thought, 'Gees, can you recognize me from when I was *seven?* I'm on a date here. Have I not changed since then or *what?* I don't even have red hair any more!'

It was the only time I was really embarrassed to be recognized from work I'd done.

DINAH CHRISTIE
It's not who you are

It was a late summer day in 1989 when I dashed into the Copy Shop in Toronto. John Brooks was just about to start printing off an order for a tall blonde woman as I burst in.

'Hi, Dinah. How goes it?' he threw over his shoulder at me. The blonde turned to scrutinize me and nodded shyly. She had a very tanned face and her eyes twinkled. I had straightened up my papers on the counter when she approached.

'You *are* Dinah Christie, aren't you? I've got something amazing to tell you. This past winter I treated myself to a trip to the Bahamas. I'd been feeling really lousy since my marriage ended and felt I bloody deserved it. After a day or two, I went for a stroll on the beach and wandered past a lounge bar that extended out from a nearby hotel. As I glanced at the people sitting there, a man leapt up, started waving frantically, and tore down the beach towards me.

'He raced up, grabbed me, whirled me around and kissed me full on the lips! "Damn! I haven't seen you for ages. Not since that film we did in Winnipeg. It has to be fifteen years! You look fabulous!" I was dumbfounded. He said, "Oh, sorry. I was the first A.D. on the thing. Tony, remember?" Well, I told him I was terribly sorry but I didn't remember him at all. "Oh, don't worry. You can't remember everyone you meet. Let's have dinner, shall we? Are you here with someone?"

'Well, bottom line is, I finally managed to explain that I really wasn't Dinah Christie at all but thanks for the compliment. He was appropriately embarrassed and we got giggly thinking what you might think if you ever heard about this.

'He suggested that you'd be really pleased if I'd go to dinner with him, anyway. So I did. And guess what? We're still dating! So, what I really wanted to say is, thank you!'

HARVEY ATKIN
The ticket

My wife and I are on our way to do a benefit at the Hotel Triumph just outside of Toronto. We are slightly late and are in the heated 'debate' mode regarding the route we should take. The debate grows more heated to the point where we stop talking to each other. By now, we're both in a great mood for a party. Then a cop pops out of the bushes and motions us over. Great, this is all we need. We quickly buckle on our seat belts, not wanting to be fined for that infraction. I hadn't been speeding.

The cop sticks his head in the window, gives us the once over.

'Nice try. Please step out of the car.' I'm incredulous.

'For a seat belt ticket?'

'Please. Step out of the car.'

By this time my patience is at a low ebb and my fury is planted firmly on my face. I get out of the car and go over to his cruiser under the trees. He leans into his car and takes out a pad of paper and says, 'Can I have your autograph?' While I am still trying to absorb the insanity of the situation he hands me a pen and says, 'Make it out to Ruben, will ya?'

Sure. Sir.

CHRIS WIGGINS
That actor fella

The irony of being a recognizable face in Canada is that no one here quite believes that you could actually be the person they have seen on TV. Famous people are always from 'someplace else', certainly not their neighbourhood. So if someone stops me on the street because they recognize me, they think they must have met me at a party or something. However, when I have travelled in the United States or Europe, I have often been stopped and asked for autographs.

I was doing a film with James Garner out in Lethbridge, Alberta some years ago. We were to be out there for some time and I hate bloody hotels, so my wife and

I decided to take our dogs out in our camper. We stayed in a campground and had a wonderful time. It was lovely.

The first morning I went to shave part of my beard down because the part required me to have a little Van Dyck beard. So I was there shaving away over one of the fifteen or so washbowls that are lined up in a typical campground. A few other 'guys' came in and there was the usual morning chatter while they were doing their morning ablutions. They were all down at the other end of the row of wash-bowls. Suddenly I hear someone speaking.

'Do you know that actor fella, Chris Wiggins?' I stopped dead and turned around.

'Well, yes.'

'Well, you sure look like him.'

'Well, there is a reason for that.'

'Ya?'

'That's who I am.'

'Uh-huh.' He pondered that for a second, 'Well, you sure look like him.'

I had no idea what to say.

13

Early Radio and TV Days

ALFIE SCOPP
'The Voice of Doom'

Lorne Greene set up the Academy of Radio Arts at the end of the Second World War to assist returning war veterans. He wanted to give those who had missed four or five years of their working life a chance to learn about broadcasting. He provided a full curriculum, acting, sound effects, writing, and all the attendant skills. The faculty included Lorne himself along with Mavor Moore, Andrew Allan, Lister Sinclair—all the best people available. At that time almost all the professional work being done in this country was radio. There were one or two theatres but you didn't really get paid.

Some of the students who went through the Academy in the early years are Leslie Nielsen, Fred Davis, Gordie Tapp, Cec Linder, Anna Cameron, Tom Harvey and Jimmy Doohan, who played 'Scotty' in the television series, *Star Trek*. It was a great group.

I had been in the Royal Canadian Air Force. Posted to an isolation station in Gander, Newfoundland, I had done some jazz and sports broadcasting from a small professional radio station we had set up. I knew nothing about broadcasting. I'd just done it. Consequently I was quite good at it because I didn't know enough to get worried about it. I'd just breeze into the little studio, do my bit, and get finished on time. We also did all of our own entertaining there and I quite took to it.

When I was discharged, I was thinking I might do burlesque vaudeville, so I came to Toronto. I then met someone who told me about Lorne Greene's Academy of Radio Arts. Curious, I called Lorne and he invited me down to CKEY, the Toronto radio station where he was working at that time, for a chat.

We talked for a few minutes in his studio. He told me that the school was full up and he wasn't going to accept any more pupils but none the less he would give me a few minutes.

'I'm going into the control room. Read this copy.'

He handed me some copy and, of course, I was awful.

'OK, ad-lib something for a few minutes.'

I told him about hitchhiking and I had some pretty funny tales. When I was finished he called me into the booth.

'Congratulations. I'm going to accept you!'

I was really embarrassed. I didn't want to say to Lorne Greene, the Voice of Doom, as they used to call him, that I wasn't sure. He was such an important man in the business. So I said OK. He told me about the curriculum.

'I think you should take announcing, writing, and I think you should take acting.'

'Oh God, no! I don't want to be an actor.'

'Why not?'

'Well, actors are kinda "dancey", aren't they?'

And in his deepest voice, and it was deep, he said,

'*I'm* an actor.'

That's the story of how a street guy like me ended up at The Lorne Greene Academy with all these splendid people when I had never acted in my life.

ALFIE SCOPP
Forty-five dollars

Andrew Allan was one of the instructors at the Academy of Radio Arts. He wanted to show the students that there was a living to be made in radio, so at the end of the first year of his course he announced that he was going to give each of the students an opportunity to work on one of his broadcasts.

My name was selected to be the first. When I started at the Academy I didn't know the names of radio actors. I never used to listen to that kind of radio. But after a year of discussing their work on a weekly basis I was in enormous awe of these people—John Drainie, Bernie Braden, and on and on. I walked into the studio for my rehearsal call and they were all there! Barbara Kelly, Ruth Springford, what seemed like the entire upper echelon of radio.

The actors sat down around a long table. Andrew came into the studio carrying all the scripts, accompanied by his sound man. After saying good morning to every-one he called out the actor's name and the part they were playing and handed them their script. 'Mr Drainie, "Bill"; Mr Scopp, "Walter"...' etc. This was the first time I had ever been called Mr Scopp in my entire life! I was so impressed.

We didn't look at the script right away. Andrew gave a brief dissertation on what the play was about. What its background was. What Andrew was aiming for in the production. It was very impressive. Of course, I started looking through the script right away to see where the part of Walter was. I was listening but I was also curious. I flipped through the whole darn thing and I couldn't find Walter anywhere. I was sitting beside John Drainie who looked over to me and said,

'What's your problem?'

'Oh, I can't find my part, "Walter".'

'Walter? He said "Waiter".'

By this time Andrew was looking over at me and this was not good. The direc-tor of the Stage series was God and I was interrupting him. I eventually found 'Waiter' somewhere around page 42. My scene consisted of the sound effect of a restaurant, dishes clattering, then the lead, John Drainie, was to come rushing through the restaurant. He was to see the waiter, me, and say,

'Waiter, can you tell me where Joe Smith is?' I was to reply with the line:

'Yes, he's over there, sir.'

That was it. Five words. But I was completely thrilled with them.

'How much do you get paid for this?'

'Forty-five dollars.'

Forty-five dollars! That was an enormous amount at that time. It would keep you for a month. I was living on sixteen dollars a month from the War Vets. But, forty-five dollars wasn't *my* salary, surely.

'Yes. Everybody gets paid the same, if you have a speaking part.'

That was the way at the CBC then. Very egalitarian, nobody was to be a star.

'Wow! That means I'm getting nine dollars a word!'

'Maybe we can make it even better than that.'

I didn't know what he meant but it sounded good to me.

After the first day of rehearsal I went back to my digs and, of course, all the Academy was gathered to hear the story of what it was like. And I was Mr Big Shot, telling them all about it: and Oh, yes, John said this and Barbara said that. I was completely impressed with myself. And I told them what my five words were. Then they all had advice as to how I should play them.

The day after the rehearsal was the live show. I'd phoned home to tell them to listen out for me. The word went all round my big family in Montreal. In those days when you came for the broadcast you got dressed up because it was considered a very prestigious event. I had to borrow a jacket and tie. We did the dress rehearsal. As it got closer and closer to the show, my nerves got up.

The show started. My, it was wonderful to watch those people and to see how confident they were. The way they made everything work was an eye opener. I waited for my line, getting more and more excited as it came closer and closer. I stood up and went to the single standing microphone—too early. Drainie moved me, very kindly, out of the way and motioned that he would bring me in at the right time. The moment arrived. He brought me to the mike. The restaurant noises started. The cue was given to John to say his line, he came rushing in and said,

'Waiter! Have you seen Joe Smith?'

'Uh...'

'It's OK. I see him.'

He'd cut me right off! The cast were highly amused. Even Andrew had a smile on his face. I was so disappointed. As soon as the play ended there was a roar of laughter from the cast and Drainie came over to me, sitting disconsolate in my chair, and said,

'You see, I told you. Now you'll be paid forty-five dollars and you didn't even have to open your mouth!'

That was my inauguration. Ironically, because it was such a funny story, and people who were there told other people, I became a known person around the CBC. I started to get work right away. But the best line belongs to my mother who said, when I phoned home afterwards, 'You must have been wonderful because I didn't recognise your voice!'

SANDY WEBSTER
Communing

After WW II, instead of studying hard at Queen's University for a good solid grounding in General Arts, I confess I spent a great deal of my time at the excellent Drama Guild. In my final year my group had a Sunday night ritual of listening to the radio program CBC *Stage*. We'd go to a friend's boarding house; he had a very ample room and a very tolerant landlady. One of us was training to be a doctor, one was a science man, and two or three were in Arts. We would darken the room and listen, religiously.

I think the most impressive and moving experience of all was when we heard Mavor Moore in the play *Socrates*. I can remember, as if it were yesterday, sitting and listening to the drumbeats at the end. 'Socrates' takes the hemlock and talks to his students as the poison creeps through his system and, finally, he dies. We listened to Lucio Agostini's wonderful music and then a great kettle drum began to play: 'Boom...Boom...Boom...' It moved into his heartbeat as he was slowly fading—'Boom...Boom...Boomph...' Dead silence.

After what seemed like a very long time Elwood Glover came on and said 'Socrates' with Frank Peddie in the title role, and did the credits. We would listen right to the end to learn who had been part of this. Then we turned the radio off. We must have sat there, in the dark, for ten minutes. Nobody could say anything. We just sat there and communed with Socrates.

MAVOR MOORE
On double entendres

In the early days a well-known women's commentator at CBC radio, Toronto, had a daily program. She had been a newspaper woman and had a great voice and a very warm personality. Two occasions combined to get her fired. They are perfect examples of what can happen on radio with its strange power of double entendre. On the first occasion she had a guest from the entertainment world. She introduced the man. She mentioned him by name and said what a great magic show he was doing at whatever theatre and then she said 'But, ladies, wait 'til I tell you what he does! It is simply wonderful. He has these balls and he turns out the light and juggles with them in the dark.'

Frank Willis was the producer and he was in the booth going—no, no, cut, go on to something else. She realized what she had said and tried to recover herself as best she could.

Some weeks later (this time I was in the booth with Willis) she was absolutely determined to make it perfectly clear who it was she was interviewing. In this case it was a champion archer. She began by saying 'Now, my guest today, ladies, is someone very special...' She mentioned his name, where he was from, that he was a champion, but somehow never actually mentioned the word 'archery'.

She started the interview.

'Now, Mr so and so, have you brought it with you?'

'Yes. I've got it right here.'

'Can I hold it?'

'Certainly.'

'Oh, my, it's big and strong.'

'Not really, just regular championship size.'

Willis was desperately gesturing to her in the booth but she just kept going.

'Do you mind if I pull it?' On and on with nary a mention of a bow, arrows, archery, nothing. It was just a disaster.

The poor lady was let go by the CBC after this but became a great success as a commentator on radio elsewhere.

DON (ACE) MacDONALD
The sing-ger

I had been in the navy during the last part of the War (WW II), and after, went to the Lorne Greene Academy of Radio Arts, first as a student electrical engineer. I switched in mid-stream when I heard that 'God' had spoken. Lorne had invited me down. I thought actors could make a good living in Canada in those days and I did very well indeed in commercials and acting and on radio.

I was the youngest announcer ever hired by the CBC out of CKUA in Edmonton where Bob Goulet, Fred Diehl, Arthur Hiller (who became a famous director in Hollywood) all worked. Arthur was an announcer, the worst announcer in the world. We used to strip him naked while he was reading the night news. I once went in and lit his newscript on fire and he just laughed...on the air, couldn't stop laughing. He wasn't fired but they put me on as the regular news reader.

Bob Goulet came on board there as a disc jockey at about the same time I did. He and I became quite good chums. We'd finish work at night and there would be a bevy of twenty-five, thirty groupies...for *him*. He used to tell me a story a week in a different dialect. He was the best stand-up comic I ever heard. He was a very funny guy. I asked him later why he never worked his comedy into his singing act. He said, 'No, I don't want to use comedy. I'm a sing-ger.'

At the radio station he would practise his singing over the records...*on air*. They gave him hell for it. What they wouldn't give to have him sing over the records now.

DAN MacDONALD
They don't make 'em like that anymore

A wonderful old English actor, H. Leslie Pigot, lived for many years in Halifax, Nova Scotia. Mr Pigot, as everyone called him, was a mainstay of the theatrical community at the time, highly respected as an actor, teacher and repository of professional knowledge, behaviour and custom. Mr Pigot did a great deal of radio drama, CBC Halifax being the most active anglophone centre outside of Toronto in those days. He was in every radio show, or so it seemed, and he was very good.

He had, however, the unnerving habit of nodding off while others were performing, sleeping soundly in his chair until his next cue arrived. Thereupon, he would move quietly, and unhurriedly, to the mike, arriving just in time to deliver his next bit of script. Flawlessly.

I worked with him a great many times under the direction of Peter Donkin and was fascinated with Pigot's unique ability. Each time I thought, 'Ah, this is it...', but it never was. These were the days of 'live' radio, so you can imagine how twitchy we were, seeing him snoozing happily while we fretted over whether he would wake up in time, *this* time.

One evening, while a serious drama was being emoted across the 'Trans-Canada Network of the CBC', it seemed Mr Pigot might, finally, have cut it a bit too close. I edged over to his chair and was just about to rouse him when, without a twitch, one eye flipped open at me. He stared briefly, and whispered, 'An actor must be able to catnap when he can.' He winked and added, 'But make very sure you keep your ears open!' as he started towards the microphone.

LISA LANGLOIS
Casting 101

Early in my career, my agent called to inform me that I was booked on a radio play.

'But I don't know what I'm supposed to do. I've never done voice work.'

'Just do what you did for the audition.'

'But I never did an audition for a radio play,' I said.

'Well, the producer wants you.'

It was the right thing to say to an actor so I suited up, showed up, and acted 'as if'. Throughout recording, the producer seemed quite pleased with my work. In fact, as I was signing out, he stopped me.

'I am so glad that I hired you because I remembered you from the audition. You had so much depth to your voice.'

DONALD DAVIS
Plummy tones

A friend and I were driving back from visiting my aged father in hospital and we were listening to a play on CBC radio. It was about a famous artist and I found it very interesting. The story was curiously familiar, as if I had read something about his life before. The play was intriguing but I didn't care for the actor who was doing the narration. He had that CBC pretension about his speech, more British than the British. I was complaining to my friend about him, about how I deplored the loss of 'Canadian' speech, and wondering just who it might be.

I pulled into my driveway and stayed a few minutes longer to hear the credits. To my great surprise the narrator was myself! I had been so preoccupied with my father's health that I forgotten all about the little job I'd done for CBC some few weeks before. It was me. A lesson indeed.

JOHN REEVES
The railway station

Broadcaster Otto Lowy, a resident in Canada since the 1940s, is a fine example of an immigrant who makes a valuable contribution to life here. But he never lost his connection to Prague, where he grew up. To be uprooted, as he was, as a refugee leaves an abiding sense of loss. In his case, he came to terms with it in part by writing about it, notably in a radio script entitled *Going Home*. Among other things it describes his flight from Czechoslovakia when the Nazis invaded. There was a touching scene set in the Prague railroad station where he said 'Goodbye' to his mother who could not be persuaded to come with him to England where he was to enlist in the RAF. He would never see her again. He lost her and all of his immediate relatives in the Holocaust.

Otto was not only a good writer but an accomplished actor. In the production of his script, he played himself as a young man. Other members of the cast were drawn from the Czech community in Toronto so that the text would be performed with authentic accents. Otto's mother was played by Hana Malinovsky, a senior actress from Bratislava who had escaped to Canada in 1968. The scene between them had unbelievable poignancy from the very first read-through.

After the whole text was recorded, the actors popped into the control room, as was customary, to say 'goodbye' and 'thank you'. But Hana lingered after the others had gone and asked for a moment. She was worried that she might have overplayed the station scene because it had meant so much to her personally.

'You see,' she said, 'when the Russians invaded in 1968, I managed to get away...by train. And I tried to persuade my son, who was a young man, to come with me. But he insisted on staying. So we had to say goodbye...on the station platform. And I will probably never see him again.'

DAN MacDONALD
Suiting Mom

In the short time it took Martin Lager to realise his talents lay in the writing, rather than acting, area of the business, he appeared as a 'bit player' in several early television and stage productions. His first television appearance was a 'walk-on' on CBC. Marty played a bedraggled, down-and-out bum sitting on a park bench.

When the night of the telecast arrived, his whole family gathered to watch his debut, making the appropriate noises of approval during his scene. After the show, everyone bubbled with compliments on the fine job he had done, and how proud they were to have a real, professional actor in the family. Everyone, except his mother. As Moms will, she fretted.

'But Martin, why didn't you wear your good suit?'

DOUGLAS CHAMBERLAIN
This Shakespeare stuff

I remember doing a live television show of *Macbeth* in the early days. Barry Morse was playing 'Macbeth' and Patrick Macnee was playing 'Macduff'. I carried a spear but, because I had also been an acrobat, I was hired mainly to do a piece of stunt business, falling down 32 stairs after a sword fight.

I had the fight with Barry at the top of the stairs, then fell as if dead, head over heels. I fell down 32 steps four times that day in rehearsal.

All my family were sitting up to see my big moment on TV. It was a big deal to them but my bit didn't come till the end of the play. They waited and waited but they were all bored out of their minds when by twelve o'clock, I still hadn't done my thing. The play was long, long, long. By the time it got to my fight and I did my bit, they had turned out the box and gone to bed.

BARRY MORSE
Christmas, you say?

My wife, Sydney Sturgess, our children and I had arrived in this country a few months in advance of the very moment that television was gearing up to burst upon an astonished Canada in the fall of 1952. As fate would have it, I was one of the few professional actors living in Canada at that time who had ever appeared in a television show. I had done a good deal of it in the UK before coming across.

In 1936, when I first started to work for BBC television in London, the medium was not at all popular. Most actors who were in any way established wouldn't be seen dead on television. That was partly because it was so miserably badly paid but also because nobody believed that television could ever become a wide spread, universally popular public entertainment!

I remember an older, well-established actor saying in sonorous tones, 'Morse, what is this I hear you are doing during the day, then?' I replied, 'Well, it's for the BBC, sir.' You always called older actors 'sir' in those days. 'Oh yes, yes, yes. It's the wireless, isn't it?' 'Well, no, sir, it's not exactly the wireless. It's like the wireless but with pictures.' His face took on an appearance of intense disgust and he said. 'Oooooh yes, I've heard of that rubbish. Called the te-le-vision, isn't it? Well, you're a bloody fool wasting your time with that twaddle. Don't you understand? It's just a fad like the yo-yo. The public will have forgotten all about it by Christmas.'

DONALD HARRON
Loose lips

Actors live in constant fear of forgetting their lines. I did my first television drama back in 1951 for the BBC in England. Several actors were also having their maiden voyage on this new medium and the atmosphere was tense when we went on air for ninety minutes live. One of the actors was a man well over seventy-five, a key player in the dramatic scene at the end of the piece. Unfortunately, he forgot his lines. But fortunately, for him, he had enough sense to keep his lips moving as if he was speaking. He did this for about four minutes before anyone had the insight to interrupt his silent monologue.

During those four minutes the BBC switchboard was lit up with hundreds of callers complaining that they had no sound to go with the picture on their set.

MAVOR MOORE
There ought to be a law

In 1954 I was producing a big variety show for CBC television called *The Big Revue*. These shows at that time were live to air. I had hired an Australian magic star, an absolute madman in his mid 30s, who was a sharpshooter and a hypnotist and did all the other mental tricks that go along with that. Peter Mews from *Spring Thaw* was the Master of Cermonies.

The mad magician had been up all night by the time he arrived in Toronto and I was concerned. He was to do a number of sharp-shooting tricks with his assistant. She seemed to take it all in her stride, but a man who had been up all night and very probably drinking into the bargain, shooting at someone, had me considerably worried. When we did the live broadcast, we got to the end of the first segment and he did his hypnotism bit. He started by asking for volunteers from the audience and also from some of the performers. One of the people he picked was Peter Mews. Nobody knew, at the time, perhaps not even Mews, that he was particularly susceptible to hypnotism.

The magician put all his volunteers to sleep, then was to clap his hands to wake them up. I was up in the booth. The commercials were being done out of another small studio, Studio B. Keep in mind the commercials were also live. The magician had these hypnotized people do some stunts, then clapped his hands to wake them all up and we cut to a commercial.

Mews would not wake up. My MC was out like a light. They stood him up, they slapped his face, they tried everything to get him awake so we could carry on with the show. Meanwhile I was watching the commercial come to an end and had no MC to cut back to. So I got on the intercom to Harvey Hart, directing the commercial in Studio B, to tell him to keep the commercial going. 'What?' asks Harvey. 'Keep it going. I can't cut back to Studio A. Do anything you like but stay in Studio B.' So he started panning the camera around and playing some music while they were desperately trying to bring Mews around in the other studio.

Finally the camera came up on Mews. He stood there smiling, his eyes wide open, barely awake, trying manfully to cue the next number. The upshot of the whole thing was, not only had we put Mews out, we had put several viewers to sleep as well!

The issue ended up in the House of Commons and there was a law passed. Ever since that day it has been illegal to do hypnotism acts on Canadian television.

ARTHUR VORONKA
I'm ready for my closeup

I first met Michael Kane in Montreal in the late 40s. We used to do Canada's first radio soap opera, *Laura Limited*. It was on at 11:45 to noon, every day. We became buddies. When he moved to New York, I would often see him there. By then he had graduated into live TV soap operas.

Robert Goodier, Henry Ramer and I gave him a call one day and he said come on up to the studio while he did his show. He confided that he was having a hell of a time with the director, who was in love with the actress playing Michael's love interest. *She* was ending up with all the close-ups.

As the shows were live, they had portable changing rooms set up, just off camera, for the actors to change in, because time was of the essence. On that day, when Michael had a quick change, he reappeared, beautifully coiffed, a nice shirt and tie, and no pants. The director had no choice but to 'stay close on him' that day.

JEAN CAVALL
The toast

There was a 'live' TV musical show that left me in a rather disastrous predicament. I was supposed to be competing with several other artists in a search for new TV 'stars' on the variety show *Pick the Stars*. I sang the song *You Go To My Head* seated at a night club table and toasting the 'lady' opposite me as I sang. 'She' was the TV camera, thus making the viewing audience the 'person' I was toasting. While I sang and looked lustfully into the lens, I took an uncorked bottle of champagne (ginger ale) from a bucket and pretended to pour some in her glass and then really poured some in mine. Oh, so romantic.

As the song was reaching its amorous end, I gestured a toast to her (touching the camera lens) and brought my glass to my lips and took a sip. At that instant, I coughed explosively and couldn't stop!

There I was spluttering, with 'champagne' ginger ale on my face, making all sorts of unromantic faces. Disaster! What an embarrassment! The song was unfinished so the camera was on during the whole scene broadcasting live. After what seemed forever, the commercial light finally went on.

What had happened? It had been a very hot summer day. The old TV studios on Yonge Street had once been an automobile showroom, with no air conditioning.

When the dress rehearsal was over, someone had gone around the studio spraying bug spray on the sets to keep the flies from buzzing around while we were 'on the air'. Apparently, the champagne bottle had been left uncorked the whole time. When I took a sip from my glass, I had noticed too late a dead fly and scum in the glass. Before I could stop swallowing, I gagged and spewed everywhere.

GORDON PINSENT
Cod tongues

I was invited by my good friend Bruno Gerussi to join him on his television program *Celebrity Cooks*. I was absolutely delighted, so I made the plane trip up to Ottawa to do the tapings. I thought it would be an excellent opportunity to show off some Newfoundland recipes. My roots, as it were. I was to shoot two shows. As they shot several episodes a day, it was almost like the old live TV days, one time through and that was it. I was ready. Bruno and I cooked up a storm as the cameras rolled. My first meal was Cod Tongues.

I don't know at what point that Bruno realised he should have asked me if I knew how to cook before he'd asked me to appear on a cooking show.

After completing the first session, I saw him go over and have a few hurried words with the producer. They came over to tell me that they'd decided to put a hold on the Cod *Cheeks* episode and that I could go home now.

SUSAN CLARK
On the birth of *Webster*

Alex [Karras], my husband, and I had our own production company and had, at that time, completed three movies for CBS. We were in Orange County on location doing a commercial, staying at the Disneyland Hotel, when two agents from William Morris came banging at the door to announce that 'we' had a deal.

'We are going to get you on the air with a new series but you have to sign with us.'

We asked what the deal was. They said that they did not know, but could we be at ABC for a meeting the next week?

Alex and I presented ourselves as agreed at ABC and were ushered into a room full of people including several execs from William Morris, more from Paramount, and five or six from ABC including a scruffy-looking guy in an old baseball cap. This was Stu Silver, a very talented writer who had done 60 episodes of *Soap*, a hugely successful satirical sitcom. They turned on a video screen and up came a cute little black boy doing a commercial. They explained that they wanted to do a series with this boy and us, and asked if we would like to meet him. In came this sweetheart, Emmanuel Lewis, from the next room with his mother. He was twelve at the time but looked barely five years old.

There was no premise, nothing to begin with at that point and we had never done a sitcom before. The executives said to us, 'Stu Silver over there is going to write something. We don't know what he is going to write. We're going to shoot it at Paramount...and we do it in a month. So you guys go off and work out what you are going to do.'

So Alex and I, Emmanuel, Stu, and one of the execs from ABC went out to a Chinese restaurant and talked about nothing in particular. Stu made notes. Later, he called each of us separately. He asked me what kind of character I wanted to play if this series went for five years. I gave it some thought, and when we met again, I described a career woman who had not considered having children, who was involved and concerned about her community, and inept at housework and cooking. In 1983, there were not many women on TV fitting that description, so in many ways the character of 'Catharine' became a prototype. It was the same for the character of 'George', who was better at the domestic life of the family, cooking and organizing.

They came up with the idea that George was a career sportscaster who had previously agreed to become godfather to the son of a friend of his. Some time later, he and Catharine met, fell in love, and impulsively married. On returning to begin their life together, they discovered 'Webster', whose parents had been killed in a car crash, on their doorstep. George took his responsibility as a godparent very seriously and adopted Webster, thereby creating an instant, unexpected, and somewhat unorthodox nuclear family.

There was some political backlash at the beginning because some people objected to the implications of two white parents raising a black child. But it was short-lived, and our feeling was that we were not making a political statement. We were talking more about the characters as people than as representatives of their respective races.

The show ran for six wonderful years.

14

Stunts and SFX

CHRIS WIGGINS
On *The Last Of The Mohicans* with Lon Chaney Jr

Our first chance to do a filmed TV series came in 1955-56 when an American company came up to do *The Last Of The Mohicans* with a powerful handsome silver-haired guy named John Hart as 'Hawkeye' and Lon Chaney Jr as 'Chingachgook'.

Nearly every actor in Canada at the time did something on the series. I was lucky enough to do five of them. I thoroughly enjoyed it. It was a bit scary at first. Being used to theatre and long rehearsal periods it was an adjustment to have to read through the script once or twice and then you were on. Then we'd finish that and they'd say, 'That's it.' Then we'd move on to the next scene which we read once and then shot, and went on.

The two men who were the producers, or the producer and the director who were partners, apparently had been Keystone Cops. They certainly knew how to shoot quickly.

Lon and I got on very well and became friends. Usually I was getting beaten up by John which was good because he was a first-class stunt man and we could usually work out a pretty good fight between us. It was great fun for me to learn to do the stunt fighting especially. I almost got used to being smashed into the snow.

In those days 'extras' came from just about anywhere. There were no agencies or no central casting places here. They were just guys out of work looking to pick up a few bucks. They came out and were given a form asking them if they could ride a horse, would they be willing to get wet or be naked to the waist in the dead of winter playing Indians, willing to get their head shaved in the Mohawk style, whatever. Everyone signed and said 'Yeah, sure', anything for another $15. It kind of fooled the Americans who thought it was great that there were all these people who could do all of this. But this was Canada. Why not? So they went to the Circle M Ranch and hired 40 horses. They lined them up on the plain.

Sam, the director, was a great character. He used the famous 'F' word so often that it was rendered meaningless, more like punctuation. There he was giving the Indian 'extras' instructions for the scene.

'OK, I'm gonna fire the fucking flare, you see the fucking light go off, you dig your fucking heels into the fucking horses and ya come fucking over the fucking toppa that fucking rise there.'

They put all of these guys dressed up like Indians on the horses, bareback. Sam fired off the pistol and the forty horses all charged forward. Within five or six steps there were only three guys left on their horses. Riders were falling off all over the place, landing on their heads. Some poor guys were getting stepped on. It was a mess.

'Ah Geeziz Keerice, all right. Patch 'em up, put 'em on their fucking feet and we'll do it as a foot charge.'

So they took the horses away and shot it as a foot charge.

A few weeks later we were called into shoot something else. Several of us were to prepare in this scene to bushwhack somebody or something that was coming along the road. We were all hiding in the bushes and trees, or behind rocks with our guns at the ready. John Hart as Hawkeye walked up and down in front of us and made his speech about waiting for the signal before firing and so on. Then finally he said, 'Here they come!', jumped behind the bushes and said, 'FIRE!' and we all levelled the guns and let go with these flintlocks. Well, there was nobody there to shoot at. I found out later why.

The cost of the failed horse charge was sufficient that they had to somehow use the footage in some other episode. So they sent us out to provide the 'reverse' angle that might have justified a scene with all of these Indians falling off their horses. We who were shooting at nothing, would eventually end up shooting all of these Indians off their horses in another episode when it was all cut together.

The people from Hollywood were thrilled with the footage and wondered where in the world the producers had found these amazing stuntmen who were falling on their heads, diving off horses, being dragged along.

The 'stuntmen/extras' were not unhappy about it. They got paid for two days' work instead of just the one.

SHAWN ALEX THOMPSON
Straitjacket

As a kid, I would study library books and learn magic moves. It's a very solitary experience. I would practise the moves for hours in front of a mirror until I had perfected them to the point where they were invisible. The problem is that then no one really appreciated how much I had learned. Being a magician is very frustrating that way. It's different from being a guitar player where you can see how good someone is. They may play effortlessly but you see the talent and the time spent practising. Magic's about not letting them know you're doing anything at all.

As a professional magician, by the age of 16 I had played every dive, bar and convention, Elks Club, you can name. I also worked *Puck's Circus* for several years, off and on. *Puck's* was billed as 'the smallest tent circus in the world'. My act was escaping from a straitjacket while being hung upside down from a burning rope. I'd walk out into the ring wearing a pair of skates. They'd put a hook through the blades and hoist me upside down to the top of the tent. Then they'd light the rope on fire. I would have to escape from the straitjacket in under a minute. There's no trick to this stunt. You just learn how to wiggle out of the jacket. I used the same rope every time I did it. It was a big piece of rope that had cotton batten wound around it and it was the cotton that burned. The rope itself was never on fire.

However, I didn't realise, in my youth and stupidity, that the rope was actually baking. I did some fifty performances with the same rope. On a hunch the circus ringmaster took the rope one night and just broke it like spaghetti. I really used to wiggle around on the rope while I was getting out of the jacket and there was no net. If I had done a couple more performances on the thing I could have snapped the rope and plunged 80 feet to the pavement. He saved my life.

That's about the time I began to think acting would be safer. When I left the circus I gave my dog to the people who ran it. He was a fabulous dog and understood a lot of words. I had taught him some tricks and they taught him some more. The next year the dog earned $35,000 doing his tricks and I earned $12,000 doing mine.

NORMA DELL'AGNESE
Meatballs

Soon after graduation, I answered an ad for a film about a summer camp. I figured the place would be chock full of nubile babes on high school vacation looking for their big break. And who could compete with that? What they probably needed was a 'nerd'. And that's how I went. Turned out, I was the only support performer cast from the cattle call; the rest were submitted by agents, experienced actors with a confident 'cool' attitude. Pretty intimidating, but I kept my fears to myself. Years later I discovered that, isolated up north shooting our first feature film, we were all terrified...and all very secretive about it. They ended up calling the film *Meatballs*.

A lot of the script was created as we went along. One call sheet announced that I was in the 'new' tennis scene.

'What tennis scene?'

'Oh. Jack [Blum] and Keith [Knight] are writing right now, so if you want any lines you better get over there.'

By the time I got there, of course they'd written the best stuff for themselves. So I got an outfit in town, and decided to go for the physical. I would run backward to hit the ball, and pratfall into the fence. But when I went to do it, I passed the asphalt, slipped on the gravel, and landed in that lovely bony part of your lower back. KLUNK! Limbs akimbo, I lay there stunned.

Big silence. Then I heard the director's voice. 'CUT!... Are you all right?'

Apparently I was. We did the scene a few more times, with proper padding, but I never did capture the spontaneity of the first take. And that's the one that ended up in the film.

DIANA PLATTS
The semi-Siamese cat of *Cats*

With no solo lines but lots of leg and talent, Lyne (sex goddess) Tremblay, who *was* 'Cassandra the Siamese Cat', became the definitive crowd favourite. In fact, the only question more unwelcome and asked more often than 'How long does it take you to do your make-up?' was 'Who were you? The "Siamese cat"?'

Filling in one night as Cassandra for the Goddess herself, yours truly was to saunter out into the spotlight to seduce the 'Tugger', on tip toe, hips swaying, hands seductively running through his yak-hair wig. He would casually pop an Elvis hip-thrust in my direction. Of course, the sheer testosterone of it all causes the desired effect and Cassandra would fall into a dead faint...straight backwards, supposedly into the waiting arms of 'Alonzo' who then, in keeping with her sleek character, would gracefully toss her back up into a classy spin and recovery. After all, the Siamese is just naturally better than us all.

No such luck on my big night. My Alonzo also turned out to be an understudy and he couldn't get his tap shoes off in time to re-enter and cover his part (the catching part) of the stunt. The back-up, already safely blocked on stage, was also an understudy but he had no idea that he was expected to cover the stunt, in case of, say, a quick wardrobe change problem. Gravity, however, never misses a cue. The entire cast was frozen in place with all on-stage focus (plus 4000 paying eyes) duly riveted on the set-up for Cassandra's bit.

I was 105 pounds of pure BOOM!

Thank God for that yellow belt in high school karate. Before the shocked dance captain could sprint from the back of the house to the wings, the stunned and not so high and mighty 'Siamese' was up off her butt (pure adrenalin) and on to the next cue.

It was not my splashiest debut, but certainly memorable.

TONY ROSATO
A dubious distinction

We used to keep a list backstage at the Firehall that noted all of the various bizarre milestones that had occurred over the years. Robin Williams, Marty Short, and I have the dubious distinction of being among the very few who have wiped out badly off the Second City stage. When Robin first came up to do Second City with us he was not used to the stage in the dark. Once when he was trying to leave the stage between scenes, he stepped off the edge of the stage and took out a table of five. Flattened the whole table. And Marty once did a pivot on the edge of the stage, lost his balance and fell backwards into the audience. Fortunately a few people caught him so no one was hurt, but he took them all down with him.

In my case, it could have been a lot worse than it turned out to be.

The cast that I worked with included Derek McGrath, Mary Charlotte Wilcox, Ditch (Don) Dickinson, Maggie Butterfield, and Robin Duke, and was directed by Joe Flaherty. We were doing a sketch called *Immigration*. It involved various characters in a game show scene where everyone was trying to correctly answer skill-testing questions in order to win a 'green card' or landed immigrant status. I was playing an unwilling contestant who didn't really want to come out. Ditch had to push me through the curtain, with my hands tied behind my back.

However, just before we performed, the stage had been redesigned and reshaped slightly, leaving a smaller playing space. The edge of the stage now dropped off into the audience, who were seated at tables that were almost touching the stage.

We had done this sketch many times before and we all knew what to do. But we were not yet quite used to the new stage. So when Ditch pushed me through the curtain, he did it with the same force that he had used when the stage was larger. As I headed through the curtain, I realised that I would not have enough room to stop myself before I would run out of stage. I was about to catapult into a couple at a small table that was full of drinks. I could *not* stop, and I could not protect myself or the people I was about to crash into because my hands were tied!

I saw myself heading straight for the woman. I could see her face getting closer to my face and I realised that she was frozen, not quite realising what was happening. I fell right into her head and actually saw the immense pain that the blow had caused her. I thought, 'Oh my God, I've killed her.' My head glanced off her head and smashed into a glass on the table. Somehow my hands came untied by the time I hit the floor. Broken glass was everywhere. I got up and I remember saying, 'Wow...sorry to pop in so unexpectedly.'

The room was so quiet that you could have heard a pin drop. I got back up on stage and slowly there were little nervous titters and then some laughing. I think I did every conceivable bad entrance joke in the world right up until I sat down again. 'Never let it be said that I don't know how to make an entrance...' etc. etc. and a handful of other riffs on the situation, trying to take the heat off for myself as much as everyone else.

As we continued the scene, I suddenly felt a slow drip of blood hitting my hand. I must still have been pretty stunned because it took a second to absorb the idea that I might have been hurt badly. I reached up to my chin and realised that my finger had gone *into* my chin. 'Hmmmm', I thought, 'I must have a really deep cut.'

We finished the scene. People were applauding wildly, probably because they couldn't believe that we actually kept going to the end of it. I think some of them were still not yet quite sure whether or not it was part of the show. We got off stage and I was rushed to the hospital. I got seven stitches in my chin and they bandaged me up as best they could so that I could get back to the show for the second half.

When I got back, everyone in the cast had put on big bandages in the same place that I had mine, and they wore them for the rest of the show. And not incidentally, I was very relieved to hear that the woman I had hit was not badly hurt after all.

TIMOTHY FINDLEY
Making the leap

It was exciting news. In 1953, I was among those chosen to be part of the acting company in the opening season of Canada's Stratford Shakespearean Festival. I was only twenty-two, and would be working with some of the most talented people in Canadian and British theatre—including the director, Tyrone Guthrie.

One of my roles was 'Catesby', the King's henchman, in *Richard III*. This meant that I had to make an explosive entrance into the scene in which Alec Guinness, alone on the battlefield, was to cry, 'My kingdom for a horse!' Guthrie wanted this entrance to be physically alarming, having already devised some entrances for other actors that were pretty spectacular. Pacing around the stage, he looked up at the balcony—and, while my heart sank, asked if I could burst through the drapes that covered its entrance, jump up onto the balustrade—and leap down onto the stage. That's right. A ten-foot leap through the dark...and *not* land on Alec Guinness, whose single spotlight was the only light there was. What else could I say but 'sure'. I tried it and, to my dismay, it worked. This meant I had to do it in every performance! Somehow both Guinness and I survived.

It was only in later years, looking back, that I realized how well that single move summed up what had happened that summer. Canadian theatre took a leap into the unknown and, to judge from what's been achieved since, it landed on its feet.

TOM KNEEBONE
And I'm not kidding!

This was a classic mid-'70s pre-Broadway try-out musical experience where it seemed like practically everybody was being fired and we had re-writes every minute. You'd walk in of a morning and there would be a different conductor. In the cast were Dorothy Loudon, George Grizzard, Carole Shelley, Arthur Mitchell, the great, great black dancer, and myself.

When we opened out of town there was no time to work on the playing of the show. No time to do anything but change costumes. They had to put changing tents in the wings. They'd throw you in, change you, and throw you out again. All you could think about was the next costume change. I had thirty-five of them. We each had to have two dressing-rooms, one to hold the costumes and one to use for changing.

We played out of town, then came into New York to rehearse with a new director. On the evening of the first New York preview, after rehearsing changes all day, I went to the dressing-room to get ready for the performance. My dresser was looking sheepish and I heard Arthur screaming from next door, 'Where are my costumes?'

It turned out that they had, without our knowledge, cut all the costumes. The costumes had been taken away. Instead, the men had been given G-strings with genitals painted on the fabric. Out of the thirty-five costumes I'd had, I was left with a G-string and a caftan. Imagine the expense, apart from anything else.

The show had three titles: first, *And Now, Noel Coward.* Then it was, *Here's Noel Coward.* It ended up as *Noel Coward's Sweet Potato.* It included such numbers as one of Coward's most romantic songs, 'I'll Follow My Secret Heart', done as a mugging in Central Park.

Just before the preview performance, Arthur and I were given a new way of doing a number based on *Private Lives,* a piece that we were to try out on the raked stage for the first time that night. The new choreography put us on roller skates. Neither of us had ever roller-skated before and certainly not on a raked stage. It was a hair-raising experience. We lost control. We were clinging to one another. Arthur grabbed me and said, 'I'm going to fix this. We're getting off.'

We went careening offstage, into the wings, and took a tremendous tumble into someone standing backstage, watching. We felled the poor man. It was George Balanchine. We nearly killed George Balanchine!

We received the reviews of all time. Wonderful, wonderful, wonderful. We transferred from the Barrymore to the Booth. By that time I didn't care, I just had to get out of it. And I couldn't. We played for three more months.

Dorothy Loudon and George Grizzard told stories from this experience around New York for years and nobody would ever believe them.

SAUL RUBINEK
Playing bad guys

A film called *Highpoint*, directed by Peter Carter and starring Richard Harris and Beverly D'Angelo, became famous for a stunt jump that was made by stunt man Dar Robinson off the CN Tower. Maury Chaykin and I played inept bad guys who were chasing Richard Harris's character.

We were crazy in those days. We would do *anything.* This was before the *Twilight Zone* tragedy that killed Vic Morrow and two children. There was a sequence in this movie where we were in a speeding limousine standing up through the sun roof and firing machine guns at a helicopter that was flying not more than twenty feet directly over us. We thought we *were* the characters. I don't think we had any idea how dangerous this was. We just trusted everyone who was doing this, the stunt crew, everyone.

Later on, we were filming another scene at the restaurant level of the CN Tower, which is no big deal if you are inside the building. Maury and I, however, were hustled *outside* onto a window-washing rig which brackets the restaurant windows and can be winched around the entire pod. It's just under a quarter mile off the ground, open to the air, with a grate at the bottom of the rig that allows you to look down past your feet to the ground...*far* below.

We were terrified. But because we were on camera, we were willing to risk our lives for a laugh. Neither of us could be described as *light* on our feet, but Maury decided that it would be amusing to *jump up and down* on this rig...for a laugh.

The director, Peter Carter, the camera and crew were inside shooting this insanity, which was not, of course, ever in the script. We just did it. Peter laughed so hard he fell off the camera dolly. This went on for about ten or fifteen minutes. But the absurd thing to me was that I *stayed* outside on that rig, terrified out of my mind, with the grid shaking under me, and remained in character, playing the scene!

What was really depressing was that none or very little of this was used in the final movie. Even worse, the final movie wasn't released for nine years and it never had a theatrical release at all. Maury and I did, however, manage to get the complete out-takes from that day's shoot and put them on our reels.

MONICA PARKER
Adrenalin rush

One of my first movies starred John Gavin as the father of a very pretty pristine young girl who was marrying some guy in a hippie '60s commune. I was playing her bridesmaid, also a member of the commune.

I was new to acting and quick to 'method'. I didn't wash my hair for days, I wore a bright pink polyester dress and I took the bouquet and just smashed it, to give it that ragged look. It was just hideous.

In this scene, Michael Kirby and several others who were in the wedding scene were to have a great big fight in the commune. We were to throw food and wreck the place. Michael was supposed to pick up a chair, a break-away chair of course, and break it over my shoulder. We rehearsed this carefully over and over. It worked perfectly.

We came to shoot the scene. The second they said, 'Roll 'em! Action!' Michael's adrenalin was pumping. He went berserk, lost everything we had rehearsed, and became an animal. He started picking up furniture, and food, chipping the walls with plates. He jumped on the table and broke it. Then somehow he remembered that he was to pick up a chair and break it over me. He brought down a *real chair* across my back with full force and knocked me out cold.

I don't remember take two...if there was one. Poor Michael must have been mortified.

TED FOLLOWS and TONY VAN BRIDGE
Touché

The sword fights at Stratford are a basic part of mounting plays written in an era when homicide was a domestic art. There is always a fencing coach in residence, to work with the Company, and during some rehearsal seasons the corridors and the lawns outside are steadily a-jingle with the sounds of fencing practice.

The swords used on Stratford's stage are definitely steel, and clear steel. Although they are not whetted to a sharp edge, their edges are yet sharp enough to cut. The points of rapiers are unbated. There are no masks, and no padding and no defence save the actor's skill. Further, these duels are fought within a few feet of the audience, with audience on three sides of the ones who fight. On a proscenium stage, with audience on only one side, swordsmen can clink their blades together for sound effects, but miss their thrusts by a mile and still have the fight look vicious. Not on this stage. There can be no tricks to suggest a duel; this stage was not designed for trickery. The duels must be fought.

They are choreographed in advance, of course, and must be, because on that stage they must be fought up and down three steps, and it's not the place for improvisation unless you want a corpse to crumple at the Governor-General's feet. They are also planned because the play progresses more smoothly when the right man wins. But despite the planning and the steady coaching, despite a minimum of forty-five minutes' daily rehearsal per fight to keep in trim, the duels as fought on the stage at Stratford depend entirely on the actors' skill. The place is rife with tales of accidents from other years, told lightly, and not much accented because they know they have been fortunate.

One story concerned Ted Follows fighting in a battle scene with Tony van Bridge. In the thrust and parry of battle, one thrust went an inch awry. With the weight of Ted's fighting arm behind it, the blade ran through Tony's heavy costume, and apparently through Tony himself. Tony fell, as he was supposed to fall in that sequence, and Ted in the scurry of battle rushed offstage.

There he flung himself, sword in hand, on Jack Hutt [the stage manager], crying, 'I think I got him! I think I killed him. I felt the sword go in.'

[In the early days there was no spot backstage at Stratford from which the stage itself could be seen.] The prompter's box in the roof (in nine years there has never been a prompt at Stratford) was too far away for the alerted Stage Manager there to see if Tony was breathing or not. Since corpses, as well as furniture, have to be carried offstage, there wasn't a thing to do.

'We'll have to wait till they bring the body off,' said Jack [Hutt] with his usual composure, while Ted paced frantically about the backstage area.

When said body was duly delivered and rose to its feet, Ted went off into a gale of relieved laughter and popped around to Wardrobe to apologize for the rents in the costume. Lest anyone else be inclined to laugh too lightly, be it noted that Tony did have three cracked ribs and a beautiful gash, as souvenirs.

Tony's own description of the incident is charming. For a moment he, too, thought that he had been killed, 'and even as I fell, onstage, with the lights upon me, I couldn't help thinking, "What a perfect way to die!" It was quite a come-down when I hit the stage and found out I was breathing. I doubt I'll ever have another chance for an exit like that!'

TEDDE MOORE
Powys and Paddy

I played a buxom wench and general oddsbody in a remarkable 1968 Stratford production of *The Three Musketeers* in which Powys Thomas was playing 'Athos'. Athos has a huge speech in the middle of the play where he drunkenly confesses information and events that explain the entire plot. Powys often lost track of where he was in the speech. But he talked on and on in such a remarkably interesting, often amusing, way that the company took to crowding around the backstage speakers to hear what fabulous tale Powys would spin that night. Many times this tale would be illogical but, such was Powys' skill as an actor, it always seemed that he was speaking perfect sense.

This was also a production filled with stage fights and Athos was supposed to be the pre-eminent sword master and win all these wildly hectic fights. Powys was very short-sighted and as this was still early days for contact lenses, he had not yet acquired them. This posed a certain problem for the fight director, Patrick (Paddy) Crean, who had been Errol Flynn's double and fencing master in Flynn's swashbuckling movies. Paddy so cleverly staged the fights, with Powys hardly moving and all the other actors going berserk around him, that at the end when the villainous Cardinal's men lay in heaps around him, all Powys had to do was lean over in exhaustion and you absolutely believed that he had just annihilated them all.

MARCEL SABOURIN
Unsure and uninsured

G.A. Martin Photographe was a film about a travelling photographer in the last century. A great deal of the story involved the characters travelling in a covered wagon drawn by a team of horses. I had never worked with a team of horses or driven a wagon. I was asking all the time about the safety of the wagon. 'Oh, yes,' I was assured, 'it has been built by someone who knows wagons well.'

We shot most of the film on private land here and there in Quebec, but we were to try out the wagon on a piece of land owned by the National Film Board, their back lot. My first attempt to drive the wagon with my co-star, Monique Mercure, aboard was scary because as I tried to turn the wagon around it nearly went over. Monique, who won the best actress award at the Cannes Festival for her role in this film, was frightened but there were no injuries and the wagon didn't break. The horses were calm. They just stopped and turned and looked at me as if I was an imbecile.

After a certain time I became very good with these horses. One day I was asked to take the wagon, with Monique aboard, down an extremely steep hill. We couldn't have a stuntman because the shot was a close one and our faces would be clearly seen. Also, we were not insured. The National Film Board never insures because the Queen doesn't insure.

When you are filming as an actor there is a rule. If you do something dangerous, that you know is dangerous, without asking any questions about it first, you alone are responsible for your actions.

'This is dangerous and if you want me to do this stunt I must have a letter from the producer that he will take the responsibility.'

The producer was not on the set. They called him and while we waited for him to arrive, I talked to the horse wrangler. At first he said that to take the wagon down the hill was not that dangerous. After a while I asked him if he would get into the wagon and ride with us, looking through a small curtained window. If something went wrong he could take the reins. He wouldn't do it. He was too frightened! He had tried it himself a couple of times and indeed, the horses had had a hard time. They were braking so hard, each facing opposite sides of the road, they formed a V figure. By this time we had waited for two hours for the producer. He hadn't come and we were short of time and money. Finally I said all right, I'd do it.

We did it. I was like a cowboy. They got the shot. Everyone was very happy. When they showed us the finished film this shot was not there! This scene, that took so much courage, had been cut.

KERRIE KEANE
My most frightening stunt

I have never been so scared working on a movie as I was a couple of years ago. I was in London, England doing *The Return of Sam McCloud,* with Dennis Weaver. One of the stunts required Dennis to ride a horse, with me on the back, from Buckingham Palace down the mall and through Trafalgar Square, jumping several barriers along the way. Dennis is a great horseman, with a lot of experience with riding for the movies and television, but the horse they brought onto the set was a huge, powerful, young, black Spanish stallion. The horse was so gorgeous it had a mythic quality. I could imagine fire shooting from its nostrils. Dennis said that it was the most frightening horse he had ever tried to handle.

I was to get up onto the back of this horse...with no saddle...no stirrups...and no reins, and I was told I couldn't hold onto Dennis. It's hard enough to stay on a galloping horse but all I had to hold onto were two tiny little leather straps.

This was a very high-spirited creature. Every time I would get onto his back he would buck me off. It took several tries to get the horse under enough control to point him down the mall, with me on the back. When we finally did, the horse took off as if he had been shot full of 'speed'. We rode at a full gallop down the mall with the cameraman shooting from the back of a motorcycle in front of us. We were charging down so fast that the motorcycle couldn't stay ahead of the horse. At one point Dennis felt me going off and grabbed the back of me while still trying to control the horse. We continued down the mall and even more amazingly, *jumped the barriers*. To this day, I don't know how I stayed on that horse.

Dennis got off the horse and said, 'You better have gotten that because I am not doing that again. It is just too damned dangerous.' He said it was the most frightening experience working with horses he had ever had in his long career, going back before his *Gunsmoke* days. If he had lost control of that horse and one or both of us had fallen, we could easily have been badly injured or killed, not to mention the possible injury to crew and extras.

I smartened up after that and decided to leave the stunt work to the professionals.

JONATHAN WELSH
Summer of '73

I auditioned and got a role, along with so many others, in the CBC's *The National Dream*. The show filmed out west for almost two months.

I was 'Albert Rodgers', nephew of 'Major Rodgers' (James Douglas), who together explored the Selkirk mountains of B.C. looking for a southern passage. We were to board a raft and 'drift' along the Illecillewaet River outside Revelstoke. Camera angles were plotted and set up along the proposed route as our film caravan snaked across the interior of B.C. A particular spot looked good enough so we were put on a makeshift raft. Later, in a publicity photo of Jimmy and me about to launch, I believe I saw the terror in my eyes and the incredulity in Jimmy's.

After some rehearsal, we disembarked for make-up touch ups. The raft chose that moment to slip its mooring and immediately sink. It emerged 40 yards downstream shooting straight up 50 feet in the air and completely disintegrating upon landing. All that was left were bits bobbing downstream. Filming was suspended for the day as we regrouped.

A week and a half later we found ourselves on the Fraser River outside of Yale, B.C., just a few miles up from Hope, with a spare morning to try to get the raft shot again. The two natives who had joined us, Chief Lawrence Battle and another fellow from outside of Calgary, had purchased beer for the morning because they couldn't believe anybody would voluntarily embark on such an escapade, filming or no! James Murray, the producer, was in the boat pulling another CBC prop raft with second unit cameraman Vic Sarin. We pushed off in tow. Someone had the great idea to cut us adrift so as to get a better shooting angle.

The minute they let go, the raft immediately spun around with its makeshift-CBC-rudder now facing forward. Shades of the earlier mishap were dancing before our eyes. We kept glancing over at the camera boat manoeuvring out in the fast water for the optimum shot. They kept waving at us to not look at the camera!

Smack in the middle was a swift flowing rut filled with debris and deadwood, all unobservable from a distance. Couple that with hidden obstacles like boulders. We were suddenly presented with the terror and sucking swell of a whirlpool about 40 feet across! The 'rudder' dipped as in a cocktail glass, spun the raft around once in a full circle pitching me out, then flipped back into the river stream leaving me spinning in the water circling downwards.

We were equipped with flimsy lifebelts around our waists and I made use of it by blowing and puffing my stomach out like a ball. It was that or plunge into the vortex and hope to be spat out downstream with the deadwood. I said no—I'll take my chances trying to buoy myself upward and out of the vast whirlpool. I couldn't see above the rim but blew and puffed and kicked my legs up and climbed the lip of the whirlpool and plunged out into the stream. I had gone around four times all the while clutching my hat and saying to myself 'if I lose this hat, continuity will kill me'.

The boat finally picked me up 200 yards from where I went in, the water was moving that fast. The natives laughed and immediately named me 'little friend of the whirlpool' in Coast Salish.

KERRIE KEANE
Train-hopping training

On the television series *Hot Pursuit,* the character I was playing was an automotive engineer. She was the one who worked on the engines, drove the cars and speed-boats in the chases, and so on. It was an action series and I insisted that I do as much of my own stunt work as possible.

In one scene, Eric Pierpoint, who played my husband, had just freed me from a police car that was taking me to jail. The two of us were running to try to catch a moving train, with me still in handcuffs. The stunt was this; he would jump up on the flatbed and then he would lean down, put his arm through my arms and lift me up onto the train as I swung myself up. It was a hard move because I was off balance without the free use of my arms, I had to run, and the timing had to be just right when I swung my body up or it would be a disaster.

Kenny Johnson, the director, was up on the flatbed looking through the camera during the rehearsal making sure that the shot was just right. As Eric tried to swing me up onto the flatbed, I couldn't quite do it and he dropped me. All Kenny could see through the lens was me falling down out of frame. He said later that it was the most heart-stopping moment of his life because it looked to him that I had fallen under the wheels of the moving train. Of course I hadn't. I was just down beside the track. Everyone came flying off the train to see if I was all right. I was fine, so we backed it up and did it again.

It occurred to me later that there probably were not too many people who had a lot of real-life experience with jumping trains in handcuffs any more. I wonder where you would get training for that?

WAYNE BEST
On *K2*

They hired someone to teach us how to do the mountain climbing for the Studio Theatre production of *K2* at Hamilton Place. The *K2* set was a section of the side of a mountain which we had to actually climb during the play. Our teacher was a real climber but he had had no experience in theatre.

As is anyone who is deeply attached to one passion or another, to outsiders these climbers seem a little nuts. We put the harnesses on in the theatre the first day, then later they took us out to Rattlesnake Point to have our first lesson in climbing on a real rock face, just to see what it was like. This guy climbed up about forty feet, made a belay station, and let the rope down so that the other actor could belay me from the ground. He was not comfortable with heights and did not want to climb, so all he had to do was take in the rope's slack as I went up.

So I started to climb. I got about 10 or 12 feet up the side and was about to dive for the next hand hold when my fellow actor below got anxious and pulled the rope in. The belay station to which the rope was attached to support me if I fell, came off the side of the rock face, leaving me climbing free. I'd like to think that if I had started from the top to rappel, that our mountain-climbing expert would have checked it before I had leaned out over the edge, but apparently it had not been checked for my climb. In any case, my confidence in our expert waned.

Nevertheless, we moved onto the set. In this play, 'Taylor', the character I was playing, climbs up about 12 feet off the deck to a ledge where we play a lot of the scenes, then I climb up another fifteen feet and out of sight of the audience while the play and the dialogue continues. At one point Taylor realises that he is going to fall and drops some fifteen feet. I was to be stopped by the safety rope which would then allow us to continue the scene while I was dangling. They rigged a system, measured the rope, and as a precaution set up a big crash pad out of the audience's visual range, in case there was an accident.

We were in rehearsal, getting ready to work on this drop. I was psyched and ready. The climbing consultant had measured the rope and we were all set, so I started up assuming that I would be testing this stunt. But our climber told me that, no, he would try it out first to make sure it was safe. Up he went, climbing up as we watched him. He got out over the ledge, jumped...and landed *smack!* into the crash pad.

I looked at our expert sprawled on the pad and realised that I would have to do a stunt that this man had devised every night of the length of the run. It was not a happy thought.

SAUL RUBINEK
Making points

In a film called *I Love Trouble* I was required to do an eighty-five-foot drop back-wards on a descender. It was a high angle shot looking down a glass and steel build-ing into a huge interior atrium. I was to be hanging onto the edge of a catwalk, with my face in close-up, and I was to drop away from the camera. You could see behind me in the shot, all the way to the floor of the building, ninety feet below.

I have a fear of heights.

To begin with, it meant a lot to me to try to overcome my fear. Also, there were a couple of scenes later in the film that I felt needed some rewrites. I needed to make some points with the producer/writers in order to get my way. They could not do the shot unless I agreed so that's why I said I'd do it.

A descender is a device used by stuntmen that allows you to effect a controlled 'fall' off a building at perhaps eighty per cent of free-fall speed. You are never actu-ally falling when you are on a descender. It lowers you. As you get closer to the ground, the descender gradually slows your descent until you arrive like a feather on the ground. Ken Baker, the stuntman who had done the free fall out of a helicopter in *Demolition Man*, owned the descender. The stunt team was the best in the business. I trusted them. And they prepared me for weeks. They got me used to the feeling of the descender from lower levels. Slowly they increased the height so that I could get the feeling of how the fall would be.

Since I was only going to be falling at eighty per cent of free-fall speed, they would be speeding up the fall in the post-editing process. That meant I also had to learned to flail my arms in slow motion when I was doing the stunt so that the adjusted speed would look natural on film. I did not have the abdominals to hold myself in the proper position to keep the wire from getting between my face and the camera, so they made a fibreglass harness to hold me in position. By the time we were ready to do the shot, all I had to do was concentrate on my arms as I went down. They did everything else.

The only thing that could go wrong was if the thimble-sized attachment that connected me to the rig broke.

On the day, I think I was too busy concentrating on my slow motion flailing to be thinking about the height. The drop itself took about seven seconds...but I had to do the stunt seven times.

When they finally edited it together, it looked OK. A stuntman had done a real free fall for me as well which was cut into the final edit. There were a lot of angles and lots of cuts. The part that I had done was so short, it barely seemed worth it in the end result.

Of course I made the producers think that doing the stunt was much harder to do than it really was, so I did finally get my way in the scenes that I had wanted changed.

But I'm still afraid of heights.

NORMAN BROWNING
Ascension

During an ill-fated production of *Knock, Knock* at the National Arts Centre, Janet Wright starred as 'Joan of Arc' with Gregory Reed and Jackson Davies.

In one scene, Joan of Arc has to fly, literally rise off the ground as she experiences one of her fantasies or religious epiphanies. Janet, who was a rather substantial Joan of Arc, had to be strapped into a harness and winched off the ground. An assistant stage manager was in charge of the winch.

On one occasion, this young ASM accidentally managed to get her sweater caught somehow in the mechanism just as Janet had ascended about ten feet. Our Joan was then stuck...moving neither up nor down and completely out of reach of any assistance from the ground. There was Janet, *suspended*. And because she was no longer moving up or down, she started to spin slowly, helplessly around in a circle. Of course, those who know Janet would be not at all surprised to learn that this completely cracked her up. She lost it. There she was in her 'moment of transcendence' slowly spinning and laughing so hard that her wings were falling off. Through all of this, Gregory and Jackson were desperately trying to find a way to reach her and get her down, to no avail.

This went on for what must have been fifteen or twenty minutes. The audience was in hysterics. I honestly can't remember if we finished the play.

NORMA DELL'AGNESE
Odd jobs

The producers and director of *Quest For Fire* were looking for a voice to dub 'Ika' (played by Rae Dawn Chong on screen). They needed an other-worldly quality to match her appearance. At the audition, I gave them all kinds of weird sounds, as well as the impression that I was an old hand at this kind of work (of course, I'd never done it before). I got the job and, in preparation, listened to the rhythms of her 'dialogue' (it was a pre-historic language created by Anthony Burgess) for days at home.

In the sound booth, I spend the first two days doing background vocals with Inuit and Asian language speakers, to immerse myself in their guttural sing-song qualities so dissimilar to Western speech. Then it was my turn up to bat.

I was asked which dubbing method I was used to. Panic-stricken, I blurted out the only one I'd ever heard of, 'The beep method?' 'Oh, we're all set up for slash, we'll have to switch.' ('Beep' being an aural cue, 'slash' was a visual one, in fact a coloured diagonal line on a black and white print of the film.) 'Oh no, it's OK, I'd like to learn the slash.'

So I was tutored in 'slash' and started to work. Now, no matter how hard I tried, I couldn't seem to please the producers and director and I was getting progressively worried about my secret inexperience. This went on for a long frustrating time. My self-esteem rapidly plummeted, when I noticed they kept contradicting themselves. Eureka! It wasn't that I couldn't give them what they wanted at all. They didn't *know* what they wanted! With this little revelation, the power paradigm abruptly shifted in my head. I was transformed into an equal player, experimenting to my heart's delight, so we could discover it *together*.

Creating her laugh was a hoot, but the most fun part was dubbing the scene in which the Everett McGill character injures his groin area. Ika lifts his loin-cloth and, like a child soothing a sore spot, applies her mouth to suck it better. Well, for inspiration, they provided me with an assortment of professional tools—cucumbers and bananas, etc.—but in the end, the old hand ended up producing the best result. They needed a sucking sound interspersed with constant babbling. The effect was that of an incessant chatterbox nonchalantly performing an utterly innocent 'good deed'.

With my secret still intact, I completed the work to their satisfaction, but if you really listen to this scene in the film, the character starts off with my voice, and switches to Rae Dawn's. To this day, I know not why. I can only assume that the higher-ups found my sucking sound to be too lascivious and/or humorous, and it had to be cut midstream. Oh well. 'Twas truly a one-of-a-kind experience.

And that is how I came to perform The World's First, and perhaps only, Prehistoric Blow Job.

BARRY FLATMAN
Soap opera hell

Let me put shooting a television daytime drama into perspective. Filming a feature film one would shoot approximately three or four pages of script in one day's work. Shooting a television show or a movie of the week averages around 11 or 12 pages a day. On *Family Passions,* a daytime series in which I had a lead role, we would shoot an average of 95 pages a day!

Because scripts were being written as the show went along we didn't receive our pages until the night before we were to shoot them. We also didn't use Teleprompters. That meant you had to draw on your skills at improvisation if you lost track of where you were, one take being the norm. The sets were gigantic because, of course, the people the story was about were all high flyers and fabulously wealthy. Also, the freedom you have as to where you can go with the plot, well, the sky's the limit.

I played 'Connor McDeere', the head of a Canadian car manufacturing family. He was a one-legged, ex race-car driver and company magnate. Susan Hogan played 'Libby', my tempestuous wife, herself a strong-willed business mogul. Our two characters fought endlessly and made up endlessly. One of our fights was 12 pages long and was done in a single, continuous shot. It took place through four different sets using four cameras rolling all at once. In order for the camera focus to be accurate we would have to precisely hit dozens of marks on the floor as we were having this hysterical fight. And my character had only one leg.

In the first episode we shot, we were just working out the way to play the one leg since I am, unbelievable but true, a two-legged actor. Libby's and my first fight took place after I had removed my artificial leg. In an effort to establish the one-leggedness of Connor, I tied one of my legs up behind me and wore a dressing gown. Libby was to taunt me by waving my artificial leg just out of my reach. The fight was to start on the upper floor of the house and come down the grand staircase, consisting of 30 stairs, through the foyer and into the living room. This was not done in one take or even two.

For *two hours,* over and over again, I hopped down 30 stairs, yelling and screaming, into the living room and hopped, on one leg, over the coffee table, all the while hitting my marks. I couldn't sit and I couldn't stand. Every time we did it again, I had to hop back up 30 steps to the top of the staircase.

Oh, the romantic life. I had to have major knee surgery when I finished my year limping around as a one-legged magnate. But, I had a great time. When you are working under pressure with other good actors, which I was, you can really fly. Wouldn't have missed it.

JENNIFER PHIPPS
On ice

When I was in Leon Major's company at the St Lawrence Centre, Richard Monette, Monique Mercure, I and various others were doing a Toronto Arts Production of *Electra*. Kurt Reis was directing. Kurt had decided rather daringly that I, as 'Clytemnestra', would be pregnant, though there is no mention of that in the classical text.

This was one of the first times that dry ice was used in a production. We really had no idea what to expect. In the first dress rehearsal the mist from the ice was to come from the front of the stage and cover all the actors. Suddenly, the crouched cast, who were supposed to be 'rocks', started to pop out of the mist with complaints that their eyes were in difficulty. Those with contact lenses were unable to stay down at all.

Well, I thought that this was terrible. After all, this was the theatre! One must suffer for one's art. How difficult could it be to shut one's eyes, for heaven's sake. Really! These chorus people!

We continued with the dress [rehearsal] until we got to the scene after Clytemnestra and her husband were killed. I, as the Queen, and my husband were pulled by our legs out of this marvellous cave on stage and left there in full view of the audience as the dry ice mist came up over us. Now it was my turn to shut my eyes. I was going to show them how a professional manages these things.

As it came across us, the supposedly dead Queen, lying prone and in all her glory, suddenly jumped up from under this ice mist and shouted, 'What the hell was that? I can't stand this stuff! Get this stuff *off my face!*' I couldn't breathe. It was as if I'd drowned. It was terrifying.

Of course we did learn to manage it. We would close our eyes and hold our breath, count to ten or such, and by then the stuff had rolled over and gone.

Later in the run, the man who was playing my husband, a non-speaking part, had occasion to find someone to replace himself for one show. I asked him if he had told this new chap about the ice and what to do. He said that oh yes, of course, of course he had.

That night, the new king-for-a-day and I were lying there dead, side by side, while the dry ice rolled over us. Suddenly, I heard this pained, shallow gasping and wheezing beside me. I thought, my God, this poor soul. He's going to go. He's going to panic. I know he is going to pop up if I don't *do something*. We were shrouded by the mist at this point, so I rolled over, pregnant padding and all, right on top of him to keep him from jumping up.

Of course, I didn't have time to roll *off*, so what the audience saw as the mist rolled past us was this 'dead' queen rather unexpectedly lying on top of her 'dead' husband. We must have looked rather lusty...for a couple of corpses.

CHRIS WIGGINS
Shot

Often on the series, *The Last Of The Mohicans*, a handful or so of extras would have the opportunity to volunteer for some 'special business'. On this occasion someone was required to be shot with an arrow and die. As usual fifteen hands went up...because it would mean more money. It didn't matter how horrible the scene might turn out to be. They finally chose some little pudgy guy.

The next I heard of all of this was when Lon [Chaney Jr] came over to the bus where most of us were huddling trying to stay warm. No honeywagons in those days.

'Have you ever seen somebody shot with an arrow?' he said to me.

'No.'

'You'd better see this. It's really quite interesting. The special effects man is very good.'

What they would do was strap a block of wood over the heart of the person who would be shot. There was a hole pre-drilled halfway into the block of wood where the arrow was to end up. This prevented the arrow from bouncing out of the wood once it had hit. From the centre of this hole a nylon line was threaded through the shirt which was then put back on the victim over the wood block. The line was then taken behind the camera, threaded through the shaft of a hollow arrow and tied to a tree. When the arrow was shot from a bow beside the camera, it would slide along the line directly to the dowelled hole. It was simple but incredibly effective.

So this rolypoly extra was set up for the stunt. He was playing a soldier guarding the fort, marching back and forth in front of the palisade when he's shot. Very simple. The extra decided that this was his big opportunity because he had a solo shot. Suddenly he became very self-conscious about being singled out and was anxious to 'do it properly'. He marched ridiculously up and down, the rifle smartly up on his shoulder. Apparently he was now a guard at Buckingham Palace! Sam, the director, who was known for his colourful language, walked over.

'Look, just walk up and down the fucking ground, willya? Don't fucking go on like that. You're not a fucking peacock. You're bored, you're tired, you want to go to bed for fuck's sake.'

'Oh...oh yeah, yeah right.'

'Just take three or four steps one way, then turn around and go the other fucking way. '

'Right. OK, I got it.'

When action was called, the guy looked down at his feet and counted.

'One, two, three, four...'

'CUT!...Look, you don't have to do *exactly* three steps. Just walk up there, turn around and come back.'

'OK. I'm OK now.'

So he did it but when he got to the turn, he turned *away* from camera, the wrong way, having forgotten that the nylon line was strung from the front of his shirt. Now this line was wrapped around his back, making it impossible for the arrow to hit him without circling around behind him and coming in from the front. So Sam ran over and explained that he had to keep the line free so that the arrow could slide along it to hit him from his camera side. He'd have to turn the other way. The fellow nodded. OK.

Now this fellow was walking back and forth and turning the right way but he was walking in a straight line instead of an arc which was needed to keep the line taunt. The arrow magically scooped down the sagging line and up again to the intended victim's heart at the other end. Sam's normally colourful language was now becoming more than usually brutal.

'Nah, what the fuck! Ya have to keep the fucking wire *tight!*'

This poor little tubby guy by now was getting more and more rattled.

'Oh, yeah. I get ya.'

Sam was ready to kill him.

Now he had to remember not to count, turn the right way, keep the line tight, and walk back and forth. So he tried again, but by that time he was so nervous, his walk looked stiffly crab-like as he was trying to keep the wire tight. At this point no one could keep a straight face. Lon was nearly on his knees weeping with laughter. Sam's eyes were bulging.

'Look...' He took a long deep breath, 'Just-take-four-steps' and he said to the archer with the bow, off camera beside him, 'Shoot the S.O.B. on the second step...and if he screws it up again, shoot him anyway!'

So the extra took two steps and fwoosh! the bowman let it go. And it looked bloody marvellous. It hit POW! right into the block. But the second it hit that poor little guy, you could see on his face the sudden realisation that he was shot and he now had a solo 'death scene'. So the gun was *flung* in one direction, his hand went into the air, 'Ah! ah! ah!' and the other hand clutched the arrow as he fell *backwards...directly away from camera.* But of course, he *couldn't* fall backwards because the wire was still attached to the tree off camera. So instead, he bounced, boing! boing! on the end of this nylon line.

Lon Chaney completely lost it. He sat on the ground and just howled with laughter, eyes streaming. Sam was livid.

'Hold my arms back. I'm gonna kill him!'

It was the one out-take that I would love to have had. Someone must have kept them. The look on that guy's face had to have been one of the all-time classics.

15

Pranks and Escapades

FRANCES HYLAND
Bouquets

One of my favourite 'opening night gift' stories is about two great ladies who were dear friends, Kate Reid and Barbara Hamilton.

Kate was at Stratford doing two plays. One was about to open and the second was in rehearsal and would not open for some weeks. Barb was at the same time in Charlottetown playing either her first or her second 'Marilla' in the stage production of *Anne Of Green Gables*. Kate had her opening night first and Barby sent her an enormous horseshoe-shaped wreath of Kate's favourite flowers, gardenias as I recall. When I say enormous, I mean it was the size of something that would go over the neck of a race horse.

Time passed. Kate kept this great 'thingummy' in her dressing room until the flowers started to go all brown and greasy the way flowers do if they are not watered. Barbara's opening night was coming up, so Kate had this decidedly unpleasant looking horseshoe boxed up carefully and shipped back to Charlottetown. She also arranged through friends to have a horse delivered to the stage door at Charlottetown, completely bedecked in this dreadful looking gardenia horseshoe-shaped collar.

A little more time went by after Barbara's opening, and Kate was then about to open in her second play at Stratford. Sure enough an exquisitely gift-wrapped package arrived from Barby in Charlottetown. It contained an enormous horse turd.

BENEDICT CAMPBELL
The water cannon warriors

Joe Ziegler, Colm Feore and I were at the Stratford Festival together for a few seasons in the mid-80s and we formed a trio that came to be known as the Geek Patrol. We arrogantly, but facetiously, took on the roles of arbiters of company standards. If we felt you had fallen below a certain standard you were immediately hosed down with whatever water weapon was at our disposal at the time.

We were constantly on the look out for more deadly and accurate weapons. The pinnacle of success was achieved when Colm invented what came to be known as 'The Killer Cane'. It was an old weed-killer tube that had been drained of its poison; with a large piece of dowelling inserted it could be used as a giant syringe. When you pushed the piece of dowelling towards the opening at the bottom you could expel about a gallon of water in the blink of an eye, all with pinpoint precision. The Killer Cane became the feared weapon backstage.

I was always a bit too shy and Joe a bit humorous to use it completely effectively. Colm, as the inventor, possessed just the proper balance of good nature and malevolence to make his assaults with The Killer Cane a humiliating experience for whoever felt his wrath. There were many great evenings backstage: rivalries between dressing rooms, surprise attacks, conferences about which older members of the company would find our attack humorous and which would simply seek some way of getting us fired. We usually went for the ones who would try to get us fired.

On one particular occasion we had been planning an attack on a dressing room we thought was particularily deserving of our wrath. As we crept down the hall with weapons in belt clips and strung over our backs, people came to their dressing-room doors as if waiting to see the showdown at the OK Corral. We kicked open the offenders' door and realized to our horror that they had been waiting for us. We were doused with water from head to toe. It was coming at us from all directions. Suffice it to say, there was water everywhere. We retreated to our dressing room to regroup. Before we had time to launch a counterstrike our dressing room door was pushed in and there stood the stage manager who had a reputation for chewing out even the most elevated members of the acting company. We were just chicken feed to her. She gave us a severe dressing down.

'We have all put up with this ridiculous behaviour for long enough. There are thousands of dollars of costumes that could be destroyed by your foolishness. You will come out in the hall and clean up this mess. I don't care if you're here for two more hours, you will get it done. And this absurdity will never happen again, is that clear? Am I making that plain enough for you?' The dressing down continued in a much more thorough manner than I am able to remember, but it was harsh and it was fierce. There was a moment of silence as she waited for an answer.

'Would you like me to be a little plainer for you? This kind of behaviour is over as of tonight.'

She fixed me with an icy stare and I felt a cold chill run up my spine, extremely reminiscent of being terrified by the school principal in grade two. Colm just pretended that nothing was going on and he had better things to do with his time, but I think he was just as terrified as me. Joe, the spiritual leader of the group, had stood silently listening attentively, never blinking an eye.

'Have I made myself clear to you, Joe?'

In his usual laconic Minnesotan way Joe said, 'Oh yeah. You've made yourself pretty clear.' ...At which point he raised his still fully loaded water pistol and proceeded to hose this person down with total irreverence and reckless disregard.

LOUIS DEL GRANDE
Tissue toss

Now and then, understudying can be a little tedious. You have to be at the theatre and have little to do. Often you will have a small part which is generally undemanding and you are supposed to learn whatever part you are to understudy in your extra time and during the few understudy rehearsals.

I was an understudy for 'Friar Lawrence' in *Romeo and Juliet*, and as usual was trying to keep myself amused. On this occasion, I was tossing a brand new roll of toilet paper back and forth like a football with Chris Berneau. It's fine to keep yourself alert in any way you can, but we were tossing it back and forth much too close to the entrance, just flipping it, waiting to go on. The tomb scene was in progress on stage. Somehow the roll of toilet paper dropped through the entrance and *onto the stage*, stopping just short of the coffin! Christopher Walken as 'Romeo' was kneeling beside 'Juliet' grieving desperately over the apparent suicide of his love, and must have blocked it from the audience's view. I doubt that they ever saw it. However...the stage manager *did* see it.

At Stratford the stage manager, Thomas Bohdanetzky, had a book in which he would write your name if you were late or did anything wrong. I think he had to get an extra book just for me. I was sure I would be fired after this episode. But when he came to find out who had tossed that roll on to the stage, God bless him, Leo Ciceri who was playing 'Mercutio' covered for us. He said that no one knew who had done it and that it must have fallen by accident.

LOUIS NEGIN
At liberty

Years ago Canadian actors used to be able to collect unemployment cheques. Then the government gave us a 'deal' in which they traded us unemployment insurance for some tax write-offs. What can I say? Before the 'deal', if you were collecting an unemployment benefit cheque and the government could get you a job, you would have to take the job. And the system required you to pick up your cheque in person.

One morning Angela Leigh, Maureen Fitzgerald, and I went down together to collect our cheques. Maureen had been up all night at a party. She came to the line-up still wearing a low-cut black Balenciaga gown. All her eye make-up was melting. Angela was doing arabesques in the line. We're all kibitzing. Then came my turn at the counter.

The lady said to me, 'Oh, yes, an actor. Now, what *else* can you do? Because we can give you a temporary job doing something else.' It was Christmas. Where was she going to find me a job? Never mind, I didn't want one. I looked her in the eye and said, 'I'm a shepherd.'

Well, that floored her. I got my money.

BARBARA HAMILTON
Coming through

My first *Spring Thaw* was either 1955 or 1958, I forget which. What I do remember is that it was Bob Goulet's last year.

The cast had kind of jerry-built dressing rooms. They were up on planks along the back wall of the Avenue Theatre on Eglinton Avenue. A small curtain separated the men from the women and another curtain separated the women from the lighting board. Every time Lyle Anton, our lighting man, wanted to get to his board he would first go through the men's dressing room and, as he approached the women's dressing room, would stand outside the curtain and in a gentlemanly way would say, 'Close your eyes, girls. I'm coming through.'

For about the first three weeks, in various forms of undress, I would squeeze my eyes tight shut while he made his way through. One night I heard uncontrollable laughter. And as I opened my eyes, I saw the entire men's dressing room holding open the curtain and roaring with laughter at my gullibility. I realized how stupid I had been and Lyle Anton never let me forget it.

NICHOLAS HARRISON
Rose in the audience

I was working in England during the time of the Gulf War, and needless to say London's West End had been hit fairly hard. *Into the Woods* had closed and many other shows would soon follow. Our company was doing *Love of the Nightingale* at the Lyric Hammersmith Theatre.

Houses hadn't been the best and we hoped for better through an increase in publicity, although some splendid reviews hadn't much improved attendance.

I remember being in the dressing room when our director burst in beaming, 'You'll never guess who's in the audience tonight, luvvies!' We all began to wonder who might have come for one of our midweek shows so we asked 'Who?' with equal enthusiasm. 'Rose!' That's all he said, expecting us to know who 'Rose' was. I had no idea. So I asked, 'Rose who?' To which he replied, tongue firmly implanted in cheek, '*Rows* of empty seats, luv. *Rows* of bloody empty seats!'

JAMES EDMOND
Less than great expectations

I joined the permanent company of Theatre Calgary under Chris Newton for the 1969-70 season. It was a good company and an interesting selection of plays. Our opening show was Joe Orton's *Loot*. We had a wild set-to with that. A stage adaptation of Dickens' *Great Expectations* was next. Revelling excitedly in the vagaries of *Loot* ('It isn't fur, it's fluff.' 'It feels like fur.' 'It's fluff.'), I began feeling somewhat trammelled, by day, rehearsing the role of the lawyer's clerk, starchy 'Mr Wemmick' in *Great Expectations*. With limited resources and time at our disposal, I thought we were hard put to do justice to the book (after the marvellous film version, too) though I ought to have remembered that Chris Newton always has a trick or two up his sleeve.

Dana Ivey playing termagant 'Mrs Joe Gargery' wasn't too enthusiastic either, I discovered, so we two put our heads together. I suggested playing a joke. Dana, who was as willing as I to muddy the waters a little when the spirit moved her, agreed. As I see it, due to the malign shenanigans let loose in *Loot*, the old Nick in me was set free too.

We concocted a telegram purportedly from the Dickens Fellowship in New York. The fellowship informed Theatre Calgary that they controlled stage rights to *Great Expectations* and were refusing permission for the production to proceed. Dana had a New York friend she telephoned and asked to send the wire for us from there. It was a jape, a diversionary tactic, not intended to do harm. I don't even remember if there ever was a 'Dickens Fellowship' or if we made it up entirely. We let one person into our confidence, Neil Munro, who was playing 'Pip', and he seemed as tickled as we were.

One morning, a few days later, the stage manager, rather than call rehearsal, gathered us in the auditorium. Chris walked onstage, solemn and serious as only he can be, and informed us that due to an absolutely unforeseen circumstance we would be prevented from continuing with our production of *Great Expectations* and went on to tell about the wire. Amid gasps of shock and incredulity from the company, Dana and I looked at each other white-faced. Sick in my stomach, with Dana right behind me, I took Chris aside and made a clean breast. He then issued a further announcement, that the edict had just been revealed to him as a hoax played by two members of the company, this uttered with sad reproach. He might have fired us, but he didn't. I went back to work remorseful and considerably crestfallen. For a day or two the rest of the company put the two smart asses in Coventry. Our backs now to it, the show did go on to be a modest success.

Sometime later, Neil Munro revealed to Dana and me that another hoax had been played on us! Clever old Chris had been no more serious about cancelling his show than we were to have it cancelled. He had been let in on the joke. Sensible to its possible repercussion, Neil had gone to him and told him what we were up to...and we had our comeuppance.

CHRIS WIGGINS
Lunch!

In one episode of the TV series *The Last Of The Mohicans*, Arch MacDonald was playing some poor innocent who had been stripped to the waist in the freezing cold and lashed to a stake. Faggots of wood were piled up all around. The Indians were going to burn him.

The director and camera crew got it all lined up and ready to shoot when someone called, 'Lunch!' So the cast, the crew, all pretended to forget about poor

Arch freezing to death tied to this stake. We all started to wander away and in the distance, as we walked away, we could hear Arch in a cold, reedy voice calling after us, 'Light the faggots...!'

MICHAEL KANE and ARTHUR VORONKA were in an elevator once
with a pretty woman who was looking everywhere but up. Michael was
very handsome and a great wag. He told her not to look at his feet.
She demurred and said that indeed she had not been looking at his feet.
He said, 'I don't actually care but I hate it when you lie about it.'

DOUGLAS E. HUGHES
Black like Sven

In 1983, Ron Ulrich had just taken over as Artistic Director of the Huron County Playhouse and was directing *South Pacific*. It was a big cast of about 35, most of who did not know each other at the beginning of rehearsals but we ended up having the most wonderful time.

I was sharing a dressing room with this mulatto actor in the chorus, named Bruce Tubbe. We discovered, about two weeks into the run, that all the sailors in the chorus had character names. They weren't written in the script but someone had put them in the programs. Bruce's name was 'Sven Larson'! We just thought this was hilarious. The one black guy in the company and his name is Sven Larson.

There was a little bit of business in the show where something was heaved off-stage. You'd hear a thump and Bruce would say, offstage, 'Hey, who the hell threw that?' Well, the night Bruce found out he was Sven, and the thing went flying off-stage, we heard—thump, 'Heya, whoo da haell trew dat?' Everybody onstage was, of course, toast.

LOUIS NEGIN
Oedipus

The first season I was at Stratford we mounted *Oedipus Rex* by Sophocles. The costumes were by Tanya Moiseiwitsch and they looked incredible but they were very difficult to wear and we had huge masks as well. We were very, very hot and it was difficult to see where we were going.

At one point in the first act the chorus came on stage as supplicants carrying twigs of varying sizes. Of course, everyone wanted a little twig. You didn't want to come on with a great tree-like twig as well as coping with everything else. They were also very cumbersome to get through the tunnels to the stage. The goings on over the twigs just got sillier and sillier.

One night I got to the theatre early and hid all the twigs. The smoke bombs began onstage, it was time for our twig entrance, and it was chaos backstage. People were screaming at each other if someone found a twig, 'That's my twig!' They were fighting each other over twigs!

I was sick, I was laughing so hard.

RICHARD MONETTE
Carrying Joan

In *Henry VI* I remember playing one of two soldiers who had to burn 'Joan'. I had to carry Joan, who was played by Martha Henry, off, then come back up the tunnel and whisper in Bill Hutt's ear (I think he was playing 'Warwick') that the deed was done. She was of course burned at the stake.

One day, I came up with gloved hand full of ashes and I said 'My Lord, ...phoooooh...(and blew the ash toward him)...Joan.' Of course, Bill Hutt, being enormously disciplined, kept a perfectly straight face. Unfortunately, I didn't.

WILLIAM WHITEHEAD
Target practice

At Toronto's Crest Theatre, in a production of 'the Scottish play', I played the 'First Murderer'—and doubled as 'Young Siward'. In the latter guise I was killed towards the end of the play. My corpse lay on the stage as 'Macduff' made his triumphant entrance bearing the head of the slain title character, and threw his trophy onto the battlefield. The head, in this case, was a large and heavy cabbage in a burlap sack.

Macduff, played by John Vernon—whom I had known when we were both growing up in Regina—delighted in seeing how close he could make that head come to my lifeless body. One night, he hit the bull's-eye; the head/cabbage landed squarely on my face. That was the moment when Young Siward came briefly to life with a series of unrehearsed and violent death throes—while the rest of Macduff's lines took on a measure of suppressed hysteria.

ALAN PEARCE
Play it again, Phil

My career as an actor started when I was nine. I was hired by a stock company in Vancouver called the Allen Players. We would do a new play every week and while we played one we rehearsed another. You were always on the go. This play was called *Mrs Wiggs of the Cabbage Patch*. I remember it vividly. I played a boy called 'Phil' who had only one leg. I had to have my leg strapped up behind me for each performance. I also had to play the violin.

At one point in the play we were all onstage in the set of a kitchen. Someone would say, 'Oh, let's hear you play the fiddle, Phil.' So I would pick up the fiddle and play a few bars of *The Irish Washerwoman*, a song known by everyone in the English-speaking world at that time. I had only learned the first five bars; when I was finished the actors would say 'wonderful, great', and applaud—and the scene would continue.

One matinee, I finished and waited for the applause from the other actors onstage. There wasn't any, just dead silence. Then one old character actor said 'Oh, that was great, Phil. Play the rest of it.' As I didn't know the rest of it I went back to the beginning and played the first five bars again. 'Good. More. More.' I must have played through those same opening bars about five times. All the other actors were in on the gag. It was the kind of thing pros used to do back then on matinee days and there weren't many people in the audience. That's when you had fun.

DOUGLAS CHAMBERLAIN
Flashlights

At the Charlottetown Festival Kate Reid and I were in Don Harron's adaptation of Earl Birney's book *Turvey* and Mavor Moore's adaptation of Gogol's *The Inspector General* that he called *The Ottawa Man*.

Turvey is a comedy about Canadian soldiers in World War II and Jack Duffy was playing 'Turvey'. In the second act there was a front-of-curtain scene between Kate and Barbara Hamilton, playing two air raid wardens. They were meant to be outside with flashlights and the stage was black. Every night before their scene Barbara would admonish Kate.

'Now Kate, every time I talk, make sure you shine the flashlight in my face or no one will see me.'

'Of course, Barbara. Do you think I'm stupid?'

The thing was, while *Kate* talked, Barbara was shining the light everywhere but Kate's face! It was about five weeks before Kate realised what Barbara was doing. Everybody used to stand in the wings and just kill ourselves laughing. As soon as Barbara started to talk, Kate was right there shining the light on her face. When Kate started talking, Barbara would shine the light all over the place.

DOUGLAS E. HUGHES
Beach blanket bongos

I did *South Pacific* at the Huron Country Playhouse in 1983 and it was one of those magical times when the whole group just bonded. It was like six weeks of *Beach*

Blanket Bingo. Everyone was having affairs all over the place. This huge six-week-long love-in carried over into the show in a lot of ways I'm sure the stage management wished that it hadn't. I've never done a show where there was so much 'stuff' going on, both on and off stage.

One of the things that spread like a disease was flashing. In the number *There Is Nothing Like A Dame* we, the chorus of sailors, had to watch all the nurses jog across the stage during the middle of the song. We would all watch them go and at that exact point came the whistling part of the song. One day they all jogged by, got offstage, turned to look at us and, as one, threw off their tops. There we were, 12 guys onstage blowing air, *absolutely* unable to whistle.

GRANT COWAN
The hat rack

We were opening a new theatre on Bloor Street in Toronto with *Dames At Sea* starring Yvonne de Carlo. The show never really took off and Yvonne de Carlo used to horse around a lot, as did all of the rest of us in the company.

We were trying to keep sane in spite of everything. One night I thought I'd go and stand in the wings with just my sailor hat on and that's all, to see if I could break Yvonne up. So I stood there, naked except for the hat on my head. Then I gradually got a bit self-conscious and thought 'Oh, my God! Maybe my privates aren't good enough for this gag.' It's amazing how your mind works. I suddenly remembered a story I'd heard years ago. Noel Coward was asked what he thought of the new renovations in his club in London—they'd redone the bathroom in mirrors and chrome and everything—and he said 'It does make one's privates look so insignificant!' And that's what I thought—his line went through my head—so I grabbed my hat and covered 'em up!

The story went around town that I'd hung my hat on my privates!

ANTHONY BEKENN
Impressing Kate

I was doing *Arsenic And Old Lace* with Kate Reid towards the end of her life. She was very ill but always, always had that amazing wicked twinkle in her eye. Charmion King and Louis Negin were in the cast as well. Louis and Kate especially were always trying to break each other up. Kate was notorious for flashing the cast from offstage. I myself was a victim at least once.

Onstage there is a box large enough to hold an adult body. It has a trap entrance from back stage. Louis decided one night that he had a great idea for a prank to play on Kate. He knew that she would, at one point in the play, be required to look into this box so he decided that he would get into it totally nude and get himself aroused. He was sure he'd crack her up.

Kate came to the box finally, opened it up, eyed him up and down...and without a flicker on her face, shut the box and continued on with the scene. Poor Louis was so disappointed.

KEN DELISLE
The trouble with Smurfs

While I was still an amateur actor with a local Winnipeg group, we were doing an Alan Ayckbourn comedy, in which I played a slow, silent, child-like man. In the play there is a mad scene in which all the characters sit down to eat a hastily prepared stew.

On closing night, one of the stage hands decided to be funny and hid little plastic Smurf dolls throughout the set. The actors could see them but the audience could not. The cast contained themselves and never lost character until the supper scene. There were Smurfs in the stew! One female character started to grin and then laughed. She was joined by a second cast member. Of course their giggling was completely inappropriate to the scene and their uncontrolled outbursts forced them to try to say their lines between bursts of laughter.

I was getting annoyed. While the rest of the cast was lost in laughter, I was the only one who had not broken character over this trick. In a valiant effort to return us to the true purpose of the scene and away from these silly Smurfs, I jumped to my next line. I delivered the line calmly, then realised what a mistake I had made. My focus was not to last. The line was, 'What are these lumpy things in the stew?'

DOUGLAS CHAMBERLAIN
Kate the great

Kate [Reid] and I worked together many times. We hung around together a lot the summer the Charlottetown Festival did *Turvey* and *The Ottawa Man*. Kate had a wonderful house to live in that summer, by the water. It was a grand old home in front of the court house.

A double decker bus used to take the tourists around town to see the sights. Every time the bus went by the house, unbeknownst to Kate, the guide would point out that this was the house 'where the well-known actress, Canada's Kate Reid lived'.

One afternoon we had all been to the beach and had come back to the house right around the time the bus was to go by. I had an idea.

'Kate, I'd love to get a photo of you and the whole family on the lawn. Everybody's here and we're all relaxed now and we could get a great picture.'

We got everyone out on the lawn and set up the picture. I could see the bus winding its way along and I was fussing with the posing to stall for time. Kate was getting impatient.

'Oh for Chrissake. Take the picture.'

I could see the bus out of the corner of my eye getting closer and closer,

'OK. Now just do a little wave thing.'

The bus came along, Kate and the kids are waving away and all of a sudden we heard the loudspeaker blaring.

'And coming up is the home of Canada's Kate Reid...Why, there she is now on the lawn!...Waving!'

They must have thought Kate did this every day as part of the deal. My gag worked like a charm. She was ready to kill me.

VERNON CHAPMAN
The mad queen

In the early nineteen fifties, Dora Mavor Moore hired a young man to sweep up and empty waste paper baskets in the office and studio of the New Play Society. He was an actor from England named Gary Montgomery and was the nephew of Field Marshal Montgomery. Eventually Gary was promoted to other functions, and when I left the New Play Society he replaced me as a teacher in the NPS school. One Saturday Mrs Moore asked him to take over her Saturday afternoon children's class. He refused. She told him she had a pressing engagement that she had to keep, and insisted that he teach the class. Gary still refused. Mrs Moore began to get irate and Gary said:

'Mrs Moore, I'm going to paint your wagon.'

Mrs Moore put on her 'mad queen face', as he described it. Now she was fuming and said, 'How dare you speak to me like that?' Gary did not immediately understand why she was so angry. Then it dawned on him.

'Mrs Moore,' he said, 'You don't understand. I am going to see *Paint Your Wagon* at the Royal Alex this afternoon.'

Mrs Moore reluctantly agreed to find someone else to take over her class.

NICOLA CAVENDISH
Spotlighted

The Queen Elizabeth Theatre in Vancouver is one of those civic theatre complexes where more than one theatre shares a backstage area. This means the cast of one show may, on time off, scoot across the hallway to the other theatre, and watch from the wings whatever is happening on that stage.

Around 1977 I was playing the nurse in the Playhouse production of *Equus*. I was wearing a traditional uniform with cap. White from head to toe. Phillip Clarkson, a respected designer and close friend, dropped by one night just at the time I had a long break in the show. Next door in the big theatre the Royal Winnipeg Ballet was giving the première performance of a new piece, *The Bare Stage*, narrated by Paul Scofield.

With twenty minutes off I suggested to Phillip we go over and watch the ballet for a few minutes. As we quietly opened the door to the backstage we could see the large main stage curtain was down. This was great! We'd come at their intermission. We hoped it was almost over as time was not really mine to claim and I had to get back for my cue in my theatre.

Philip, a very tall, elfin man with a thick head of red hair, and I in my nurse's cap and gown, stood there a couple of minutes in the dark. I whispered to Phil, 'Where is everybody? I don't see any dancers or even stage hands.'

Suddenly the mainstage curtain slowly started to rise. One by one the sold-out seats revealed themselves in their sold-out splendour until we could see the entire theatre and they could see us! To make matters worse, a huge spotlight aimed directly upstage cast a fifty-foot shadow on the upstage wall of a bushy-haired giant elf and an equally giant nurse. At that exact moment the divine voice of Paul Scofield came over the sound system describing for the audience the beauty of the bare stage!

Frozen with terror we noticed the stage hands and members of the company crouched and hiding in the extreme corners of the wings. Under my breath I said to Phillip, 'Don't move.' We were part of their ballet number whether they liked it or not. Whether *we* liked it or not. Then the curtain legs started coming down, affording us an escape which we made ASAP.

The next day as I was walking down Granville Street, I bumped into Colin Thomas, of late the theatre reviewer for the *Georgia Straight*, who said, 'Nicky! Caught your performance with The Royal Winnipeg Ballet last night. Loved it.'

I thought I'd ruined it forever, the privilege of going across to the other theatre and experiencing the wonderful artists, rock concerts, and road shows that would pass through the Queen Elizabeth Theatre. But it was all OK. Those of us working in adjoining theatres still have the best seats in town.

DAVE THOMAS
Second City nights out

When a famous female impersonator was appearing at Toronto's Royal Alexandra, we wanted to go, but you had to wear a suit to get in. We didn't have our own suits with us and we didn't have time to go home. So we [Marty Short, some other cast members, and I] took the prop coats and prop ties from the green room, none of which fit, and went to the Royal Alex looking like an Italian street gang without any money. We looked like hit men who couldn't do anything right, but the people in charge at the Royal Alex knew who Martin Short was so they let us in.

When it was over, Short and I were out in front [of the theatre]. He's saying, 'So you're the famous American, eh? I understand you can make all kinds of mugs and faces.' I said, 'Yeah, well, how's this?' and made a face. He said, 'Oh, that's easy, have you ever done one of these?' and he did one. They got bigger and broader and sillier, and we were with four other people who were getting fed up. We didn't stop until Steve Kampmann and Peter Torokvei picked me up—I forget who picked up Short—and carried us away, facing each other, in sort of prone positions. 'You haven't seen the last of me.' Making faces, into the night, grown men.

GEOFFREY D. MILLER
The great train arrest

Blood of Youth was a low-budget independent film written and directed by Tim Ziegler, and shot on location in Toronto and Las Vegas, Nevada.

It was Tim's first feature-length film with most of the budget coming from his pocket. The story was about a broke and recently unemployed college student who, at wit's end, hops a freight train to Las Vegas in order to win his tuition, and pay a few bills. There is more to the film's story but the train is the important part here.

As I said, it was a low-budget film. No stunt people. No insurance. The train company wanted two million dollars insurance coverage before they would consider letting us film. Of course this was impossible, so we would have no co-operation from the folks who actually owned the train, and no permission to film. In short...nothing unusual from the way a lot of low-budgets are made. Except perhaps the moving train!

We knew of a place in Scarborough where the trains were stationed, and where it would be possible to board them. The cinematographer had to work at his 'real' job that day, so the director decided to film the train shots himself. The crew consisted of the director with the camera, film and other bits, and myself with the costumes, props, and a few other bags. That was it.

After we had decided on which kind of train and what track, we settled in to wait for one to come. We had no way of knowing where or even when the train we hoped to hop would stop. Sure enough along came our train. At the time, I couldn't stop thinking about the giant, roaring wheels that were grinding next to me as the train started to pull away, and that I could only be insane to want to do this for a film.

As Tim ran along the track next to the moving train, he grabbed for the ladder on a grain car and pulled himself up. The problem was that he had grabbed the ladder at the front of the car, which meant that since the train was moving I had to grab for the ladder at the back of the grain car. Miraculously, we both made it on to the same car with all our equipment and our legs still attached. But we were on opposite ends of that same grain car. The director was in the front with the camera and film, and the lead (me) was in the back with...nothing to do. Ten minutes went by, and all we did was hang our heads around the side of the train and stare at each other. Then something happened. Something that would only happen on a film like this.

While I was waiting, thinking that I had got myself into a ridiculous situation and that the train was probably going to end up in Mexico, suddenly Tim jumped down beside me. He had run *over* the moving train car and then climbed down the back—with the camera and backpack! He had risked his life, just to get this shot.

After my heart resumed beating, we filmed for about twenty minutes, before the train began to slow down. It stayed still for another five minutes or so, then it snapped together, stretched out, and slowly began to move. We were just beginning to resume our filming when out of nowhere jumped a huge man with a radio and a hard-hat. He gathered himself together on the ladder, and grabbed his radio.

'Well, boys!' he yells, 'I hope ya had fun...cause you're goin' to *jail!*'

By the time I had come to, the hard-hat man was talking into his radio and the train was slowing down.

'Yeah, we got 'em. Pull up to the station and we'll turn 'em over there,' he barked, then turned to us. 'You boys are in a lot of trouble. A lot of people saw you on your little ride, you know...including the cops. Ah, well...we got ya now. And you're going to *jail*, boys.'

He kept saying that word, 'jail'. It conjured up vivid images of burly tattooed hulks calling me, 'Hey, Bitch!' I wouldn't last a second. The thought was paralysing. All I could think of at that moment was that I was going to jail for a film that I wasn't getting paid for and my gravestone was going to read, 'Here lies "Bitch". R.I.P.'

When the train slowed to a stop, the hard-hat man got down and a truck full of other hard-hatted men pulled along the other side—to block our escape, I suspect. The police were there as well, but quickly left after we had been detained. It appeared that we would now wait for the very special 'Train Police'. It was their job to take us in and process us. The hard-hat men told us that the 'Train Cops' have their own guns that are better and more deadly than the already deadly guns that the 'Normal Cops' carry.

As the Train Cop (singular) finally arrived (one short and not very scary guy), the hard-hat men asked us what we were doing and how far we had ridden. They thought, wow! that that was a long way to go before being caught. Then they said that maybe we wouldn't really go to the dark, small, private little jail that they have for just such offenders after all. The Train Cop laughed, gave us each trespassing tickets that totalled $110 and told us not to do it again.

No jail. No court. No one calling me 'bitch'. And in the end, we got the shot. It adds a huge amount of production value to the film and makes the filming in Las Vegas worth more...which is not to say I would recommend this method to anyone who is not already insane.

And, by the way, the film is called *Heroes,* last I heard at any rate.

SUSAN DOUGLAS RUBES
My early days in movies

The first movie I ever made was called *The Private Affairs of Bel Ami.* The film was directed by Albert Lewin and starred George Sanders. Angela Lansbury, Ann Dvorak, Frances Dee and I were among the victims of the lead character's seductions. I was a naïve nineteen-year-old, playing an innocent fifteen-year-old, and completely in awe of all of these marvellous people.

The first day on the set I had a very long speech, a monologue directed at George Sanders' character during a dinner scene. He was supposed to be trying to eat his soup but every time he was to take a sip, I would interrupt him and say, 'Isn't that so, Monsieur?' Throughout this whole monologue he never got to taste his soup. We did the rehearsal, the timing was difficult and I was very aware that I must do the best I could in this formidable company. We prepared to shoot it.

For many actors there is a kind of sixth sense toward the end of a scene or a long speech when you know that it is going well. Everything was working perfectly, the timing, the rhythm, everything. Just before I said the last 'And isn't that so, Monsieur?', George Sanders picked up a fork and put it down the front of my dress, spoiling the take. Well, everybody laughed. Of course, it was very funny for everyone but me because I had to do the whole thing all over again.

I found out later that George had a reputation for being a prankster and was on occasion quite thoughtless about it. I was also warned that George would try to ask me for a date and that I should stay away from him. Which I did.

ART HINDLE
The '70s in L.A.

In Los Angeles in the '70s there was an enormous amount of drug use in the business from the top on down. Producers in those days actually encouraged it by supplying to the actors. But the first time I ran into it was on a set when I was working for the first time with an Academy Award nominee, who shall remain nameless.

We were playing two guys who were supposed to be buddies. His first day on the set, we were introduced. He asked me if I wanted to play some backgammon in his Winnebago. I said, 'Sure. Sounds good. Anything you like.' Obviously, we were trying to find some way to get to know each other, to find a relationship that will work well for the film. This was a way to start, so there was no chance that I could or would say 'No'.

In the trailer he pulled out a doobie.* I asked him what he was doing because I was a little surprised. He said that he was trying a new relaxation technique, a mild tranquillizer that apparently calmed his first-day, new-set nerves.

So he pulled on this spliff* and we played backgammon until he looked at me and asked me if I wanted some. Now I was in an impossible situation. If I said 'No', then the possibility of offending him and jeopardizing our relationship on set was very real. If he thought that I judged him for using an illicit substance, then he would likely get paranoid about where I was at. So I said, 'Sure. OK...yeah.' The two of us got stoned.

Later that day, we had a very intense scene together. We had a lot of dialogue, a lot of very important exposition. Everything was very significant, talking and talking, mostly in tight two-shots, very close. They cut, they wrapped, and at the end of it, we were pretty pleased with the day's work. It felt fantastic! We said to each other, 'Ahhhh. Wow! That was great! Fabulous!'

The next night, we went to see the rushes and it *stank!* It was boring, unfocused, and completely meaningless. What were these people doing? I swore I would never be under the influence of *anything* again while I was working, no matter how important it was to someone else.

* Slang for marijuana cigarette.

TONY ROSATO
The taxi 'trip'

In the late '70s or early '80s I was going out with an American girl. Her sisters had come up from Pittsburgh to visit for the long weekend. They all thought it would be fun to introduce me to LSD. It was my first exposure to any kind of 'recreational' drug. I had a show to do at Second City that night and I didn't want to mess up my head, but they assured me that it would be out of my system in a few hours, in plenty of time for the show. So they gave me a little blotter of 'acid'. I didn't feel anything at all for the whole day until I was about half way through the show that night. I should have known that I was in trouble because the girls came to the show that night and were the only ones laughing in very bizarre places. The show continued until Ditch Dickinson and I got to the taxi sketch.

The sketch started out with a man, an out-of-towner, getting into a cab at Union Station and asking the cab driver, played by me, to take him to The Royal York Hotel (a hotel immediately across the street from Union Station, taking up the entire block). I think my opening line was, 'We'll just hop onto the Gardiner Expressway right here and we'll get you right there.' The sketch would continued as I drove him along the Gardiner, the 401, the Don Valley Expressway, and back down to the hotel.

So there we were, doing this sketch and I was thinking to myself that this acid stuff is not so bad, it's really quite manageable. It was actually enhancing the experience of improvisation. Why, I could almost visualise the route that I was driving. And in my head, I did that. I visualised the entire route, but in *real time*. I could see the streets, make the turns, feel the acceleration as I got on the highway, everything. And completely forgot about Ditch and the sketch. I had no idea that my own personal tour was eating up eons of time until I felt this hand smacking at my shoulder. Ditch was behind me going, 'Tony...! Where the fuck *are* you! *Stop driving! The scene's going on!*' through clenched teeth under his breath. I looked over my shoulder and saw this intense look of panic on his face. I looked at the audience and they were kind of confused so I said, 'You'll have to excuse me, man, I just dropped some acid before I came in today.' So we made a joke and got this huge laugh.

At that moment, a waitress carrying a huge full tray of drinks, fell and dropped the entire thing. It suddenly gave me something to focus on and play with. 'Oh my god! What the hell is that waitress doing in the middle of the highway! Who would put a restaurant here!' and so on. We did a whole routine. At that point, Ditch dropped a lit cigarette in my lap and we got into another whole riff trying to get that under control. I thought we had succeeded, until a few seconds on into the scene I looked down to see that my shirt was smouldering. A small little bonfire was building up beneath my shirt. All I could think about at the time was, 'Wow...look at the pretty colours in the flames.' I thought finally that I'd better put it out. All the while we are doing a million one-liners about the whole thing. It was very weird. Finally we got back to the 'Royal York Hotel' and finished the sketch.

Later people came up to me and said that they thought it was one of the best sketches that we had ever done. Unfortunately, when I came off stage I was kind of panicky and I didn't know quite how to deal with it. Obviously, it was something that we could never duplicate, so it was all lost.

16

Myth, Mayhem, and Magic

SCOTT WENTWORTH
The Scottish play

There are powerful superstitions about the play *Macbeth* and, as actors, we respect them. Many actors won't say the name out loud. They refer to it as 'the Scottish play'. We had a dreadful accident during the Tech Dress rehearsal of a recent production at Stratford. It was during the apparition scene which made it even spookier. The apparitions were all dressed alike in long white robes and big masks.

I was playing 'Macbeth' and was downstage. I heard a kind of thud behind me, as if someone had dropped a prop or something. Suddenly the lights came up and there was this crumpled little bundle on the stage. Then I saw blood and everything went into high gear to get help. At first I didn't know who it was because the mask was covering the actor's face. It was Joyce Campion, one of the country's veteran actresses. She had fallen off the very high stairs and was very badly hurt. She spent some months in the hospital and, remarkably, returned to the show.

I bumped into Douglas Campbell later that day who said 'That damn play.' I said I didn't know he was that superstitious. He replied, 'I'm not. But the whole play takes place in the dark. Every single scene. When they moved it from the Globe, from the outside, into indoor theatres, people felt it was necessary to create this malevolent darkness. I'm sure that's when the superstitions started. When they did it outside probably nobody got hurt.'

THOMAS HAUFF
Almighty Voice

In the act of theatre we experience many moments of magic. In 1974 Clarke Rogers hired Diane D'Aquila, Hardee Lineham, Richard Moffat and myself to tell the story of the aboriginal hero Almighty Voice, a young Cree who had been arrested in 1887 for stealing a cow. He eluded the RCMP and the Canadian army for three years until he was cornered with two other native youths and slaughtered. The members of his tribe who witnessed what was the last native uprising until the barricades of the 1990s, saw three deer running from the forest on the hill where the boys were killed. The concept of transference and spiritual relationship to animals is at the core of native belief systems. It is believed that the eagle is the closest to the spirits, followed by the hawk.

We four white actors worked on the story of *Almighty Voice* as a collective creation for a Theatre Passe Muraille Seed Show. As we rehearsed we discovered that we were touching a magic that was directly associated with the story and our commitment to it. We knew our research, here in Toronto, could only give us so much. So we went to Duck Lake where the events took place.

One day, driving around the Batoche area in the middle of winter, in very deep snow, we stopped to look at an old horse barn. Richard and I left Clarke behind in the van while we went in to investigate. We found a frozen hawk. We took it out of the barn and I carried it back to the van. As the snow was over my head, what Clarke thought he saw from the van was an eagle standing on someone's hand, coming towards him. In his mind, it was Almighty Voice. As I got closer, he realized that it was me.

We felt that the Grandmothers and Grandfathers had given us a profound gift. We purchased a scalpel and skinned the Hawk and tanned it with lemon juice. We had it preserved and it watched over our rehearsals.

Later, during rehearsal in the rehearsal hall, Diane D'Aquila was sitting on a chair in the middle of the hall, looking into an imaginary mirror. She had her back to a set of prop stairs that was the only real prop in the hall. Hardee came walking down the stairs, stopped, and spontaneously saluted her. Diane saw his reflection in this nonexistent mirror and, equally as spontaneously, saluted him back!

The Hawk watched over all the presentations of this story to the people of Saskatchewan and Manitoba. Clarke has left us but I know he is dancing with the Grandmothers and Grandfathers now!

DEREK McGRATH
Stranger things

We were doing *Godspell* in Winnipeg. Robin White was playing 'Jesus'. I can't remember what I was playing on this occasion because I played several of the male parts at different times.

The director had started out as a dancer/choreographer so this particular production had a lot of dancing in it. It was physically very tough to do because we never stopped moving. Who knows, maybe fatigue had something to do with this incident.

We opened each show wearing grey sweatshirts, kneeling and doing a kind of Bach fugue as each of us got up and became various philosophers spewing their ideas. I was doing 'Martin Luther'. During the matinee of the last day of our run, I got up to do my Martin Luther bit, marching downstage towards the audience singing, 'And God Almighty has made our rulers mad...'

As I did that, I saw, in front of me, facing towards the audience with their backs to me, two identical beings about six feet in height. They were definitely not part of the cast. They did not move and though they were well defined, I couldn't tell if they were wearing clothes or had hair. There was a ghostly look to them like a thick smoke. And I could *see through them.*

What was interesting was that they did not unnerve me or frighten me. I actually got a very positive feeling from seeing them, a wave of positive energy. I knew that part of me was really seeing these beings while another part, the sceptical, intellectual side of me was thinking, 'Wait a minute, this can't be.' I reasoned that maybe two people had been standing in the light and moved quickly and what I was seeing was the outline of their energy, an optical illusion of some kind. Then I realised that everyone had been kneeling from the top of the show and that no one had been standing there, or should have been standing there.

As I turned to march from stage right to stage left, I went on with the number which by then I knew so well I didn't have to think about it. I could not take my eyes off these beings. It was as if I had a kind of split consciousness. We finished the scene and left the stage to change for the next number. As we were all changing into our clown costumes in the stairwell, I said to the cast, 'I wouldn't worry about the show today. We have angels on stage with us.' They said, 'What?' I said 'Oh, nothing.'

The first act was fantastic that day. Enormous energy. I felt ecstasy from beginning to end. Finally the first act came down and we went backstage.

During the intermission, I went into Robin's dressing room and I asked him if he happened to notice anything on stage in the first act that was out of the ordinary. He asked what I meant and again, I asked him if he had seen anything unusual.

'You mean the Munchkins?'

'Munchkins?'

'Beings? Did you see something on stage like "beings"?'

I told him I had and asked him if he had seen them too. He nodded and smiled.

'Is this was the first time that you've seen them?'

'Yeah. What are they?' He shrugged.

'They've been here almost every show or every other show since the beginning of the run. I'm surprised it's the first time you've seen them.'

He suggested that I not mention it to the rest of the cast because they would likely think I was nuts.

'Why do you called them "Munchkins"?'

'These guys are bigger than the ones I usually see, but I have had experiences where I have woken up at night and they are surrounding the bed. But they are always little guys so I call them "Munchkins". They're harmless.'

We went on with the second act, but I never saw the beings again.

SHELLEY PETERSON
A small vision

When I was not yet ten years old, I got hooked on theatre. After much whining and cajoling, I was enrolled in classes at the Grand in London, and I felt my life had truly begun.

We put on a production of *Pinocchio*, and I was thrilled beyond belief to play one of the townspeople. As I sat staring up into the balcony at the dress rehearsal, picturing the crowds that would soon fill the seats, and imagining how all eyes would be on me (even though I had no lines nor individual action!) I saw a dull white light glowing. It moved slowly down from the top tier, travelled down the aisle furthest stage right, and settled in the *second* seat from the aisle. I watched, fascinated. The director had been trying to get my attention, meanwhile, and I was mortified to discover that all eyes were indeed on me.

He asked if I could explain why I was so decidedly not paying him heed. I stammered out something that sounded stupid even to my nine-year-old ears, about a glow up in the balcony. The director looked stunned. He asked what seat. I told him. He slowly turned and looked up. All the actors were silently peering into the balcony.

There was no sign of the light. I felt miserable as I waited for the ridicule. Instead, when he turned back to me, his face was delighted and bright. 'What you saw was the ghost of Ambrose Small.'

Somehow any other career choice seemed dull after that.

JAMES EDMOND
A visit from Ambrose

During the years preceding its renovation and emergence into regional theatre eminence the Grand Theatre, in London, Ontario, was a shabby, green-painted, vastly agreeable old place inhabited by the London Little Theatre. It had been one of the theatres built by the infamous Ambrose Small and was also said to be inhabited by his ghost...but who paid attention to that?

In the summer of 1957 Joan White, a small, chubby, bustling, entrepreneurially minded English actress, director and, in this case, producer leased the Grand for a season of stock. She recruited a company that included Drew Thompson, Charmion King, Deborah Cass, Norman Welsh, Muriel Ontkean (Michael's mother), and myself. I was not long returned from England. Also, the cast included the marvellous Cosette Lee whose Canadian professional career pre-dated the 1930s when she appeared in stock at the Uptown Theatre on Yonge Street.

We were a merry troupe and laughed a good deal of the time, particularly during rehearsals for Agatha Christie's *Ten Little Indians*, a play whose absurdities reduced us to almost non-stop hilarity, so much so that Joan once threatened to kill us all if we didn't stop laughing.

It must have been during the run of this play that, one afternoon at the end of rehearsal for the following week's play, we broke for food and rest for a couple of hours before the evening show. Everybody else went out to eat, but I stayed to rest on the rehearsal furniture not yet removed from the stage. I stretched myself on a settee and fell asleep.

A while later, I awoke with a blast of cold air coming at me from the balcony. I looked up and a door swung open. Thinking someone in stage management had returned, I called but there was no one, only the swish of cold air on a hot summer's night...*inside* a closed theatre...and the door slowly opening. My flesh crawled as I realised that something or someone, an unseen person stood there, looking down on me.

I was never before subject to any ghostly visitation nor have I been since. It has stayed with me going on forty years that for the very short time it took me to get off the stage and out into the alley, I was alone in the theatre with the ghost of Ambrose Small.

DIANA BARRINGTON
Theatre lights

One of the most difficult plays that I have ever done was Sharon Pollock's *Blood Relations*, which is basically the story of axe murderess Lizzie Borden. I played the actress who investigates her story as preparation to play her. The play revolves around the dual role, 'Actress/Lizzie'.

It was the opening night performance at the Bastion in Victoria. As the lights came up on the opening tableau of characters, the stage was awash in a glorious palette of autumnal colours seen through a leafy scrim. It was a breathtaking image. As I stood frozen in my position on stage, prepared to begin, I felt the lightest touch of a hand on my left shoulder. I thought it strange as there was no other member of the cast close enough to have touched me and we were all still supposed to be in tableau. I had the distinct feeling of a presence that was not of this reality. A chill ran down my spine.

Later in the run, during the opening of the last act when Actress/Lizzie delivers a monologue of incredibly heightened awareness of Lizzie's situation, I saw a torch light moving slowly from left to right and then back again across the rear of the house behind the audience. The same sensation as I had had during the opening night tableau rushed through me. It was unmistakable and not a little unnerving. But I still could not understand what it was that I sensed.

I asked the stage manager, Kathy, please to tell whoever it was who had walked across the theatre with a light not to do it again as I found it somewhat distracting. She assured me that no one had been walking through the theatre with a light during the performance. However the same thing happened several more times during the run. Each time Kathy investigated and each time she assured me that there was no one who could have done such a thing.

At the end of the run, during a chat over a drink, she suggested that I might have seen the ghost that was associated with the Bastion, an actor who had had a passion for the theatre. It seemed his life had been extinguished but his light had not.

LOUIS DEL GRANDE
Remembering Jane Mallet

Jane Mallett was the kindest most marvellous woman I think I have ever met. I first met Jane years ago, when I was a young writer at CBC Radio with Jack Humphrey. She had liked a couple of episodes that I had written for a radio show, *Travels with Aunt Jane,* in which she appeared, so she asked that I come along to one of her parties at her Rosedale home. For a kid, new to Canada, living in a rooming house, this was a big occasion. Even then she was a legend. Later, she graciously agreed to come on *King of Kensington* for me and also appeared in *Ghosts* which I directed at Passe Muraille. It was her first time on stage in years.

She was loved by the entire community. She was known for her generosity and warmth and was active in starting up the Actors Fund to help actors who were in need.

Eventually, some years later, I also moved to Rosedale, not too far from where Jane had lived before she died. Six months or so after she had passed, I walked my dog past her house and was reminded that I had never said a little prayer for her. She was such a wonderful person that I just thought I would like to say a little personal prayer quietly as I walked. It was late fall, there were no gardens in bloom at that time, but as I walked and thought of Jane, I experienced an incredibly strong and unmistakable scent of flowers. I looked around trying to find the possible source of this bouquet. There was nothing. As I continued to walk, the fragrance stayed with me for 20 or 30 minutes. It was a very strange experience.

When I got home, I told my wife, Martha about it. She said that historically an experience like mine, involving a scent of flowers associated with the person who has died, was supposed to mean that that person was a saint. In Jane's case, I would believe it.

TOM WOOD
Don't shoot!

Nicky Cavendish and I were in a show where we played 129 characters. Nicky was playing a maniacal woman who was clawing her way up at the TV studio. At one point she murdered everybody in the show. Then she held auditions for acts for the TV show. In the time frame of three minutes, I played five different acts. I played a gorilla on a motor scooter, I played an apache dancer, and at one point I played 'Carmen Miranda'. It was absolutely wild.

This particular night there had been a lot of squeaky floor noises at the front of house. I am very sensitive to offstage noise while I am working so when I had a second during my quick change into Carmen Miranda I ran out to the box office person standing in the box office.

'Will you keep it down!' I hissed at her and then I rushed back to the show.

I found out later that at the very moment I ran in, she was being robbed at the point of a gun! I didn't see the person doing the robbing. He got away with all the box office receipts.

Afterwards I started to shake, thinking, 'I could have been shot in the drag outfit and be brought to the hospital as Carmen Miranda!'

LYNE TREMBLAY
French slaps stick

I was playing 'Sally Bowles' in *Cabaret* at the Mogador in Paris. It was somewhat difficult because I felt the other members were taking a long time to accept this Québécoise in their midst. I could almost hear them think, 'Why her and not one of ours?'

My partner, playing 'Cliff', was a notoriously unpredictable actor. One night, he walked on stage with whiskey breath and a murderous look in his eyes. Did he want to make fun of me or just give me the jitters? We came to a physical scene where he was to push me, but he did it with a bit too much energy. I reacted instinctively, out of character. From deep inside me came this huge slap across his face!

Monsieur froze, mesmerized and speechless. Overcoming my emotion, I started to dread the last act, knowing his character had to slap me. I was worried because he usually played it 'for real' with his other 'Sallys' and hurt them, even when he had no provocation. I had just done what many actresses in that role had only dreamed of doing. I thought, 'Boy, am I going to get it!'

Came the feared moment...but, to my surprise, he remained seated. I watched him and saw big tears rolling down his cheeks. I couldn't believe it.

That night I won the company's respect, including his. With an instinctive gesture, I had turned stage fear into stage magic.

MICHAEL AYOUB
Mr Bones and George Luscombe

In Toronto, I auditioned for *Che Guevara* for George Luscombe at Toronto Workshop Productions. TWP was, at the time, the only alternative theatre operating here and it was close to going under. I wanted the job very badly and was thrilled to be hired. It paid $50 a week. George, who had been a student of Joan Littlewood, was to become my third mentor and very different from my earlier influences. I will never forget George one day exploding at me in rehearsal, 'Method acting is shit! Method acting is garbage! The best actors in the world are the Marx Brothers!' This confused me since I had been trained at The Neighborhood Playhouse as a method actor. He wanted me to change my whole approach. But George was a visionary, an innovator. He brought socialist, revolutionary theatre to Toronto. Working with him would have a huge influence on me and, on at least one occasion, threaten to get me into trouble.

One of the plays we did at TWP was *Mr Bones*, notoriously remembered for being the first play to say aloud in public the word 'fuck'. During the previews one person complained. That was enough to bring the morality squad to the theatre for our opening night. We were told that they were threatening to charge us with violating obscenity laws! We had a choice. We could change the word or drop it, mouth it or say it as written and rehearsed. Being the young defiant revolutionaries that we were (it was the '60s), we naturally decided right away that we were not going to be intimidated. We did the play, four-letter word and all, as we had rehearsed and at the end of it I remember being flanked by two black guys doing a defiant Black Panther salute as we looked out at the suits and uniforms standing at the back of the theatre. It was a memorable opening night.

As it turned out, we were not taken to jail that night nor were we ever, but George did have to go to court and pay a fine.

BRIAN McKAY
The mad bomber

A number of years ago, at the Charlottetown Festival, I had the great pleasure of doing a show for Mr Alan Lund called *The Legend of the Dumbells*. The tremendously talented cast of actors included Douglas Chamberlain, David Warrack, Scot Denton, Gerry Salsberg, Barrie Wood, Stan Lesk. It was a wonderful show based on the First World War troupe of soldiers organised to entertain the men in the trenches very close to enemy lines.

One night, we arrived at the theatre to be told that there had been a bomb threat. We should remain at the stage door until the backstage area could be swept. Apparently they had already taken care of the theatre as patrons were arriving without the slightest concern. At any rate, about fifteen minutes went by and we were informed that all was well and, as suspected, it was a simple, if very misguided, hoax.

Without any more thought and only the odd, probably vulgar, reference to the perpetrator, we dressed hastily and the curtain went up only a few minutes late. The performance was going along extremely well for about eight minutes at which point we arrived at 'The Inspection' scene. All the soldiers lined up bravely. As I, as 'Captain Plunkett', began my stroll down the line, I found that I could no longer see any of the men. The theatre was in total darkness. It remained that way for what seemed like hours but was really eight or nine seconds.

The notion that the bomber was cleverer than we thought was forming itself in subtly various ways in the minds of all on stage. When the lights were finally restored not a man had moved a muscle. No one, except one of the lads who on the return of the lights was discovered in a crouching position mid-way between the stage and the orchestra pit. His move from that position back to the line cannot be described in any theatrical terms with which I am familiar. I won't name the actor, but the look on his face will keep him dear to me forever. The 'mad bomber' turned out to be someone no more threatening than Reg Thompson, our lighting board operator, whose elbow had inadvertently slipped and hit the master switch on the board.

We all bought the drinks that night. Reggie bought the most.

WILLIAM NEEDLES
Fly away home

Once, during a dress rehearsal of *Henry the Fifth* at Stratford in the mid sixties, which I think was one of the best productions we have ever mounted here, Tony van Bridge was mid speech when the door at the back of the auditorium was suddenly swung open and someone called down, 'Tony! Your house is on fire!' Tony dropped everything and started up the aisle, and Michael Langham said, 'You can't leave. This is a dress rehearsal.' Tony shouted back, '*My house is on fire!* I'm leaving.' And off he went across the field in full costume.

KENNETH WELSH
There are always these angels in your life that do things,
that take you places. If you just relax and let it happen
all these angels will do it for you.

SARAH POLLEY
My favourite job

My favourite working experience is a toss-up between two films, Atom Egoyan's *Exotica* and the recent *Joe's So Mean to Josephine*. These are the *only* two things that I have ever done that were completely Canadian. Both of them were entirely Canadian, all-Canadian cast and crew, no foreign money involved, and very low budget.

It was amazing for me partly because I had, for the first time, a lot of creative input. The actors were much more respected as 'partners' in the process. I didn't feel like a puppet for a multinational corporation. In my experience, Americans usually come up here for economic reasons and tend to treat the actors who live here badly because we work so cheaply.

I'm not saying that all Canadian producers are angels, but somehow when there is a small budget, everyone really wants to make the movie and everyone knows that they have to work together to get it done. The attitude is much better, and I know that my own work is better because of it.

The experience on these two films has helped me decide for now that I don't want to work any other way. It's given me a new love for acting, which I had lost for a while. It taught me a great deal about what acting was and could be under the right circumstances.

SHARON DYER
We done it all

In the summer of 1977 down at Charlottetown, I was doing a lot of music theatre. We were doing a musical called *Windsor*, written by David Warrack, about Wallis Simpson and King Edward VIII.

I had had a duet with Sharry Flett who was playing the lead, 'Wallis', which was cut the night before we opened. This had been my only song in the show, so of course I was disappointed. David had promised me a song, a number of my own. That night he phoned me and asked me if *I* could think of anything. I told him, No! I'm not a songwriter. He said, 'OK. Leave it with me.' David was notorious for doing stuff at the last minute.

The next morning he showed up with 3/4 of a song on tape, a few chicken scratches on the page, and lyrics sort of half written out. It was to be a solo for me at the end of the second act. Then he promptly went off to be interviewed by the CBC somewhere. About an hour later he phoned with the final verse of the song which he sang over the phone as I madly typed the words!

The song was called '*We Done It All*'. I was playing an older person, and the song was about young people who think that they are the first to do things. I was to sing that years ago we older folks had already done everything that the young were just now discovering. It was a good song, but we had less than a day before we opened!

Left with the orchestrator, I had to translate the lyrics from the tape and type them out so I could learn them while the orchestrator was rushing in and out of the office, doing the score for the number. We were frantic! Alan Lund came in about 4:00 p.m. and choreographed it. He had me standing right at downstage centre, alone. They decided that because it was a new song that I had better have cue cards. So Shirley Third, who was assistant stage manager in those days, would be down in the orchestra with the cards.

We opened that night. We worked through the show and it came to my big solo. I was all alone on stage with no one to back me up. Shirley was ready in the pit with the cards. I was terrified. In order to read them, I had to go right down front and look down. The audience could only see my half closed eyelids. I must have looked downright sleepy but I was anything but!

Shirley was madly tossing cue cards as I sang because David had written lyrics with no breaths. It was solid lyrics. I just had to *keep on going* through the whole thing. Amazingly, I got through the song, walked off stage and fainted into stage-hand Jimmy Constable's arms. The nervous tension was just...well...I collapsed.

Within three nights I was doing it from memory. It turned out to be one of the better songs in the show and the audience loved it. But those first nights I had to do it from the cue cards completely alone on stage. If I had failed I felt as if the whole show would go down. But I did it and after that I felt as if I could do anything.

TEDDE MOORE
French Shakespeare

Part of my first season's contract at the Stratford Shakespearean Festival in 1968 was to understudy the role of 'Juliet' in a uniquely Canadian production of *Romeo and Juliet* directed by Douglas Campbell. The concept was to have the warring houses of Montague and Capulet divided by culture. Juliet was to be played by the internationally famous French Canadian actress Geneviève Bujold and all the rest of the house of Capulet were to be played by actors from Quebec. At the last minute Mlle Bujold had to withdraw and the artistic directors, Jean Gascon and John Hirsch, had to find a replacement. At the Théâtre de Nouveau Monde in Montreal the brightest ingenue was the beautiful young actress, Louise Marleau, and it was she they invited to play Juliet.

Ultimately, the original French/English concept was more or less abandoned but Mlle Marleau was our Juliet. Before rehearsals began M. Gascon took me aside and said, 'Now, I'm counting on you to spend as much time as possible with Louise to help her with her English because she doesn't speak it.' I thought he meant doesn't speak it very well. He meant exactly what he said. At the beginning of rehearsals Mlle Marleau had very few words of English.

The production also starred a new John Hirsch discovery named Christopher Walken as 'Romeo'. An actor since childhood, he had recently been a hoofer on Broadway. It was while performing as a back-up dancer for Mae West that he got the name Christopher, bestowed by Ms West herself. So there we were with a Juliet who couldn't speak the language and a Romeo who had never played Shakespeare.

As an understudy I was required to be present for all the rehearsals and it was a particular privilege. The first-rate cast included Amelia Hall as the 'Nurse', Bernard Behrens as 'Friar Laurence' and Leo Ciceri as 'Mercutio'. Walken worked with passion and commitment and in the end he was a graceful Romeo. I will never forget him taking Juliet's inert body out of the grave, lifting it high over his head and lowering her lifeless arms down his back in a macabre embrace.

But it was watching the magnificent Marleau wrestle her challenge to the ground that really affected me. She worked incredibly hard. One can only imagine what doubts she may have had, but piece by piece she learned the words by rote. She bent her francophone tongue around this unfamiliar language and created a troubled, intelligent, fiery Juliet.

Louise went on to play a number of roles in the English theatre as well as to have an international film career. Some years later I had the pleasure of working with her again when she played 'Irina' in Chekhov's *Three Sisters* at the St Lawrence Centre in Toronto. We shared a dressing room and during one performance she excitedly confided that she'd had a real break-through. She could finally think in English as she was acting in English!

Remembering her performance as Juliet it was hard to imagine what she had had to do. Think in French and act in English iambic pentameter verse, on a thrust stage, for the first time. I am still impressed.

GRAHAM JARVIS
My introduction to Stratford

In 1953, I was a twenty-year-old doing odd jobs, stage managing and the occasional on-stage part in an off-Broadway company. When the company failed and disbanded, I wanted very much to stay active somehow in the theatre. But I was at a loss, until I remembered Aunt Glassy.

Margaret (Peggy) Glass, who I knew as Aunt Glassy, was connected to the London Little Theatre that was performing in the Grand Theatre. She had been a dear friend of my mother's. On an impulse, I called Glassy up and told her I was looking for an apprenticeship. That was how I ended up back in Canada, in my home town, London, Ontario.

On my one day off during the week, I went to the brand new Stratford Shakespearean Festival. I saw *The Taming of the Shrew* which starred William Needles and Barbara Chilcott, also Alec Guinness as *Richard III*. I had been in New York for some time and was even then a pretty experienced theatre-goer, but I had never seen anything quite like Stratford. I was awe-struck.

Those first couple of years the performances were mounted in a tent. There was absolutely no seating for latecomers until the end of the first act. So audiences were religiously on time. (In those days, Broadway productions would seat you during the first blackout, so this was very impressive to me.) The audience would be called in from the surrounding lawn with a blast from a row of cornets. As curtain time approached, audience conversation would become slowly quieter.

A pale yellow canvas wall rimmed the seats and separated them from the 'lobby' area of the tent. On this inner wall was a series of rust-coloured curtains across the entrances to the audience seating. At a signal, the ushers stationed at these entrances would, beginning at the far right, *whisk* their curtains shut in rapid succession, creating a *whish-whish-whish-whish-whish-whish!* effect sweeping around behind the audience. Then, you could feel the compression of the air in the tent a fraction of a second before you would hear the *BOOM!!* of the cannon out on the lawn. You could feel the anticipation and excitement of the audience as their chatter rose. Suddenly, the band outside would begin a stirring *God Save the King*. We all stood and sang and sat down again as a hush settled over us.

It was the most brilliant opening for a theatrical event I have ever experienced. My God, if they didn't 'have you' by then, they were never going to have you! I was nearly blown off my feet with admiration. I thought, 'Wow! These guys know what they are doing!'

ELIZABETH SHEPHERD
Field of love

We toured Russia and Poland with Stratford in 1973. We took them *King Lear*. William Hutt was 'Lear' and I was 'Cordelia'. As we got further east in Poland, and particularly in Russia, there was a problem of echo while we were doing the production. Everybody had their headphones on their laps! They didn't need a simultaneous translation. They knew the play better than we did.

The emotion that came from the audience! At the beginning of the scene towards the end of the play, Lear is mad. I, as Cordelia, find him and decide I must cure him. I stood at the top of a flight of stairs and ran down to him. Butch Blake was playing 'Kent', wonderfully, as always. There were Lear and Kent and Cordelia and the whole heart of the audience, beating inside the auditorium. The love was absolutely potent. You could feel it.

As I ran down those stairs, there was no way that we weren't going to cure him, all of us together. It was the most powerful feeling of rapport and emotion. The audience were one with us, with Lear, with Cordelia. I ran down the stairs into this field of love.

SHIRLEY DOUGLAS
On 'attitude'

I lived in Los Angeles for more than ten years before moving back to Canada. What struck me most about Canada and Canadians on my return was the general negativity, for everything...except hockey. We do not seem to value ourselves in this country and I found it very disturbing. I don't know why it exists or what to do about it but we must get over it because we, all of us, are defeated by it before we start.

Those of us in the theatre somehow seem to assume that the best work is always being done somewhere else, in New York, or London, or Stockholm. It is *not*. Some of the very best work in the world is being done right here. We are *very* lucky...and yet we are still quick to dismiss ourselves and our work.

Interestingly, this is not the case in French Canada.

One of the most wonderful periods I have ever spent in the theatre was at The National Arts Centre in Ottawa. I was a member of the English company headed by John Wood. It was a rare opportunity to get to know each other as a company over several months and then to return the next season to work with the same company again. It was a revelation for those of us who were used to three-week rehearsal periods, a modest run and then we'd scatter. Working with John Wood and that company was marvellous experience for me.

The brilliant Jean Gascon headed the French company. The companies were in the same building, so we often met in the halls and got to know each other. What interested me about the French company was the enormous reverence that existed for the artists. When M. Gascon walked into the room, you could feel the love they had for this man. In Quebec, there is a more European view of artists. When I was in Europe, in Italy or France, if an artist or a poet walked down the street, there was, not uncommonly, polite and genuine clapping from people as he or she passed. There is no mobbing or interfering with them, simply a show of affection, appreciation, and respect. That is how it is in Quebec, but unfortunately, it does not exist in English Canada. It is not at all about flattering the ego. It is about feeling that the work and the passion that has gone into a work does not go unnoticed or unacknowledged.

We, the anglophone artists at the Centre, were afforded the same respect from the francophones that they held and demonstrated for each other. We were addressed formally, as they were, never by our first names, always 'Madame' or 'Monsieur'. Occasionally we would comment on each other's work, always constructively, always with tremendous love and generosity, because we all knew how hard it was to do what we all were doing. I can remember feeling so tremendously encouraged and nurtured by the sense of respect that was part of that environment. It just made you want to do more, do better work, to risk trying something that may or may not work, but it gave you the strength to try at least. It was wonderfully stimulating, a very nurturing environment. And it showed in our work. The audiences responded and when they did, it made us want to work harder for them as well.

If there is one thing that I could do for the acting community, it would be to remind them that they are among the best in the world.

WILLIAM NEEDLES
Rain delay

Performing in the original tent at Stratford could be quite a challenge sometimes. Acoustically it was difficult. There were interruptions, noises from outside, baseball games behind the theatre, and trains whistling by. One night as the 'Chorus' in *Henry Fifth* I said the line 'Hear the shrill whistle which doth order give to sounds confused' and toot! There was a very nearby train whistle right on cue. That stopped the show for a while.

Rainstorms caused enormous problems because of the sound of the rain on the tent. When it got really bad an announcement would be made that the play would stop until the rain had cleared. One year there was a near hurricane that was very frightening. The tent was rocking from side to side. No one could go outside at intermission, the rain was too heavy, so the management sent the orchestra out to calm the audience. I think they must have played *Nearer My God To Thee*! It lasted for almost half an hour and it rained so hard the mist was coming through the tent itself and audience members were sitting in the auditorium with their umbrellas up.

CHRIS HUMPHREYS
Bard on the beach

It was the closing night of Bard On The Beach's second season in Vancouver in 1991. We had a packed house, including many friends who were there to see this production of *A Midsummer Night's Dream* for the second or third time. It had been a very successful season.

In those days the tent in Vanier Park faced straight out towards the entrance of English Bay. The audience was completely covered but the back of the stage area was not. As we came to the end of the first act, out over the bay we could see a storm heading toward us. As the music for Act II came up, it hit.

I was playing 'Oberon', all Persian pyjamas, face paint, and feathers. As I ran up the back I was deluged within seconds. Nonetheless I felt, as King of the Fairies, that this was *my* weather so I threw myself into the storm as if I had called it for the occasion. The raked stage quickly became slick with rain. The downpour pounded on the tent roof so loudly that 'Puck' (Scott Bellis) and I were forced to stand downstage and shout our lines at the audience. The Lovers struggled on. When I cast my spell on 'Demetrius' (played by Jeffrey Renn), I closed my eyes. When I opened them I saw Christopher Gaze, the Artistic Director, who was also playing 'Bottom', genuflecting before me and imploring me to leave the stage. Of course, Bottom should not have been in that scene so my first instinct was to zap him with my fairy powers. But since this obviously was not going to work, I realised that we would have to bow to the storm and the play would have to stop.

I turned and ran for my upstage right exit. I had always used it to launch myself, my arms and feathers flying, into the sky and drop out of sight onto a mattress a few feet below. Except this time, at the very moment that I leapt, silhouetted against the stormy sky...the entire horizon flashed white with sheet lightning! The audience gasped in almost eerie unison, as if they were fused by the vision. The actors were speechless. I rolled and ran for the tent.

I had no idea what they were reacting to. When I asked someone what all the fuss was about, they explained to me the stunning impact of my exit, courtesy of God, the ultimate lighting director. I was the only one who had missed it.

We temporarily suspended the show until the rain let up. The company all wandered into the house and sang madrigals with the audience. When the worst had passed, we hit the slippery slope again. That night the company played as if every speech was lightning-lit. Every weather reference was cherished. With uncanny timing, the storm wound down along with the play. It was truly magical.

Every actor in that cast has a story from that night. It was the most extraordinary experience I have ever had in the theatre. There was, for that moment, no division between the actors and the audience. We were joined in something unique, and forevermore, I can say, 'I was there!'

TODD WAITE
The theatre's tears

This is not so much a story as a theatre image I will always remember. The Royal Alexandra Theatre has two balconies and, therefore, two balcony railings. Each night many people would be moved to tears by Victor Hugo's story and the wonderful music of *Les Miserables*. During the show the two railings would gradually become covered in wet tissues that people placed there (Lord knows why on the railings, but there you are). At the end of one evening, when the railings were unusually full of tissues, and the audience was particularly generous, everyone leapt to their feet in applause. The movement wafted the tissues in a beautiful slow cascade from both railings onto the audience below. No one in the seats appeared to notice but it seemed to us on stage as though the building wept that night.

17

The Family Album

DAVID DUNBAR
Home away from home

My mother was a wonderful pianist. She found herself in a very unhappy marriage with three children and although she was never able to do much with her music outside the home she would always play for us at night. She would harmonize with the piano in a lovely mezzo voice, playing perhaps to soothe herself because our home was a violent one.

My brothers and I were shuttled off to the Anglican church choir where we practised Tuesday and Thursday nights and Saturday mornings. After that I would go to the movies. I remember becoming addicted to the movie *Charade* with Audrey Hepburn and Cary Grant. I'd watch the two o'clock show and the four o'clock show and then I'd hide in the bathroom because in those days, at that age, you were not allowed in the movie theatre after six without an adult. Then I'd sneak back in to see the six and eight o'clock shows.

Because of their own troubles, my parents were often unaware of my where-abouts so I would just come home as late as possible and crawl into bed. But those Saturdays I felt safe. I had my imagination stirred, even though I had seen the movie a million times. It was comforting and although I was alone, I wasn't lonely and I didn't have to listen to or be part of the violence. This was the beginning of my understanding that theatre or movies could provide an escape.

By the age of twelve or so I was asked to sing at the Moose Lodge Talent Competition. My piece was the Frank Sinatra song *It Was A Very Good Year*! Alas, I didn't win. That honour went to Gloria Gunderson and her Flaming Unicycle. Around that time I noticed in the paper an open call for an amateur production of the musical *Oliver*. I auditioned with my signature song and got a part. It was a happy accident because in doing amateur theatre I found a place. Everybody was friendly and caring. They seemed to be happy all the time for some reason that I didn't understand but it felt awfully good. People even touched you in an affection-ate way and the director or choreographer treated you as if you were something of worth.

Now, later in my life, I realise that the theatre became my home away from home. I love to do summer stock. There isn't much time in that situation so there is an immediate bonding that takes place. Everybody gets together, good, bad, indifferent or Diva, and there is this fondness, this instant family—we're all going to do this together and we will have a good time doing it! This is not a false thing but it is, realistically, limited to the life of the season, or the show.

At the end of a run I have a little ritual. I go out on the bare stage alone with the work light on and I stand there and look out into the empty house and I remember everything. If there is an unlocked piano, I play it. I get teary-eyed because I know it's over. But I also know that in our life there is always the opportunity to do it all again—'another opening, another show'.

DAN MacDONALD
The Christmas gift

God bless Stan Rogers! At each hearing of his poignant 'First Christmas Away From Home' I recall cherished memories of a particular Christmastime—and some extraordinary people. My Vancouver 'theatre family' remains so special to this then-young Maritimer, alone on the West Coast during his first Christmas away from home.

I had struck out for the 'other' coast to pursue various summer classes in theatre and haply some work as well. Later in the fall, I found myself hard at work constructing, rehearsing, and plotting a tour of *The Three Bears* for Holiday Theatre Company, Canada's first professional theatre for children. By Christmas week, we already had two successes under our belt, and Holiday's *Bears* tour would open on Vancouver Island in January.

The days and nights of rehearsing, set building, promotion, and performing seemed to whiz by with unmarked hardship. There was little money being made by anyone. It didn't seem to matter. It was exciting work. We were doing what we wanted, what we felt was important for ourselves, for Canadian theatre, and for all the arts in Canada. I was learning a great deal in the company of talented, respected, and dear friends. So what if there was a constant shortage of money. Rehearsals were going well. I eagerly rushed between holding a paintbrush in the workshop and a script in rehearsal hall and back again.

One day, I noticed the others were leaving soon after lunch and, as they called out 'Merry Christmas. See you Boxing Day', it dawned on me that it was December 24th. They were leaving early to begin Christmas celebrations with their families. I had been happily working every day and night—eating, drinking, sleeping theatre with no thought of what day of the week it was or what I would be doing tomorrow. I realized, with a shock, tomorrow was Christmas and I had no place to be on Christmas Day!

Peter Mannering, another founding member of Holiday, asked what I had planned. My shyness, my Maritime abhorrence of being burdensome, and my

Scottish independence all conspired to prevent me from admitting I would be spending Christmas all alone. I mumbled something about being prepared for the day, trying to assure him, and the few others still there, I'd be just fine and 'Thank you very much'.

Peter was spending the feastday with his mother, in North Vancouver, and (so he said) Mrs Mannering insisted he ask me to join them. Deceiving myself I'd be doing her a favour, I agreed, reluctantly, to have Christmas dinner with them. I promised to interfere as little as possible, arriving on Christmas morning after Midnight Mass and leaving after the noontime dinner. Peter arranged to pick me up about 1 o'clock in the morning, at the Cathedral.

It was drizzling as we drove over the Lion's Gate Bridge and towards North Van, but snow started falling during our climb up Mount Seymour to the Mannerings'. By the time we arrived at the large, rustic lodge Peter's late father had hand-built many years before, the snow had stopped and the temperature lent a healthy crispness to the air. The stars were out and we stood for a moment admiring the bright, twinkling lights sprinkled all over Vancouver and the many decorated ships in her harbour. Then, we went in to say hello to 'Mum'.

She was alone in the large livingroom of the lodge when we arrived. She had me efficiently settled down with some food and a drink almost before I had my jacket off. Then I noticed she *wasn't* alone. Out of the kitchen, Joy Coghill joined us. Russ Williamson also appeared, then suddenly Jessie was there, and Sidney, Gwen and Lloyd, Jack, Myra, John. Everyone was here! The whole company was present, even a few who were not involved in the present production! Soon we were singing, laughing and telling lies as boisterously as any other theatre get-together.

I knew that some of them had planned to leave Vancouver for a few days' holiday by car; one even had a flight booked. So, to say all of this was a surprise is an understatement. I was stunned. These wonderful people had disrupted their own and their families' lives in order to bring some Christmas cheer to a lonely, seventeen-year-old Herring Choker, thousands of miles from home for the first time.

BETH ANNE COLE
Far and wide

In drama school at the start of our performing lives we often make very strong attachments with our fellow students. For me it was a kind of first family away from home.

I went to LAMDA [London Academy of Music and Dramatic Art] in London, England, to a special course designed for overseas students. During the first week of school one of my classmates, Yossi, who was from Israel, glued an Israeli postage stamp onto the front page of my trusty *Collected Works of William Shakespeare*. For this reason, although I lost touch with him for over twenty years, I thought of him every time I opened the book.

Yossi was doing battle with Shakespeare's language. He barely spoke English, but his work was really touching because all his attention was in saying the words, not in imposing anything else. We became very good friends. We were all young artists in exile. When we left, he went back to Israel and I to Canada.

A few months ago, while writing a song for my new CD, I developed a sudden passionate desire to go to Israel, where I'd never been. One night at midnight, the phone rang.

'This is Yossi.' In a voice I hadn't heard since we left school he said, 'We are having a Festival in Israel this year. Someone mentioned your name, could it be you? Will you come and sing?'

There's no punch line to this story. His voice over the wires made the past and our young selves immediate and reclaimable, and like the stamp in my *Collected Works*, there for always.

TIMOTHY FINDLEY
On Amelia Hall

Everyone in Canadian theatre—everyone of a certain age, that is—has a Milly Hall story. Amelia Hall, that incredible actress/manager with Sam Payne, started Ottawa's Canadian Repertory Theatre. 'I get no kick from Sam Payne; Amelia Hall doesn't thrill me at all...' We all used to sing it—because we loved her...and Sam.

RICHARD MONETTE
Saved bacon

I was in London, England. And Barbara Hamilton was there as well, doing *Anne Of Green Gables*. I was struggling as a young actor, poverty stricken. The only person I knew in London was Barbara. I had an audition that was way across town and I didn't have enough money for the tube...the subway. It was an important audition, so I went to Barbara.

'Can you just...can I borrow money just to get there and back?'

I don't know how much the fare was, but she gave me a five-pound note, which was then an astronomical amount of money for me. It was a wonderful thing to do. It literally saved my bacon. I went to the audition, came back, bought food, and lived off the rest of that five-pound note for an entire week.

Years passed. She had long since returned to Canada. When I came back from England, I brought her a bottle of her favourite perfume. The wrapping was a five-pound note.

CHARLOTTE MOORE
Grateful to Brent

After Brent Carver won his Tony Award for *Kiss of the Spider Woman* and was the toast of Broadway, after he starred in the same show in London and was the toast of the West End, he came back to Canada. I believe he thought it was time to come home. He missed his friends. He missed his life.

Over the years, I have had a lot of colleagues ask me, 'Why are you still in Canada?' or 'Why didn't you ever move to the States?' or 'You could have had a *real* career in New York!' (Yes, somebody said that.)

For years I have floundered around (read: flaoondered araoond) looking for an answer they might comprehend. 'This is my home' or 'Well, I live here' never seemed to work.

Now, I reply to these questions with another question, 'Why did Brent Carver come home?' If they smile and nod their heads, I know they'll understand. If they don't, I could talk until I'm blue in the face and I know they'd never get it. I just smile and nod my head and leave them to ponder the obvious.

JAYNE EASTWOOD
My first film

The first film I ever did was *Goin' Down The Road* (1969), a beautiful Canadian film about two young men from the east coast trying to make it in the big city of Toronto. I was paid $500.

It was a very low-budget film. There was no crew. We had a director, Don Shebib, a camera-man, Richard Leiterman, sound man Jim McCarthy, and us, the cast: Doug McGrath, Paul Bradley, Cayle Chernin, and myself among a few others. The movie, written by William Fruet and Don Shebib, was made for about $80,000, but it was an instant hit and has become a legend in Canadian movie-making history.

It also launched my career in show business. I was very lucky and did a lot of work over the years, including *Godspell* and Second City, plus a lot of movies and television. Ironically, years later I was to parody myself in a take-off of *Goin' Down the Road* on *SCTV*. John Candy and my brother-in-law Joe Flaherty played the two down-and-outers as a doctor and lawyer looking for 'doctorin' and 'lawyerin' jobs in the big city. And my main concern was that I was just 'bummed out about a mouse in the house'. People still talk about the movie and that sketch.

One of the best things about being a Canadian actor is working with other Canadian actors. They are, in general, a rare breed of gentle loving people who truly appreciate each other's talent.

WANDA CANNON
Carrying on

I was part of a company preparing an original musical called *Hometown* for production at Hamilton Place theatre. Rob Iscove [Canadian choreographer, film and theatre director] was up from Hollywood to direct it and Kimball Hall, Dinah Christie, Michael Burgess, Tabby Johnston and I were part of a huge cast. I was playing the young Dinah, so we were the female leads and our roles were large.

We had one preview before the opening and my husband, Bob Cannon, had come down from Toronto to see it. I had taken a hotel room for the next few nights because I didn't want the extra strain of the Toronto-Hamilton commute on top of the long days. After a bite to eat with us, Bob drove home to Toronto. Tabby Johnston asked me if I would mind if she stayed as well so I offered to share my hotel room. We went back to the hotel and fell into bed, exhausted.

About 1:30 a.m., when we were sound asleep, the phone rang. It was Bob, who had just arrived back at our home in Toronto. He told me that he had some very bad news. My father had just been killed in a farm accident in Saskatchewan. The first words out of my mouth were these:

'OK, but can we talk about this in the morning? I just can't deal with this right now. I have an opening night tomorrow. I absolutely refuse to deal with this right now.'

'Wanda, hear what I'm saying. Your father is gone. You have to phone home. You have to deal with this.'

'No, I can't. Bob, just phone me in the morning, OK?'

By then reality was starting to beat at the door of my sleep-filled head and Tabby was sitting up in bed understanding that something really serious was going on.

We were up the rest of the night. I called Dinah because I didn't know what else to do. She and Tabby spent the whole night in my room trying to help me deal with what had happened. Rob Iscove came in about 3:00 a.m. to talk to me.

'Well, Wanda, phone the airline first thing in the morning, get on the plane and just get home. This is real life and we are only "playing" here.'

I don't know if it was that I felt I couldn't let them down, or that this was the way I could survive the grief. In retrospect it is kind of blurry, but I felt it would be best to do the opening night. So that's what I did. I spent the day with these caring people around me. Dinah had just taken a grieving course so she made me do all sorts of things I didn't want to do, like talking about my feelings, but I got through the run-through that day and then the opening of the show that night.

With new shows the script is somewhat fluid. You get new pages, new staging and business every day because you are trying to make it better all the time. Colleen Winton came in that same day to take over for me. She had to learn everything in one day and all she had to work from was some scribbles on what existed of my script. It was an extraordinary event in both our lives.

SCOTT WENTWORTH
The long chain

A few years ago at Stratford I was covering Colm Feore as 'Richard III' in the play of the same name, and I asked to be able to do a couple of performances as Richard late in the season. I'd had an unfortunate experience the year before, covering Brent Carver as 'Hamlet' when I had never had a costume fitting. I thought this way, if I definitely perform it, everyone will know the hump will have to fit me!

I thought it would be fun to take a whack at a role without long rehearsal, like they used to do in the nineteenth century. Just learn the part, decide what I would do here and there, and go on and do it. I was regularly playing 'Tyrrell', a small two-scene part. So when my dates to perform Richard came, Colm and I just switched parts. He was just great. He would meet me backstage like a coach and would say things like 'You've got four minutes now, sit down, have a glass of water, time for one cigarette.'

During the run I was over at Bill Hutt's house having a martini and we were talking about *Richard III*. Despite the fact that this is a play Bill has been in several times, he has never played Richard. I was asking him about the play, I knew he had been in the first Stratford season when Sir Alec Guinness played Richard, and I knew he had played 'Clarence' at some point. Bill said, 'Never play Clarence. It's a terrible part. If you can't play Richard, play Buckingham. If you can't play Buckingham, play Tyrrell.'

Then he stood up, in his living room, to illustrate something that Alec Guinness had done when he had played the part some forty-five years ago. He did the entire opening speech, as Guinness, with Guinness' blocking. He thought perhaps I could use some of the ideas. It was amazing. There I was getting Alec Guinness' business from Bill Hutt: information and creative ideas still alive in someone's memory. We actors share a remarkable chain of connection with each other.

CHARLOTTE MOORE
The generous of spirit

When I first went to the Shaw Festival in 1989, I had a nice part in the musical, a nice part in a main stage show, and one fabulous understudy, of Nora McLellan in the Moss Hart comedy, *Once In A Lifetime*. Some weeks into the season Nora had to leave the show and I got bumped up. All of a sudden I had a lead! On the main stage! With only a couple of rehearsals to do it in.

On the day I got the news I went home in a panic. When I sat down to try to digest what was happening, l heard my roommate, Brian Hill playing the piano and singing, *No-one Is Alone*.

During the course of the run I had kibbitzed with Nora and complimented her on the great lipstick she was using for her make-up for the part. At the curtain call of her final performance, in full view of the entire company, she handed me that lipstick. It was as if she was passing the baton.

A class act is a class act.

MARCEL SABOURIN
The danger chain

Acting is a dangerous craft. All people who do dangerous things like soldiers at war, flyers, acrobats, or politicians, all these people are superstitious and are very close to each other. They have to fight together. They are doing something dangerous together. Theatre, especially, is something dangerous. There you are. Alone on the stage, anything can happen.

Also we have all played intimates with each other. We have been one person's brother, one person's husband, one person's son, one person's lover. Our work creates links. If I hear that someone I have worked with is ill or has died, it is as if my real mother has passed away, or my real brother is dying. Perhaps I haven't seen them for years but I feel it as if it happened yesterday. Of course it is only a percentage of reality but this work creates a bond that you don't have in other crafts.

In our world, whether the scene ends up in the film or not, the emotion of the experience remains forever.

RON HASTINGS
Passing the torch

In the sixties I was working at the Neptune Theatre in Halifax. Another actor and I had a break and decided to hop over to P.E.I. to see chums who were working at the Confederation Centre in Charlottetown. This was the second season for them, and our friends had a matinee of *Anne Of Green Gables*. I had no particular desire to see it but, having nothing else to do, we decided to go to the show.

By the time 'Mathew' died, my friend and I were gripping each other's arms and shaking with very real emotion. We were so pulled into the play, so affected by the warmth and love and caring. It was one of the most thrilling experiences of my life in the theatre. I had worked with Peter Mews, the actor who originated Mathew, so I knew him and was able to go backstage and talk to him about the profound effect the show had on me. When I left, I thought to myself, 'I can't wait until I'm old enough to play that role.'

Twenty years passed. It was at Peter Mews' funeral that director Alan Lund offered me the role of Mathew.

ROBERTSON DAVIES
On Robert Christie

[Reprinted posthumously with permission from the Davies family]

I first met Bob Christie in 1939. We were both members of the Old Vic Company. The war had brought about the closing of the Old Vic's own theatre, but the company was playing a varied repertoire in some provincial cities, and in theatres in the suburbs of London. It was when we were at one of these, in Golder's Green, that Bob and I found ourselves often on the same bus making its way back to Central London in the black-out. As the bus groped its way along the darkened streets, we usually sat in the front seat in the upper deck, and Bob unfolded to me what was at that time his great ambition.

It had a Tolstoyan splendour. He wanted to return to Canada, whenever that might be possible, and assemble a company of actors and theatre artists who would work as an artistic commune. The ideal place for it, he thought, would be on a farm in the West, perhaps not too far from Winnipeg, where the barn could be converted into a theatre, admirably equipped but retaining superficially the simplicity of the barn. And there, gradually developing a discriminating audience, drawn from the nearby city, the company would present the great plays of the world's drama, done with the devotion and the psychological penetration similar to that of the Moscow Art Theatre, under the domination of Stanislavski and Nemirovich-Danchenko. The actors, living together and knowing one another intimately, would have a sympathy and intuitive collaboration impossible in the commercial theatre where companies were assembled for a single production, and dispersed after it had played itself out.

The question hovered in the air; how was the venture to be financed? Aha, said Bob, his face transformed by a beautiful smile, that was at the very root of the adventure. The theatre was on a farm, and the farm would be cultivated, and maintain itself and much of the expense of the theatre by producing and selling all that a farm can offer. A specialty might present itself—pigs, for instance, or sheep, for which there would be an obvious demand. And of course, the theatre artists would feed healthily and amply on the vegetables, the eggs, the bacon, doubtless the beef, that the farm would produce.

The beauty of the plan, its nub, so to speak, was that the artists would themselves work the farm, and the healthy toil so demanded would give them a robustness of physique which few city actors could boast; this abounding health would infuse their theatre work, and give it a true, a physical realism, which even the Moscow Art Theatre could not hope to have, with its citified players, open to all the temptations of a bohemian life. This would be a theatre literally with its roots in the ground, a theatre drawing upon the very stuff of life. The physical toil would lift the company far above the jealousies, the spites, the pettiness of citified, physically underdeveloped player folk. It would be unmistakably Canadian in its vigour and clarity of vision.

The plan was splendid, almost stupefying in its Tolstoyan grandeur, and I was properly awed. If I had doubts about its practicality, I did not speak of them. The plan was so immense, so inclusive, it would have been gross to do so. Of my own fitness for such a life, I had misgivings. An unworthy aversion to pigs, perhaps, stood between me and participation.

Later in our lives, Bob and I often met in theatrical ventures, and his deeply lovable nature and the whimsical invention which he brought to such characters as the 'Pedant' in Tony Guthrie's 1954 production of *The Taming Of The Shrew* never failed to delight me. His theatre commune has never come to pass, but his contribution to our theatre has nevertheless been imaginative and enlarging to who can say how many artists and audiences.

SHELORA FITZGERALD
Actor, teacher, friend

Powys Thomas was a much loved teacher and founder of the National Theatre School. Though he had performed across Canada, he had never received the recognition he deserved as an actor. In 1987, after years of secondary roles at Stratford, Powys Thomas was playing 'King Lear' at the Queen Elizabeth Playhouse.

The director was a brilliant Englishman, Philip Hedley. Under his direction, Powys played the mad scene like 'Ophelia' in *Hamlet*, dancing about amongst flowers and totally fey. It was brilliant! And amazing (as I realised when I went backstage to see him) given that he was very ill. He was by then in the final stages of liver dysfunction, guzzling Gatorade to keep himself functioning. Despite that, he had given a magnificent performance in a stunning production, the culmination of the man's career and yet so few in Canada seemed to realise it. An exception was John Hirsch.

On the last night of the production, John Hirsch, then in Winnipeg, heard about the show.

'Why didn't anyone tell me Powys Thomas was playing Lear!' he roared.

He promptly got on a plane and arrived at the theatre in Vancouver in time to catch the third act of the final performance.

That was in January. Powys died in Wales surrounded by his family that June. As they wheeled him into the operating room he said simply, 'Don't worry. I am very philosophical about these things.' He was 52.

There is an oak tree in the Shakespeare Gardens in Stanley Park dedicated to his memory, because he always said that if he came back it would be as an oak tree. I have made a point of visiting it on Midsummer Night's Eve every year. Two years ago a tree fell on it and severed one side of the branches. But it is still standing sturdy, a testament to a wise and wonderful man who influenced theatre immeasurably in this country.

MERVYN 'BUTCH' BLAKE
Powys Thomas, adieu

Powys Thomas was a marvellous man, a marvellous actor, and a dear, dear friend. Whenever he had trouble remembering his lines he had this knack of looking completely innocent. He would dry up and yet he would look at you as if it was your fault and it would be you who ended up with egg on your face!

At the end, he knew he was fatally ill with cancer. He had had two marriages and several kids. They all went to Wales, where he was from, to his first wife Anne Morrish's farm and they all stayed together there, the two wives and all the kids. One night in the middle of a great feast of a meal he suddenly stood up and said 'I must go and check on the chickens.' Well, the others tried to dissuade him with admonishments that the chickens would undoubtedly be all right. But he was insistent and off he went. When he did not return his son went out into the yard to find him collapsed from a massive haemorrhage. He was still alive so they rushed him to the hospital. As they wheeled him in he lifted his head and said to his anxious family, 'Don't worry. I often do these things.' He died a few hours later.

LOUIS DEL GRANDE
George McCowan's favourite story

George McCowan directed most of the episodes of *Seeing Things*, especially in the last couple of seasons. He told me this story once when we were talking on set.

The actor Arch MacDonald was a very close friend of Jane Mallett and her husband. When Jane's husband died, Arch called George, who was a constant smoker and by then had emphysema, to tell him. George, who had known Jane and her husband well, was saddened and asked how old he had been. Arch said, 'Eighty-eight' and added, 'If only he wouldn't have smoked!'

ROBERT BENSON
Claude Bede remembered

When I heard tonight that that lovely man Claude Bede had died, my first recollection was not of Claude the wonderful actor, but of Claude the reluctant spectator.

It was during my first year in Leon Major's company at the St Lawrence Centre—a season of modified rep: two plays in each half of the season. On Christmas Eve there were to be a final technical dress and then a dress rehearsal of a new play, the day's work to be separated by a Christmas party for the entire company including those who, like Claude and me, were not involved in The Effort lurching towards its audience. The buzz in the company was that things were not going well.

Claude and some others in the company had gathered at his house for a little Christmas cheer before repairing to the St Lawrence for the party. With all the preparations for his guests, Claude had neglected to have any food all day. He arrived at the festivities slightly glowing, and after a bit more Christmas cheer—the party food having been somehow unaccountably delayed—he was very merry.

After the drinks, the food, the speeches (few and terse), and the exchange of token gifts, all of which were then whisked away to the Sally Ann, everyone went into the theatre to watch the dress rehearsal.

It was a shambles. Almost nothing went right technically. The process was repeatedly stopped and restarted, and in the midst of all this it became apparent to Claude that he was witnessing a travesty unlike the satirical travesty intended by the revue style of the piece. After about forty-five minutes of the nonsense Claude rose majestically in his seat and in that melodious voice of beaten bronze cried out, 'You can't DO this to my friends! THESE PEOPLE ARE ARTISTS. You can't TREAT artists like this. They are WONDERFUL artists, and they are my FRIENDS, you can't TREAT my friends like this...' And on and on in the same outraged vein. The entire company on the stage paused yet again in the business of the evening, this time listening with rejoicing in their hearts, as someone at last was saying publicly what most had been saying among themselves for some time.

Leon Major, not directing the show but in attendance as Artistic Director, descended on Claude and gently and with great tact shepherded him into a taxi and sent him home.

Claude was purple with remorse in the morning, but all through that Christmas day company members, the author and director conspicuous by their absence, phoned to thank him and wish him well, telling him they had visions through the night not of Sugar Plums but of Diogenes.

Claude Bede was a fine actor, a generous friend, and a lot more than words and labels adequately define. And in that moment on Christmas Eve a quarter of a century ago, he became a bit of a legend. We are richer for his life, his talent, and his outrage.

LYNNE GRIFFIN
A tribute to my Mum

So what's wrong with being a stage mother? My Mum [Kay Griffin] was. She loved the stage and she always made me believe she loved being the mother of an actress. She was an actress herself and continued to appear in amateur stage productions, as well as commercials and TV shows for the CBC. So I had something to live up to: her savvy as an actress, a mother, and an agent.

Yes, she was also my agent for many years, selling me to casting directors, producers, and directors with great gusto. She was responsible for my first appearance at Stratford and at many other theatres. To my chagrin, I once overheard her telling another of her clients who was complaining about a lack of auditions, 'Well, my daughter hasn't had an audition in weeks, and she's the best actress in Canada!' Oh yes, embarrassing to relate now, but oh, how I miss her.

She was always there to help me learn lines, insistent on my being letter-perfect, and ever unable to resist giving a wee bit of direction. No one was more excited when I got a part than she. She was indefatigable in taking me as a child to audition after audition, waiting around on sets, and driving me daily to the CBC for a kids show I did in my teens.

She liked to sit in the front row to watch me closely and, again, give me direction. She once came to see a play I was in *seventeen times*. There were sixteen other actors in the show and the first time she came to see it she only had watched me. So she came back to give the other sixteen actors an equal viewing.

On another occasion, she was so moved by a performance of mine she actually got up from her seat, arms outstretched to embrace me...and joined me onstage for the curtain call! Horrifying at the time, but I remember it now with great fondness.

She kept scrapbooks of my career from my very first professional photos (in baby clothes and children's underwear), and every review, both good and bad. She once accepted an award for me when I couldn't be there in person; she always said that was a high point for her.

Mum died peacefully in her sleep in the spring of 1996. Even now, every job I get, I know she's in God's face demanding he get me that next audition, that next great job, that part of a lifetime. She was a force. She made it all happen for me in life, and I know that she continues to do so from up above on the heavenly stage.

MONICA PARKER
On Barbara Hamilton

This is my favourite recollection of the amazing Barbara Hamilton.

When I was very young, when I was brand new, I mean just out of the egg, I had done some show, I've forgotten what it was. Out of the blue, there was a phone call. It was Barbara Hamilton. Now I had never even met Barbara Hamilton personally, though of course I knew who she was. Even then, she was one of the biggest stars in Canada. So I picked up the phone and I heard this deep, unmistakable voice.

'Hello, this is Barbara Hamilton. Is this Monica Parker?'

'Yeah.'

'I just saw you in (something or other) and I wanted to tell you I thought you were bloody marvellous. That's all I called for.'

I was so stunned and touched that someone would actually do something like that, that all I could say was, 'Thanks...Thanks very much.' And that was it. She hung up.

It was great.

JOHN REEVES
Memories of John Drainie

A few days before his death, John Drainie came to Studio G at CBC with his wife, Claire Murray, to do some taping for a drama anthology. For a long time he had been on painkillers but decided to discontinue them the day before he came in. He was afraid that they might blur his concentration and loosen his grip on his vocal technique. Rather he should attempt his best at the price of pain, than settle for less than his best but be pain-free.

When he arrived at the studio, he could barely walk, let alone stand at the microphone to perform. We gave him a lounge chair so that he could perform lying down and hung a microphone over him on a boom. I knew John to be a consummate professional whose judgement of both text and timing I trusted implicitly. There was no point in wasting his fragile energies on rehearsals. My own concern was to make John as comfortable as possible artistically and to contrive the best possible microphone pick-up with the least possible fuss.

John was obviously in great pain. It was clearly a strain for him to carry on any kind of conversation. But when I gave the cue to start taping, I was utterly unprepared for what came out of his mouth. It was as though, by some unimaginable act of will, he had banished the cancer to another room. The old John Drainie was suddenly there, at the height of his powers from the first line to the last, flawless, compelling.

And so it went throughout the session. Between takes we kept company with a dying man nailed to the agony of his flesh. Every time the tape rolled we sat in awe of the world's greatest radio actor doing his unique justice to one of the world's finest languages.

That was John Drainie's final performance. Days later, on the last day of his life he sat in his living room and talked about his career to a visiting film crew well into the evening. Then he went upstairs to his bedroom and died as he would have wished, working to the very end. He was just fifty years old.

ALFIE SCOPP
Remembering Gerry Sarracini

Gerry grew up in Toronto in a large family, owners of a grocery store. Thank goodness they did because his mother used to make enormous bowls of spaghetti for us and we all ate there. She was a great lady. They were a great family.

Gerry and I met at the Academy of Radio Arts while we were students. He had always wanted to be an actor. In my own long career, I have been fortunate to know many talented and gifted performers and people in the entertainment business, and there has never been anyone to top Gerry. I still think he was the most widely talented person I ever knew. He could do everything, be it character actor or leading man. He sang and he wrote well. At the time of his death he was playing 'Romanoff' in Peter Ustinov's *Romanoff and Juliet* on Broadway. He was thirty years old.

In some ways he was a self-made actor. He was a street talker and he was very aware that he had to change his speech. He did this by sitting at the piano and singing all the notes, lower and lower. In two years he had the most marvellous instrument.

During our studies at the Academy, the New Play Society mounted a production of a play called *Joan of Lorraine* by Maxwell Anderson, about Joan of Arc and starring Mona O'Hearn. I managed to get Gerry the small part of a soldier who only had one scene and one line, 'The horses are ready.'

The play was performed at Toronto's Museum Theatre, a tiny space with only 435 seats. The stage itself was like a postage stamp and the actors had to enter by side doors that were visible to the audience.

At that time Gerry was a big cumbersome guy. On opening night when he made his first ever stage entrance, at the beginning of this impassioned scene, he stumbled on the stairs to the stage. As a result, the entrance drew titters from the audience. He managed to hit his mark and the scene continued with Gerry's face growing ever redder from embarrassment. Mona began her long speech and at the first pause she made, Gerry came right in with his line. The problem was that they were only a third of the way through the scene and ages from his real cue.

Mona looked at him and went on with her speech. She had about five different pauses and every time she paused Gerry said, 'The horses are ready.' The last time he said it he even asked it as a question, 'The horses are ready?' But, she still had the climax of her speech to deliver! Mona finally finished her speech. By this time Gerry was so terrified, and the audience was so conscious of him, he didn't dare say a word. Mona paused for his line and when nothing was forthcoming she said in frustration, 'Now! Are the horses ready?' To which he said a meek, 'Yes.' The audience had a tremendous laugh which was not the intention of the scene at all.

While Gerry was appearing in *Romanoff and Juliet* in New York, he stopped off at a bar for a Christmas drink. It was Christmas Eve so he invited his black taxi driver in to join him. After a drink or two, Gerry went to the washroom, and when he came back the driver wasn't there. The bartender told him that the driver was having an argument with some guys and he had told them to get the hell outside and settle it there. Gerry went outside and when they were just starting to square off, he stepped in between them. The other guy swung and hit Gerry. He fell back and hit his head on the edge of the curb in such a way that it killed him. He died the next day. It was a terrible thing.

The odds were against such a thing happening but it did, and it happened to a wonderful guy who had beaten the odds and was on his way to the very top.

JOHN NEVILLE
A final bow

One of the great experiences of my life was working in a remarkable production of *My Fair Lady,* at Stratford. It was directed by one of the very, very great men of the Canadian theatre—Jean Gascon. He was great as an actor and truly great as a director.

Everyone loved him and we became dear friends. We in the cast had known that he was not in perfect health and that he was frail, but had no idea how ill he was. Sadly, he died before we opened. It was horrible, a dreadful loss. He never saw our first night.

That opening night was like none I have experienced, as the cast...played for Jean.

TONY VAN BRIDGE
The real stuff

[*This story comes from Tony's experiences in the provinces in England, doing repertory theatre with the Bainbridge company as a 'character juvenile', circa 1940.*]

Our character lady...Lillian Drake was a delicate and delightful woman who in her younger days had made quite a name in the music halls. As she had advanced in years and lessened in demand, she had become a 'character lady'. A sad but ever-hopeful echo of the young music-hall star, Lillian Drake now made a living by playing cooks, grandmothers, and aged aunts.

For reasons best known to himself, the Captain [Bainbridge] celebrated some event or other by presenting a Variety evening. We performed sketches, somebody played an instrument, I sang a rusty ballad, another actor gave some impressions, and the Captain recited something from Dickens. But at all this kind of stuff we were a bunch of amateurs. It was Lillian who showed us what it was all about.

Somewhere in the depths of a theatrical trunk her vaudeville costumes had been preserved, and, with them, tattered copies of her songs.

For a few imperishable moments the Lillian Drake of the music halls, the Lillian Drake that none of us kids had ever known, came magically to life. The tender figure, the lined face, the voice thin and uncertain, responded with an indescribable spirit. The old eyes flashed vivaciously at the audience as Lillian Drake stepped back in time. It was a kind of resurrection. The years, the disappointments, the frustrations, fell away from her as she twirled a parasol and slipped into the whisper of a soft-shoe dance.

We theatre people are simple in our sentiment, and we cling to kind of fairy-tale immortality. On that night, Lillian convinced us that we would never die, that we would not even fade away like old soldiers but that always, somewhere, there would be a theatre, an audience, a thunder of heavenly applause. All this was over fifty years ago, and Lillian was elderly even then. But I am sure that somewhere she is still doing that soft-shoe dance, still singing those songs, still smiling at the celestial applause.

NICHOLAS PENNELL
Adieu et merde!

[Nicholas Pennell, one of our leading actors and a 23-year staple of Canada's Stratford Festival passed away February 22, 1995 after a brief battle with cancer. His final letter to the Stratford Festival Theatre Company at Stratford, Ontario, delivered two days before his death, serves as eloquent testimony to a life in the theatre and is reprinted here as inspiration to us all.]

A Letter To The Company On The First Day Of Rehearsals

February 20, 1995

My dearest company, stage management and crew,

I wanted to write something to you on the occasion of your first day, from one who, for the first time in 24 years, cannot be there.

Each year the miracle renews. We band of artists are released into the adventure again, to renew the act of faith in the recreation of the spirit of imagination. For it is that unique gift that is ours (our joy and our sorrow too), to delve into the stuff of our lives, and dig up with absolute fidelity and accuracy our happiness, our ecstasy, our pain, our misery, our laughter, our ironies, our intimacies passionate and identifiable—hot or icy cold: all unguarded and uncensored, free and truthful. And, through the medium of the text, allow the audience to receive the transubstantiation of our truth into their truth, their reality.

'To hold as 'twere a mirror up to nature.'

For that is what we must do as artists: demonstrate the shared wholeness of the human condition to our audiences, in order that together we may arrive where we started from and know the place for the first time.

That demands from us, our hearts, courage, endurance, energy and commitment of an impossibly high order. But look around this rehearsal hall and take heart. A room more full of talent, generosity, wit, speed, laughter, thievery, meanness, ambition, chutzpah and Bill Hutt is impossible to imagine...unless Monette has stepped out for a cigarette!

My love, my passion, my bliss and my joy, and...my pea-green envy are, and always will be, with every one of you.

Now, take Bill's hand, he's a stranger in Paradise! What are you waiting for? Fly, my darlings!

I love you,

Nick

Contributors

DAMIR ANDREI
Mr Andrei was born in Zagreb, Croatia, grew up in Montreal, and now lives in Toronto. An actor since 1977, he also directs and produces, and is remembered as 'Ed "the Doberman" Werner' in the CBC movie *Breaking All The Rules*.

MAJA ARDAL
Born in Siglufjördur, Iceland, actor/director Ms Ardal is the award-winning Artistic Director of Young People's Theatre in Toronto. She was seen for seven seasons as 'Mrs Potts' in the CBC/Disney TV series *The Road to Avonlea*.

PAT ARMSTRONG
A Montreal-born actor/director, Ms Armstrong trained at the Bristol Old Vic Theatre School and began her career in Winnipeg with John Hirsch. She has performed in England, South Africa, and across Canada, including the Stratford and Shaw Festivals.

HARVEY ATKIN
Mr Atkin, a Toronto-based character actor, has worked in television, film, and radio. He is known for his voice work and animation characterizations for *Super Mario Brothers, Alf, Stunt Dawgs, X-men, Rupert Bear*, and *Tintin*.

MICHAEL AYOUB
Born in Timmins, Ontario, actor/director Mr Ayoub has appeared in many television and film productions including leads in two comedy series, *Michael and Mary* and *Mixed Doubles*. He was co-founder and Artistic Director of the Muskoka Festival.

YANK AZMAN
Mr Azman has been a professional actor since 1969 and has been booed off some of the best stages in Canada. Consequently he now hides solely behind recorded media.

BARRIE BALDARO
Born in Warwickshire, England, Mr Baldaro is a satirist, writer, and actor for many CBC TV shows, among them *Nightcap* and *This Hour Has Seven Days*; and on CBC

radio, *Funny You Should Say That*. He was inducted into the TV Comedy Hall of Fame in 1995.

LESLEY BALLANTYNE
Ms Ballantyne has had a wide-ranging career in the Canadian entertainment industry as a performer, director, choreographer, producer, teacher, and administrator.

DIANA BARRINGTON
Born in Simla, Northern India, Ms Barrington studied at RADA in England and came to Canada in the '60s. She debuted in the title role of *Yerma* and has since appeared in numerous roles for CBC TV and radio, as well as in leading roles in theatres across Canada.

HENRY BECKMAN
Character actor born in Halifax, Nova Scotia, Mr Beckman has performed in every medium across Canada and the United States. He has won Best Supporting Actor awards and the Queen's Medal '79 (for contributions to Canadian culture). He celebrated his 50th year in show biz in February 1996.

CLAUDE BEDE
Mr Bede hailed from Halifax. He played across Canada and the United States and was especially known for his work with the Dominion Drama Festival, the Canadian Players, and the Stratford Festival.

BERNARD BEHRENS
Born in London, England, Mr Behrens planned to be in the movies from the age of eight. He made it into 16 Hollywood films, before he built another career playing at such theatres as The Old Vic, The Stratford Festival, the Guthrie, and the Neptune.

ANTHONY BEKENN
Mr Bekenn was born in Tanzania. His first professional role was in *Equus* in 1976. Among his favourite appearances are *Taming Of The Shrew* with his wife, Sharry Flett, and *Arsenic And Old Lace* with Kate Reid. He has been seen more recently in the TV series *Wind At My Back*.

ROBERT BENSON
Mr Benson, born and raised in Denver, Colorado, immigrated to Canada in the '70s. His work across Canada includes five seasons at the Stratford Shakespearean Festival and seventeen seasons at the Shaw Festival. He has also appeared in film and TV productions.

MARIAM BERNSTEIN
Ms Bernstein is a Winnipeg-based actor/director. She has worked in theatres from Nova Scotia to Saskatchewan in pieces ranging from Shakespeare, to adaptations of children's stories by Robert Munch, to new chamber operas.

WAYNE BEST
Born in Saint John, N.B. and a graduate of Ryerson Theatre School, Mr Best has a long list of TV credits and has spent the last six seasons on stage at the Stratford Festival.

MERVYN 'BUTCH' BLAKE

Born in India, Mr Blake made his career there until coming to Canada in 1957. He has appeared in film and television and toured with The Canadian Players. 1997 marked his forty-second year with the Stratford Festival. In 1983 he received the Queen's Medal and in 1995 he was made a member of the Order of Canada.

DOMINI BLYTHE

Born in Liverpool, England, Ms Blythe came to Canada in 1972. She has performed leading roles at the Shaw Festival, the Stratford Shakespearean Festival, the St Lawrence Centre in Toronto, in the States and in England, and in film and television. She performs in French and in English.

DAVID BOLT

Born and educated in Toronto, he has worked as an actor across the country in all mediums but he is best known for his work in new plays in the Toronto 'underground' theatre.

SARA BOTSFORD

Born in a small mining town near Kirkland Lake in northern Ontario, Ms Botsford studied theatre at York University and began her career at the Stratford Festival. She has starred in many feature films and on Broadway, and in the TV series *E.N.G.* She has also become a producer and film director.

MARILYN BOYLE

A native of Regina, Saskatchewan, Ms Boyle plays 'Hattie Olsen' in TV's *Wind At My Back*. She is also a familiar face at Winnipeg's Rainbow Stage and in the theatre in Lindsay, Ontario. Two of her own plays have been produced in Lindsay: *Relative Strangers* and *Better Offer*.

BERNARD BRADEN

A preacher's son from Vancouver, Mr Braden was a gifted entertainer who moved to Toronto in the '40s as one of Andrew Allen's B.C. radio 'Mafia'. He and his wife and fellow performer Barbara Kelly then went to London, England to try their luck for 'one year'. Almost supernatural success in radio, theatre, and then television anchored them to Britain.

MARK BRESLIN

Mr Breslin is an institution in Canadian stand-up comedy. He is a performer, writer, entrepreneur, and a manager for many other successful comics. His chain of comedy clubs, Yuk Yuks, is the largest in North America.

DAVE BROADFOOT

Born in North Vancouver, B.C., Mr Broadfoot is an internationally known stand-up comedian and a veteran of CBC's *Air Farce*. He has won fourteen awards for writing, performing, and producing comedy including the Queen Elizabeth Silver Jubilee Award and the Order of Canada.

NORMAN BROWNING

Born in Vancouver, Mr Browning has appeared on TV, radio, and film and in major

Canadian theatrical venues for more than 30 years, most often at the Vancouver Playhouse, The Arts Club Theatre, and the Shaw Festival. He is the recipient of three 'Jessie' Awards for best actor, a Peoples Choice Award, and an ACTRA Award for Best Actor in a Radio Drama.

BENEDICT CAMPBELL
Born in Stratford, Ontario, Mr Campbell has worked in all mediums and has become very familiar for his work in Toronto's many theatres, several seasons at The Stratford Festival, and his five seasons at the National Arts Centre.

DOUGLAS CAMPBELL
Glasgow-born Mr Campbell began his career with the Old Vic. He was one of the original British stars invited by Tyrone Guthrie to come to Canada to start the Stratford Festival in Ontario in 1953. One of the country's best known and respected performer/teacher/directors, he will also be remembered as *The Great Detective* on CBC television.

NICHOLAS CAMPBELL
Mr Campbell was born in Toronto and raised in Montreal. He has become familiar to Canadian audiences from leading roles in mainly television and film, notably as series leads in *The Insiders* and *Diamonds*. He has recently directed his first feature film, *Booze Can*.

WANDA CANNON
Born in Wilkie, Saskatchewan, and a performer from the age of five, Ms Cannon glided into acting from singing and has been happily doing both ever since. She was 'Mom' in the television series *My Secret Identity* for three seasons.

LEN CARIOU
Mr Cariou was born in Winnipeg, graduated from the first class at The National Theatre School, and was an original member of Manitoba Theatre Centre under John Hirsch. He won a Tony Award for the title role of *Sweeney Todd, The Demon Barber Of Fleet Street* in 1979. A veteran of Stratford, he has most recently appeared on Broadway as 'Ernest Hemingway' in *Papa*.

JEAN (JOHN) CAVALL
M. Cavall was born in Grand-Mère, P.Q. and has had an eclectic career in the US, Britain, and Canada as a singer, actor, host, comic actor, and children's entertainer. He presently produces bilingual children's recordings and provides bilingual services to the film and TV industry.

NICOLA CAVENDISH
Born in Cirencester, Glouscestershire, England, Ms Cavendish is best known for her national tour of the play *Shirley Valentine*. In twenty years as an actress she remembers fondly her stint on Broadway with the late, great Geraldine Page in *Blithe Spirit*.

DOUGLAS CHAMBERLAIN
Born in St Joseph's Hospital, Toronto, Ontario, Mr Chamberlain has spent 40 happy years as a performer in Canada.

VERNON CHAPMAN

Mr Chapman was Hamilton-born and raised in Toronto. In 1946 he and four others joined Dora Mavor Moore to form the New Play Society. He has acted and directed coast to coast and performed in radio, TV, and films. Chairperson of Equity for six terms, he has also served on the board of ACTRA.

MAURY CHAYKIN

Mr Chaykin began life in Brooklyn, N.Y. and his acting career in Canada. He won a Best Actor Nellie Award for *Hal Banks: Canada's Sweetheart* and a Genie for *Whale Music*. He is also remembered for his work in the films *Dances With Wolves* and *Unstrung Heroes*.

DINAH CHRISTIE

Ms Christie was born in London, England of Canadian actor parents who were then performing at the Old Vic. She acts, sings, writes musicals, directs opera, performs an original evening, and has been in the theatre since she was born.

GORDON CLAPP

Mr Clapp was born in New Hampshire and became a landed immigrant to work at the Neptune Theatre in Halifax. He has appeared in many film, TV, and stage productions in both Canada and the United States, but is best known as 'Medevoy' on the TV series *N.Y.P.D. Blue*.

SUSAN CLARK

Sarnia-born Ms Clark, known for her work in TV and film, moved to Hollywood in the late 1960s. She met her husband Alex Karras while shooting *Babe,* the biographical film about Babe Didrickson Zaharias, a role for which she won an Emmy. They worked together again on the long-running TV sitcom, *Webster*.

BETH ANNE COLE

Born in Winnipeg, Ms Cole is a singer, actress, and songwriter, performing at the Shaw Festival, in her own concerts, and in cabaret performances. She was in the original company of the musical *Jane Eyre* at the Royal Alexandra Theatre in Toronto, and has recorded two solo albums, *Song Under The Stair* and *Gifts In The Old, Old Ground*.

CORINNE CONLEY

Ms Conley hails originally from Batavia, N.Y. She is a veteran of the stage and a pioneer performer for CBC TV in the '50s. She has performed on Broadway, in the West End of London, and Hollywood. Recent Toronto credits include *Salt Water Moose, Wind At My Back,* and *Flash Forward*.

ERNIE COOMBS

Mr Coombs was born in Maine, where he studied art, became a scene designer, and later an actor. He came to Canada in 1963 and became the perennial children's favourite 'Mr Dressup' in 1964. A Canadian citizen, he was made a member of the Order of Canada in 1996.

GRANT COWAN

Musical comedy and character actor Mr Cowan, originally from Winnipeg, was

'Snoopy' in the Canadian production of *You're A Good Man, Charlie Brown* for a five-year tour of Canada and the United States. Part of the first season of the Manitoba Theatre Centre, he has done 16 productions of *The Fantastiks* and lately has played 'Maurice' in *Beauty And The Beast*.

JACK CRELEY

Mr Creley was born in Chicago. He came to Canada in the early 1950s. Jack has appeared in over 2500 television shows, numerous films including *Doctor Strangelove*, and many stage productions including Stratford, Shaw, and Broadway. He is also a director. 1997 marks his sixty-first year in the business.

RICHARD CURNOCK

Originally from London, England, Mr Curnock has been acting and living here since 1970, more on than off.

JENNIFER DALE

Ms Dale was born in Toronto. In the 1970s, in a film called *Susanne*, she met her husband-to-be, Robert Lantos. One of Canada's most accomplished and sexiest film and TV stars, she is a recipient of both Gemini and Genie awards.

ROBERTSON DAVIES

Mr Davies was born in Thamesville, Ontario and began his acting career in England before he became a writer/editor of the Peterborough *Examiner*/founding Master of Massey College and author of more than thirty books with translations into 19 languages. He died in 1996.

DONALD DAVIS

Mr Davis, the founder of one of Canada's first professional theatres, The Crest, was born in Newmarket, Ontario. He premièred such major theatrical works as Beckett's *Krapp's Last Tape* and *Ohio Impromptu*, J.B. Priestley's *The Glass Cage*, and Timothy Findley's *Stillborn Lover* on stages from London's West End to Broadway and across Canada's main stages.

IAN DEAKIN

Mr Deakin is a native of Worcestershire, England. He began his stage career at the Neptune Theatre, Halifax, and has appeared in more than 150 productions across Canada.

LOUIS DEL GRANDE

Born in New Jersey, Mr Del Grande first came up to Canada to the Stratford Festival. He participated in the alternate theatre community in Toronto as an actor/director, notably at Passe Muraille. He wrote for TV and radio before creating and starring in the CBC TV series, *Seeing Things* with his wife Martha Gibson.

KEN DELISLE

Mr Delisle was born in Windsor, Ontario. He has co-founded and served as Artistic Director for two amateur theatre companies: Townhouse 9 Productions and Interesting Theatre. He is a United Church minister currently working with the Winnipeg Church of the Deaf.

NORMA DELL'AGNESE
A native Torontonian, Ms Dell'Agnese is a 20-year veteran and a 'Dora' Award winner for Best Musical performance in a Brecht/Weill Cabaret. Film credits include *Meatballs, Margaret's Museum, Agnes Of God* and *Atlantic City.* She wrote, produced, and performed two one-woman shows, *Notre Dame Diva* and *The World's Oldest Profession.*

JOHN DEVORSKI
Mr Devorski originated the role of 'Smudge' in *Forever Plaid* in Toronto for which he won a Dora Award. 'Billy' in *Carousel* at the Stratford Festival, he has also appeared at the Persephone Theatre, Rainbow Stage, Young People's Theatre and the Elgin Theatre in Toronto.

MARCIA DIAMOND
Born in Calgary, Alberta, Ms Diamond is a character actor well known for her recurring role, 'Mary', on *Street Legal,* and her performances in the TV movie *The Queen Of Mean* and the feature film, *Sam And Me.*

WENDY DONALDSON
Ms Donaldson has made her career mainly on stage across Canada and the US, although she has appeared in film, television, and radio. She is a graduate of the University of Victoria and the Vancouver Playhouse Acting School. A highlight of her career is Pinter's *The Birthday Party* with the inmates of William Head Prison.

RICHARD DONAT
Born in Kentville, Nova Scotia, Mr Donat has spent his adult life as an actor in film and theatre and has become a director as well. He created the role of 'Cuirette' in Michel Tremblay's play *Hosanna.*

LEN DONCHEFF
Mr Doncheff began life in Toronto, Ontario and is Macedonian in descent. He learned his craft from George Luscombe and has appeared on stages from Halifax to Vancouver and in the United States as well. He also appears on television and in films.

JAMES B. DOUGLAS
Born in Cape Town, South Africa, Mr Douglas has had a long and varied career in England, the US and Canada. As well as acting he has been an Artistic Director, director, and a writer, and helped create several new Canadian plays and musicals.

SHIRLEY DOUGLAS
Ms Douglas was born in Weyburn, Saskatchewan, daughter of former NDP leader Tommy Douglas. At the recommendation of Michel Saint-Denis, she went to England to study at RADA. She is well known to stage and television audiences, most recently for the TV series *Wind At My Back*, for the CBC.

DAVID DUNBAR
Calgary-born Mr Dunbar's fondest memories include being a member of Robin Phillips' Grand Theatre Company, four seasons with Stratford, playing 'King Arthur'

in the Chicago production of *Camelot,* and being part of the New York company of *Tamara.* David also teaches singing.

ROSEMARY DUNSMORE

Ms Dunsmore's work has ranged from 'Katharine Brooke' in TV's *Anne Of Green Gables* to her TV series *Mom P.I.* to the doctor in *Total Recall* and 'Stella' in *Streetcar Named Desire.* Edmonton-born, she has premièred new Canadian plays and played at the Stratford Festival. She was recently selected for *Maclean's* magazine's Honour Roll of Canadians Who Make a Difference.

SHARON DYER

Ms Dyer was born in Toronto, and her theatrical career has taken her to stages across Canada, notably a tour of the musical *Thin Ice*, and *O.D. On Paradise* at Theatre Passe Muraille. She appeared in the CBC TV series *9B*, and garnered an ACTRA nomination for *Slim Obsession*.

JAYNE EASTWOOD

During Ms Eastwood's more than 30 years in show business, she has won four awards and several nominations. She was an original member of the *Second City Troupe* and *SCTV*, was in the original cast of *Godspell*, and recently was seen in Toronto's Broadway-bound production of *Showboat*. Ms Eastwood will be long remembered as 'Betty' in the Canadian film classic, *Going Down The Road*.

JAMES EDMOND

Mr Edmond is a Walkerton, Ontario native, raised in Kitchener. He trained and worked in England after serving there in WW II, returning to Canada in the mid '50s. He has been an actor for 48 years.

RALPH ENDERSBY

Montreal-born Mr Endersby began his career as a child actor in TV's *The Forest Rangers* and continued as an adult in such features as Don Shebib's *Rip Off*. He is now a producer/creator of the TV movie *The Challengers,* recipient of six international awards, and executive producer of *ParticipACTION, The Energy Station*.

GERALDINE FARRELL

A native Montrealer, Ms Farrell currently resides in sunny Los Angeles, California with a pack of dogs who've been kind enough to take her in. In addition to her work as an actress, she is also a writer and director.

DENISE FERGUSSON

Born in Timmins, Ontario, Ms Fergusson has performed at major theatres across Canada and in the United States. Presently an associate professor in the Theatre Department of Memorial University in Newfoundland, and a regular performer at the Charlottetown Festival in P.E.I., she is also involved there with actor training.

DAVID FERRY

Mr Ferry is a Newfoundlander who lives and works in Toronto, Ontario as an actor, director, and arts activist. Responsible for *Canajun, Eh?,* an audio collection of Canadian dialects for the actor, he has been nominated for a Genie and a Gemini and won an Nellie Award for radio performance.

JOY FIELDING
Born in Toronto, Ontario, Ms Fielding has lived and worked there all her life, with the exception of a 2½ year sojourn in Los Angeles. She long ago switched from acting to writing. Her novels include *Missing Pieces, See Jane Run,* and *Kiss Mommy Goodbye.*

GARY FILES
Mr Files is an Australia-born Canadian who began his acting career as a graduate of the National Theatre School in Montreal. He is well known to Canadian theatre audiences and has performed in Australia and England as well.

TIMOTHY FINDLEY
After two decades as an actor, now as an award-winning writer of fiction, drama, and documentary for radio, television, and film, Toronto-born Mr Findley is working on his fifth play.

SHELORA FITZGERALD
Ms Fitzgerald, MEd, was born in Toronto. In 1960 she became the youngest student accepted by the National Theatre School in Montreal. Later she taught acting at the Vancouver Playhouse, Studio 58, and Simon Fraser University. Currently she is an independent producer.

BARRY FLATMAN
Mr Flatman is a native of Victoria, B.C. A Toronto-based performer, a Gemini Award nominee, writer, director, producer, and teacher, he is a familiar face in numerous TV shows and series as well as films, commercials, radio, and animated children's shows.

MARIE-HÉLÈNE FONTAINE
Mlle Fontaine, originally of Drummondville, P.Q., is familiar to both English and French audiences in film, TV, stage, and radio. She is remembered for her work in *Hal Banks: Canada's Sweetheart* and *Escape From Iran.*

TED FOLLOWS
Ottawa-born Mr Follows has been an actor/director for more than 50 years and a company member of The Straw Hat Players, *Spring Thaw*, and The Canadian Repertory Company.

COLIN FOX
Mr Fox was born in Canada and attended the National Theatre School in Montreal. He is a veteran of film, TV, radio, and stage—winning in 1971 a Best Actor Award for his role as 'Lord Durham'. Recently he has appeared in the TV series *The PSI Factor*, and in the feature film *Daylight* opposite Claire Bloom.

DON FRANCKS/IRON BUFFALO
Charles Chaplin was Vancouver-born Mr Francks' mentor, Thelonius Monk and Johann Sebastian Bach his music teachers. Model Ts and motorcycles are his hobbies and mother nature his healer.

ROBIN GAMMELL
Montreal-born Mr Gammell began his acting career in the Stratford Festival's tent days with Tyrone Guthrie. He is especially remembered as 'Hitler' in *The Incredible*

Rise Of Arturo Ui (Guthrie Theatre), in many TV series, and recently in the CBC movie as 'Con Smythe' in *Net Worth*.

DAVID GARDNER
A native of Toronto, Mr Gardner has been a familiar presence in radio, film, TV, and theatre for more than 50 years. Recently he has been seen in continuing roles on *Traders* and *Robocop*. He also holds a PhD in Canadian Theatre History.

MARILYN GARDNER GASCON
Mme Gascon was born in Montreal and grew up in the theatre watching the likes of Christopher Plummer, John Colicos, Leo Ciceri and Eric Donkin. She had a marvellous 30 years married to Jean Gascon, and now resides in France.

ANGELA GEI
Ms Gei was born in Toronto, Ontario. She has been an actress performing in TV, film, radio, and on stage for more than twenty years, and has also been an associate producer for the stage and radio. She is also the proud mother of two little boys.

BRIAN GEORGE
Mr George was born in Israel, lived in England, and immigrated with his family to Toronto in the late '60s. Part of the Second City Troupe, he is known for his work in commercials in Canada. He has lived and worked in Los Angeles for more than 10 years, appearing in many TV shows such as *Seinfeld* and *Quantum Leap*.

MARTHA GIBSON
Ms Gibson was born in Elizabethtown, Illinois and, with her husband Louis Del Grande, began her career in Canada during the 1960s explosion of small theatres. She is most familiar in the CBC TV comedy mystery, *Seeing Things* and from appearances on stages across Canada. She and her husband became citizens of Canada in 1990 and now reside in Nova Scotia.

MARION GILSENAN
Ms Gilsenan was born and raised in Britain. A drama student from an early age, she came to Canada on the first leg of a round-the-world trip in the '50s and never got any further. She married, raised three children, and returned to the stage in Ontario. She has been nominated for both Gemini and Dora Awards.

LINDA GORANSON
Toronto-born Ms Goranson was trained at LAMDA in England, and has since performed in all media in Canada and the US. She starred in the Oscar-nominated short *The Painted Door*, and won the Yorkton Best Actress Award for it. She is remembered for her work in TV's *The Newcomers (The Irish)*, *The Rowdyman* and *Traders*. She won the Best Actress award for CBC's *Spike in the Wall*.

BARBARA GORDON
Ms Gordon was born in Montreal and grew up in Alberta. She has played theatres from Vancouver to Montreal. Her Canadian films include *Dead Ringers*, *Beautiful Dreamers*, and *White Room*. She was a regular on TV's *Judge*, *Street Legal*, and *Great Defender*. Married to writer Douglas Roger, she is the mother of Dougal and Melody.

JOYCE GORDON
Born in Montreal, Ms Gordon came to Toronto in 1957. She studied acting at Ray Lawlor's Acting Studio and has been an Equity and ACTRA member since 1960, performing in all media at most major theatres across Canada. She has also appeared in scores of TV and radio commercials, films, and television productions.

ROBERT GOULET
Mr Goulet, born in Lawrence, Massachusetts, grew up in Edmonton, Alberta. He began his singing and acting career there, before studying and performing in Toronto. He has since become well known in Canada and the US in film, television, on stage, and as a headliner in Las Vegas. His Broadway debut as 'Lancelot' in the original production of the musical *Camelot* made him an international star.

ALLAN GRAY
Mr Gray has been a member of the Shaw Festival acting ensemble for seven seasons and the Stratford Festival for three seasons. He was nominated for a 'Dora' Award and won a 'Jessie' Award for his role as 'Lyle' in *Whale Riding Weather.*

BRUCE GRAY
Mr Gray was born in San Juan, Puerto Rico to Canadian parents. He is an award-winning actor (Dramalogue Award, Philadelphia Critics Award) who has performed on stage, screen, radio, and TV in Britain, Canada, and the U.S. He is recently familiar to Canadians for his work on the TV show *Traders.*

LYNDA MASON GREEN
Born in Sarnia, Ontario, Ms Green first performed on stage at the age of five. She is best known for her TV series regulars such as 'Susanne McCullough' in *War of the Worlds,* 'Fleece Toland' in *Night Heat* and 'Dory Quimby' in *Ramona* and has also appeared in many films and episodic TV, on stage and on radio.

GRAHAM GREENE
Mr Greene was born on the Six Nations Reserve in Ontario, and is a full blood Oneida. He began his career in television, film, and radio in 1976. He won a Best Actor Dora Mavor Moore Award for his work in *Dry Lips Oughta Move to Kapuskasing* and was nominated for an Academy Award for Best Supporting Actor for the role of 'Kicking Bird' in Kevin Costner's *Dances With Wolves.*

DAWN GREENHALGH
Born in Shanghai, China, Ms Greenhalgh has been a founding member of many Canadian theatre companies. Her international career as leading lady has spanned forty-five years and all her four children are in the business.

BRUCE GREENWOOD
Mr Greenwood began his career onstage at the Arts Club theatre in Vancouver where he worked for several years before moving to California. He makes feature films and is perhaps best known for his work on the television series *St Elsewhere,* and *Nowhere Man.*

LYNNE GRIFFIN
Toronto-born Ms Griffin has worked on stage, screen, radio, and TV across Canada

and the US. She will be remembered for her roles in *Strange Brew* and *Obsessed*. She has recently repatriated from Los Angeles and has been seen regularly in *Wind At My Back*.

GARRICK HAGON
Born in London, UK, Mr Hagon grew up in Toronto, and earned a BA in English at the University of Toronto. He played at the Stratford Festival for eight seasons, and has acted in TV, films, and theatre in Canada, the US, Europe and, recently, China.

REX HAGON
Mr Hagon was born in Toronto in 1947 and has been a professional actor from the age of five and a half. He was one of the stars of the first colour television series filmed in Canada, *The Forest Rangers* and he has been President of Toronto Branch of ACTRA.

AMELIA HALL
Born in Leeds, England, and brought to Canada at the age of five, she graced our stages for 38 years until her death in 1984. She was the first woman to speak on the Stratford stage, as 'Lady Anne' opposite Alec Guinness's 'Richard the Third'. Ms Hall appeared in almost every stage venue in the country as well as on radio, television, and film.

BARBARA HAMILTON
Ms Hamilton, who died in 1996, was one of the few genuine stars born in and working almost exclusively in Canada. She was acclaimed in Canada and Britain for her 'Marilla' in *Anne Of Green Gables* and was a perennial favourite in *Spring Thaw*. Her last performance was on the stage at the Royal Alexandra Theatre, in the musical *Crazy For You*.

NICHOLAS HARRISON
Mr Harrison was born in Prince George, British Columbia and trained/worked in London, England. Recent work includes *A Promise Is A Promise* at Kaleidoscope Theatre, *Beau Geste* in Chemainus, *The X-Files, Highlander,* and *Sliders* television series. He continues to work as an actor, fight director, and director.

DONALD HARRON
Born in Toronto, Ontario he began his career while still a student. A member of the New Play Society and also of the first Stratford company Mr Harron went on to work in London's West End, and at the American Shakespeare Festival and toured as 'Jimmy Porter' in *Look Back in Anger*. He adapted *Anne Of Green Gables* for the stage and appeared in countless radio and television shows.

RON HASTINGS
Mr Hastings was born in Guelph, Ontario. A founding member of several theatre companies including The Neptune Theatre and Lennoxville, he has spent 10 consecutive seasons with the St Lawrence Centre and 8 seasons at the Stratford Festival, and has been a familiar presence in many other theatres across Canada including the National Arts Centre.

THOMAS HAUFF
Mr Hauff was born in Bad Ischel, Switzerland and came to Canada when he was six years old. His TV, film, and stage credits include *Scales Of Justice, Spike Of Love,* and *As You Like It* for the World Stage Festival.

MICHAEL HEALEY
Mr Healey was raised in Brockville, Ontario. As an actor, he has worked across the country. He has written several plays (*Kicked, The Farm Show*), some journalism, and two works of theatre fiction (*Dear Mr. Newton, Sincerely Michael Healey* and *An Actor's Diary*).

ELLEN-RAY HENNESSY
A native Torontonian, Ms Hennessy has been in more than 100 plays in Canada, the US, and Europe. She is a regular on the Disney series, *Flash Forward* and has appeared on *FX, Goosebumps, Mighty Jungle, Conspiracy Of Fear* and *Shoemaker* among many others.

ART HINDLE
Mr Hindle was born in Halifax and raised in Toronto. A familiar face on Canadian and American TV in the last quarter century, he is best remembered for his portrayal of 'Mike Fennell' on *E.N.G.* and for *Liar, Liar.* He has been a Genie Award nominee.

MICHAEL HOGAN
Born in Kirkland Lake, Ontario, Mr Hogan studied at the National Theatre School. He was very much involved with the development of the 'underground' theatre scene in Toronto in the '70s and has worked extensively in theatres across the country as well as in leading roles in radio, television, and film.

SUSAN HOGAN
Born in Agincourt, Ontario, Ms Hogan began acting in high school, and went from the National Theatre School straight to the Shaw Festival, then to leading roles in television, radio, and movies. She is often recognised from her work as 'Nicole' in *Night Heat.*

ELVA MAI HOOVER
Ms Hoover is from Toronto and attended the National Theatre School of Canada in Montreal. Some of her better known roles have included her Genie-nominated role as Betty Fox in *The Terry Fox Story* and Stacey in *Anne's Story* for the CBC. She also appeared for four years as Elvira Lawson in *Road To Avonlea.*

LARRY HOROWITZ
Mr Horowitz has appeared on *The Joan Rivers Show, Late Night with David Letterman,* and *An Evening at the Improv,* and has opened in concert for Smokey Robinson, Melissa Manchester, Dionne Warwick, and Paul Anka, among others. He also has performed in movies, published humour books, and written comedy material.

ERIC HOUSE
Mr House was one of the original members of the Stratford Festival and the Crest Theatre. After appearing in London, England in, among other things, the world

première of Jean Genet's *The Balcony*, he returned to Canada to act here as well as in New York, Boston, and Minneapolis. He has also appeared in films, and directed and written for television.

DOUGLAS E. HUGHES

Mr Hughes was born in Richmond Hill, Ontario and has been an actor for more than 17 years, performing on stages across Canada including at the Stratford and Shaw Festivals. He has also appeared in television, in film, and on radio. More recently he and co-writer Marcia Kash have been writing plays, among them *Bedroom Farce* and *A Party To Murder.*

CHRIS HUMPHREYS

Mr Humphreys is a native of Toronto who lived and worked in London, England until 1991. He has since returned to perform across Canada in such roles as 'Don Pedro' in *Much Ado About Nothing,* 'Marlow' in *She Stoops to Conquer*, and 'Geoffrey' in *The Sisters Rosensweig*. He presently resides in Vancouver.

WILLIAM HUTT

Born and raised in Toronto, Ontario, Mr Hutt has played in over 90 productions at the Stratford Festival, and in countless television, radio, and films. A multiple award winner, he has received honorary degrees from three universities. Mr Hutt was the first recipient of the Governor General's Lifetime Achievement Award, and holds the Order of Ontario and the Order of Canada.

PAM HYATT

Ms Hyatt was born in New York City and trained at RADA and LAMDA. She is a veteran of Canadian theatre, notably the Stratford Festival and the Muskoka Festival. She is also a very familiar face in Canadian television productions, commercials, and Canadian and American films shot here on location.

FRANCES HYLAND

Among Canada's most celebrated artists, Ms Hyland was born in Shaunavon, Saskatchewan. Her 47-year career in theatre, TV, film, and radio began in England and continued in the US on Broadway and in Canada. She has two Best Supporting Actress Awards, a 'Dora' and a 'Nellie', and a 'Jefferson Award' for Best Actress. She is a member of the Order of Canada and a recipient of Lifetime Achievement awards from the Governor General and the Toronto Arts Foundation.

MICHAEL IRONSIDE

Mr Ironside was raised in Toronto and had his first big break in David Cronenberg's film *Scanners*. He has since gone on to appear in more than 65 films including *Total Recall* and *Free Willy*, and to star in many TV series including *E.R.* and *DSV Seaquest*. He lives in Los Angeles, California.

ROBERT ITO

Mr Ito was born in Vancouver, B.C. to second generation Japanese Canadian parents who loved the arts. He danced with the National Ballet for nine years. The first Asian member of the cast of *Spring Thaw*, he went from there to Broadway to perform in many productions including *Flower Drum Song*. He may be best remembered for his work as 'Sam Fujiyama' on the TV series, *Quincy*.

TANJA JACOBS

Ms Jacobs is an actress and director living in Toronto. She has been an active member of the professional theatre community since 1981.

GRAHAM JARVIS

Mr Jarvis was born in London, Ontario, cousin to Hume Cronyn. He began as a young actor in New York City, eventually performing in many Broadway and Off-Broadway productions. Well known to film and TV audiences, he is perhaps most remembered for his work in *Mary Hartman, Mary Hartman*.

NOLAN JENNINGS

Born in Dartmouth, Nova Scotia, Mr Jennings has performed across Canada in most of the regional theatres as well as in TV, film, and radio. He appeared at the Stratford Festival for six seasons and continues to reside in Stratford, Ontario.

TED JOHNS

Mr Johns is an actor and playwright. Born and raised in Southwest Ontario, he still lives and works there, largely at the Blyth Festival.

CLARK JOHNSON

Mr Johnson was born in Philadelphia to a show business family. He immigrated to Canada with his family in the '60s. He began his acting career as a child actor in Broadway touring companies and has become well known as a regular on such series as *Night Heat*, *E.N.G.*, *Brewster Street* and *Homicide: Life In The Street*.

MARTIN JULIEN

Mr Julien, born in Montreal, was in the original cast and the touring company of *Goodnight Desdemona (Good Morning Juliet)* and the Theatre Columbus adaptation of *The Barber of Seville* among many others. He was nominated for Dora Awards in 1995 and 1996.

MURRAY KASH

Mr Kash is a native of Toronto, a liberal arts graduate of University of Toronto and of The Lorne Greene School of Radio and Television Arts. He spent thirty years living and working in England, notably in *Goodnight Mrs Puffin* in the West End of London, and various films starring Noel Coward, Alec Guinness, Charlie Chaplin, and Sean Connery. He is also a Voice and Image consultant.

KERRIE KEANE

Ms Keane was born and raised in Vineland, Ontario. She has been seen mainly on television and in film in Canada and the United States. A leading lady in such TV series as *Yellow Rose*, *Star Trek: The Next Generation*, and *McCloud*, she was nominated for a Best Actress Genie for *Obsessed* and also for *Perry Mason* and *Perry Mason Returns*.

CHARMION KING

Ms King is a 40-year veteran of acting in every medium in Canada, England, and the

United States. She is a Gemini nominee as Best Supporting Actress in *Broken Lullaby* and a Jane Mallet Award winner for her portrayal of 'Jessie' in *Jessie's Story*. She is seen regularly as 'Mrs Whitney' in CBC TV's *Wind At My Back*.

TOM KNEEBONE
Born in Auckland, New Zealand, Mr Kneebone has appeared with the London Old Vic, The Stratford Festival, The Shaw Festival, and The Canadian Opera Company among others. He is presently the Artistic Director of Smile Theatre.

GREG KRAMER
Mr Kramer is a Toronto-based actor and broadcaster. His fascination with the theatre has led to many exciting roles across the spectrum of his craft from Shakespeare to Neil Simon.

MARTIN LAGER
An actor for some of his life—he's toured with the Canadian Players—Mr Lager has been a writer for most of it, writing or story-editing many TV series, feature films, and stage plays. He was Executive Producer of drama at CTV for five years.

LISA LANGLOIS
Ms Langlois was born fifth, after four brothers, to a French Canadian father and a Scottish Canadian mother in North Bay, Ontario. She was raised by her mother in Hamilton but schooled in French, and was discovered by French director Claude Chabrol. Her extensive career has been in film, television, and theatre.

JEAN LE CLERC
M. Le Clerc was born in Montreal, and appeared on stage and screen throughout Quebec and Ontario, in New York City, Los Angeles, and London, England. He is best known for his portrayal of 'Jeremy Hunter' on the daytime drama *All My Children*.

RENÉ LEMIEUX
M. Lemieux was born in St Ephrem. He toured for eight years with Le Theatre des Pissenlits. He did TV and theatre in Montreal before moving to Toronto in 1982 where he has since performed at Théâtre du P'tit Bonheur and in many shows for TVO.

MARILYN LIGHTSTONE
Ms Lightstone is a native of Montreal. She has performed numerous leading roles in Canada and the United States, winning two Genie Awards—for *Lies My Father Told Me*, and *In Praise of Older Women*—and a Moscow International Film Festival Award for *Tin Flute/Bonheur d'Occasion*.

BEATRICE LILLIE
Born and raised in Toronto, Ontario, Ms Lillie became the leading revue-comedienne of her generation. A genius at comic timing and improvisation, she rose to stardom in England. While maintaining a genteel, ladylike composure she employed eccentric and occasionally naughty bits of pantomime to ridicule her favourite targets.

ARABY LOCKHART
Ms Lockhart's career has spanned the Atlantic, touring in '60s England and across

Canada where she has acted, directed, and produced in most of the major theatres. Born in Toronto, she also works in film, TV, and in radio and has been the recipient of the Silver Ticket Award, The Brenda Donahue Award and Equity's Lifetime Achievement Award.

DAN MacDONALD
Actor/director/producer/writer and founder-member/AD/creator of theatre companies, Mr MacDonald was first President, ACTRA Performers' Guild and of CAEA.

DON (ACE) MacDONALD
Mr MacDonald grew up in Edmonton, the son of two British-born actors who were among the founders of the theatre scene in Edmonton. Ace has spent his career as an actor, announcer, host, disc jockey, director, and producer in Canada and the United States.

PAUL MacLEOD
Mr MacLeod lives in Halifax and works mainly in the Maritime provinces, the land he loves best. He has appeared several times at the Neptune Theatre and has also performed in TV, films, and radio, and in numerous commercials. He specialises in physical comedy.

THEA MacNEIL
A native of Winnipeg, Manitoba, Ms MacNeil was a member of the original casts of *Cats* and of *Napoleon* at the Elgin Theatre in Toronto. She has played 'Anne Shirley' in Charlottetown's *Anne Of Green Gables* for three seasons. Children will recognise her from her work as 'Cleo' on TVO's *Join In*.

PETER MacNEILL
Mr MacNeill was born in Campbellton, New Brunswick. His work has been seen on stage, on television, and in the cinema. His TV credits include *Traders*, *Psi Factor*, *Street Legal*, *E.N.G.*, and many other popular series. Recent films include *Crash* and *Hanging Garden*.

DAVID McCLELLAND
Mr McClelland was born in Sheffield, England, and is now proud to call Nova Scotia his home. Since arriving in Canada he has worked extensively in the Maritimes with appearances at Neptune Theatre, The Atlantic Theatre Festival, and Live Bait Theatre.

DEREK McGRATH
Mr McGrath, born in Timmins, Ontario, was a member of the Second City troupe in the '70s. He toured in *Godspell* and *You're A Good Man, Charlie Brown* and has become a familiar face on television, guest starring on shows such as *Cheers* and as a regular in *The Client*.

BRIAN McKAY
Mr McKay was born in Greenock, Scotland but was put on an English boat at three and the Canadian stage shortly thereafter. He has since written, appeared in, or

directed well over 150 productions in Canada and in the US including Broadway. He was twice nominated for a Dora. An ACTRA award winner, he is currently Artistic Director of the Huron Country Playhouse.

PATRICK McKENNA
Mr McKenna was born in Hamilton, Ontario and continues to call it home today. He co-stars in TV's *The Red Green Show* as the nerdy techno-geek nephew 'Harold' and as 'Marty Stephens' in the critically acclaimed TV series *Traders*.

SEANA McKENNA
Toronto, Ontario born, and trained at the National Theatre School, Ms McKenna has performed across Canada and the US since 1979 in many of the major classical and modern roles for women including 'Juliet', 'Cordelia', 'Lady Macbeth', 'Portia', 'Rosalind', 'Cleopatra', 'Candida', 'Eliza Doolittle' and 'St Joan' (for which she won a Dora Award for Best Actress in 1991).

SUSAN McLENNAN
Born in Edmonton, Alberta, Ms McLennan has appeared in TV's *Party Of Five*, *The Commish*, and *Highlander*. Her stage credits include 'Agnes' in *Agnes Of God*. The recipient of ACTRA's Joseph Golland Award, she is currently a writer/producer for television.

ARLENE MEADOWS
Ms Meadows was born in Brandon, Manitoba. In her long and varied career she has performed in opera, operetta, musical theatre, cabaret, comedy, and drama on the stage, TV, radio, and film. In her spare time she writes poetry and short stories.

JACK MEDLEY
Born in Barnsley, Yorkshire, England, Mr Medley was part of the famous CS Entertainment Unit in the British Army during WW II. He came to Canada in 1960 to work happily with the Canadian Players and the Neptune Theatre among others. He has been a permanent member of the Shaw Festival for 20 years.

MICHAEL MILLAR
Mr Millar has appeared on stages throughout Canada, more than 70 commercials, 20 movies, and countless TV shows. He also runs *It's A Mystery to Me*, a comedy improv troupe that performs throughout Southern Ontario.

GEOFFREY D. MILLER
Mr Miller was born in Toronto and has been seen in numerous independent feature films, most recently in the feature length film, *Joe Schmoe*. He has also produced and directed local comedy shows including *Monty Python's Flying (AIDS) Benefit* and *Buzzed Beyond Belief*.

RICHARD MONETTE
Born in Montreal, Mr Monette made his stage debut at 19 playing 'Hamlet' at the Crest Theatre in Toronto. He has made his living as an actor for more than 30 years. Since 1994 he has been Artistic Director of the Stratford Festival.

CHARLOTTE MOORE
Toronto-born Ms Moore is a musical theatre performer, Dora Mavor Moore Award winner, and former 'Fantine' in *Les Miserables*.

FRANK MOORE
Born in Bay de Verde, Nfld, Mr Moore was an original cast member of the Canadian productions of *Hair, Tommy,* and *Les Miserables*. A familiar face in numerous TV and film productions, he won Best Supporting Actor as 'Tom Thomson' in *The Far Shore*. NBC recently produced his script, *The Secret She Carried* as a Movie of The Week.

MAVOR MOORE
Toronto, Ontario-born playwright, actor, director, producer, composer, critic, teacher, and the first artist to chair the Canada Council, Mr Moore is now Research Professor, Fine Arts and Humanities, at the University of Victoria, B.C. He was made a Companion of the Order of Canada in 1985.

TEDDE MOORE
Born in Toronto, Ontario into an acting family that includes her grandmother, father, sister, son, and daughter, Ms Moore has been acting professionally since the age of thirteen and enjoys the success of her role as 'Miss Shields' in the film *A Christmas Story*.

BARRY MORSE
Mr Morse was born in London, England. His career has spanned more than 60 years and more than 2000 parts including 'Lt Gerard' in the TV series *The Fugitive*, and his series-leading role in *Space 1999*. His favourite part is 'the next one'.

SEAN MULCAHY
Born in Bantry, Republic of Ireland, Mr Mulcahy is an actor, teacher, and director. He was artistic director of the Citadel in Edmonton for its first five years. In 1977 he received the Queen's Silver Jubilee Medal for 'worthy and devoted service to the arts'.

WILLIAM NEEDLES
Mr Needles was born in Yonkers, N.Y. and was trained at the Goodman Theatre and the Art Institute of Chicago. His first professional work was with the Holden Players in Winnipeg in 1939. A founding member of the Stratford Festival, he has played for the Festival's audiences for a remarkable 38 seasons.

LOUIS NEGIN
Mr Negin was born in England but grew up in Montreal. He has had a long career playing 'exotics': 'I just don't look WASP.' He played 'Gandhi' for the television series *Witness To Yesterday* and was in the original production of *Fortune And Men's Eyes* in London, England.

JOHN NEVILLE
London-born Mr Neville spent his early professional life in England as an actor/director and ran the Nottingham Playhouse. Invited to Canada in 1972 by Jean Roberts, head of the English Theatre Company at the National Arts Centre, he

shortly after decided to bring his family to Canada permanently. He is well known for his work in theatre, films, and television, and especially for his portrayal of 'Baron Munchausen' in the feature film, *The Adventures Of Baron Munchausen*.

SHARON NOBLE
Ms Noble began her acting career at Theatre Winnipeg. She subsequently appeared on stage across Canada as well as in television (*Seeing Things*, *Street Legal*, etc.), film, commercials, and radio drama. In Los Angeles she does character voice work for two cartoon series and has appeared on *Days Of Our Lives*, *Punky Brewster*, and *The World's Oldest Rookie*.

JACK NORTHMORE
Mr Northmore has been a familiar presence to audiences across Canada on stage, in film, TV, and on radio for many years. Though he is retired and living in Lindsay, his backstage and onstage wit is remembered fondly and missed.

TRISH O'REILLY
Ms O'Reilly is a Toronto actor in 'straight' theatre, musical theatre, and opera. Her favourite credits include two new Canadian plays at the Blyth Festival: 'Clare' in *Ballad For A Rumrunner's Daughter* and 'Sheilah' in *This Year, Next Year*; 'Lucy Lockit' in *The Beggar's Opera* (Bathurst Street Theatre), and the 1993 Fringe of Toronto collective *Women In Utero*.

MONICA PARKER
Born in Glasgow, Scotland, Monica Parker came to Canada at 14 with her family. She has made her career as an actor, host, comedienne and, in the last ten years, as a successful screenwriter and producer in Los Angeles.

ALAN PEARCE
Born in Calgary, Alberta, Mr Pearce began his working life aboard steamships travelling the world. Upon his return to Canada he became an actor and writer for radio, TV, stage, and film in Vancouver, Winnipeg, Montreal, Toronto, and England.

NICHOLAS PENNELL
Mr Pennell was one of America's leading actors and a 23-year veteran of Canada's Stratford Festival. He passed away in February of 1995 after a brief battle with cancer. His final 'Letter to the Company', included herein, was delivered two days before his death.

SHELLEY PETERSON
Ms Peterson was born in London, Ontario and was educated at Dalhousie University, University of Western Ontario, and the Banff School of Fine Arts. Her career in theatre, film, and television has spanned 25 years. She also writes novels and raises horses along with her three children.

JENNIFER PHIPPS
Born within the sound of Bow Bells in London, England, Ms Phipps studied at RADA on scholarship and, after ten years of West End, rep, tours, film, radio and TV, came to Canada in 1960. She has had the continual blessing of company work with the

Toronto Arts Foundation, Stratford Festival, and the Shaw Festival, and has won a Gemini and a Dora Mavor Moore Award.

GORDON PINSENT
Mr Pinsent was born in Grand Falls, Newfoundland. His career has spanned thirty-five years in theatre, radio, television, and film, notably *Quentin Durgens MP*, *A Gift To Last*, *The Rowdyman* and *John And The Missus*. The recipient of the John Drainie Award for overall contribution to broadcasting, other awards, and three Honorary Doctorates, Mr Pinsent was made an Officer of the Order of Canada in 1980.

DIANA PLATTS
An actress, dancer, singer, Ms Platts was a member of the original Canadian cast of *Cats* as well as the national tour of the same production—the first Broadway musical to be produced in Canada with an all-Canadian cast. Ms Platts continues to perform and has also taken on chairperson responsibilities for ACTRA's Women's Committee.

CHRISTOPHER PLUMMER
Mr Plummer, born in Quebec, is one of the most highly regarded classical actors in the English-speaking world. His extraordinary career has been a testament to his talent and versatility. He is the recipient of numerous acting awards and honours including being named a Companion of the Order of Canada.

SARAH POLLEY
Ms Polley was born in Canada, the daughter of actors Diane and Michael Polley. She is best remembered for her leading role for seven seasons on TV's *Road to Avonlea*. Recently she has won critical acclaim for her work in such films as *Exotica* and *Joe's So Mean To Josephine*.

MILES POTTER
Actor/director Mr Potter came to Canada in 1970 from the United States and became involved with the alternate theatre scene. He has since directed more than 45 plays and has performed in most of the major theatre companies across Canada.

JOHN REEVES
Born in 1926, in Merritt, B.C., the sometime actor and producer of CBC radio drama 1952-1990 was awarded the Italia Prize for Radio Drama in 1959. He is the recipient of the John Drainie Award 1977, 'for distinguished contribution to radio drama'.

DEAN REGAN
Mr Regan, from Vancouver, B.C., started as a dancer, then moved into comedy, singing, and acting. He created the role of 'Gilbert' in the musical *Anne Of Green Gables* as well as doing several seasons of *Spring Thaw*.

KATE REID
Born in London, England and raised in Toronto, Miss Reid performed at all the major theatre festivals, on Broadway, in films and countless radio and television productions. Plays were written for her by Tennessee Williams, Arthur Miller, and Edward Albee. She received an honorary PhD and was made a member of the Order of Canada.

NICHOLAS RICE
Mr Rice is a Toronto-based actor who is proud to say that in 1994 he fell off the Neptune Theatre stage...twice.

RUSSELL ROBERTS
Especially familiar to audiences in Western Canada, Mr Roberts has played in *Noises Off* at the Bastion, *A Flea In Her Ear* at the Citadel and *A Midsummer Night's Dream* at Bastion and Northern Lights. He and his wife, actor Colleen Winton, have two sons.

WAYNE ROBSON
Mr Robson was born in Vancouver and has been a professional actor for thirty years. He has two Best Supporting Actor Gemini Awards ('Wally' in *Then You Die* and 'Christie Logan' in *Bye Bye Blues)* and has been nominated twice for Genies for *The Grey Fox* and *Bye Bye Blues*.

TONY ROSATO
Mr Rosato was born in 1957, in Fontanorosa, a small town in the province of Avellino in Italy, and came to Canada with his family when he was eight. Part of the company of *Second City* and on *SCTV*, he also spent 3 1/2 years as a performer/writer on *Saturday Night Live* in New York City. He has appeared as a regular on *Amanda-By-The-Sea* with Bea Arthur, *Night Heat*, and *Diamonds,* and in various parts in several movies.

JEAN-LOUIS ROUX
Born in Montreal, M. Roux began studies as a medical student but completed them in France as an actor. Unpon his return to Montreal he founded Le Théâtre du Nouveau Monde in partnership with Jean Gascon. A classical actor, fluent in both French and English, he has had a career in all media as an actor and a writer. He has been awarded many distinctions, including the Order of Canada, and he is the first actor to be appointed to the Canadian Senate.

DIANA ROWLAND
Ms Rowland is an actor who has been working in theatre, film, and television since the early '70s. She has been writing and had a short story published in a recent issue of *Chatelaine*.

JAN RUBES
Born in Voyyne, Czechoslovakia, Mr Rubes began his performing career as an opera singer and came to acting much later in life. He has since appeared in many TV shows and films, earning five Best Actor and Supporting Actor nominations and winning a Best Actor Gemini for *Two Men*. He has also been presented with an Earl Grey Award, a Queen Elizabeth Award, and the Order of Canada.

TONY RUBES
Mr Rubes, the son of actors Jan and Susan Rubes, was born in New York City. He has been working in theatre, film, and TV since the age of eight, in everything from school tours to features shot as far away as Prague.

SUSAN DOUGLAS RUBES

Ms Douglas Rubes was born in Vienna and lived in Czechoslovakia until 1939. She has lived in England and New York, becoming a Canadian citizen in 1974. She is remembered as 'Kathy Grant' on the daytime drama, *The Guiding Light*, and won a Tony award for best debut on Broadway. Actor/producer and the founder of the Young People's Theatre in Toronto, she is a recipient of the Order of Canada.

SAUL RUBINEK

Mr Rubinek was born in a United Nations refugee camp near Munich in 1948. He grew up in Canada and has appeared on stage, in films, and on TV in Canada and the United States. He appeared in such feature films as *The Unforgiven* and *Bonfire Of The Vanities* and is a regular on the TV series *Ink*.

MELODY RYANE

A Vancouver native, Ms Ryane is an accomplished veteran of Canadian and US stages including the Stratford Festival and the Shaw Festival. She now has her own business in Los Angeles as a dialogue coach for TV and film and as a manager of child actors.

MARCEL SABOURIN

M. Sabourin grew up in Montreal and has played extensively on stage and cinema in both French and English. He was co-writer of *J.A. Martin Photographe* (in which he also appeared) and Godbout's *Les Troubles de Johnny*. A teacher at the National Theatre School, he also writes songs, including lyrics for 12 songs that became hits for Robert Charlebois in the '70s.

GUY SANVIDO

Born in Guelph, Ontario, Mr Sanvido is a 40+ year veteran of theatre across Canada, playing everything from 'Barney Cashman' in *Last Of The Red Hot Lovers* to 'Willy Loman' in *Death Of A Salesman*. He has appeared in more than 200 TV and film productions and 182 commercials.

GILLES SAVARD

M. Savard was born in Témiskaming, Quebec. He studied at the Conservatory in Montreal and in Paris. While shooting a movie in Montreal he fell in love with Monica Parker; they married and have had a son. Gilles, when he is not acting, now designs clothing for the film industry and film and TV personalities in Los Angeles.

AUGUST SCHELLENBERG

Born in Montreal, Mr Schellenberg studied at the National Theatre School there. His first and only theatre audition was for the Stratford Festival. He has performed across the country on stage, in television, and in film. Mr Schellenberg, a Genie winner for best supporting actor in the feature film *Black Robe,* has co-starred in the films *Iron Will* and *Free Willy*. His acting family includes his wife Joan Karasevich and daughters Reena and Joanna.

ALBERT SCHULTZ

Born in Port Hope, Ontario and raised in Okotoks, Alberta, Mr Shultz has worked as an actor/singer/host in theatres across Canada and is known to television audiences for his continuing roles on the CBC series *Street Legal* and *Side Effects*. He has played at The Stratford Shakespearean Festival as well as many other theatres.

DAVID SCHURMANN
Born in the United Kingdom, Mr Schurmann, a fifth generation Canadian, returned 'home' to Canada in 1966. He begins his 15th season at the Shaw Festival in Ontario in 1997.

ALFIE SCOPP
Born in Montreal, Mr Scopp has been an integral part of Canadian television, both as a writer and as an actor. He was 'Clarabell' in the Canadian production of *Howdy Doody* which also starred Peter Mews, Barbara Hamilton, and Robert Goulet.

CHUCK SHAMATA
Mr Shamata made his stage debut at the famous Crest Theatre in Toronto, after which the Crest closed forever. He is a Toronto native, an award-winning actor who has appeared in diverse film and TV productions such as *Mod Squad, Joshua Then And Now*, *The Tai Babilonia Story*, *Death Wish 5*, and on stage with Peter O'Toole in *Uncle Vanya*, *Battering Ram*, and *A Doll's House*.

WILLIAM SHATNER
Born and raised in Montreal, Quebec, Mr Shatner had an extensive theatrical and television career in Canada before moving to the United States and starring on Broadway. He became famous as 'Captain James T. Kirk' in the series *Star Trek,* first on television and then in several movies. He has had a full career as writer and director as well as actor.

NOAH SHEBIB
Born in Toronto, Ontario, Mr Shebib has been a professional actor since the age of ten when he starred in the television series *The Mighty Jungle*. Among his other credits he appears regularly in the TV series *Wind At My Back*. He is a fourth generation professional Canadian actor.

ELIZABETH SHEPHERD
Ms Shepherd was born in London, England but was raised in Burma by her Methodist missionary parents. She came to Canada in 1972 to appear at Stratford. Although she works in all mediums, in all three English-speaking countries in the Northern Hemisphere, she makes Toronto, Ontario her home.

MARTIN SHORT
Born in Hamilton, Ontario, Mr Short was a member of the legendary Canadian production of the musical *Godspell*. A singer and dancer as well as an accomplished actor, he rose to international fame as a member of the TV shows *SCTV* and *Saturday Night Live*. He is now a first-string Hollywood character actor.

FRANK SHUSTER
Mr Shuster and the other half of the beloved comedy team of Wayne and Shuster, Johnny Wayne (now deceased) were both born and raised in Toronto. Internationally famous for their long comedy sketches on CBC and *The Ed Sullivan*

Show on CBS, Wayne and Shuster were often asked but rarely tempted to make it big somewhere else.

BRENDA SHUTTLEWORTH

A native of Courtney, B.C., Ms Shuttleworth (née Pennock) graduated from the Playhouse Acting School and is now a resident of Calgary with her husband Daryl.

DARYL SHUTTLEWORTH

Mr Shuttleworth was born in New Westminster, B.C. and graduated from the National Theatre School. He has appeared in theatres from Fredericton to Victoria, in film and television, and in CBC radio dramas. He now resides in Calgary and often performs for Alberta Theatre Projects.

SONJA SMITS

Ms Smits arrived in this world via Sudbury, Ontario. She is well known to Canadian audiences as the female series lead in both *Street Legal* (for which she won a Gemini Award for Best Actress) and, more recently, *Traders*. She will also be remembered for her role as 'Morag' in Margaret Laurence's classic, *The Diviners*.

PAUL SOLES

After more than 50 years as an actor and broadcaster, Toronto-born Mr Soles has graduated into the senior ranks. He created the role of 'Grandfather' in the musical, *Ragtime,* was nominated for a Genie for his role as 'Harvey' in the film *Falling Over Backwards,* and starred as 'Nat' in the major Canadian production of *I'm Not Rappaport.* He is a licensed pilot and avid canoeist.

GEORGE SPERDAKOS

Montreal-born Mr Sperdakos has been working professionally since the early 1950s. In 1953 he hitch-hiked to Stratford to try to get into the company and ended up helping to build the tent. He was a charter member of the acting companies of the Neptune Theatre in Halifax and the St Lawrence Centre in Toronto.

HEATHER SUMMERHAYES (CARIOU)

Ms Summerhayes was born in Brantford, Ontario. Her Canadian theatrical career includes the St Lawrence Centre company, Stratford Festival, the Manitoba Theatre Centre, Press Theatre, and Hamilton Place Theatre. Her American career includes theatres in Washington, Philadelphia, and Delaware and appearances off-Broadway. She is a founding member of the Ontario Youtheatre, and a published essayist.

AILEEN TAYLOR-SMITH

Born in Brownsville, Tennessee, Ms Taylor-Smith came to Toronto in 1952. She has been a resident ever since. She has worked as an actor in many of Canada's theatres including Manitoba Theatre Centre and Theatre New Brunswick. The Artistic Director of Huron Country Playhouse for three years, she also created the Young Players troupe there.

DAVE THOMAS

Mr Thomas is an alumnus of the *SCTV* television series where he created his half of the famous Canadian duo 'Bob and Doug' and distinguished himself as an exceptional mimic. He has appeared in several films and is the co-star of the American TV series, *Grace Under Fire*.

SHAWN ALEX THOMPSON
Born in Berwick, Nova Scotia, airforce brat extraordinaire—from magician to actor to writer to fame in one short lifetime. He has just recently directed his first film.

LINDA THORSON
Ms Thorson was born in Toronto, Ontario and studied at RADA in London, England. Best known as 'Tara King' on the late '60s television series *The Avengers*, she has continued to perform in theatre, film, and television productions on both sides of the Atlantic, and is often recognised as 'Julia Medea' from *One Life to Live*.

SARAH TORGOV
Toronto-born Ms Torgov's first acting experience was in CBC's *Drying Up The Streets* for which she won a Nellie Award. She subsequently appeared in *Meatballs* and *If You Could See What I Hear* among many others. She is also a happily married mom living in Los Angeles.

LYNE TREMBLAY
Born in Lac St Jean, P.Q., Ms Tremblay is a singer, dancer, and actor, recently seen in her one-woman cabaret, *Gauche*. She appeared in *April One* and *Atlantic City*, the TV series *The Newsroom, Street Legal*, and *E.N.G.*, and was memorable as the original 'Siamese Cat' in *CATS* in Toronto.

KATE TROTTER
Born in Toronto, Ontario, Ms Trotter is remembered as 'Jane' in *Joshua Then And Now*, and 'Captain Karen Simms' in *Kung Fu, The Legend Continues*. She was nominated for an Ace Award for her work in *Alfred Hitchcock Presents, The Hunted* and won a 'Dora' Award for 'Sarah' in *Translations*.

TONY VAN BRIDGE
Born in Battersea, Mr van Bridge came to Canada in 1954. He has been an audience favourite at both the Shaw Festival and at the Stratford Festival—North America's two biggest repertory theatres—appearing for fifteen seasons with each company.

ARTHUR VORONKA
Born in Montreal, Mr Voronka began his career as an actor at the Mountain Playhouse, then became a producer, designer, director, and writer. He has directed or produced a dozen feature films and hundreds of commercials, and was the creator, producer and director of the series *Witness To Yesterday* hosted by Patrick Watson.

VLASTA VRANA
Mr Vrana was born in Norway to Czech political refugees. He has worked in Canada as an actor for 25 years and calls the country near Montreal home. He has appeared in many films and television programs and lends his voice to documentaries and commercials.

TODD WAITE

Mr Waite is a Canadian actor and director best known for his work as a member of the Shaw Theatre Festival and for originating the role of 'Enjolras' in the Canadian première of *Les Miserables*. He is also strongly associated with the works of Michel Marc Bouchard.

RATCH WALLACE

Toronto-born Mr Wallace began his acting career in *The Offering* and will be remembered as 'Kenny' on *Seeing Things*. As a writer, his work has been produced on radio, TV, and film. As well, he is a licensed Great Lakes captain and a marine specialist for the film industry.

JERRY WASSERMAN

Born in Cincinnati, Ohio, Mr Wasserman is Professor of English and Theatre at the University of British Columbia and editor of *Modern Canadian Plays*. His résumé also includes over 100 TV and movie roles from *The X-Files* to *Alive*.

ALBERTA WATSON

Ms Watson was born and raised in Toronto. She moved to Los Angeles and worked steadily there. Her breakthrough movie into feature films and television was an independent film, *Spanking The Monkey*. She has recently appeared in *Gotti* for HBO with Armand Assante.

RICHARD WAUGH

Born and raised in London, Ontario, Mr Waugh has worked extensively in theatre, television, and radio since the age of fifteen. He has spent six years with the Shaw Festival and is a multiple award winner for his work in commercials. Richard can be seen on television in *F/X The Series*.

AL WAXMAN

Mr Waxman is familiar to audiences world wide as co-star of the TV series *Cagney and Lacey*, 'Larry King' of *King of Kensington*, and more than 1000 appearances on TV, radio, and in films. He has appeared in London's West End, New York's Off Broadway, and Canadian regional theatres. He won the Earl Grey Award for Best Actor for the title role in *The Winning of Frankie Walls* and a Best Actor Award for *King of Kensington*, and recently received the Order of Canada.

SANDY WEBSTER

Born in Thunder Bay, where he grew up watching cowboy pictures in the city's only theatre, Mr Webster has built a successful career as a character actor on stage and in films across the country. Canadian TV audiences will remember him from CBC's *The Great Detective*. He is 'still at it some years later'.

JONATHAN WELSH

Mr Welsh was born in St Catharines, Ontario and is a familiar face to viewers from his many leading roles as continuing characters in such TV series as *Sidestreet, Adderley, E.N.G.*, and *The New World Wine Tour*.

KENNETH WELSH

Born in Edmonton, Alberta and an international film, TV, stage and radio actor,

Mr Welsh loves Shakespeare and is familiar to TV audiences as 'Colin Thatcher' in *Love And Hate* among many others. 'A little powder, a little paint, turns you into something you ain't.'

SCOTT WENTWORTH
An actor, director, and playwright who was born in Baltimore, Maryland, Mr Wentworth moved to Canada in 1985 to join the Stratford Festival where he played such roles as 'Iago' in *Othello,* 'Sky Masterson' in *Guys and Dolls,* and the title role in *Macbeth.*

WILLIAM WHITEHEAD
A Hamilton, Ontario native, Mr Whitehead was educated in Saskatchewan as a biologist and after five years in the theatre became a documentary writer for radio and television. He is now retired.

KENNETH WICKES
Born in Iver, Buckinghamshire in England, Mr Wickes came to Canada in 1957. He has performed in Canada, most often at The Shaw, The Stratford, and The Charlotteown festivals and also in the United States. Recently he has appeared at Manitoba Theatre Centre in Steve Martin's *Picasso At The Lapin Agile* as 'Gascon' and as 'Mr Drimmond' in *There Goes The Bride.*

CHRIS WIGGINS
Born in Blackpool, Lancashire, Mr Wiggins came to Canada in 1952. He is remembered for his continuing lead roles in the TV series *Swiss Family Robinson* and *Friday 13th* and as the voices of 'No-Heart' in *The Care Bears* and 'Cornelius' in *Babar The Elephant.* He continues to work steadily in radio, TV, and film.

TOM WOOD
Mr Wood hails from Dawson Creek, British Columbia and graduated in fine arts from The University of Edmonton. His theatrical career over the last 30 years has spanned Canada. Most recently, he has appeared in *Angels in America* in Toronto. As a playwright, his work includes *North Shore Live, B Movie, The Play* and *The Theatrical Adventures of Justin Fair.*

Index